The New System of National Accounts

Recent Economic Thought Series

Editors:

Warren J. Samuels
Michigan State University
East Lansing, Michigan, USA

William Darity, Jr.
University of North Carolina
Chapel Hill, North Carolina, USA

Other books in the series:

The New System of National Accounts

edited by

John W. Kendrick
George Washington University

KLUWER ACADEMIC PUBLISHERS
Boston / Dordrecht / London

Distributors for North America:
Kluwer Academic Publishers
101 Philip Drive
Assinippi Park
Norwell, Massachusetts 02061 USA

Distributors for all other countries:
Kluwer Academic Publishers Group
Distribution Centre
Post Office Box 322
3300 AH Dordrecht, THE NETHERLANDS

Library of Congress Cataloging-in-Publication Data

The new system of national accounts/edited by John W. Kendrick.
     p. cm.—(Recent economic thought series)
  Includes index.
  ISBN 0-7923-9602-2 (hb: alk. paper)
  1. National income—Accounting. I. Kendrick, John W.
II. Series.
HB141.5.N49 1995
339.3—dc20

                              95-22205
                                  CIP

Printed on acid-free paper.

Printed in the United States of America

Contents

Contributing Authors

Derek Blades
OECD
2 rue André Pascal
75775 Paris, CEDEX 16
France

Carol Carson
International Monetary Fund
Washington, DC
Mailing Address:
5410 Surrey Street
Chevy Chase, MD 20815

Uma Datta Roy Choudhury
50, Shivalik Apartments
Pocket A, Alaknanda Kalkaji
New Delhi
India 110019

John Dawson
Department of Economics
Grinnell College
P.O. Box 805
Grinnell, IA 50112

Erwin Diewert
Department of Economics
#997-1873 East Mall
University of British Columbia
Vancouver, British Columbia
V6T 1Z1 Canada

Robert Eisner
Department of Economics
Northwestern University
2003 Sheridan Road
Evanston, IL 60208

Luisella Goldschmidt-Clermont
OECD
74 Rüe de Versoix
F-01210 Fervey Voltaire
France (Fax 33.50.42.96.58)

Robert Gordon
Department of Economics
Northwestern University
2003 Sheridan Road
Evantston, IL 60201

Anne Harrison
97-99 Boulevard Rodin
92130 Issu-le-Monlineauz
France

Sir Jack Hibbert
180, Kings Hall Road
Beckinham, Kent
BR3 1LJ England

Peter Hill
Broadwater
The Street Flordon
Norwich NR15 1RN
England, United Kingdom

T. Homenko
Statistical Commission of the
  Commonwealth of Independent
  States
c/o Jan van Tongeren
National Accounts Branch
DESIPA, Statistical Division
Room DC2-1720
United Nations, UN Plaza
New York, NY 10017, or

Statistical Committee of the C.I.S.
39, Myasmts kaya St.
Moscow-103450
Russian Federation

Charles Hulten
Department of Economics
3115 Tydings Hall
University of Maryland
College Park, MD 20742

Youri Ivanov
Statistical Commission of the
  Commonwealth of Independent
  States
c/o Jan van Tongeren, or

Statistical Committee of the C.L.S.
39, Myasmts kaya St.
Moscow-103450
Russian Federation

John W. Kendrick
Department of Economics
George Washington University
Washington, DC 20052
Mailing Address:
6363 Waterway Drive
Falls Church, VA 22044

Yoshimasa Kurabayashi
Toyo Eiwa Women's University
32-1, Miho-Cho, Midori-Ku
Yokohama-Shi
Kanagawa, 226
Japan

Jonathan Levin
8620 Rayburn Road
Bethesda, MD 20817

Heinrich Lützel
Statistiches Bundesamt
Gustav-Stresemann-Ring 11
Postfach 5528
D-6200 Wiesbaden 1
Germany

Harry Postner
Apt #309
1343 Meadourlands Drive
Ottawa, Ont.
Canada K2E 7E8
Ottawa, Ontario
Canada K1A 0T6

F. Graham Pyatt
Institute of Social Studies
P.O. Box 29776
2502 LT The Hague
The Netherlands

Peter Reich
Fachhochschule Mainz II
An der Bruchspitze 50
55122 Mainz 1
Germany

Richard Ruggles
100 Prospect Street
New Haven, CT 06511

Albert M. Teplin
Federal Reserve Board
20th and C Streets, NW
Washington, DC 20551

Jan van Tongeren
Chief, National Accounts Branch
DESIPA, Statistical Division
Room DC2-1720
United Nations, UN Plaza
New York, NY 10017

Rob Vos
Institute of Social Studies
P.O. Box 26776
2502 LT The Hague
The Netherlands

Allan H. Young
824 Aster Blvd.
Rockville, MD 20850

Acknowledgments

In late 1991, Professor Warren Samuels, editor of this Kluwer series, invited me to prepare a volume on national income and product accounts. I was receptive to this proposal since the textbook I had written with Carol Carson two decades previously, *Economic Accounts and Their Uses* (McGraw-Hill, 1972) was out of date. Further, the United Nations and four other international organizations were near completion of a second revision of the *System of National Accounts (SNA)* first published in 1948 as a basis for consistent international reporting. I thought it would be useful to devote a volume of essays to explaining and critiquing what was to be published as *SNA 1993*.

I met with Samuels and the senior editor at Kluwer, Zachary Rolnik, at the American Economic Association meetings that winter and signed a contract to produce the book of readings. I am grateful to both gentlemen for initiating the project and for their encouragement and support throughout.

It was my hope that Carol Carson might coedit the volume since she was one of the chief participants in preparing *SNA 1993*. Although her position then as director of the Bureau of Economic Analysis, which is responsible for preparing the U.S. national income and product estimates, precluded her serving formally as a coeditor, she did write the important chapter on the design of economic accounts. She also advised me on the topics to be treated in the volume and the experts to be invited to serve as authors and discussants of each of the chapters. More than half of the contributors are from countries other than the United States.

It is, of course, on the work of the authors and discussants that the worth of the volume depends. I believe that their essays make a significant contribution to the socioeconomic accounting literature and will influence the content of any future version of the SNA.

The royalties on this book are being contributed to the International Association for Research in Income and Wealth, to which most of the contributors belong. We and the purchasers of the volume can take pleasure in helping the IARIW, which plays an important role in advancing our discipline through its biennial international meetings and its quarterly journal, the *Review of Income and Wealth*.

Finally, I express my appreciation to the staff members of the Economics Department of the George Washington University, who have facilitated my communications over many months with the many persons involved in producing this volume.

John W. Kendrick

The New System of National Accounts

1 INTRODUCTION AND OVERVIEW

John W. Kendrick

National income estimates date back to the latter seventeenth century. But it has been only in the past half century or so since World War II that economic accounts have developed in their present form, becoming an indispensable tool for macroeconomic analysis, projections, and policy formulation. Furthermore, it was in this period that the United Nations issued several versions of a system of national accounts (SNA) to make possible international economic comparisons on a consistent basis. The latest version, *SNA 1993*, published in early 1994 (United Nations, 1993), occasioned this collection of essays and commentaries by recognized experts in the field.

The volume has three chief objectives. The first is to enhance understanding of socioeconomic accounts generally and of *SNA 1993* in particular. Second, the essays and commentaries critique *SNA 1993* and offer constructive suggestions for future revisions of the system that would make it even more useful for the national and international purposes it serves. A third is to serve as a textbook or book of readings in conjunction with *SNA 1993* for courses in economic accounts. This use is one reason for inclusion of the next two topics in this chapter.

The next section covers some of the uses served by socioeconomic accounts, which underline their importance. Then we shall survey the development of national income and product estimates and accounts, particularly in the modern period since the outbreak of World War II, which saw the introduction of the accounting approach, development of an integrated system of accounts by industry and sector, and the movement toward international comparability. This underscores the evolutionary nature of the accounts and the value of a critical view that looks forward to further improvements of economic statistics in the future. In the final section of this chapter, we indicate briefly the contents of the other essays contained in this volume.

The following statements taken from the textbook I wrote with Carol Carson in 1972 *Economic Accounts and Their Uses* applies as well to the present volume (Kendrick and Carson, 1972, p. 2): "Despite the rapid strides in economic accounting since the 1930's it must be emphasized that the economic accounts of the United Nations (UN) are far from 'finished.' . . . Changes reflect a growing understanding of economic accounts as well as insights into better modes of presentation to accommodate the known uses of accounts (which themselves change). They also reflect dynamic changes within the economy itself, changes in concepts and definitions, changes in the quantity and quality of underlying data and methodology. The unfinished nature of economic accounts explains the critical approach of this volume."

1.1. Uses of Economic Accounts

As economies become larger and more complex, it is increasingly important to have good economic statistics organized in an analytically meaningful way to provide an empirical counterpart of those economies across time and space. Economic accounts have evolved to become the centerpiece of such a system of statistics enabling decision makers to see where the economy has been and its recent status as background for projections of where it may be going and the kinds of policies necessary for governments and private groups or individuals to achieve their objectives.

Figure 1.1 illustrates the role of information systems. The process depicted there is an interactive one, beginning with the real world, physical and social, including particularly, for present purposes, the economic transactions whereby people satisfy their current needs and wants and provide for the future. First, data must be collected about the transactions—flows of factor services, incomes and outlays, saving, investment and financial transactions—during successive periods and stocks of tangible

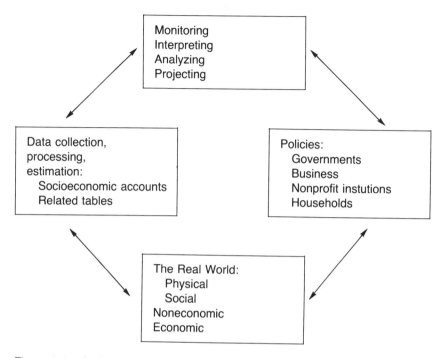

Figure 1.1.   An Interactive Information System: Socioecomomic Accounts

and financial assets, liabilities, and net worth at the end of successive periods. Wherever possible, data on quantities and prices should be obtained if values are to be estimated in both current and constant values. The values, including imputations for nonmarket transactions where feasible and desirable, are aggregated by significant types of flows and stocks. The economy is classified by meaningful sectors and subsectors, and flows between a given economy and the rest of the world are recorded.

Indeed, an important use of the system of accounts is as a coordinating framework for economic statistics in two senses: (1) as a conceptual framework for ensuring consistency of definitions and classification used in different fields that are integrated with the income and product core accounts, and (2) as an accounting device for ensuring the numerical consistency of data drawn from different sources. The most useful concepts and classifications, including sectoring, evolve with experience in using accounts, particularly in analysis. As to data collection, processing, and preparation of estimates, each country must decide on the tradeoffs it is willing to make between accuracy and costs. But it must be remembered that misleading statistics can also be costly if they result in inappropriate policy measures.

Although not all economic data fit into the accounts, the use of supplemental tables and the satellite accounts of *SNA 1993* can make the system quite comprehensive.

The accounts for successive periods are very valuable in monitoring and interpreting economic behavior over time within and among nations and in analyzing relationships. This involves the cyclical and secular movements of aggregates and the changes in their composition by product, industry, and source of income. The numbers make possible econometric analyses of intertemporal or cross-sectional relationships between and among variables, such as the consumption (or saving) function and various multipliers. On a quarterly or monthly basis, the statistics facilitate analysis of causal forces and temporal sequences in business cycles. Annual estimates in constant prices make possible decomposition of economic growth into input and productivity components and the relationship of the latter to intangible capital outlays and stocks and other causal variables. The quantitative analysis is guided by theory, and it helps to improve theories and bring them into closer uniformity with facts.

By increasing understanding of economies, the accounts become a more useful framework for planning and projecting economic developments. Aggregate projections can be broken down by final product and then, by use of input-output matrixes, translated into output projections by industry. These can be converted to employment and capital requirements by projections of productivity by industry. The projections are useful not only to enterprises in the various industries but also to governments in planning outlays for infrastructure, education, training and retraining, and so on. The financing accounts can be used in conjunction with the income and product accounts to project requirements for various types of financial instruments and thus the demand for services of the financial intermediaries.

Needless to say, predictions can seldom be made with precision, and allowance must be made for possibly large margins of error. But policy makers are in a far better position to devise effective policies given the existence of economic accounts and the analyses and projections they make possible than they were before.

The chief impetus to the development of economic accounts has come from central governments, which probably remain their chief users. By monitoring economic movements, policy-making agencies including the central bank can see if they are on track with respect to national objectives regarding growth, price inflation, the trade balance, unemployment, and so on, and if not, they can take appropriate actions. Projections may suggest preemptive measures if the likelihood of unfavorable developments seems high. Econometric models based on the accounts make it possible to predict the impacts of alternative policies so officials may choose the most efficient ones. Budgeting for one or more years ahead is typically done within the framework of economic accounts, which serve as the centerpiece of economic reports of successive administrations.

State and local governments have little influence on the national economy, but they must plan their budgets in the light of general economic conditions, particularly with respect to projected revenues. More relevant at the subnational levels are regional economic accounts where these are available.

International organizations make extensive use of economic accounts of the member nations in economic analyses and projections. Dues of the United Nations are assessed by a formula that includes income per capita—which was a factor in the rapid spread of economic accounts after World War II and in the development of the original SNA. Estimates of income or product per head of various countries are used by the World Bank and others to determine eligibility for loans or aid and to determine the terms or conditions on which funds are made available. To convert the estimates to a common currency, purchasing power parities are used since there is a systematic bias in exchange rates. Comparable national estimates are used to evaluate the relative success of economic policies. The international time-series and cross-sectional data are also valuable for econometric estimation of functional relationships, including foreign trade flows in relation to the incomes of nations.

Within individual nations, firms are generally able to relate their sales to the disposable income of the nation or the industries and regions in which they operate, if such statistics are available. The larger firms often have their own economists to track and project the business climate; others may subscribe to various economic forecasting services to provide inputs into their decisions regarding investments, financing, hiring, and so on. Organizations such as labor unions and other nonprofit institutions also find it in their interests to monitor and project GDP and selected components and related series.

As average levels of education and income rise, an increasing number of individuals also find it useful to track the economy as revealed in economic accounts in making decisions about their careers, real and financial investments, and other economic matters.

The policy measures by governments and decisions made in the other sectors all react back on the economy, as shown in Figure 1.1. Forecasters have to factor in what they think the net effect of the policies of one period will be on the economy in the next period.

Economic accounts have become so indispensable a tool in the ways described that it is hard to imagine how we would get along without them. They have been called the greatest invention for economic analysis of the twentieth century. But they are not an invention; they have gradually developed over several centuries, although that evolution accelerated at the time of World War II, as is described in the next section.

1.2. Early Historical Development

The first estimates of national income were made in the latter seventeenth century by Sir William Petty and Gregory King in England and by Pierre Boisguille and, subsequently, Marshall Vauban in France. From then until the 1920s individual scholars in at least a dozen other countries prepared discrete estimates for a variety of purposes such as estimating tax revenues, comparing the material strength of certain nations, and assessing income distribution (see Kendrick, 1970, pp. 284–315; Kendrick and Carson, 1972, ch. 2).

Between 1925 and 1939, a number of countries began to prepare continuing "official" estimates of national income and related series to strengthen the information base for economic policy decisions. This process was accelerated by the great depression. In its *World Economic Survey* for 1939, the League of Nations for the first time published national income estimates for twenty-six countries covering all or part of the period 1929–1938, nine of which were governmental. It was recognized that the estimates were not fully comparable. The League's Committee on Statistics considered the problems of achieving international comparability, but work in that direction was slowed down by World War II.

Up to 1940, work had been concentrated on the estimation of national income and to a lesser extent on the expenditure side of national product or at least selected components thereof. Within the next half dozen years, development took a quantum leap with the formulation of integrated economic accounting systems. Yet the work of individual economic statisticians and the early governmental estimates of national income were important in developing concepts and methodology, particularly since the production account is the cornerstone of an accounting system.

Although the earliest national income estimates were based on a comprehensive view of production, Quesnay and the French physiocrats sought to limit the scope of production to the output of agriculture and other extractive industries. It was in reaction to such a narrow view that Adam Smith argued that manufacturing and distributive industries were also productive in processing raw materials and distributing the finished products. Yet Smith excluded services from national income, since there labor does not "fix itself in vendible commodities that can be accumulated as capital for future periods" (Studenski, 1961, pt. 1, p. 18). Ricardo and J.S. Mill followed Smith's definition. So did Karl Marx, since he could then more readily develop his theory of the materialization of surplus value into capital. Marx's concept was subsequently implemented by the Soviet Union and other Communist nations in the *material product system* of national accounts that prevailed until the breakup of the USSR and the end of its domination of eastern Europe.

The narrow Smithian concept of national income came under increasing attack in the United Kingdom and on the continent. The final blow was struck by Alfred Marshal in his *Economics of Industry* (1879). Marshal firmly identified production with the creation of utility, comprehending direct services as well as tangible commodities. He also clearly distinguished between national income gross and net of depreciation as well as net of the using up of intermediate products (Marshall, 1948, p. 523): "The labour and capital of the country, acting on its natural resources, produce annually a certain net aggregate of commodities, material and immaterial, including services of all kinds."

The neoclassical economist A.C. Pigou (1932, p. 11) gave further direction to estimates by defining national income as comprising goods and services that "can be brought directly or indirectly into relation with the measuring rod of money." Some individual statisticians had tried to include estimates of unpaid economic activity such as housewives' services. But most government statistical agencies felt it was prudent to confine national income and product estimates largely to final goods bought and sold in organized markets, with imputations of value confined to those nonmarket transactions with significant market counterparts from which unit values could be derived. Thus, the imputed values of food produced and consumed on farms, and the rental values of owner-occupied residences are generally included, but the value of unpaid economic activity taking place in households (for which adequate continuing data are usually lacking) is not. To avoid suspicions of slanting their estimates, statistical agency personnel try to use objective data as much as possible, minimizing the kind of judgements often involved in imputations. The assumption of responsibility by governments for national economic accounts has increased collection of more and better basic data through periodic economic censuses and continuing surveys.

1.3. The Development After 1939 of Comparable Economic Accounting Systems

During World War II and the succeeding couple of decades there was a tremendous leap from national income estimates to the development of economic accounting by sector and the integration of related accounts, notably input-output, financial (flow-of-fund) accounts and balance sheets.

Zoltan Kenessey (1994, esp. pp. 109–123), in a recent review of the development of national economic accounts, credits Irving Fisher with the "original intellectual influence" in suggesting the use of double-entry bookkeeping in his work *The Nature of Capital and Income* (1906). Fisher also referred to the possible aggregation of individual accounts to national levels.

The accounting approach was expounded in the United States in the 1930s by Morris Copeland and Robert Martin. Eric Lindahl in Sweden was well aware of Fisher's attention to accounting and probably influenced Frisch's work in Norway. J.R. Hicks was likewise influenced and is credited by Richard Stone with being the first to use the term *social accounting*.

But it was the concrete work on national income and product estimates in the United Kingdom early in World War II that established the economic accounting approach. In December 1939 a Central Economic Intelligence Service (CEIS) was created in the United Kingdom, one of whose assignments was the compilation of national income estimates for the United Kingdom. Professor Bowley and associates prepared an annual series 1924–1938. James Meade, who had worked at the League of Nations as an economist, joined CEIS and in 1940 prepared a secret paper containing national accounts estimates using double-entry bookkeeping methods. When a Central Statistical Office was formed in January 1941, Meade continued to work on national accounts estimates using double-entry bookkeeping methods, together with Richard Stone, whose interest in the field had been stimulated by his Cambridge tutor, Colin Clark. Their work pleased Keynes, who recommended that a White Paper based on national accounts estimates be appended to the U.K. budget in April 1941. It was the first of a series. Although Meade moved on to other work, Richard Stone continued the development of economic accounts.

The new estimates were methodologically significant in that they were grossed to include not only depreciation but also indirect business taxes so that valuations represented market prices. More important, factor income (costs) plus other charges against product and gross national expenditures were viewed as the two sides of a double-entry production account. Formulation of consistent government revenue and expenditure estimates was also significant not only for war-time planning but because it led Stone and his colleagues at the Central Statistical Office to the idea of constructing income and outlay accounts for each major sector of the economy connected with the national production account by debit and credit entries for the various components. The results of this work were incorporated in a White Paper published in 1946.

Similar work was going on by Jan Tinbergen and J.B.D. Derksen in the Netherlands and in Norway under Ragnar Frisch and Petter Bjerve. Because of the German occupation, the Dutch and Norwegian systems were not published until after the war.

In the United States, the first national income estimate had been made in 1843. A succession of individuals followed suit until 1932, when Congress authorized the Department of Commerce to prepare official estimates, which began publication in 1934. The Department was assisted in this by Simon Kuznets, who had made national income estimates at the National Bureau of Economic Research. Kuznets, and a few others in the 1930s (especially Clark Warburton, who is credited with being the first American economist to use the term *gross national product*) (Carson, 1975, pp. 153–181), also began working on components of final expenditures and again assisted the Commerce Department in developing such estimates beginning in 1940. After the United States entered the war in December 1941, it took only a few months for the Department to publish an annual series of the gross national product from both the income and expenditure sides, essential for wartime planning of resource allocation between the public and private sectors and for other policy matters.

Quarterly estimates followed in latter 1942. The next year, receipts and expenditures of the general government sectors were shown, together with gross saving estimates. In 1944, representatives of the British, U.S., and Canadian statistical agencies met to discuss concepts and methods of estimation and presentation to make their estimates comparable and more useful (see Denison, 1947). Subsequently, the United States and Canada accelerated development of interlocking sector accounts, published in 1947 and 1948, respectively.

Concerned with promoting the spread of economic accounts throughout the world on a comparable basis, at the end of 1945 the League of Nations convened a group to develop guidelines. A memorandum prepared by Richard Stone based on his work in the United Kingdom was a landmark. It was published as an appendix to the Report of the Sub-Committee on National Income Statistics of the League's Committee of

Statistical Experts: *Measurement of National Income and the Construction of Social Accounts* (Geneva, 1947). This served as the basis for the first *System of National Accounts (SNA)* formulated in 1952 and published in 1953 (United Nations, 1953). In addition to providing guidelines for nations beginning economic accounts, the System provided a uniform basis for countries to report national income for publication in the *Yearbook of National Accounts Statistics*. The U.N. Statistical Office also provided technical assistance to the nations in process of developing national accounts. It became generally recognized that economic accounts were necessary to perform the quantitative analysis needed as background for projection and policy formulation.

The 1953 SNA provided a systematic framework for recording and presenting the main flows involved in production, consumption, accumulation, and external economic relations. There was a set of six accounts simple enough to fit on two printed pages. It went beyond the set of five accounts used in the United States, which was more consolidated with respect to the production and saving-investment accounts. A set of twelve supporting tables took various entries in the basic accounts and subdivided them. The estimates were to be entered in terms of current prices.

While there was a conscious effort to keep the accounts relatively simple, the authors also wished to construct a framework that could be elaborated in various directions. Already by 1952, progress was being made on economic accounts related to national income and product: input-output, financial (flow-of-funds), balance sheets and wealth statements, and estimates in constant prices. But the U.N. Statistical Office did not think the time was ripe to integrate the several types of accounts into one system since many countries lacked such accounts or were in early stages of developing them. In the United States, in 1957 an integration of the various accounts was strongly recommended in a report of the National Accounts Review Committee (1957) of the National Bureau of Economic Research chaired by Raymond Goldsmith at the request of the Office of Statistical Standards of the U.S. Bureau of the Budget.

Half a dozen years later, international discussions were begun based on experience in related accounts leading to appointment of an expert group by the U.N. Secretary-General to develop an improved and expanded *SNA*. Richard Stone again played a leading role in this project. No more concise statement of the revised *SNA* can be devised than is given in the preface to the 1968 U.N. report *A System of National Accounts* (United Nations, 1968, p. iii):

> The new SNA provides a comprehensive and detailed framework for the systematic and integrated recording of the flows and stocks of an economy. It

brings together data ranging in degree of aggregation from the consolidated accounts of the nation of the old SNA to detailed input-output and flow-of-funds tables into an articulated coherent system. The production account of the old SNA is disaggregated into input-output accounts in respect of industries and commedities and the flow "net lending or borrowing" is dismembered into the transactions in financial assets and liabilities of the institutional sectors and sub-sectors of an economy. The income and outlay and capital accounts are subdivided into the corresponding accounts for institutional sectors and sub-sectors; and balance sheet accounts for these categories of transactors, and the nation, are added to the accounts of the old SNA. The new system incorporates additional classifications in respect of the activities of government and private non-profit bodies and transfers of income so as to furnish much more adequate tabulations of data than the old SNA concerning the effects of these bodies on the economy, the provision of social and community services, and the redistribution of incomes. It also integrates constant-price data in respect of the supply and disposition of goods and services into the structure of the system.

The first four chapters of the report set forth the objectives, structures, and concepts of the 1968 SNA. In the next four chapters, the framework of the system is elaborated into standard accounts and tables with full definitions and classifications. The final chapter suggests ways in which developing countries might adapt the new SNA in the light of their own needs and capabilities.

1.4. The 1993 SNA Revision

In 1975, a U.N. study was made of the experience of various countries in preparing estimates for and using the SNA. The United States was one of the few major countries that had not adopted the SNA, although it had integrated the input-output matrix into the production account. But it had not integrated the Federal Reserve Board's flow-of-funds and balance sheets, although it did prepare tangible wealth estimates consistent with its investment estimates.

Those involved in planning for a *SNA* revision decided that major conceptual changes or extensions would not be made; rather, the revision would update the 1968 SNA, clarify and simplify its presentation, and harmonize the SNA with other international guidelines such as the IMF's *Balance of Payments Manual*. The process was funded and planned by the United Nations together with four other international organizations, which formed an Inter-Secretariat Working Group. The Group arranged a series of topical "expert group" meetings beginning in 1986 that reviewed issues and made recommendations for revision. Issues were also discussed in regional meetings and forums such as the International Association for Research in Income and Wealth. A number of experts attended all the meetings and formed a coordinating group for the final revision process.

The revised SNA manual was submitted to the U.N. Statistical Commission in February 1993. It was adopted by the Economic and Social Council on July 12 and published by the United Nations and four other international organizations in early 1994 under the title *System of National Accounts 1993*. A series of handbooks providing more detailed guidelines were to be prepared and issued subsequently to help make the system operational but have not yet been issued (Inter-Secretariat Working Group on National Accounts, 1993, ch. 2).

A good many of the differences betweent the 1968 and 1993 SNAs are related to the clarification and refinement of concepts and definitions with respect to statistical units, sectors and subsectors, financial instruments, valuations, and so forth. Other differences are more basic and are described below. They will be discussed in greater depth in some of the subsequent chapters. Annex I of *SNA 1993* is entitled "Changes from the 1968 SNA"; several dozen changes of greater or lesser importance are described there. The SNA volumes have become successively longer since 1953 (see Harrison, 1994, pp. 169–197).

Gross domestic product (GDP) remains the key aggregate in the revised SNA, but gross national product (GNP) is also shown. Since GNP includes net factor income from abroad in addition to domestic income and other charges against GDP, it is viewed as an income concept and called gross national income (GNI). Methods of deflating both aggregates to eliminate the effects of price changes are described. To deflate national disposable income, it is suggested that the implicit deflator for net national final expenditures (final consumption expenditure plus net capital formation) be used.

The new SNA clarifies the boundaries of production, particularly with regard to household activities, but the change would not significantly alter the magnitude of GDP estimates in most cases. As before, produciton is defined largely in terms of goods and services produced for and traded in markets. With regard to production of goods for consumption within the same households, the boundaries have been expanded and the handbook contains an extensive list of goods typically produced for own-account consumption. Production of household services on own account continues to be excluded, except for those rendered by hired workers and the rental value (imputed) of owner-occupied residences (but not that of major durables, which are counted as consumption rather than investment). The rationale is that the excluded services are incapable of being marketed since they result in current household consumption; they are difficult to measure, particularly in output units; and valuation of neither the nonmarket input nor output can be done precisely.

It is recognized that own-account household production is important in all countries and that its relative magnitude differs among countries and changes over time. Estimates of nonmarket production have been prepared by various respected economists (see Eisner, 1989), and household surveys have improved in accuracy and scope. The revised SNA does suggest that "in satellite accounts an alternative concept of . . . GDP be elaborated which is based on an extended production boundary, reflecting estimates for household production of services for own use" (United Nations, 1993, pp. 522–523, para. 35).

The revised *SNA* recommends the identification of imputed transactions and reroutings, particularly if they are significant, for the benefit of analysts interested only in monetary aggregates and components. This was not done in the 1968 *SNA*.

Volunteer labor outside the home is to be valued on the basis of actual compensation paid, even if well below the competitive market rate.

The 1968 SNA did not provide clear guidelines on the coverage of illegal or underground activities. But the revision makes it clear that the illegality of an activity or transaction is not a reason for excluding it from the accounts (United Nations, 1993, pp. xxxiii, 77, paras. 3.54–3.56). In fact, if the legal expenditures come out of receipts from illegal production, both sides of such transactions would have to be included to prevent accounting imbalance. It must be observed, however, that differences among nations in the extent to which they include illegal transactions or changes in the proportions would adversely affect international and intertemporal comparisons.

A major departure of the revised *SNA* from its predecessor is the introduction of the concept of actual consumption of households and government to supplement the concept of consumption expenditure. This involves breaking government expenditures into two parts: (1) expenditures that augment consumption of individuals, as indicated by the functional composition data, and (2) collective consumption—services provided to the community as a whole. Household consumption expenditures plus the individual consumption provided by governments plus the expenditures by private nonprofit institutions serving households equals household consumption. Government consumption is confined to the collective services.

The broader concept of household consumption is useful in welfare studies, particularly comparisons across time and countries, in the face of differences in the public and private mix, such as for health services.

SNA 1968 did not provide much guidance on the balance sheets of the system, including the coverage of assets. In the revised SNA, produced assets include not only tangibles but also intangible assets such as mineral exploration, computer software, and entertainment, and literary or artistic originals. The nonproduced assets include tangibles such as land, water, subsoil assets, and noncultivated biological resources and intangibles such as patented entities, leases and other transferable contracts, and purchased goodwill. Capital formation comprises net expenditures to acquire these assets, the value of work in progress (changes in inventories) until completion in the case of assets with long production periods, and the value of the growth of agricultural crops and livestock and cultivated assets. Net purchases of valuables (precious metals, gems, and so on) are included.

The concept of government capital formation has been expanded to include military durables except for weapons and the accumulation of all goods as inventories—not just strategic items.

Paradoxically, purchases of consumer durables will continue to be treated as consumption expenditures, although it is recommended that stocks of consumer durables be entered as memorandum items in balance sheets.

There was considerable discussion in the expert groups as to whether to count research and development outlays as investment. It was decided not to, although it was recommended that R&D outlays be identified and possibly be elaborated in a satellite account. Human intangible investments such as education and training are also not counted as investment, and the resulting human capital is not included in balance sheets.

SNA 1993 recommends provision of a change in the net worth account to recapitulate the transactions, other changes in assets, and revaluations that result in changes in the balance sheet. The revaluation account reflects changes in the value of both financial and real assets that stem from both relative and general price changes.

1.5. Overview of the Volume's Contents

Following this introductory chapter, the next chapter, "Design of Economic Accounts and the 1993 *System of National Accounts*," was written by Carol S. Carson, then director of the Bureau of Economic Analysis at the U.S. Department of Commerce. Mrs. Carson was actively involved in preparation of *SNA 1993* (as were her discussants), To use her own words in her letter of transmittal of the essay: "My paper is certainly not an 'easy read,' but I believe that it makes a contribution in explaining the basic structure of the SNA, which is not easy to get out of the 711-page publication. I hope I held to my own design: to take a reader step by step through the SNA's basic structure." The author starts with the building blocks of the system: institutional units combined into five major sectors, establishments combined into industries, then the accounts, proceeding from current accounts and accumulation accounts (flows) to balance sheets (stocks at beginning and ends of periods). The sequence and content of the accounts are summarized in her balance Tables 2.3 and 2.5.

She discusses various significant aggregates and then explains the supply and use (input-output) tables. Carson emphasizes that the integrated economic accounts, and the SNA generally are conceptual systems providing a framework for consistent reporting by various nations. But the specific content of the accounts will depend on the instructions and definitions in the questionnaire to be circulated by the U.N. Statistical Division.

Peter Hill, the first discussant of Mrs. Carson's chapter, also played a major role in the *SNA* revision as an official of the Statistical Directorate of the Organization for Economic Cooperation and Development (OECD). He supplemented Carson's "clear and concise description of the design and structure of the central system of the 1993 *SNA*." He then discussed the various ways in which the values of assets and liabilities held by institutional units may change over time. This accounting marks a significant improvement of *SNA 1993* over its predecessor.

The other discussant of Chapter 2, Jan van Tongeren, chief of the National Accounts and Statistical Classifications Branch of the U.N. Statistical Division, also was influential in the design of *SNA 1993*. In his discussion, van Tongeren emphasizes the flexibility of the system, which is the forcus of Chapter 3.

In Chapter 3, Professor Robert Eisner of Northwestern University points out that expanding the production boundary of GDP to include nonmarket economic activities would significantly affect its levels and movements. The effects on GDP would differ in different countries. Redefining investment to include nontangible and nonbusiness investment would have a much larger relative impact. But as a practical matter, Eisner felt that modified accounts would be prepared as supplements rather than substitutes for the existing ones. The vehicle proposed by the SNA 1993, satellite accounts, would permit "the use of complementary or alternative concepts . . . when needed to introduce additional dimensions to the conceptual framework of national accounts" (p. 489). The report suggests setting up such accounts in a variety of functional areas. Of these, Eisner discusses three major areas in some detail: household, research and development, and environmental accounts.

The Chapter 3 discussant, Graham Pyatt, of the University of Warwick in Coventry, England and, temporarily, the Institute of Social Studies in The Hague, questions whether the concerns of Professor Eisner and others who favor broader definitions of investment and production "should be consigned to a variety of satellites which orbit around a refurbished central system" He offers an alternative view that there should be a succession of GDP aggregates, as is now the case with the money supply, ranging from a Yo relating to the monetized economy to a Yx representing the opportunity cost of all human activity within which the other concepts are nested. Pyatt then discusses a number of particular issues such as the treatment of personal maintenance, human investment, and government outlays.

In Chapter 4, "Household Sector Income, Consumption, and Wealth," Heinrich Lützel of the German Statistisches Bundesamt first considers the coverage of the household sector and its subsectors and their role in national income accounts. He notes that household production, most of it nonmonetary, would be treated in satellite accounts where the production boundary must be specified, and household income defined. In discussing household final consumption, Lützel pays particular attention to the *SNA 1993*'s inclusion of individualized consumption outlays of general government and nonprofit institutions, and the inclusion of consumer durables rather than the volume of their services. He concludes his essay with a consideration of the issues involved in constructing household balance sheets.

In her comments on Chapter 4, Luisella Goldschmidt-Clermont concentrates on household production for own consumption, particularly that outside the SNA boundary. She questions the SNA boundary, but approves the use of a satellite account for estimates of household production. She compliments Lützel and his associates for their thorough estimates that demonstrate the great importance of non-market production.

In Chapter 5, "Capital and Wealth in the Revised *SNA*," Charles Hulten, professor at the University of Maryland, explains the SNA treatment of saving and investment, wealth and capital stocks, and capital income and services within the framework of capital theory. He applauds the 1993 system as a major advance, providing an internally coherent set of guidelines consistent with the neoclassical model of production and consumption. Aware that "the devil is in the details," Hulten discusses a number of the practical problems met in implementation of the SNA guidelines. He notes the controversial nature of the boundary lines drawn between investment and consumption, particularly in the non-business sectors. But he observes that the *SNA 1993* document recognizes the evolutionary nature of economic accounts and has left some issues unresolved.

The Chapter 5 discussant, Derek Blades, works for the OECD Statistical Directorate and participated in many of the expert groups that helped prepare *SNA 1993*. He congratulates Professor Hulten on "a cogent and insightful analysis of the theoretical underpinnings of the 1993 *SNA* treatment of this complex area." He further discusses issues involved in sectorization, categorization of investments, definition of capital and accounting for quality changes, and the perpetual inventory and alternative methods of estimating capital stocks, gross and net. He suggests that analysts in more countries conduct the type of empirical study done by Hulten and Wycoff on the prices of secondhand tangible assets of differing vintages.

The challenges of measuring government activities and interactions with other sectors, given the peculiar features of general governments, are discussed in Chapter 6, "Goverment in the 1993 *System of National Accounts*," by Jonathan Levin, until recently with the International Monetary Fund. He treats the problems of valuation, allocation of consumption, defining the line between market and nonmarket production, sectorization, distinguishing capital from current expenditure, and application of national accounts analysis of public finance. Levin is not uncritical of the treatments adopted in *SNA 1993*, such as the omission of implicit interest on public capital from the costs in terms of which government production is valued. But in general he believes that the changes introduced by the new *SNA* "must be viewed as a considerable achievements."

Utz-Peter Reich of the Fachhochschule Mainz considers Levin's chapter to be a "useful summary" of the materials relating to government scattered through the *SNA 1993* volume." But he would like to have seen a more critical evaluation of the SNA treatment of the governmental role in economic accounts. So his discussion is directed at some of the controversial issues. He notes the inconsistency between valuing outputs at market price and at cost without allowance for a property return as is the case with most general government services. He also discusses issues raised by identification of intermediate outputs of government, the treatment of social security funds, inconsistencies in the timing of transactions, and the classification of tax revenues.

In Chapter 7, "Financial Intermediation and Financial Accounts,"

Albert Teplin calls for continual flexibility and adequate detail in compiling national financial accounts. He draws on his experiences as chief of the Flow of Funds Section of the Division of Research and Statistics of the Board of Governors of the U.S. Federal Reserve System to point to developments that have blurred classification schemes—notably, the decline in the relative importance of traditional intermediaries and the rapid movement of funds into stock and bond mutual funds and a stream of innovations in markets that securitize financial assets and that may call for entirely new categories. Although Teplin thinks *SNA 1993* has the potential for flexible financial accounts, the generalized discussion in Chapter 11 of the U.N. report leads him to warn against hiding useful information within large categories of transactions and of sectors.

In responding to Chapter 7, Professor John Dawson of Grinnel College first comments "that finance has finally arrived in the *SNA 1993*" with its integration of financial accounts and balance sheets into the system and with its discussions of the functions of finance and the nature and uses of financial analysis. Dawson then deals with analytical problems raised by the evolutionary developments described by Teplin and suggests that we need some new conventions for measurement of financial intermediations. Finally. Dawson explains why to-whom and from-whom financial tracing is more feasible than is suggested by Chapter 11 of the U.N. report.

For the measurement of the volume of production and of productivity, *SNA 1993* provides guidelines for estimating real GDP and real stocks by industries and types of products. Comments on those guidelines, particularly the price index numbers used to deflate values, are provided by Professor Erwin Diewert of the University of British Columbia in Chapter 8, "Price and Volume Measure in the System of National Accounts." When current values cannot be decomposed into physical units and their prices, the report recommends deflation by a composite of prices of relevant baskets of goods and service or of assets or by an index of the general price level. It is recommended that the price deflators be annual chain indexes or fixed-base indexes when volume components must be additive, but with seriadic releasing. Diewert, a recognized expert on index numbers, discusses the issues systematically. He is cognizant of the importance of the price indexes for analysis of inflation and for revaluation accounts. He views the 1993 report's treatment of both price and volume indexes as generally satisfactory.

Chapter 8 by Diewert is discussed by Professor Robert Gordon of Northwestern University. He concentrates on quality changes as a source of error in price and volume measures. His own extensive investigations of changes in the quality of consumer and producer durable goods for the National Bureau of Economic Research indicates that the price indexes used to deflate outlays for durables have a significant (1.5 to 3 percent) upward bias, so the volume measures have a corresponding downward bias.

Chapters 9 and 10 deal with adaptations of the SNA for developing and transition economies. In Chapter 9, "Adaptation of the Revised *SNA* for Developing Eoonomies," Uma Datta Roy Choudhury, senior consultant at the National Institute of Public Finance and Policy in New Delhi, thinks that *SNA 1993* provides a large part of the analytically useful reporting requirements of developing economies. She does, however, call for more meaningful definitions of the concepts such as "modern" and "traditional" modes of production and "formal" or "informal" and "organized" and "unorganized" subsectors. She also suggests a few extensions of the system that might make it more useful for developing economies without impairing its value for advanced countries.

The discussant for both Chapters 9 and 10 on adaptations of the revised *SNA* for developing and transition economies is Anne Harrison of the OECD Statistical Directorate, who participated in many of the deliberations of the expert groups. She notes that there was unanimous rejection of the idea of having a special version of the SNA for developing countries; rather, it was considered more appropriate to have a single system with adequate flexibility. She then comments on the various needs of particular relevance to the developing world as identified by Mrs. Choudhury—the need for a household sector production account and a category of "mixed income"; the several types of output; and the distinction between monetary and nonmonetary output, urban and rural, modern and traditional output, and formal and informal activities. Harrison notes that these distinctions affect most economies to some degree, which underscores the appropriateness of having a single system of accounts.

In Chapter 10, "Adaptation of the Revised *SNA* for Transition Economies," Yuri Ivanov, deputy chairman of the Statistical Committee of the CIS, and T. Homenko discuss the relatively slow and uneven progress of the countries in transition in introducing the *SNA* over the past several years and the problems that arise in adapting it to conditions there, including the collection and processing of primary data. They also discuss the links between the former material product system and the *SNA* which will help in introducing the latter. Finally, they assess the prospects for progress in transition from the MPS to the *SNA*, which they expect to accelerate during the next five years.

In commenting on Chapter 10, Anne Harrison notes that in the latter stages of the *SNA* revision, it was clear that the SNA would supplant the material product system, so particular attention was paid to the needs of countries making the transition from command economies. She underlines the problems of basic data collection, noted by Ivanov and Homenko, and sectorization. There were not many conceptual problems; Harrison mentions the provision of social and cultural services by enterprises to employees, consumer subsidies, privatization, and the treatment of central banks. Two major practical problems of implementing the *SNA* are hyperinflation and the measurement of informal activities. Despite the problems, Harrison thinks the transition to the SNA will come more quickly than Ivanov expects, though the usefulness of the new accounts will depend on how well compilers and users of the accounts are reeducated.

Rob Vos, member of the Institute of Social Studies in the Hague, points out in Chapter 11, "The Foreign Sector: Toward a World Accounting Matrix," that *SNA 1993* has come close to harmonization with related systems of macroeconomic accounts, notably the International Monetary Fund's balance of payments statistics, but that some problems remain. Further, he describes a global accounting framework that would provide a continuing consistency check of international transactions and enable improved analysis of economic linkages among countries. He illustrates the nature of the framework with his world accounting matrix (WAM) for 1990. The WAM shows significant discrepancies between global trade receipts and payments. His reconciled accounts show, for example, much lower U.S. trade deficits and Japanese savings surpluses than do national data sources. If one accepts the rates and assumptions Vos uses to achieve global consistency with present data, it is clear that analyses and policy measures could be palpably affected by application of the WAM. Ultimately, of course, the underlying data sources must be improved.

Professor Yoshimasa Kurabayashi of Toyo Eiwa Women's University in Yokohama discusses four aspects of the Vos chapter. In the first, he explains why he likes the *SNA* clear definition of residents of a nation, necessary to delineate transactions with the rest of the world (nonresidents). Second, Kurabayashi makes several points in favor of the *SNA* 1993 sectoring of the economy versus the 1968 treatment. Then he points out the ways in which reconciliation between *SNA 1993* and the IMF'S *Balance of Payments Manual* (BPM) has been advanced, but he finds difficulties in the treatment of services of financial intermediaries. Finally, Kurabayashi discusses the approach to WAM by Vos that he believes should be encouraged. For this, he considers that international cooperation and coordination of research among countries would be indispensable.

In Chapter 12, "The United Nation *System of National Accounts* and the Integration of Macro and Micro Data," Richard Ruggles notes the importance for analytical and statistical purposes of such integration. In the 1968 *SNA*, imputations for nonmarket transactions and rerouting of market transactions were made at the macro level without separate identification, which precluded any attempt to develop micro data sets that would replicate the aggregates. But in the 1993 *SNA*, Ruggles shows that it is possible in each of the institutional sectors to identify separately the actual market transactions. Further, he argues that major advances in the technology of data processing and storage now make it feasible to edit and adjust data explicitly at the micro level, making possible the matching of the micro and macro totals. The advantages of being able to conduct consistent analyses using integrated macro and micro data are recognized in *SNA 1993*, but considerable work will be necessary to realize that objective.

Harry Postner shares Richard Ruggles' disappointment that the question of integration of micro and macro data was treated only briefly in *SNA 1993*. Ruggles had noted that in national accounts macroeconomic aggregates are not merely sums of microdata sets; they must be adjusted and reconciled to satisfy national accounting concepts and balance identities. But these adjustments and identities are rarely carried back to the microdata. Postner suggests that whereas purely conceptual adjustments could be carried back, there would be strong opposition to forcing the reconciliation adjustments on the microdata. Further, the aggregate estimates undergo a series of revisions, and it would be difficult to make a case for numerous revisions in the basic data for the sake of alignment. Provision for macro-micro data links would also increase the problems of reaching consensus on international standards. Micro data are obviously not available for macro estimates of the informal and illegal economies. Despite his recital of the problems posed by micro-macro integration, Postner does suggest it would be beneficial if the relevant statistical agencies documented the statistical gaps existing between comparable micro totals and macro estimates.

Finally, in Chapter 13, "Reliability and Accuracy of Quanterly GDP Estimates: A Review," Allan H. Young, former director of the Bureau of Economic Analysis, defines *reliability* with reference to successive revisions in the estimates. *Accuracy* refers to the total measurement error from defects in source data and estimating methodology. Accuracy can be only partially observed, and assessments must rest on close knowledge of sources and methods. Young believes that levels and swings in the statistical discrepancies are of limited use for assessing accuracy. He also looks at the differences in real product changes stemming from different methods of deflating current values to correct for price changes.

Allan Young's chapter is discussed by Sir Jack Hibbert, formerly with the U.K. Central Statistical Office. There the data on which national income and product estimates were based—administrative records, censuses and surveys, centering largely on micro data requirements—were taken as largely predetermined, and users made the best of them. Young maintains that producers and users need to understand the nature and size of errors. But Hibbert points out that to the extent producers can reduce or correct errors and biases, it is of less value for users to understand them. Ideally, the users, particularly government policy makers, should specify the degree of reliability and accuracy adequate for their uses and then try to influence the levels of resources devoted to producing estimates of the desired quality. But this influence is exerted sporadically, usually after officials have been seriously misled. Hibbert discusses various sources of error, noting that they may be greater in certain periods, such as where major changes in prices and quantities occur, making estimates in constant prices more problematical. He also argues that given a certain degree of reliability, analysis of current economic developments and their portent for the future becomes more important than further refinements of the data.

In general, the authors have tried to give their own views of the subjects they were assigned and describe and critique the new *SNA* treatment of the issues. In addition to critiquing the essays, the discussants often reveal different views of *SNA 1993* than the authors.

One purpose of this book is to promote the understanding of socio-economic accounts generally, and of the 1993 revised SNA in particular. Another purpose is to provide constructive criticisms of the SNA as it now stands that would be useful in a future revision as experience with the current system accumulates and as circumstances change. The ongoing goal is to make economic accounts even more valuable for the important uses discussed at the beginning of this introduction.

References

Carson, Carol S. (1975). "The History of the United States National Income and Product Accounts: The Development of an Analytical Tool." *Review of Income and Wealth*: 153–181.

Denison, Edward F. (1947). "Report on Tripartite Discussion of National Income Measurement." *Studies in Income and Wealth* (Vol. 10). New York: National Bureau of Economic Research.

Eisner, Robert. (1989). *The Total Incomes System of Accounts*. Chicago: University of Chicago Press.

Harrison, Anne. (1994). "The SNA: 1968–1993 and Beyond." In Z. Kenessey (ed.), *The Accounts of Nations* (pp. 169–197). Amsterdom: IOS Press.

Kendrick, John W. (1970). "The Historical Development of National Income Accounts." *History of Political Economy* 2 (Fall): 284–315.

Kendrick, John W. and Carol S. Carson. (1972). *Economic Accounts and Their Uses*. New York: McGraw-Hill.

Kenessey, Zoltan. (ed.). (1994). *The Accounts of Nations*. Amsterdam: IOS Press.

Marshall, Alfred. (1948). *Principles of Economics* (8th ed.). New York: Macmillan.

National Accounts Review Committee. (1957). *The National Economic Accounts of the United States: Review, Appraisal, and Recommendations*. Washington, DC: Joint Economic Committee of Congress, Subcommittee on Economic Statistics.

Pigou, A.C. (1932). *The Economics of Welfare* (4th ed.). London: Macmillan.

Studenski, Paul. (1961). *The Income of Nations*. New York: New York University Press.

United Nations. (1953). *A System of National Accounts and Supporting Tables*. Studies in Methods, Series F, No. 2. New York: United Nations.

United Nations, Inter-Secretariat Working Group on National Accounts. (1993). *System of National Accounts 1993*. Brussels/Luxembourg, New York, Paris, Washington, DC: Commissions of the European Communities-Eurostat, International Monetary Fund, Organization for Economic Co-operation and Development, United Nations, World Bank.

2 DESIGN OF ECONOMIC ACCOUNTS AND THE 1993 *SYSTEM OF NATIONAL ACCOUNTS*

Carol S. Carson

The *System of National Accounts*, or *SNA* as it is widely known, is a set of guidelines with two dimensions. As a set of guidelines for economic accounting, the *SNA*'s purpose is the same as that of economic accounts in general: to show how to organize information about the flows and stocks that represent an economy in an analytically useful way. To serve this purpose, the SNA provides concepts, definitions, classifications, accounting rules, and accounts and tables. Together they make up a comprehensive, integrated framework. In its second dimension, as set of guidelines for international use, the SNA's purposes are to guide contry statistical offices in the development of their own economic accounts and, in the interest of international comparability, to serve as a framework in which countries report their statistics to international organizations.

This chapter is about the design of the recently revised *SNA*. Design has been discussed by some giants in the field of economic accounting. For example, and citing only those who specifically wrote about design, George Jaszi (1958), in his landmark review of the U.S. national income and product accounts, "The Conceptual Basis of the Accounts," included a section on accounting design. Edward Denison (1971) also included a section on accounting design in a review of the U.S. accounts. Ingvar

Ohlsson (1961), in his book *On National Accounting*, had a chapter on "The Accounting Design." Nancy Ruggles and Richard Ruggles (1970) wrote a whole book, *The Design of Economic Accounts*, on the subject. All wrote about the economic units whose activity is to be recorded and how to group those units for presentation, and about transactions that represent economic activity and how to group them. Several also wrote about other topics—for example, consolidating and combining accounts, the role of aggregates within the accounts, and the competing virtues of simplicity and completeness. These and similar topics are at least as relevant in discussing the 1993 *SNA* as they were earlier. Even if agreement has been reached on some topics, the increasing comprehensiveness of the *SNA*'s coverage and the breadth of its applicability keep open many questions about design.

This paper deals mainly with the tables and accounts of the 1993 *SNA*. The concepts, definitions, classifications, and accounting rules that are the other elements of the 1993 *SNA* are discussed only in the context of the design of the accounts and tables. For example, the paper will not discuss the merits of recording production net or gross of consumption of fixed capital, but only how the tables and accounts are structured to implement the conclusion embedded in the *SNA*'s concepts. The paper outlines the underlying structure of the accounts and tables, shows how they fit together, and clarifies other features of their design. By this approach, the paper aims to make the tables and accounts, and thus the *SNA* of which they are part, more readily understood. This review of the accounts and tables lays the ground for assessing the contribution of their design to the *SNA*.

The *System of National Accounts 1993* (as a publication, hereafter referred to as *SNA 1993*) describes a very broad system (United Nations, 1993). The system is shown in Table 2.1. Of the three elements shown in the first column, this paper focuses on the central framework (or system, as it is called in the publication). The role of the satellite accounts and social accounting matrices, the other two elements, is to provide flexibility. That flexibility is part of the grand design, so to speak, of *SNA 1993* and is the topic of Chapter 3 in this volume. The central framework consists of the five parts shown in the second colum. To narrow the focus further, the paper concentrates on the last two of the five parts—the Integrated Economic Accounts and the supply and use table—as representing the basic design of *SNA 1993*. The other three parts can be viewed as providing additional depth to the basic design.

The paper first briefly describes some of the factors that influenced the system that emerged in 1993 from a decade-long revision process. It then proceeds step by step. It starts with the building blocks—flows and stocks and their grouping into activities and then into accounts, and units and their grouping into sectors and industries. The description of building blocks leads into the Integrated Economic Accounts. The main aggregates—that is, the widely used summary indicators from within the accounts—are then described. The paper next describes the supply and use table. Finally, the paper closes with some remarks, from a historical perspective, about the contribution to the understanding of a comprehensive and complex system of national accounts made by the design of the accounts and tables of the 1993 *SNA*.

By necessity, simplifications are made, but many of them are noted in footnotes to the text and tables. Terminology is a special problem. Not only is it necessary to use a number of technical terms, but some terms have meanings unique to the *SNA*. Many of the more gneral terms are defined in the text. In addition, a glossary of terms found in the tables is provided in Appendix 2.A.

The description and discussion throughout are structured to ease the way for persons mainly familiar with the U.S. economic accounts, the national income and product accounts in particular. Although the early development of the *SNA* and the U.S. national income and product accounts had much in common, for a number of years beginning in the mid-1960s the U.S. accounts evolved along their own course—the NIPA's and input-ouput at the Bureau of Economic Analysis, the flow of funds and balance sheets at the Board of Governors of the Federal Reserve System. In the 1980s, U.S. interest in the ongoing revision of the *SNA* and, more important, the increased concern for the international comparability of the economic accounting measures of puoduction, saving and investment, and trade coalesced as support for moving the U.S. accounts toward the *SNA*. The Bureau of Economic Analysis is working actively toward that goal.

2.1. Factors That Influenced the Design of the 1993 *SNA*

The 1993 *SNA* represents the latest stage in the development of international guidelines in the field of economic accounting. Three major factors influenced the design of the system that emerged from the decade-long revision process.

First, and pervasive in any discussion of design, the *SNA* is a conceptual system. *SNA 1993* describes the *SNA* as such a system, highlighting that it is a comprehensive, integrated, and consistent system of economic

Table 2.1.   Telescoping schematic of the *System of National Accounts, 1993*

1993 SNA, consisting of	*Central framework, consisting of*	*Integrated Economic Accounts, consisting of*
Satellite accounts Accounts that organize information to suit a particular analytical focus, but maintain links to the main accounts. They may add detail, or they may use concepts and definitions that, while internally consistent, differ from those in the main accounts.		
Social accounting matrices A matrix presentation of the SNA that incorporates detail of special interest (to date often about the household sector).		
Central framework	Population and employment tables Tables that show population data, to calculate per capita product and consumption aggregates, and labor input data, to use with output to calculate productivity. Functional analyses	

Tables that show four groups of transactions according to an international classifications by purpose or function: Individual consumption (food, beverages and tobacco; etc.), outlays of government (defense affairs and services, etc.), outlays of nonprofit institutions serving households (education services, etc.), and outlays of producers (current production programs, repair and maintenance, etc.).

3-dimensional analyses of transactions and holdings of financial assets and liabilities Tables that show not only a transaction or asset (or liability) category and one party to the transaction or holding the asset (or liability), but also the other party.

Supply and use table

Integrated economic accounts

Institutional sector accounts

Rest of the World accounts

Transactions accounts

Assets and liabilities accounts

Note: Shaded areas show parts of the 1993 SNA discussed in this paper.

accounts. The publication does not attempt, for example, to provide guidance on the format of the accounts and tables a country should use to present its accounts and tables. As a conceptual system, the *SNA* is meant to serve a wide range of analytical and policy needs. *SNA* also serves a statistical funcion; it is a framework around which a statistical system can be constructed and improved.

Because *SNA 1993* describes a conceptual system, from the outset of the revision process the intent had been to provide practical guidance and specialized guidance in supplementary manuals and compilation guides. Several of these are already in preparation. Further, it should be noted that just as the tables and accounts in *SNA 1993* are not meant necessarily to be used by a country to present its accounts, they are not meant to be the tables and accounts filled in by countries for reporting to international organizations. A separate questionnaire is being constructed by the international organizations for that purpose.

Second, over the *SNA*'s long history as a system of economic accounts and an international guideline, the comprehensiveness of its coverage and the breadth of its applicability have increased substantially. To go back only as far the 1968 *SNA*, that system had incorporated the statistical pictures of production provided by input-output accounts and of lending or borrowing provided by flow of funds accounts, and it laid the ground for balance sheets for the sectors and the nation. Further, it introduced constant-price data for goods and services. (For a fuller history, see United Nations, 1993, "Perspectives on the 1993 System of National Accounts: Looking Back and Looking Ahead.") The preface of *SNA 1993* notes four points about the ways in which the 1993 *SNA* builds on the 1968 system and reflects the overarching role the *SNA* has come to play in statistics:

- The 1993 *SNA* provides a more comprehensive view of an economy. It completes the integration of balance sheets, thus providing a fuller picture of the resources at the economy's disposal. It consolidates some important information—for example, on population and labor force, and on purchasing power parities— that previously had been separate from the economic accounts.
- The 1993 *SNA* is expected to the applied almost universally. Its framework was meant to be applicable to developed and developing economies alike, and special efforts were made to include explanations and clarifications that would ease the transition to the *SNA* by countries that had previously used an accounting system based on Marxist theory.

- The 1993 *SNA* reinforces the lead role that national accounts play in international statistics. National acccounts serve as a point of reference in establishing international guidelines for related statistics, such as the balance of payments. Harmonization of the statistical guidelines encourages efficient use of statistical resources and enhances the analytical power of statistics available to a variety of users.

- The 1993 *SNA* recognizes both the need to facilitate international comparisons and the need to encourage the SNA's use in economies that differ widely. It seeks to reconcile these sometimes conflicting needs by providing a framework thought to be widely applicable and by emphasizing flexibility. It provides, for example, alternative classifications, hierarchical structures, and other features that encourage flexibility.

Third, the purposes of the revision that led to the 1993 *SNA* were to update the 1968 system to fit new circumstances, to clarify and simplify it, and to harmonize it more completely with other international statistical guidelines. The updating included changes to recognize the emergence of inflation as a major policy concern, the changing role of government in many countries, the increasing importance of service activities, the increasing sophistication of financial instruments and markets, and the increasing concern with the environment's interactions with the economy.

2.2. Building Blocks

Economic accounting emerged from the older study of national income as a single aggregate with the recognition that a powerful analytical tool could be created by organizing information about an economy's transactors and the transactions in which they engaged in a group of accounts. As Richard Stone (1947, pp. 23–24) described the process, "We shall begin by classifying accounting entities into certain broad sectors . . . distinguised by function, and at the same time consider the different sorts of accounts and different types of transactions that require to be kept distinct. The object here is to combine accounting entities and transactions as much as possible so as to be left with a relatively simple system which can conveniently be handled."

The *SNA* uses the same building blocks of grouped transactors and transactions. The starting point in describing the *SNA*'s accounts and tables is with these building blocks. The building block that Stone called "transactions" has been broadened as the *SNA*'s coverage was broadened, and it is now referred to as *flows and stocks*. Their definition and grouping into activities and accounts is described first. The building block that Stone called "accounting entities" is called *economic units* in the *SNA*. The *SNA* recognizes two kinds of economic units. One kind, institutional units, is described in this section on building blocks; the other kind, establishments, is described later in the paper.

2.2.1. Flows, Stocks, Economic Activities, and Accounts

The *SNA*, as mentioned earlier, records information about the economy in two basic forms—flows and stocks. Information relating to economic actions and the effects of events that take place within a given period of time is recorded as a flow. Flows are of two kinds: transactions and other flows. Transactions are interactions between units by mutual agreement (such as purchases and sales) or actions within units that are analytically useful to treat like transactions (such as production for one's own use). Other flows, a category introduced in *SNA 1993*, are changes in the value of assets and liabilities that do not take place in transactions. Information relating to a position in, or holdings of, assets and liabilities at a point of time is recorded as a stock. Stocks are connected with flows; they result from the accumulation of prior flows, and they are changed by flows within the period.

The *SNA* groups flows according to the economic activity to which they relate. In defining "economic activity" in an accounting context, Richard Stone (1951, p. 1) refers to three as the basic ones: production, consumption, and adding to wealth. Ohlsson (1961, p. 121) specifically breaks out income distribution for a fourfold grouping: producion, income distribution, investment, and consumption. These groupings are very general, and further breakdowns are obviously possible.

The *SNA* provides an account for each activity identified as analytically important and for stocks as the results of those activities. Before examining in more detail the SNA's specific groupings of flows and thus the specific accounts, it will be useful to reconfirm the idea of an account. An account is the most basic structural element in economic accounting. An account organizes a group of related flows or stocks to present two perspectives on that group. The two perspectives, such as flows in and flows out, are often referred to as the two sides, and the two sides are meant to balance (sometimes with an item intended to balance the two).[1]

SNA 1993 has three general kinds of accounts: current accounts, accumulation accounts (a new term to indicate they cover more than the capital and financial accounts of earlier versions of the *SNA*), and balance sheets. Each kind has distinguishing structural features. These features relate to whether the account records flows (and which kind, transaction or other flow) or stocks, the kind of entries made on the left and right sides, the basis on which separate accounts are identified, and the kind and interrelationships of items that bring the accounts into balance.

Current accounts record transactions related to production and, in separate accounts, several stages in the distribution and use of income. The accounts show transactions that are uses on the left and that are resources on the right. *Uses* refers to transactions that reduce the economic value of the unit or group of units (elsewhere these are sometimes referred to as *debits* or *outgoings*), and *resources* refers to transactions that add to the economic value of the unit or group of units (*credits* or *incomings*). The balancing item for each account, on its left, is the opening balancing item for the next account in the sequence, on its right. The last balancing item in the current accounts is saving.

Accumulation accounts open with saving, record transactions and other flows that are changes in assets on the left, and changes in liabilities and in net worth (the difference for any unit or group of units between its assets and liabilities) on the right. Separate accounts record several kinds of changes. The balancing items, as will be explained, are more complex than in the current accounts.

Balance sheets present stocks, with stocks of assets (financial and nonfinancial) on the left and stocks of liabilities on the right. There are two accounts, an opening balancing sheet and a closing balance sheet. Net worth, the balancing item, is on the right, as is standard for balance sheets.

2.2.1.1. Introducing an Account.   So far, three points have been made: the SNA records information about an economy in terms of flows and stocks, it groups the flows according to the economic activity to which they relate, and it provides accounts for each identified acivity and the resulting stocks. Table 2.2, which shows the *SNA*'s production account for the total economy, illustrates these points. (The values shown in the illustrative accounts are the same as or derived from those shown in *SNA 1993*.) The account is in a form in which entries, with their values, are shown on two balancing sides. This form, called a T-account, takes it name from the thick lines in Table 2.2, the one across the top (uniting the items shown beneath it) and the one down the center (separating the two balancing sides). T-accounts are used in presenting and explaining

Table 2.2. Production account for the total economy in T-account form

Uses	Resources
Intermediate consumption 1,883	Output 3,604

Gross domestic product 1,854
  Consumption of fixed
    capital 222
  Net domestic product ... 1,632
	Taxes less subsidies on products 133

Total 3,737	Total 3,737

Note: The values shown in the illustrative accounts are the same as, or derived from, those shown in the *SNA 1993*.

the U.S. national income and product accounts; for example, the five-account system that summarizes the U.S. accounts is in that form (see Appendix 2.A).

The production account is the first of the current accounts. In fact, some presentation of production is usually first, in recognition of the central role that production plays in an economy. Three kinds of transactions related to production are recorded. On the resources side, output is shown. In addition, the item taxes less subsidies on products is needed because of the way the *SNA* values output. In *SNA 1993*, the preferred valuation for output is at basic prices—prices receivable by the producer for a unit of output minus any tax payable, and plus any subsidy receivable, on that unit as a result of its production or sale. If output is valued in basic prices, the amount of the taxes, less subsidies, must be shown separately if the resources-side total is to be at market prices and lay the ground for the balancing item in the account to be at market prices. On the uses side, intermediate consumption—the using up of goods and services when producing this output—is shown.

Domestic product is the item that balances the account. That is, given output (and the valuation item) and intermediate consumption, domestic product will balance the two sides of the account. The balancing item is shown in two variants, net and gross, with consumption of fixed captial as the standard difference between the two. The production account in *SNA 1993* differs from many accounts that earlier carried that name; they showed the several kinds of income generated in production on the uses side. The production account in *SNA 1993*, in contrast, stops short of showing all the transactions related to production and is structured to provide the well-known aggregate domestic product as a balancing item.

In Table 2.3, the first account is a rearrangement of the production account in Table 2.2. It then shows the other current accounts, the accumulation accounts, and the balance sheets. Table 2.3 introduces two features of the presentation of the accounts in *SNA 1993*.

First, the body of *SNA 1993* uses a form of presentation called a balance statement. Balance statements are more economical than T-accounts in that they present only once, in a middle column, the names of flows and stocks that would otherwise be repeated—for example, on both sides of an account where a unit or group of units records a given entry (such as interest, included in property income), both as a resource and as a use. The choice of form—whether a T-account or a balance statement or a matrix, for that matter—is more a matter of space, convenience, and perhaps even familiarity than substance.

Second, *SNA 1993* provides a classification of transactions and other flows, assets, and balancing items. For flows, the classification is according to the nature of the flows, such as wages, interest, taxes, and so forth. Further, and fitting neatly with the strengths of a balance statement, the flows are named and defined to be neutral with respect to the unit to which they are payable or receivable. (The classification avoids entries, such as "rental income of persons" found in the U.S. national income and product accounts, that specify a payee or recipient.) A unique code, consisting of a letter and a number, is provided for each kind of entry. (These are to the left in the center column of Table 2.3.) For a flow, the letter designates the kind of flow—transactions in goods and services (that is, products) as P, for example. Nonfinancial and financial assets, respectively, are coded as AN and AF. Balancing items are coded as B. The numbers in the code are hierarchical. For example, output is P.1, and P.11, P.12, and P.13 are three subcategories of output (market, for own final use, and other nonmarket).

2.2.1.2. Introducing the Sequence of Accounts. The production account arrives at domestic product, either gross or net. It does so via output and intermediate consumption, an approach that is less familiar to those who know the U.S. national income and product accounts than one that arrives at a product measure as the sum of goods and services sold to final users (sometimes referred to as *final demands* or as *final expenditures*). (In the United States, gross domestic product is most often thought of as the sum of personal consumption expenditures, gross private domestic investment, net exports of goods and services, and government purchases;

Table 2.3. Accounts for the total economy

CURRENT ACCOUNTS

Uses		Transactions and balancing items	Resources	
Total economy			Total economy	
PRODUCTION ACCOUNT				
	P.1	Output	3,604	
1,883	P.2	Intermediate consumption		
	D.21–D.31	Taxes less subsidies on products	133	
1,854	B.1*g	Gross Domestic Product		
222	K.1	Consumption of fixed capital		
1,632	B.1*n	Net Domestic Product		
GENERATION OF INCOME ACCOUNT				
	B.1*n	Net Domestic Product	1,632	
762	D.1	Compensation of employees		
191	D.2–D.3	Taxes less subsidies on production and imports		
679	B.2n, B.3n	Operating surplus and mixed income, net		
ALLOCATION OF PRIMARY INCOME ACCOUNT				
	B.2n, B.3n	Operating surplus and mixed income, net	679	
	D.1	Compensation of employees	766	
	D.2–D.3	Taxes less subsidies on production and imports	191	
391	D.4	Property income	416	
1,661	B.5*n	National income, net		

SECONDARY DISTRIBUTION OF INCOME ACCOUNT

| Changes in assets | | | Changes in liabilities and net worth |
Total economy			Total economy
	B.5*n	National income, net	1,661
212	D.5	Current taxes on income, wealth, etc.	213
322	D.61	Social contributions	322
332	D.62	Social benefits other than social transfers in kind	332
269	D.7	Other current transfers	239
1,632	B.6n	Disposable income, net	

USE OF INCOME ACCOUNT

| Changes in assets | | | Changes in liabilities and net worth |
Total economy			Total economy
	B.6n	Disposable income, net	1,632
1,399	P.3	Final consumption expenditure	
11	D.8	Adjustment for the change in net equity of households on pension funds	11
233	B.8n	Saving, net	

ACCUMULATION ACCOUNTS

| Changes in assets | Transactions, other flows, and balancing items | Changes in liabilities and net worth |
Total economy		Total economy
CAPITAL ACCOUNT		
	B.8n Saving, net	233
414	P.51–53 Gross capital formation	
−222	K.1 Consumption of fixed capital (−)	
0	K.2 Acquisitions less disposals of non-produced non-financial assets	
	D.9 Capital transfers, receivable	62
	D.9 Capital transfers, payable (−)	−65
	B.10.1 Changes in net worth due to saving and net capital transfers	230
38	B.9 Net lending (+)/Net borrowing (−)	

Table 2.3. *Continued*

ACCUMULATION ACCOUNTS

Changes in assets		Transactions, other flows, and balancing items	Changes in liabilities and net worth
Total economy			*Total economy*
FINANCIAL ACCOUNT			
	B.9	Net lending (+)/Net borrowing (−)	38
641	F	Net acquisition of financial assets	
	F	Net incurrence of liabilities	603
OTHER CHANGES IN VOLUME OF ASSETS ACCOUNT			
27	K.3, K.4	Economic appearance of assets	
4	K.5	Natural growth of noncultivated biological resources	
−9	K.6	Economic disappearance of nonproduced assets	
−11	K.7, K.8	Catastrophic losses and uncompensated seizures	0
4	K.9, K.10	Other volume changes, nec	−2
0	K.12	Changes in classification and structure	0
	B.10.2	Changes in net worth due to other changes in volume of assets	17
REVALUATION ACCOUNT			
	K.11	Nominal holding gains/losses	
280	AN	. . . on nonfinancial assets	
84	AF	. . . on financial assets	
	AF	. . . on liabilities	76
	B.10.3	Changes in net worth due to nominal holding gains (+)/losses (−)	288

BALANCE SHEETS

Assets			Stocks and balancing items	Liabilities and net worth
Total economy				Total economy
9,922	AN		Nonfinancial assets	
6,792	AF		Financial assets	
	AF		Liabilities	6,298
	B.90		Net worth	10,416
CLOSING BALANCE SHEET				
10,404	AN		Nonfinancial assets	
7,522	AF		Financial assets	
	AF		Liabilities	6,975
	B.90		Net worth	10,951

Note: The values shown in the illustrative accounts are the same as, or derived from, those shown in the SNA 1993.

see Appendix 2.B.) *SNA 1993* records these expenditures but does so as part of a sequence of accounts. The accounts in the sequence, as noted above, are for activities or, as has become apparent, parts of activities identified as analytically useful.

Following the production account in the sequence, Table 2.3 shows two current accounts that record the distribution of income from production. The generation of income account takes the point of view of the resident producer and shows the part of the distribution directly linked to production—the part distributed to labor as compensation of employees, to government as taxes on production and imports (less the amount payable by government in subsidies), to capital as operating surplus, and to capital and labor combined as mixed income (in the case of unincorporated enterprises owned by households, in which members of the household may combine labor and entrepreneurship). The account is structured to provide operating surplus and mixed income as balancing items. These balancing items represent the return from production before considering any property income—rent, interest, or similar income from lending or renting assets for use in production—payable or receivable.

The allocation of primary income account shows the remaining part of the distribution. It records the same kinds of incomes as in the generation of income account but takes the point of view of the recipient; in addition, it show property income, both receivable and payable. (For property income, as well as for compensation of employees and several other items, the difference between the values in Table 2.3 for uses and resources presages that transactions with nonresidents will need to be dealt with to close the system.) With the inclusion of property income, the balancing item is national income.

Having been distributed, income is then redistributed. The redistribution of income occurs via current taxes and other current transfers. These are transactions in which one party provides a good, service, or asset to another but does not receive a counterpart in return. These items, mainly cash transfers, are recorded in the secondary distribution of income account. The balancing item is disposable income—the amount that is available for final consumption expenditure and saving.

The use of disposable income account, the last of the current accounts in Table 2.3, shows the allocation of disposable income between final consumption expenditure and saving. (Final consumption expenditure is the rough analog of the U.S. accounts' personal consumption expenditures and government purchases of nondurable goods and services; government purchases of durable goods and the change in government inventories are included in capital formation in the SNA.)

The accumulation accounts record, in four separate accounts, four kinds of changes in assets, in liabilities, and in net worth. They record

- Changes in nonfinancial assets as a result of transactions,
- Changes in financial assets and liabilities as a result of transactions,
- Changes in assets and liabilities as a result of events other than transactions that affect the volume of assets and liabilities, and
- Changes in the value of assets and liabilities as a result of changes in the level and structure of prices.

The capital account and the financial account record, respectively, the first and second kinds of changes. Both accounts have net lending and net borrowing as their balancing items. In the capital account, net saving and net capital transfers can be used to accumuate nonfinancial assets—fixed capital, inventories, valuables (a new category in *SNA 1993*), and non-produced nonfinancial assets. Net lending shows the amount left over, so to speak, to provide finance directly or indirectly via financial instruments; net borrowing shows the amount that must be borrowed. The financial account shows how the lending and borrowing is carried out via various financial instruments.

The other changes in volume of assets account and the revaluation account are innovations of *SNA 1993*. They record, respectively, the third and fourth kinds of changes, the changes that comprise the "other"—that is, other than transactions—categories of flows. The other volume changes include, for example, depletion of assets and destruction by natural disasters, thus opening the *SNA* to accounting for the interactions between the economy and the environment. The revaluation account records nominal holding gains and losses (sometimes called capital gains and losses), both realized and unrealized.

The balance sheets, for the opening of the period and its closing, complete the set of accounts. A total (treated like a balancing item) on the right side of the capital account plus the balancing items in the last two accumulation accounts fully "explain" the change in net worth as coming from three sources: saving and net capital transfers, other changes in volume of assets, and nominal holding gains and losses.

2.2.2. Institutional Units and Sectors

So far, the discussion has been in terms of flows and stocks and grouping them into the accounts for the total economy. The second kind of grouping that determines the basic structure of a set of accounts is the grouping of units. The *SNA* recognizes two kinds of units in the economy—institutional units and establishments. (Establishments will be discussed in the section on supply and use tables.) An institutional unit is a unit that is capable, in its own right, of owning assets, of incurring liabilities, and of engaging in economic activities and transactions with other units. Institutional units that are resident in the economy are grouped together on the basis of their principal functions, behavior, and objectives; these groupings are called institutional sectors. There are five mutually exclusive institutional sectors:

- *Nonfinancial corporations*: legal entities that are principally engaged in the production of market goods and nonfinancial services;
- *Financial corporations*: legal entities that are principally engaged in financial intermediation or in auxiliary financial activities;
- *General government*: legal entities that, in addition to fulfilling their political responsibilities and their role of economic regulation, produce principally nonmarket services for individual or collective consumption and redistribute income and wealth;
- *Households*: individuals or groups of individuals who supply labor, engage in final consumption, and, if the owners of an unincorporated enterprise, engage in the production of market goods and services;
- *Nonprofit institutions serving households*: legal entities that are principally engaged in the production of nonmarket services for households.

The five institutional sectors make up the total economy. Thus, the total economy refers to the sum of all resident units. (The definition of residency thus becomes an important aspect of defining the coverage of the accounts.)

Two important interrelated features of the design of the accounts in *SNA 1993* can now be highlighted. The first of these is that the 1993 *SNA* includes a full sequence of accounts, as just described in a simplified form for the total economy in Table 2.3, for each of the five institutional sectors. Each institutional sector is provided with a production account, for example. Within each account, however, only the flows and stocks relevant to the institutional sector are provided.

The second of these features is that *SNA 1993* emphasizes sectors and analysis of sectors (even more than earlier versions of the *SNA*), and the design of the accounts is adapted to that purpose. Specifically, the structuring of the distribution and use of income accounts serves that purpose. The most noteworthy example is the provision of accounts that record final consumption not only in terms of goods and services for which expenditure is made but also in terms of goods and services acquired (or conversely, provided) free or at nominal cost.

Table 2.4 shows these two accounts, which provide a second view of income distribution and use. The two accounts—the redistribution of income in kind account and the use of adjusted disposable income account— are uninteresting at the level of the total economy; the values for the balancing items are the same as in the secondary distribution of income account and the use of disposable income account, respectively (which are reproduced in Table 2.4 to make comparison easier). Only for sectors—for general government, households, and nonprofit institutions serving households in particular—are the entries in these two accounts analytically useful.

The redistribution of income in kind account identifies, in the entry social transfers in kind, the goods and services received (or provided) free or at nominal cost. These goods and services are of two types. For some, the recipient household either does not incur the expense at all or is later reimbursed for the expenses incurred, such as medical services. For others, such as education, the goods and services are provided largely for individual consumption (rather than collective consumption, such as defense). The addition of the value of these goods and services to the disposable income of households and the subtraction of that value from the disposable income of government and nonprofit institutions serving households provide a new balancing item—adjusted disposable income. This new balancing item opens the use of adjusted disposable income account. On the uses side, a new item appears—actual final consumption, which is the total of final consumption expenditures plus or minus social transfers in kind. Saving is the same for each sector as in the disposable income account; income and consumption are raised or reduced by the same amounts.

This presentation, an innovation in *SNA 1993*, is constructed to give a clearer picture of the role of government in the economy and a more comprehensive measure of household income and consumption than is otherwise possible. In Table 2.4, social transfers in kind are a substantial part of final consumption expenditure by government (212 out of 368). The amount of goods and services actually available to households for consumption is still dominated by expenditures (1,015 of the 1,243), but the social transfers in kind (228, mainly from government) are not inconsequential. The adjusted disposable income and actual final consumption

Table 2.4. Two views of income distribution and use

Uses — Institutional sectors								Resources — Institutional sectors					
Total economy	Nonprofit ISHs	Households	General government	Financial corporations	Nonfinancial corporations	Code	Transactions and balancing items	Nonfinancial corporations	Financial corporations	General government	Households	Nonprofit ISHs	Total economy
SECONDARY DISTRIBUTION OF INCOME ACCOUNT													
						B.5n/B.5*n	Balance of primary incomes, net/National income, net	72	19	197	1,367	6	1,661
212	0	178		10	24	D.5	Current taxes on income, wealth etc.			213			213
322		322				D.61	Social contributions	14	39	268	0	1	322
332	1		289	29	13	D.62	Social benefits other than social transfers in kind				332		332
269	2	71	139	46	11	D.7	Other current transfers	10	49	108	36	36	239
1,632	40	1,164	358	22	48	B.6n	Disposable income, net						
USE OF INCOME ACCOUNT													
						B.6n	Disposable income, net	48	22	358	1,164	40	1,632
1,399	16	1,015	368			P.3	Final consumption expenditure						
11				11		D.8	Adjustment for the change in net equity of households on pension funds				11		11
233	24	160	−10	11	48	B.8n	Saving, net						
REDISTRIBUTION OF INCOME IN KIND ACCOUNT													
						B.6n	Disposable income, net	48	22	358	1,164	40	1,632
228	16		212			D.63	Social transfers in kind				228		228
1,632	24	1,392	146	22	48	B.7n	Adjusted disposable income, net						
USE OF ADJUSTED DISPOSABLE INCOME ACCOUNT													
						B.7n	Adjusted disposable income, net	48	22	146	1,392	24	1,632
1,399	0	1,243	156			P.4	Actual final consumption						
11				11		D.8	Adjustment for the change in net equity of households on pension funds				11		11
233	24	160	−10	11	48	B.8n	Saving, net						

1. Begining with D.7 Other current transfers, the entries for nonfinancial corporations, financial corporations, and general government in Table 2.8 of the SNA 1993 are not consistent with the entries found in the corresponding tables in the chapters. The entries in this table follow the chapters' tables.

Note: The values shown in the illustrative accounts are the same as, or derived from, those shown in the SNA 1993.

measures facilitate comparisons among countries and over time, where economic and social arrangements are likely to differ.

The U.S. national income and product accounts give much less emphasis to sectors than does *SNA 1993*. The contrast is apparent in the five-account summary of those accounts. The production of all sectors is combined in one account, which also shows the income of the business sector and its use. The detail about production outside of the business sector is suppressed. (This account is shown in Appendix 2.B.) There are appropriation accounts for the personal and government sectors and an account for transactions between residents and nonresidents. Finally, there is an account that is similar to the *SNA*'s capital account in that it covers saving, capital formation (limited to business), and a version of net lending or borrowing, but it is a consolidated account for the domestic sectors.

2.3. Integrated Economic Accounts

The accounts described so far make up sequences of accounts for the institutional sectors and for the total economy. They are balanced in the limited sense of recording both uses and resources for flows by resident units and assets and liabilities for stocks held by resident units. The next step toward the 1993 *SNA*'s integrated economic accounts is to add the rest of the world account. This account is where the harmonization with the International Monetary Fund's *Balance of Payments Manual* is especially apparent. SNA and balance of payments guidance for concepts, definitions, and rules of accounting are virtually identical.

2.3.1. Adding the Rest of the World Accounts

To record the so-far unrecorded part of flows between residents and nonresidents and the related stocks, the SNA provides a rest of the world account. It treats the group of nonresidents like an institutional sector, and its recording is from the point of view of that pseudosector. Exports of goods and services, for example, are recorded on the uses side.

The rest of the world account's structure is similar to the structure of accounts for institutional sectors, but it differs in ways that permit it to focus on relevant features of resident-nonresident relations. There are two current accounts. One of them, the external account of goods and services, records imports of goods and services, exports of goods and service, and—as the balancing item—the external balance. The other, the external account of primary incomes and current transfers, starts with the external balance of goods and services and then records the other current-account flows; its balancing item—the current external balance— is equivalent in function to saving for the institutional sectors. The external accumulation accounts, in four accounts that correspond to those for institutional sectors, record only a limited number of flows. They are mainly for financial flows because, when nonfinancial assets are owned by nonresidents, the entries are recorded as though the nonresident acquired the equity in a notional institutional unit as a financial asset and that institutional unit, in turn, acquired the nonfinancial asset. The final account, the external assets and liabilities account, shows the financial assets and liabilities held by nonresidents (and thus the consolidated liabilities and assets, respectively, of the institutional sectors).

Table 2.5 brings into one table the accounts discussed so far. Working out from the center on both sides, there are accounts for institutional sectors (omitting the additional accounts introduced in paragraph 40), for the total economy, and for the rest of the world. The external account of goods and services is placed at the same level as the production account; in fact, imports and exports of goods and services are shown first. Output is shown next; output for the five institutional sectors on the resources side sums to 3,604 for the total economy. Intermediate consumption for the five institutional sectors on the uses side sums to 1,883 for the total economy. Taxes less subsidies on products of 133, the valuation item not attributable to a sector, is shown on the resources side for the total economy. The balancing item in the production account is shown as value added/domestic product, using the slash to indicate that value added for the sectors (plus the valuation item) sums to domestic product for the total economy, 1,854 gross and 1,632 net. The balancing item for the rest of the world account is shown in the row below domestic product in the production account.

Other rows in Table 2.5 include rest of the world entries as needed. For example, compensation of employees now includes, on the uses side, six distributed by the rest of the world in addition to the 762 distributed by the five institutional sectors; on the resources side, it includes two receivable by the rest of the world in addition to the 766 receivable by households.

One very important feature of the accounting design can now be illustrated: It fully "explains" the change in the total economy's position as represented in the balance sheet due to a full year's economic activity. With net disposable income of 1,632 and final consumption by households,

Table 2.5. A simplified version of the integrated economic accounts

CURRENT ACCOUNTS

Uses: Goods and services (res'ces)	Uses: Rest of the world	Uses: Total economy	Uses: Nonprofit ISHs	Uses: House-holds	Uses: General government	Uses: Financial corporations	Uses: Nonfinancial corporations	Code	Transactions and balancing items	Res: Nonfinancial corporations	Res: Financial corporations	Res: General government	Res: House-holds	Res: Nonprofit ISHs	Res: Total economy	Res: Rest of the world	Res: Goods and services (uses)
									PRODUCTION ACCOUNT								
499								P.7	Imports of goods and services							499	
	540							P.6	Exports of goods and services								540
3,604								P.1	Output	1,753	102	440	1,269	40	3,604		
		1,883	9	694	252	29	899	P.2	Intermediate consumption								1,883
133								D.21–D.31	Taxes less subsidies on products						133		
		1,854	31	575	188	73	854	B.1g/B.1*g	Value added, gross/Gross Domestic Product								
		222	3	42	30	10	137	K.1	Consumption of fixed capital								
		1,632	28	533	158	63	717	B.1n/B.1*n	Value added, net/Net Domestic Product								
	−41							B.11	External balance of goods and services								
									GENERATION OF INCOME ACCOUNT								
								B.1n/B.1*n	Value added, net/Net Domestic Product	717	63	158	533	28	1,632		
								B.11	External balance of goods and services							−41	
	6	762	23	39	140	15	545	D.1	Compensation of employees								
	0	191	0	2	2	3	51	D.2–D.3	Taxes less subsidies on production and imports								
		679	5	492	16	45	121	B.2n, B.3n	Operating surplus and mixed income, net								
									ALLOCATION OF PRIMARY INCOME ACCOUNT								
								B.2n, B.3n	Operating surplus and mixed income, net	121	45	16	492	5	679		
								D.1	Compensation of employees				766		766	2	
								D.2–D.3	Taxes less subsidies on production and imports			191			191	0	
	63	391	6	41	42	167	135	D.4	Property income	86	141	32	150	7	416	38	
		1,661	6	1,367	197	19	72	B.5n/B.5*n	Balance of primary incomes, net/National income, net								

Table 2.5. Continued

CURRENT ACCOUNTS

Column groups — Uses (left): Goods and services (res'ces), Rest of the world, Total economy, Nonprofit ISHs, Households, General government, Financial corporations, Nonfinancial corporations; then Transactions and balancing items; then Resources (right): Nonfinancial corporations, Financial corporations, General government, Households, Nonprofit ISHs, Total economy, Rest of the world, Goods and services (uses).

G&S (res'ces)	Rest of the world	Total economy	Nonprofit ISHs	House-holds	General government	Financial corporations	Nonfinancial corporations	Transactions and balancing items	Nonfinancial corporations	Financial corporations	General government	House-holds	Nonprofit ISHs	Total economy	Rest of the world	G&S (uses)
								SECONDARY DISTRIBUTION OF INCOME ACCOUNT								
								B.5n/B.5*n Balance of primary incomes, net/ National income, net	72	19	197	1,367	6	1,661		
	1	212	0	178	0	10	24	D.5 Current taxes on income, wealth, etc.			213			213	0	
	0	322		322				D.61 Social contributions	14	39	268		1	322	0	
	0	332		0	289	29	13	D.62 Social benefits other than social transfers in kind				332		332	0	
	9	269	2	71	139	46	11	D.7 Other current transfers [1]	10	49	108	36	36	239	39	
		1,632	40	1,164	358	22	48	B.6n Disposable income, net								
								USE OF INCOME ACCOUNT								
								B.6n Disposable income, net	48	22	358	1,164	40	1,632		
1,399		1,399	16	1,015	368			P.3 Final consumption expenditure								
	0	11		0		11		D.8 Adjustment for the change in net equity of households on pension funds		11		11		11	0	
		233	24	160	-10	11	48	B.8n Saving, net								
	-41							B.12 Current external balance								

ACCUMULATION ACCOUNTS

Column groups — Changes in assets (left): Goods and services (res.), Rest of the world, Total economy, Nonprofit ISHs, Households, General government, Financial corporations, Nonfinancial corporations; then Transactions, other flows, and balancing items; then Changes in liabilities and net worth (right): Nonfinancial corporations, Financial corporations, General government, Households, Nonprofit ISHs, Total economy, Rest of the world, Goods and services (uses).

G&S (res.)	Rest of the world	Total economy	Nonprofit ISHs	House-holds	General government	Financial corporations	Nonfinancial corporations	Transactions, other flows, and balancing items	Nonfinancial corporations	Financial corporations	General government	House-holds	Nonprofit ISHs	Total economy	Rest of the world	G&S (uses)
								CAPITAL ACCOUNT								
								B.8n Saving, net	48	11	-10	160	24	233		
								B.12 Current external balance							-41	
414		414	19	68	40	9	278	P.51-53 Gross capital formation								
		-222	-3	-42	-30	-10	-137	K.1 Consumption of fixed capital (−)								
	0	0	1	4	2	0	-7	K.2 Acquisitions less disposals of non-produced non-financial assets								
								D.9 Capital transfers, receivable	33	0	6	23	0	62	4	
								D.9 Capital transfers, payable (−)	-16	-7	-34	-5	-3	-65	-1	
								B.10.1 Changes in net worth due to saving and net capital transfers	65	4	-38	178	21	230	-38	
0	-38	38	4	148	-50	5	-69	B.9 Net lending (+)/Net borrowing (−)								

FINANCIAL ACCOUNT

Code	Transaction														
B.9	Net lending (+)/Net borrowing (−)	50	641	32	181	120	237	71	−69	5	−50	148	4	38	−38
F	Net acquisition of financial assets								140	232	170	33	28	603	88
F	Net incurrence of liabilities														

OTHER CHANGES IN VOLUME OF ASSETS ACCOUNT

Code	Transaction														
K.3, K.4	Economic appearance of assets	27	0	0	0	3	0	24	0	2				0	0
K.5	Natural growth of noncultivated biological resources	4	0	0	0	4	0	0		0					
K.6	Economic disappearance of nonproduced assets	−9	0	0	0	−2	0	−7	0	0				0	0
K.7, K.8	Catastrophic losses and uncompensated seizures	−11	0	0	2	2	−3	−10	−4	2	0	0	0	−2	0
K.9, K.10	Other volume changes, nec	0	0	2	0	0	1	1	1	0	0	0	0	0	0
K.12	Changes in classification and structure	0	0	0	−6	−6	0	6	17	−4	2	2	0	17	0
B.10.2	Changes in net worth due to other changes in volume of assets														

REVALUATION ACCOUNT[2/]

Code	Transaction														
K.11	Nominal holding gains/losses	0	280	8	80	44	4	144	18	51	7	0	0	76	
AN	… on nonfinancial assets	7	84	1	16	2	57	8	134	10	39	96	9	288	
AF	… on financial assets													3	
AF	… on liabilities													4	
B.10.3	Changes in net worth due to nominal holding gains (+)/losses (−)														0

Table 2.5. Continued

BALANCE SHEETS

Assets

Goods and services (res.)	Rest of the world	Total economy	Nonprofit ISHs	House-holds	General government	Financial corporations	Nonfinancial corporations	Stocks and balancing items	
								OPENING BALANCE SHEET	
0		9,922	324	2,822	1,591	144	5,041	Nonfinancial assets	AN
	573	6792	172	1819	396	3,508	897	Financial assets	AF
								CLOSING BALANCE SHEET	
0		10,404	349	2,932	1,647	145	5,331	Nonfinancial assets	AN
	630	7,522	205	2,018	519	3,802	978	Financial assets	AF

Liabilities and net worth

	Stocks and balancing items	Nonfinancial corporations	Financial corporations	General government	House-holds	Nonprofit ISHs	Total economy	Rest of the world	Goods and services (taxes)
AN	Nonfinancial assets								
AF	Financial assets	1,817	3,384	687	289	121	6,298	297	
AF	Liabilities	4,121	268	1,300	4,352	375	10,416	276	
B.90	Net worth								
AN	Nonfinancial assets								
AF	Financial assets	1,972	3,669	863	322	149	6,975	388	
AF	Liabilities	4,337	278	1,303	4,628	405	10,951	242	
B.90	Net worth								

1. Beginning with D.7 Other current transfers, the entries for nonfinancial corporations, financial corporations, and general government in Table 2.8 of the SNA 1993 are not consistent with the entries found in the corresponding tables in the chapters. The entries in this table follow the chapters' tables.

2. Following the SNA, differences between data on individual items and totals of holding gains/losses may not be consistent due to rounding errors.

Note: The values shown in the illustrative accounts are the same as, or derived from, those shown in the SNA 1993.

Simplifications in addition to those noted in paragraph 56:

• After the Production Account, the balancing items that, in principle, can be both net and gross of capital consumption are only shown net.

• Valuation of output is at basic prices; the alternative (not preferred) valuations and thus the alternative specifications for taxes are not shown.

• Names for the current Rest of the World Accounts not shown.

• Actual final consumption and adjusted disposable income are not shown, nor are subaccounts to derive entrepreurial income.

• The Financial Account does not show transactions by type of financial asset and liability.

• Revaluation Account has two subaccounts that are not shown: One shows neutral holding gains/losses based on revaluation in proportion to the general price level, and one shows real holding gains/losses based on revaluation in terms of the specific prices of the asset or liability.

• Several flow categories are combined (although the codes are shown, as in the Other Changes in Volume of Assets Account).

nonprofit institutions serving households, and government totaling 1,399, net saving is 233. Net saving plus net capital transfers from the rest of the world sum to 230 (and are the financing for net capital formation of 192 and lending to the rest of the world of 38). That 230 plus other changes in the volume of assets (such as the discovery or depletion of subsoil assets) of 17 and nominal holding gains of 288 fully "explain" the change in the economy's net worth from the opening balance sheet to the closing balance sheet.

2.3.2. Adding the Goods and Services Account

Table 2.5 also shows an account, the goods and services account, that will not be familiar to most users of U.S. economic accounts. This account is shown as two columns (at the outer sides of Table 2.5), with entries in (the relatively few) rows where there are transactions in goods and services. The sum of the entries in the left column balances the sum of those in the right column.

To those who have not encountered this presentation before, it may seem a bit odd. Why is the goods and services account in a column? So far, the accounts have consisted of groups of rows. The answer begins by noting that, within the accounts presented so far, most rows are balances for the total economy (and, when relevant, the rest of the world). These are balances either between the two sides in the same row or between one row in one account and another row with the same name in another account. For example, the sum of entries for property income as resources, in the allocation of primary income account, is balanced in the same row by total uses. A look at Table 2.5 shows that the rows for the various transactions in goods and services are not balanced in this way. For example, the row for output, in the production account, shows entries for each of the institutional sectors and for the total economy on the resources side, but no such entries on the uses side. The row for final consumption expenditure, in the use of income account, shows entries in three institutional sectors and the total economy on the uses side and no such entries on the resources side.

But why are transactions in goods and services presented differently? Transactions in goods and services could be balanced in a single row, with the sum of the resources equaling the sum of the uses. However, in addition to being part of this relationship, each kind of transaction in goods and services has relationships with other transactions that are analytically interesting. Presenting all transactions in goods and services in a single row would preclude showing these additional relationships. Thus, transactions in goods and services are not balanced in a single row so that, instead, each kind of transaction can be shown separately in the appropriate account to show these relationships. Output and intermediate consumption, for example, are shown in the production account to reveal their relationship with the balancing item, domestic product. Final consumption expenditure is shown in the use of income account to reveal the income-consumption-saving relationship, and similarly gross capital formation is shown in the capital account to reveal its role in the saving-investment relationship. Analytical relationships such as these lie at the heart of the economic process displayed in the economic accounts.

Finally, circling back, where does the goods and services account fit into this design? The goods and services account provides the balance for the transactions in goods and services shown in the various rows. It records entries reversed from the usual sides—that is, with the entries that are resources on the left and the entries that are uses on right. On the left side of the table, the values in the column for goods and services are the counterparts of (that is, provide the balance for) the resources of the total economy and rest of the world: imports and output (along with the taxes less subsidies on products). On the right side of the table, the values in the column for goods and services are the counterparts of the uses of the total economy and rest of the world: exports, intermediate consumption, final consumption expenditure, and gross capital formation. At the foot of the columns is shown an important identity: total resources equal total uses.

Although the goods and services account per se may seem a bit odd to those who have not previously encountered it, its contents are more familiar, especially when rearranged. Table 2.6 shows the goods and services account in T-account form for the total economy. By simple rearrangement, the entries sum to gross domestic product; the intermediate consumption entry is moved to the left and its sign changed (it is entered as a negative item in the balance), and the import entry is moved to the right and its sign changed. Then, the familiar final expenditure components all appear on the right.

2.3.3. Wrapping up of the Integrated Economic Accounts

The goods and services account is one of a kind of accounts called *transactions accounts*. Such an account recapitulates, for a given trans-action or group of transactions, the resources and uses. With the exception

Table 2.6. Goods and services account for the total economy

Resources		Uses	
Output	3,604	Intermediate consumption	1,883
Taxes less subsidies on products	133	Final consumption expenditure	1,399
Imports of goods and services	499	Gross capital formation	414
		Exports of goods and services	540
Total	4,236	Total	4,236

Note: The values shown in the illustrative accounts are the same as, or derived from, those shown in the *SNA 1993*.

of the goods and services account, a recapitulation drawn from Table 2.5 would be for each sector that engages in this kind of transaction. For example, a transactions account for property income drawn from Table 2.5 would show, all in the same row, resources for each of the five institutional sectors and rest of the world summing to 454 and balanced by uses for each of the five sectors and the rest of the world summing to 454. In the case of the goods and services account, as was shown, the recapitulation is at the level of the total economy plus the rest of the world.

Table 2.5 is a simplified version of the table in *SNA 1993* known as the integrated economic accounts. Several of the simplifications made in Table 2.5 are to omit visual checks and analytical conveniences (other major simplifications are listed at the bottom of Table 2.5). In the first category, it omits the columns that show as total the sum of the columns for total economy and the rest of the world. In the second category, Table 2.5 omits the recapitulation of accumulation accounts that is in a changes in balance sheet account. This kind of account, in turn, is a simplification of a kind of account called an *asset and liability account*. For a given kind of asset or liability, such an account recapitulates the four kinds of flows recorded in the accumulation accounts and the opening stocks and closing stocks recorded in the balance sheets.

The integrated economic accounts are described as being at the center of the *SNA*'s accounting framework. In fact, the appearance of *integrated* in their title carries the meaning that several kinds of economic accounts are brought together within its structure. The several kinds of accounts are presented in the integrated economic accounts only in summary form; full detail is shown distributed through the chapters that explain them and collected in T-account form in an appendix in the accounts elsewhere in *SNA 1993*. However, the principal economic interrelations are displayed there, as sampled above in describing the handling of transactions in goods and services. Further, the major aggregates are displayed there, as will be described in the next section.

The integrated economic accounts of *SNA 1993* invite comparison with the five-account summary of the U.S. national income and product accounts and the summary matrix of the U.S. flow of funds accounts (Board of Governors, 1991, pp. 10–11). All three are interlocking sets of accounts that provide an overview of their respective systems. As overviews, they are useful in gaining an understanding of the scope of the systems and interrelations that are structured within them. They are the tips of the iceberg in that a wealth of detail is provided in tables and accounts that tie into them. Of course, the integrated economic accounts are more comprehensive; they provide an overview of a system that embraces the coverage of both U.S. sets of accounts and more. A further contrast is that the five-account summary and the flow-of-funds summary matrix are overviews of operational systems, whereas the integrated economic accounts are an overview of a conceptual system.

2.4. Aggregates

The SNA provides a number of summary indicators used for analysis and comparisons over time and across countries. Most of these aggregates, which are viewed as important but certainly not the only reason for preparing economic accounts, are identified within the integrated economic accounts. Some are totals of transactions, which are summed across the institutional sectors. Final consumption expenditure and gross capital formation are such aggregates. Many are balancing items in the integrated economic accounts, either summed across the institutional sectors or for the rest of the world account.

Table 2.7 summarizes the aggregates of production, income, saving, net worth, and expenditure—the ones that are balancing items in the accounts for institutional sectors. In the *SNA*, the accounts, by design, yield these aggregates. (One result is the substantial number of accounts, even in the simplified presentation in this paper.) In contrast, aggregates appear in several ways in the five-account summary of the U.S. national income and product accounts. Some like personal saving, are like

Table 2.7. Aggregates of production, income, saving, net worth, and expenditure

Aggregate	Concept	Coverage	Value[1] and derivation[2]	
			Across institutional sectors	For total economy
Domestic product (GDP, NDP)	Production	Value added by resident producer units	1,854 = sum of value added (B.1g), gross 1,632 = sum of value added (B.1n), net	= by production: Output + taxes, less subsidies, on products − intermediate consumption = by demand: Final consumption expenditure + gross capital formation + exports of goods and services − imports of goods and services = by income: Compensation of employees + taxes, less subsidies, on production and imports + operating surplus and mixed income, gross
National income (GNI, NNI)	Income receivable as a result of participating in production or owning assets needed for production	Primary incomes receivable by resident units	1,661 = sum of balance of primary incomes (B.5), net	= NDP + taxes, less subsidies, on production and imports, net receivable from abroad + compensation of employees, net receivable from abroad + property income, net receivable from abroad
National disposable income (GNDI, NNDI)	Income available for final consumption and saving	Primary incomes receivable by resident units + current transfers receivable (except taxes, less subsidies, already included) by resident units from abroad less corresponding items payable	1,632 = sum of disposable income (B.6), net	= NNI + current taxes on income, wealth, etc., net receivable from abroad + social transfers and benefits and other current transfers, net receivable from abroad

Table 2.7. *Continued*

| | | | Value[1] and derivation[2] | |
Aggregate	Concept	Coverage	Across institutional sectors	For total economy
National saving	Disposable income not used for final consumption	Disposable income as defined for GNDI less final consumption expenditures of resident units	233 = sum of saving (B.8), net	= NNDI − final consumption expenditure
National worth	Wealth	Nonfinancial assets held by resident units and net position vis-a-vis the Rest of the World	10,951 = sum of net worth (B.90), closing	= net worth, opening + changes in net worth = closing assets − closing liabilities
National expenditure	Final use of production	Final use of goods and services by resident units	Not applicable	1,813 in the goods and services account: final consumption expenditure + gross capital formation

Simplifications

- Actual final consumption or adjusted disposable income considerations omitted.
- The adjustment for the change in net equity of households on pensions funds omitted.

1. As shown in numerical examples in *SNA 1993* and in tables in this paper derived therefrom.

2. The production, income, and saving aggregates shown can be either gross or net of consumption of fixed capital. After domestic product, only the net values are presented.

balancing items in the *SNA* sense. Some are presented as totals rather than as balancing items. For example, gross domestic product is a total. Still other measures that are aggregates in the SNA are presented as components or otherwise do not exist as aggregates in the U.S. national income and product accounts. The *SNA*'s national expenditure is an example.

2.4.1. Domestic Product, National Income, and the Attributes of the Aggregates

Domestic product is derived in the *SNA* as value added in production by resident units, the sum of value added by institutional sector (and as will be discussed shortly, by industry). For the total economy, it also can be derived in the three familiar ways: by the demand approach, as the sum of expenditures by final users; by the production approach, as output plus taxes (less subsidies) on products (assuming the use of the preferred basic prices for valuing output) less intermediate consumption; and by the income approach, as the sum of primary income distributed by resident producing units.

The design of *SNA 1993* reflects choices made about three long-discussed attributes of aggregates: whether they are gross or net of consumption of fixed capital, whether their coverage is domestic or national, and whether their valuation is at market price or factor cost.

Domestic product, and the other balancing items in the current accounts that are considered aggregates, are shown both gross and net of consumption of fixed capital. Thus, the production account shows two balancing items, gross and net value added, which for the total economy become gross and net domestic product. Showing both the net and gross values is a compromise between conceptual preference and practice. *SNA 1993* argues that value added should conceptually exclude the counterpart of consumption of fixed capital because it is not newly created value; it is really a reduction in the value of previously created fixed assets when they are used up in the production process. *SNA 1993* recognizes, however, that GDP is commonly used, in part for practical reasons. The depreciation of fixed assets as calculated in business accounting does not generally match SNA concepts, so estimates of the consumption of fixed capital must be made using the present value of the stock of fixed assets, the lifetime of various types of assets, assumed patterns of depreciation, and so on. Thus, even when these calculations are made, gross figures are more often readily available, or available earlier, and are generally considered more comparable between countries.

SNA 1993 refocuses the distinction that sometimes had been drawn between aggregates described as *domestic* and *national* on differences between production and income. The design of the integrated economic accounts highlights two points about these aggregates, one a point of similarity and one a point of difference between them. The similarity is that the aggregates are defined in terms of a single set of resident economic units, those making up the total economy. The design highlights this point by showing these aggregates (and the others) vertically in two columns. The difference is that one is part of the production process and the other is part of the distribution of income. The design highlights this point by placing the aggregates within in the sequence of accounts.

Gross domestic product records the production of the resident economic units. Gross national income is a measure of income of those same units. Specifically, it is their primary income—that is, income related to production either from participating in production or owning assets needed for production. It is the income related to the production measured by gross domestic product less the income payable to nonresident units related to that production plus the income receivable by resident units related to production abroad. Thus, gross national income is gross domestic product (or, phased in terms of income, gross domestic income) plus net primary income from abroad. In the 1953 *SNA*, that aggregate had been a product aggregate—gross national product. (Gross national product did not appear as an aggregate in the 1968 system.)[2] *SNA 1993* points out that, strictly speaking, that aggregate is a measure of income, not product, because the production abroad attributable to residents and the domestic production attributable to nonresidents is not measurable except as income. In other words, a measure that includes net income from abroad could not be a product measure and must be an income measure. (The *national* can be used to flag income measures that include net income of residents from abroad.)[3]

Gross value added, or gross domestic product, is at market prices. In fact, in many of the text references in *SNA 1993*, gross domestic product and aggregates derived from it are referred to as "at market prices." Gross value added at factor cost is not a concept explicitly presented in *SNA 1993*. *SNA 1993* argues that the conceptual difficulty with gross value added at factor cost is that there is no observable vector of prices such that gross value added at factor cost can be obtained directly by multiplying the price vector by the vector of quantities of inputs and outputs that defines the production process. By definition, "other taxes or subsidies on production," which are those that are not payable per unit, cannot be eliminated from the input and output prices. Thus, despite its traditional name, gross value added at factor cost is not strictly a measure of value added (and is a measure of income). Value added at factor cost can, however, easily be derived from value added presented in Table 2.5 by subtracting the value of any taxes, less subsidies, on production payable out of gross value added. These are the "other taxes on production" (that is, taxes less subsidies on production and imports other than the taxes less subsidies on products).

2.4.2. Other Aggregates

Two income aggregates are provided. One, national income, was already introduced as the income receivable by resident units from participating in production or from owning assets needed for production. The second is national disposable income. The transition to *disposable* in *SNA 1993* is made in terms of current transfers—by adding current transfers receivable and subtracting current transfers payable by resident units. For the total economy, this transition is made by recording those receivable and payable from the rest of the world.

National saving is national disposable income not used for final consumption; it is thus available to finance accumulation.

So far, the aggregates are within the most widely known part of the accounting structure, the production and income accounts. National worth, from balance sheets, can be viewed as the total of nonfinancial assets held by resident units and the net position of the total economy vis-a-vis the rest of the world. The derivation of closing net worth within the structure of the accumulation accounts is as opening net worth plus the sum of changes due to saving and capital transfers, other changes in the volume of assets, and nominal holding gains and losses, and it reflects the integration of the balance sheets within the overall accounting structure.

National expenditure, from the goods and services accounts, is final consumption plus gross capital formation by resident units. As a significant part of the use of goods and services, it will make its appearance again in the description of the supply and use tables.

2.5. Supply and Use Tables

Earlier it was mentioned that the *SNA* recognizes two kinds of units, and one kind—the institutional unit and its grouping into sectors—was explained. The other kind of unit, an *establishment*, is an institutional unit engaged in production, or a part of such a unit, that is situated in a single location and in which only a single productive activity is carried out or in which the principal productive activity accounts for most of the value added.[4] Units of this kind are needed for analyses of production in which the technology of production plays an important role; an institutional unit such as a corporation, for example, may produce several kinds of goods and services and is thus too heterogeneous to serve as the unit for such analyses. Establishments are grouped on the basis of their principal activity; these groupings are called *industries*.[5]

Having introduced establishments and industries, a moment's reflection might lead to the comment that, although the integrated economic accounts were described above as providing an overview of an economy, they do not provide information about industries. Such information could have been built in, however. The rows for output, intermediate consumption, value added, and the incomes generated in production might have been subdivided by industry. Similarly, the integrated economic accounts did not have detail for goods and services, but the columns for the goods and services account could have been subdivided by type of product.[6]

Instead, the supply and use table is the part of the *SNA*'s central framework that displays this information. Specifically, it presents a production account and a generation of income account by industry, and it presents the goods and services account by product.

Table 2.8 is a schematic presentation of a supply and use table. (Such a table is sometimes referred to as an *input-output table* or *matrix*.) It shows industry detail (with medium shading) plus some additional items in the columns, and it shows goods and services detail (with light shading) plus some additional items in the rows. One industry is shown in column 4, to suggest industry detail, and one product is shown in row 1 to suggest product detail; leaders are shown in other columns and rows.

The top panel presents the supply of products: the detail by industry is for output. Output plus columns for imports of goods and services and two valuation items sum to the total supply of goods and services at purchasers' prices in column 1, all by type of product. The bottom panel presents, first of all, the use of products: the detail by industry is for intermediate consumption. Intermediate consumption plus exports of goods and services, final consumption, gross capital formation, and the valuation item in additional rows sum to total uses of goods and services at purchases' prices in column 1, again all by type of product.

In Table 2.8, values have been entered for entries already encountered in Table 2.5. The total supply of goods and services in the upper panel, of

Table 2.8. Schematic of a supply and use table, reduced format

SUPPLY OF PRODUCTS

Resources	Total supply at purchasers' prices (1)	Trade and transport margins (2)	Taxes less subsidies on products (3)	Output in industries								Total industry, in basic prices (12)		Imports of goods and services (14)
				Agriculture, hunting, forestry fishing (4)	(5)	(6)	(7)	(8)	(9)	(10)	(11)		(13)	
Goods and services														
Agriculture, forestry and fishery products														
1.														
2.														
3.														
4.														
5.														
6.														
7.														
8.														
9.														
10.														
11. Total	4,236											3,604		499

USE OF PRODUCTS, PURCHASERS' PRICES

Uses	Total uses in purchasers' prices (1)	Trade and transport margins (2)	Taxes less subsidies on products (3)	Intermediate consumption in industries								Total industry, in basic prices (12)	Total economy (13)	Exports of goods and services (14)	Final consumption (15)	Gross capital formation (16)
				Agriculture, hunting, forestry fishing (4)	(5)	(6)	(7)	(8)	(9)	(10)	(11)					
Goods and services																
Agriculture, forestry and fishery products																
1.																
2.																
3.																
4.																
5.																
6.																
7.																
8.																
9.																
10.																
11. Total uses in purchasers' prices	4,236											1,883		540	1,399	414

Table 2.8. Continued

USE OF PRODUCTS, PURCHASERS' PRICES

Uses	Total uses in purchasers' prices (1)	(2)	Taxes less subsidies on products (3)	Agriculture hunting, forestry fishing (4)	Intermediate consumption in industries .... (5)	.... (6)	.... (7)	.... (8)	.... (9)	.... (10)	.... (11)	Total industry, in basic prices (12)	Total economy (13)	Exports of goods and services (14)	Final consumption (15)	Gross capital formation (16)
12. Total gross value added/gross domestic product													1,854			
13. Compensation of employees			133										762			
14. Taxes less subsidies on production and imports			133										191			
15. Taxes less subsidies on products													133			
16. Other taxes less subsidies on production													58			
17, 18. Mixed income and operating surplus, net													679			
19. Consumption of fixed capital													222			
20, 21. Mixed income and operating surplus, gross													901			
22. Total												3,604				

Note: The values shown in the illustrative accounts are the same as, or derived from, those shown in the SNA 1993.

course, equals total uses in the lower panel. This value of 4,236 is recognizable as the total at the foot of the goods and services account in Table 2.5.

Other values are also recognizable from Table 2.5. In the bottom panel, total industry uses, summed across all industries in row 22, equals that table's total output (3,604); total uses of products in intermediate consumption, summed across all industries in row 11, equals that table's intermediate consumption (1,883); and total value added, summed across all industries in row 12 and representing the total economy, equals that table's gross domestic product (1,854). In other words, a production account for industries is built into the use table. As well, a generation of income account for industries is built in. The income distributed is shown in the rows after gross value added and gross domestic product—that is, beginning in row 13 with compensation of employees.[7]

2.6. The Contribution of Design

Earlier it was noted that *SNA 1993* built on *SNA 1968*. Yet even as balance sheets and other hitherto separate elements were brought into the system, it was with the awareness that *SNA 1968* had been viewed as too complicated and too complex. In the United States, Denison (1971) expressed concern about the direction taken by *SNA 1968* in elaborating the number of sectors, types of transactions, and types of accounts (beyond current and saving and investment) and setting out the interrelations among them. His main objection was that this approach was inefficient; too many series would have to be estimated to fill in the accounts when they were of trivial or no value. Second, he felt that *SNA 1968* was so complicated that few could be expected to understand the system or the estimates it contains. Jaszi (1966), too, believed that the accounting structure was obscure and overcomplicated.

Many less committed to the tradition in which Denison and Jaszi worked also were concerned. In fact, one of the stated purposes of the revision was to simplify the *SNA*. Simplification by reducing the comprehensiveness of the *SNA* was, however, quickly ruled out; no part of the then existing *SNA* was considered expendable. With respect to complexity, some amount of detail and specificity is not only inevitable but desirable if the accounts and tables are to be useful as guides to national statistical offices. For example, a statistical office may wish to, or for reasons of data availability may have to, consider a simpler sectoring structure than provided in the *SNA*, such as combining nonfinancial and financial corporations. A conceptual system should display the information so that the sacrifice can be evaluated. Further, systems of accounts serve as a framework for statistical coordination. For example, the need for surveys and administrative records to provide data on households that have consistent timing and coverage should be considered within a system that displays the full complexities.

Thus, if the *SNA* is to be comprehensive and is of necessity complex, a substantial burden is placed on the design of its accounts and tables. This paper pointed out several features designed into the 1993 *SNA*'s accounts and tables that minimized the impact of complexity. Accepting the need both for institutional units and sectors and for establishments and industries, there are separate, but clearly linked, sets of accounts. The sets of accounts for institutional sectors, for industries (in a shortened sequence), and for the rest of the world follow the same sequence within current accounts, accumulation accounts, and balance sheets, showing only the flows and stocks relevant to the group. The major aggregates are rather easily identifiable within the accounts, many of them as balancing items. Further, some of the accounts are "nested" so that the level of detail for implementation can be matched with the analytical interest.

André Vanoli's (1985) diagnosis was that *SNA 1968* was viewed as too complex and too complicated because an important element was missing—a table that showed the general linking of the accounts and the balancing of the economy at a level of understandable detail. The integrated economic accounts go a long way in providing the missing element. They are comparable in important ways to the summary systems in the U.S. national income and product accounts and flow-of-funds accounts. If one is inclined to think, as the author does, that comprehensiveness and a degree of complexity are desirable for a conceptual system of economic accounts and that a conceptual system serves useful purposes, the integrated economic accounts are worth the investment of time and effort it takes to extract the wealth of information they provide. Further, with familiarity, one comes to respect the ingenuity of their design and thus the major contribution their design makes to the SNA.

Appendix 2.A. Selected Glossary

The entries for this glossary are taken from Tables 2.3 through 2.8. They were selected because they have meaning specific to *SNA 1993*. The numbers in parentheses indicate the paragraph numbers of the *SNA 1993* in which terms are explained in more detail.

Actual final consumption   The consumption goods and services acquired by own expenditures and the expenditures of others. See final consumption expenditure. (9.95–9.99)

Adjusted disposable income   The balancing item in the redistribution of income in kind account. It is derived from disposable income by adding the value of social transfers in kind receivable and subtracting the value of social transfers in kind payable. See social transfers in kind and disposable income. (2.123, 8.24)

Adjustment for the change in net equity of households on pension funds   An adjustment item that ensures that the treatment of pension contributions and pension receipts as transfers in the secondary distribution of income account does not affect household saving but instead affects households' financial assets. (9.15–9.16)

Balance of primary incomes   The balancing item of the allocation of primary income account. It is equal to total primary incomes receivable less total primary incomes payable. At the level of the total economy, it is described as national income. See primary income. (7.14)

Capital transfers   Transfers, in cash or in kind, in which the ownership of an asset is transferred or which obliges one or both parties to acquire or dispose of an asset. Examples include the financing of accumulation and payments of compensation for extensive damages or injuries. (2.137, 10.131–10.135, 10.139–10.141)

Catastrophic losses   The destruction of assets resulting from large-scale, discrete, and recognizable events, such as major earthquakes, acts of war, and major toxic spills. (12.35)

Changes in classifications and structure   An item in the other changes in volume of assets account that consists of changes in the classification of institutional units among sectors, changes in the structure of institutional units, and changes in the classification of assets and liabilities. (12.55)

Consumption of fixed capital (CFC)   The decline in the value, in current prices, of the stock of capital goods held by producers resulting from physical deterioration, normal obsolescence, or normal accidental damage. (2.99, 2.108, 6.179–6.203, 10.118–10.119)

Disposable income   The balancing item in the secondary distribution of income account. It is the income that can be used for final consumption expenditure and saving. See actual disposable income. (2.112, 2.121, 8.11, 8.12–8.18, 9.2)

Economic appearance or disappearance of assets   The addition of an asset (produced or nonproduced) to the balance sheet where that asset is not created by a process of production or the removal of a nonproduced asset from the balance sheet other than in a process of production. Examples include additions to, and depletion of, mineral reserves, respectively. (12.12–12.14)

Final consumption expenditure The expenditures of households, non-profit institutions serving households, and governments on individual consumption goods and services and of governments on collective consumption services. See actual final consumption. (9.93–9.94)

Intermediate consumption Goods and services used as inputs in current production excluding consumption of fixed capital. (2.216, 6.3, 6.147)

Mixed income The balancing item of the generation of income account of unincorporated enterprises owned by members of households. It measures the income earned by tangible and intangible capital, entrepreneurship, and uncompensated labor from their participation in production. See operating surplus. (2.115, 4.142–4.143, 7.8, 7.80)

Natural growth of noncultivated biological resources The growth of natural forests, fishstocks, and other biological resources not under the direct control, responsibility, and management of an institutional unit. (12.26)

Nominal holding gains and losses The change in value of assets due to (1) the change in the general price level (neutral holding gains and losses) and (2) changes in the prices of assets relative to the general price level (real holding gains and losses). (2.141–2.145)

Operating surplus The balancing item in the generation of income account of enterprises other than unincorporated enterprises owned by households. It measures the income earned by tangible and intangible capital, entrepreneurship, and other factors of production from their participation in production. See mixed icome. (2.115, 7.8, 7.80–7.86)

Other current transfers Current transfers other than current taxes on income, wealth, and so on; social contributions, and social benefits. They consist of net nonlife insurance premiums, nonlife insurance claims, current transfers within general government, current international cooperation, and miscellaneous other transfers. (8.84)

Other volume changes, n.e.c. An item in the other changes in volume of assets accounts that records the effects of miscellaneous events on the value of assets or liabilities. Examples include the writing off of bad debts, the retirement of fixed assets because of unforeseen obsolescence, and exceptional losses of inventories. (12.41)

Property income   The income that accrues from lending or renting financial or tangible nonproduced assets. (7.2, 7.88–7.89)

Primary income   The income that accrues from involvement in the processes of production or ownership of assets used in production. (7.2)

Social benefits other than social transfers in kind   Certain transfers— social benefits in cash and social insurance benefits provided under private funded or unfunded social insurance schemes—made to meet certain social needs. Examples include unemployment benefits and dependent support. See social transfers in kind. (8.77)

Social contributions   The payments made by employees or others, or by employers on behalf of their employees, in order to secure entitlement to social insurance benefits in the current or subsequent periods for the employees or other contributors, their dependents, or survivors. (8.8, 8.17, 8.66, 8.70)

Social transfers in kind   The transfers of individual goods and services (such as education and health services) provided free, or at economically insignificant prices, to resident households by governments and nonprofit institutions serving households. (3.41, 3.42–3.43, 8.22, 8.99)

Taxes less subsidies on products   The taxes payable less the subsidies receivable per unit of a good or service. Both taxes and subsidies may be a specific amount of money per unit or they may be a specified percentage of the price per unit. Subsidies may also be calculated as the difference between a specified target price and the market price actually paid by a buyer. Both usually become payable when the goods or services are produced, sold, or imported. Examples include general sales taxes, customs duties, and export subsidies. (7.62, 7.73)

Taxes less subsidies on production and imports   The sum of taxes payable less subsidies receivable on products *plus* other taxes payable less subsidies receivable on production. The latter are payable or receivable as a result of engaging in production, but they are not tied to individual units of output. Examples include taxes on the ownership or use of assets used in production (land, buildings, and so on), taxes on the labor employed, and payroll subsidies. See taxes less subsidies on products. (7.49, 7.79)

Uncompensated seizures   The seizure of assets without full compensation for reasons other than the payment of taxes, fines, or similar levies. (12.38)

Table 2.B.1.   Account 1 of the summary five-account system

Account 1.—National Income and Product Account [Billions of dollars, 1992]

Item	Line	Value	Item	Line	Value
Compensation of employees	1	3,582.0	Personal consumption expenditures (2–3)	31	4,139.9
Wages and salaries	2	2,953.1	Durable goods	32	497.3
Disbursements (2–7)	3	2,973.1	Nondurable goods	33	1,300.9
Wage accruals less disbursements (3–8) and (5–4)	4	–20.0	Services	34	2,341.6
Supplements to wages and salaries	5	629.0			
Employer contributions for social insurance (3–16)	6	306.3	Gross private domestic investment (5–1)	35	796.5
Other labor income (2–8)	7	322.7	Fixed investment	36	789.1
			Nonresidential	37	565.5
Proprietors' income with inventory valuation and capital consumption adjustments (2–9)	8	414.3	Structures	38	172.6
			Producers' durable equipment	39	392.9
			Residential	40	223.6
Rental income of persons with capital consumption adjustment (2–10)	9	–8.9	Change in business inventories	41	7.3
Corporate profits with inventory valuation and capital consumption adjustments	10	407.2	Net exports of goods and services	42	–29.6
Profits before tax	11	395.4	Exports (4–1)	43	640.5
Profits tax liability (3–13)	12	146.3	Imports (4–4)	44	670.1
Profits after tax with inventory and capital consumption adjustments	13	260.9	Government purchases (3–1)	45	1,131.8
Dividends (2–12)	14	150.5	Federal	46	448.8
Undistributed profits with inventory valuation and capital consumption adjustments (5–5)	15	110.4	National defense	47	313.8
			Nondefense	48	135.0
			State and local	49	683.0

Inventory valuation adjustment	16	−5.3
Capital consumption adjustment	17	17.1
Net interest (2–15)	18	442.0
National income	19	4,836.6
Business transfer payments	20	27.6
To persons (2–20)	21	21.6
To rest of the world (4–9)	22	6.0
Indirect business tax and nontax liability (3–14)	23	502.8
Less: Subsidies less current surplus of government enterprises (3–7)	24	2.7
Consumption of fixed capital (5–6)	25	657.9
Gross national income	26	6,022.2
Statistical discrepancy (5–9)	27	23.6
Gross national product	28	6,045.8
Less: Receipts of factor income from the rest of the world (4–2)	29	129.2
Plus: Payments of factor income to the rest of the world (4–5)	30	121.9
GROSS DOMESTIC PRODUCT		6,038.5
GROSS DOMESTIC PRODUCT		6,038.5

Note: Numbers in parentheses indicate accounts and items of counterentry in the accounts. For example, line 3 of account 1 is shown as "wage and salaries, disbursements (2–7)"; the counterentry is shown account 2, line 7.

Appendix 2.B. Five-Account Summary of the U.S. National Income and Product Accounts

"The Summary National Income and Product Accounts" (U.S. Department of Commerce, 1993) is a system of five accounts that serves mainly as a device to explain the U.S. national income and product accounts. It presents the measures of production and provides a summary picture of the production, distribution, and use of output. The configuration of the five-account system is pragmatic; the information presented was selected because of its importance for economic analysis. Table 1, the national income and product account, which sums to gross domestic product on both sides, is reproduced in Table 2.B.1.

Acknowledgments

Several people at the Bureau of Economic Analysis provided useful comments and helped in other ways in the preparation of this paper. Chris Garner, Brian Grove, Stephanie Howell, John Pitzer, and Frank Szumilo were especially helpful.

Notes

1. *SNA 1993*, as a conceptual system, does not show statistical discrepancies in the accounts and tables.

2. Gross national product did, however, appear in the 1980 "Instructions and Definitions for the National Accounts Questionnaire" prepared by the United Nations and the Organisation for Economic Co-operation and Development. Table 1.12 of the questionnaire shows a set of relations among aggregates, including: gross domestic product plus net factor income from abroad equals gross national product.

3. Gross domestic product had sometimes been described as a measure relating to the territory of a country—that is, as a geographic concept. Domestic product is defined, as just noted, as production by resident units. Thus, the extent to which it is a geographic concept hinges on whether residency is a geographic concept. Residency is defined in terms of having a center of economic interest in a country, where center of economic interest is defined, in turn, as having a location within the economic territory from which production, consumption, and so on are carried out over a long period if time. A firm resident by this definition in the home country may send employees to work abroad installing machinery, for example. The center of economic interest, and the residency, in this case remain in the home country so that the production represented by the installation is measured as part of the domestic product of the firm's home country, not the product of the country where the installation takes place. Thus, as *SNA 1993* points out, domestic product is not, strictly speaking, a geographic concept.

4. *Productive activity* here refers to processes carried out under the control of institutional units that use labor, capital, and goods and services to produce output of goods and services. Because the same goods and services may be produced by different methods, there is no one-to-one correspondence between activities and the goods and services they produce.

5. The SNA groups establishments according to the "International Standard Industrial Classification of All Economic Activities" published by the United Nations.

6. The *SNA* uses the "Central Product Classification," published by the United Nations, to classify goods and services.

7. In addition, *SNA 1993* includes an explicit shortened sequence of accounts for industries, consisting of a production account and generation of income account.

References

Board of Governors of the Federal Reserve System. (1991). *Guide to the Flow of Funds Accounts*. Washington, DC: Board of Governors of the Federal Reserve System.

Commission of the European Communities, International Monetary Fund, Organisation for Economic Co-operation and Development, United Nations, and World Bank. (1993). *System of National Accounts 1993*. Brussels, Luxembourg, New York, Paris, Washington, DC: United Nations.

Denison, Edward F. (1971). "U.S. National Income and Product Estimates: Evaluation and Some Specific Suggestions for Improvement." In "The Economic Accounts of the United States: Retrospect and Prospect." *Survey of Current Business* 51(7) (pt. 2) (July): 36–44.

Jaszi, George. (1958). "The Conceptual Basis of the Accounts: A Reexamination." In *A Critique of the United States Income and Product Accounts*. Studies in Income and Wealth, Vol. 22. New York: University Press.

Jaszi, George. (1966). "Wither *SNA*: Comments on the Revision of the Standard System of National Accounts." Paper presented at the Conference on Research in Income and Wealth, June 9–10. New York, N.Y.

Ohlsson, Ingvar. (1961). *On National Accounting*. Stockholm: National Institute of Economic Research.

Ruggles, Nancy and Richard Ruggles. (1970). *The Design of Economic Accounts*. New York: Columbia University Press for the National Bureau of Economic Research.

Stone, Richard. (1951). "Functions and Criteria of a System of Social Accounting." *Income and Wealth*, series I (pp. 1–74). Cambridge: Bowes and Bowes.

Stone, Richard. (1947). "Definition and Measurement of the National Income and Related Totals." In United Nations, *Measurement of National Income and the Construction of Social Accounts*, Studies and Reports on Statistical Methods, No. 7, Report of the Sub-Committee on National Income Statistics of the League of Nations Committee of Statistical Experts. Geneva: United Nations.

United Nations. (1968). *A System of National Accounts*, Studies in Methods, Series F, No. 2, Rev. 3. New York: United Nations.

U.S. Department of Commerce, Bureau of Economic Analysis. (1993). "National
    Income and Product Accounts." *Survey of Current Business* 73(8) (August
    1993): 54–55, table A.
Vanoli, André. (1985) "The General Structure of the System of National Accounts
    on the Basis of Experience Obtained with the French Enlarged National
    Accounting System." Paper presented at the Nineteenth General Con-
    ference of the International Association for Research in Income and Wealth,
    Noordwijerhout, Netherlands, August 26–31.

DISCUSSION OF CHAPTER 2

Jan van Tongeren

Introduction

Carol Carson, in her chapter on the "Design of Economic Accounts and the 1993 *System of National Accounts*," focuses on one aspect of *SNA 1993*—the System as a framework of concepts that are defined in relation to each other. At the same time she recognizes that the System as "a conceptual system . . . is meant to serve a wide range of analytical and policy needs." One might say that she has paid much attention to the *conceptual* SNA but has focused much less on the joint use of the concepts defining the *analytical* orientation of the system.

The analytical orientation of the System, however, is equally important as the conceptual *SNA*, for several reasons. As the number of indicators defining the System has grown since the League of Nations in 1928 "urged countries to extend the scope of official statistics to facilitate the compilation of national income estimates at regular intervals" (United Nations, 1993b, p. xxvii), an analytical orientation is needed to join this data set in a meaningful manner. The larger data set is needed because economies have grown in complexity and more indicators are needed to describe those. Also, the models and other forms of analysis to deal with those complexities have become more sophisticated and require more data. Furthermore, explicit information on the analytical orientation of the System is needed in order to guide users in deciding which analytical features they will incorporate in their national accounting system in response to analytical and policy needs.

Thus, rather than commenting in detail on the very comprehensive and excellent description above of *SNA 1993* as a conceptual system, my comments will supplement that presentation with a brief review of the main analytical features of *SNA 1993*.

Analytical Orientation of the 1993 *SNA*

The overall analytical orientation of the *SNA* is explicitly dealt with in sections I.F–J of the introduction, and furthermore, in Chapters 19, 20, and 21 attention has been paid to SAM versions, satellite extensions, and other specific adaptations of the System, in response to analytical and policy requirements. The analytical orientation, however, is also implicitly included when concepts, accounts, and tables are presented in the *SNA* manual. In particular, the following four elements determine the analytical orientation of the System.

- The hierarchical classifications of transactors, transactions and other flows, and assets that identify the concepts of the System. Thus, in the classification of transactors, transactor groupings, including nonfinancial and financial corporations, government, households, and nonprofit institutions serving households (NPISH) are identified. Similarly, the classification of transactions and other flows identifies concepts such as final consumption expenditure, capital formation compensation of employees, property income, current and capital transfers, and other volume changes and revaluations as concepts of the System. And in the asset classification are identified asset and liability concepts such as produced, nonproduced, and financial assets and liabilities or more specific categories such as buildings and machinery in produced assets, land, forests, and water resources in nonproduced assets, and bonds, deposits, and shares in financial assets. An important part of the text of the 1993 SNA is taken up by definitions and descriptions of the items identified in the classifications and accounting structure of the System.
- The accounting structure that identifies the main aggregates of the

System as balancing items that are defined in terms of the concepts identified in the classifications and in relation to each other. Thus, the accounting structure defines major aggregates such as GDP, national income, national disposable income, and saving.

- The cross-classifications of categories of industry, product, labor, and occupational, functional expenditure classifications, and *SNA* classifications of transactors, transactions and other flows, and assets that are implicit in the System or are explicitly presented and that are or can be used in structural analysis.

- Social Accounting Matrices (SAMs) and satellite extensions using alternative concepts in order to carry out alternative analyses and in particular to broaden economic analyses to social and other fields.

When countries implement *SNA 1993*, they should not only deal with adaptation of the concepts to those of the System but also select the analytical features they want to use—that is, which scope[1] they want to give to their national accounting system. In such selection, they need to decide which accounts to implement and therefore which major aggregates to compile, at which detail to use the classifications, which cross-classifications to apply, whether to apply SAMs and other satellite extensions, and, if so, which ones. When making such explicit decisions, analytical and policy uses as well as statistical feasibility should be taken into account, and the decisions should be taken in close cooperation between statisticians, national accountants, analysts and policy makers.

The consequences of adopting *only* the concepts of *SNA 1993* should be clearly recognized. For instance, if a majority of developing and some other countries with a very limited national accounts scope mainly restricted to GDP and some breakdowns would not consider an expansion of this scope, they would implicitly continue to focus their national accounts on production and growth analyses and would not be able to benefit from many of the analytical innovations that are available in the System. The conceptual approach would then contribute little to the extension of the analytical potential of national accounting in many of those countries. It is true that the reason for maintaining their national accounts model intact are statistical restrictions; however, easing some of these statistical restrictions through data expansions based on additional and improved uses of survey and administrative data should be seriously considered, given the analytical and policy benefits to be gained from it.

A similar conceptual approach in countries with more sophisticated statistical systems may have somewhat different consequences. For instance, if the United States, with a decentralized statistical system, would decide to adapt only the NIPA concepts (Young and Tice, 1985) to those of *SNA 1993* and leave unchanged all other statistical compilations (such as input-output) tables and flow of funds tables compiled by the Federal Reserve), it would be a formaidable undertaking but it would not accomplish integration of separate analyses intended in the design of *SNA 1993*. This would mean, for instance, that detailed analyses of production embedded in the U.S. input-output tables cannot be well linked to income generated, saving, investments, and net lending of different sectors identified in NIPA that carry out the economic activity in the country, as value-added components in NIPA are measured from the income side and input-output analyses are based on a production approach. Furthermore, it would not be possible for the national accounts to shed light on the relation between government consumption causing government deficits, and imports causing external deficits, as the U.S. input-output table with detailed industry and product relations between government consumption, production, and imports is not integrated with the NIPA accounts that identify these elements only as major aggregates. And finally, it would not be possible to relate effects of the money supply and other influences of the financial system on production, GDP, employment, and other economic indicators that are used in analyzing the U.S. economy, as the NIPA accounts do not include financial accounts or identify separately a financial corporate sector and are not integrated with the flow-of-funds analysis of the Federal Reserve. Thus, while maintenance of the national accounts scope and analytical orientation in countries like the United States may have the advantage of being able to continue modeling and other traditional analyses to which many analysts are accustomed, the main disadvantage is that such orientation would not benefit from the integration of analyses intended by the 1993 SNA.

New Analytical Tools Provided by *SNA 1993*

What follows is a description of three of the most important analytical features of *SNA 1993*. Not all are innovations as compared to *SNA 1968*, but most are when compared with present country practices in national accounting. They are clearly innovations as compared to the national accounting practices of many developing and other countries that restrict their compilations mainly to GDP and some breakdowns serving production analysis. In other countries, including the United States, that have applied these analytical features in separate research programs, the effects of the incorporation of these innovations in *SNA 1993* would permit integration of separate analyses into the national accounts, as was explained above.

The three analytical features are identified in the overall analytical structure of the 1993 *SNA* presented in Figure 1. The first one is the incorporation of sectoral analysis as reflected in the integrated economic accounts (IEA) for the five institutional sectors and the rest of the world that were described in detail in Carol Carson's presentation and are represented in the lower panel of the diagram. The second one is a cross-classification between industries and sectors (CCIS) of production-related

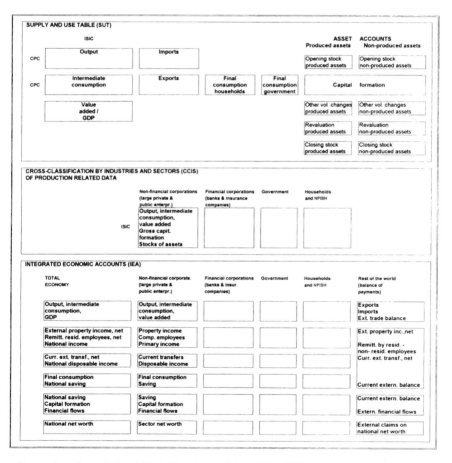

Figure 1.   Overall Analytical Structure of the 1993 SNA

data presented as the second module in the diagram; the CCIS links production analyses based on industry groupings of establishment data included in the supply and use table (SUT) in the upper panel of the diagram, to income and financial analyses based on sector groupings of enterprise or institutional unit data included in the IEA. The third important analytical innovation is the addition of so-called asset accounts of produced and nonproduced assets that are represented by two columns that are superimposed on gross capital formation on the right side of the SUT. The inclusion of the two columns for assets accounts, changes the SUT to an extended supply and use table (ESUT).

Sectoral Accounts and Analyses

The sectoral extension of the System (the third module presented in Figure 1 above) is the first data extension with analytical potential. It includes for separate sectors, data on income, saving, and finance, between which functional relations can be specified and measured. Within such a data set additional functional relations may be specified and measured for each sector beyond what is presently available in many countries only in consolidated format for the total economy. Thus, for instance, for the household sector, functional relations may be specified between income and consumption and between income and social contributions and benefits; for all sectors, between assets and liabilities in the balance sheet and receipts and payments of interest, dividends, land rent, and other property income; for nonfinancial and financial corporations and households, between income and taxes; and so on. The functional relationships defined within each sector together with identities between payments and receipts across sectors would make it possible to study, under various scenarios of overtime developments, the interaction between saving (retained earnings) and capital formation of the nonfinancial corporate sector, household savings, government deficits, and the current external balance and the resulting requirements for intersectoral and external flows of finance.

The above analysis can be further detailed when, in satellite extensions and other adaptations of the System, key economic sectors with considerable influence on the economy of a country are identified separately. The key sectors that may be distinguished range from

● Sectors that are dominated by a few large companies (such as the oil sector),

- Sectors that are dominated by very many small household units (such as coffee production, or production of agricultural products in general),
- More complex sectors (such as tourism) whose product range is relatively large and is spread over many very diverse types of establishments, and
- Very complex sectors whose production in many instances is carried out as an ancillary activity of an establishment (such as electricity, other energy production, production of computer services) and therefore would require not only identification of separate establishments but also separate identification of relevant ancillary activities within establishments.

Cross-classifications of Production and Income Data

An important data extension is the CCIS of production-related data between ISIC groupings of establishments and the sector groupings of enterprises, households, and government units, as presented in the second module of Figure 1. The CCIS, for instance, shows to what extent output, value added, and capital formation in agriculture, manufacturing, and services is generated by nonfinancial corporations and what part is carried out as small-scale household production. Thus, traditional analyses of production and growth based on establishment data can be linked to the type of income and financial analyses mentioned in the previous paragraph. The use of a CCIS coefficient matrix link opens the possibility of identifying the income, saving, and financial implications for sectors of growth of production that is analyzed by industries. In particular, it is possible to determine, the consequences of production growth for the gap between saving and capital formation of nonfinancial corporations, the saving potential of households, and the limitations that may be imposed by government and external deficits. The structure of the CCIS depends on how production in a country is organized and, as was shown above, on the type of industry and sector groupings used in the analysis.

If key sectors are identified within the sectoring of a national accounting system, as was explained in the previous section, the CCIS matrix would need to reflect this. If the key sector is very complex, such as in the last two examples mentioned in the previous section, the CCIS matrix may show to what extent characteristic production of key sectors takes place in the key sectors themselves or in other sectors. In the last example, ancillary production of sectors related to key activities is identified and reflected in the CCIS. Once the CCIS matrix is well established and reflects key sectors with their institutional sector dimension, the same link between production analyses on the one hand and income and financial analyses on the other, as described in the previous section for main sectors of the *SNA*, may also be applied to key sectors.

Other analytically useful cross-classifications are identified in social accounting matrices (SAMs). The SAMs introduce matrices converting value added into primary income received by sectors participating in production (including compensation of employees received by households and interest, dividends, and other property income by all sectors based on their capital participation in production) and secondary incomd flows and disposable income after social and other transfers, and also including the conversion of disposable income into consumption and saving. The transition or conversion matrices might be used in the same manner as the input-output matrices. They extend the input-output projections to impacts on income and subsequently establish the link with consumption and in this manner internalize consumption into input-output analyses.

Accounts for Stocks and Changes in Assets

Another major analytical extension is the incorporation of asset accounts into the System. As illustrated in Table 1, which is a further elaboration

Table 1.   Asset accounts for produced and nonproduced assets

	Produced assets	*Nonproduced assets*
Opening stocks	X	X
Capital formation	X	O
Other volume changes:		
Economic appearance of assets	O	X
Depletion and degradation (SNA: economic disappearance of assets	O	X
Destruction of assets by natural and manmade calamities (SNA: catastrophic losses)	O	O
Other	O	O
Revaluation of assets	X	X
Closing stocks	X	X

Note: X = important element; O = unimportant element.

of the asset accounts columns in the ESUT of Figure 1, they include data on stocks of assets as well as on changes in those stocks; thus, they permit using the *SNA* database for dynamic analyses. The table distinguishes between produced and nonproduced assets. Produced assets include roads, buildings, and other structures and equipment, and nonproduced assets include land, mineral reserves, forests exploited for lumbering, and other natural assets[2] and also nonproduced intangible asset such as patents, leases, and goodwill. The nonproduced natural assets are covered in the *SNA* only if they are economic assets and can be valued in monetary terms; this is the case if a market price is attached either to the asset itself or to the nonproduced products extracted from the asset.[3]

As was mentioned above, the link between the asset accounts and the SUT is capital formation. The significance of the asset accounts, as presented in Table 1, is that they show clearly that capital formation is not the only element that explains changes in the asset stocks, as is generally assumed in dynamic growth models. As the table indicates, even for produced assets this is not the case: in addition to capital formation, the stock of produced assets is also affected by revaluations of assets, as well as by other volume changes including losses of assets due to natural and manmade calamities. The table demonstrates that other volume changes are unimportant as compared to capital formation in the case of produced assets. For nonproduced (mainly natural) assets, changes in these assets due to manmade capital formation—such as improvements to land or capitalized exploration expenditures that improve the access to mineral reserves—are minor, while most changes in nonproduced assets are caused by revaluations and by two types of volume changes—that is, the addition (= first valuation) of natural resources to the stock of economic assets, such as when forest areas are brought into cultivation or urbanization or newly found mineral reserves are added to the existing reserves—and the depletion or extraction of products from the nonproduced assets, such as the extraction of minerals from mineral reserves and lumber from forests that are economic assets in the SNA sense.

Asset accounts may also play a central role in another type of satellite extension of *SNA 1993* (Van Tongeren and Becker, 1994). In these, asset accounts may cover not only nonproduced assets with monetary values as commonly covered in national accounting but also natural assets in environmental accounting and selected aspects of human capital in human resource accounting, for which no monetary valuations are available. In this wider use of asset accounts, they are the links between the stocks of natural assets and human capital (in monetary or physical terms), the changes therein (called the *effects*), and the economic transactions that are either the *causes* of the changes in the assets (for instance degradation of land, air, and water due to pollution caused by industrial activities) or the *responses* aimed at mitigating the causes (for instance, environmental protection expenses to avoid or eliminate effects of degradation, or expenses on education or health to improve human quality). The cause-response-effect relations describing the interaction between economic causes and effects on natural assets and human capital that are used in production as production factors may be presented in matrix format with a cross-classification of natural assets and human capital by selected quality characteristics, on the one hand, and a classification of causes and responses on the other (see Table 2). The cause-response-effect matrices, which could be developed for different areas of socioeconomic concern, could be used together with the asset

Table 2. Cause/response-effect matrices for nonproduced assets: selected natural assets and selected aspects of human capital

	Natural assets	Human capital
	Land, water, forests, etc. classified by quality characteristics	Classified by selected qualities of health, education, etc.
Opening stock	X	X
Economic causes:		
Depletion	X	
Changes in land quality due to changes in land use	X	
Degradation of land (except by residuals);		
Soil erosion	X	
Other	X	
Discharge of residuals	X	
Economic responses (functional classification of expenditures		
Environmental protection expenses	X	
Expenses for education		X
Expenses for education		X
Changes in assets (effects)	X	X
Closing stock	X	X

accounts of the *SNA* described above, to refine the link in growth models between (economic) production on the one hand and, on the other hand, changes in assets (including natural assets and human capital) that are (partly)used as production factors.

The incorporation of the economic responses in the cause-response-effect analysis of Table 2 is facilitated by another analytical innovation incorporated in *SNA 1993*—that is, the integration of analyses of expenditures by purpose across sectors (see Chapter 18). This analytical feature of *SNA 1993* has set the stage for integrating and harmonizing the categories of existing classifications of expenditures by households and government (and extending those classifications to expenditures by nonprofit institutions) and will facilitate identification of expenditures across sectors—by government, households, and enterprises—that respond to specific socioeconomic concerns (see also Van Tongeren and Becker, 1994). Such expenditures would be the ones to be included in the economic response section of Table 2. Furthermore, once these classifications of expenditures by purpose are linked to classifications of products on which these expenditures are disbursed and to a classification by industries (such as ISIC) producing those products, it would be possible to establish links between socioeconomic concerns such as education, health, environment, the expenditures responding to those concerns (economic responses in Table 2), and input-output analyses of industry-product relations. In other words, it would make it easier to study in an input-output context, the impact on production and imports of specific expenditures with socioeconomic connotation, no matter whether these expenditures are made by households, government, or enterprises.

Acknowledgments

The opinions expressed in this paper are those of the author and do not necessarily represent those of the United Nations. The author expresses his appreciation for the very valuable comments that he received from his colleague Mr. Vu Viet and that have been taken into account in preparing the present version of the paper.

Notes

1. Alternative "scopes" for implementing the *SNA* have been described in some detail in United Nations (1994) and Van Tongeren and Schweinfest (1994).

2. The asset accounts for nonproduced natural assets are an important feature of the system of economic environmental accounts (SEEA) as presented in United Nations (1993a, esp. tables 2.3, 2.4, 2.6, 2.7).

3. The relation between the economic asset boundary of the SNA and the valuation of nonproduced assets is described in detail in para. 10.8–10.14 of the *SNA*.

References

United Nations. (1993a). "Integrated Environmental and Economic Accounting." Interim version. *Handbook of National Accounting*, Studies in Methods, Series F., No. 61. New York: United Nations.

Commission of the European Communities, International Monetary Fund, Organisation for Economic Co-operation and Development, United Nations, World Bank: System of National Accounts 1993, Brussels/Luxembourg, New York, Paris, Washington, D.C., 1993.

United Nations. (1994). "Towards a Methodology for the Compilation of National Accounts: Concepts and Practice." Technical Report. New York, unpublished.

Van Tongeren, Jan W., and Bernd Becker. (1994). "Integrated Satellite Accounting, Socio-Economic Concerns and Modelling." Paper presented to the Twenty-third General Conference of the International Association for Research in Income and Wealth. St. Andrews, New Brunswick, Canada, August 21–27.

Van Tongeren, Jan W., and Stefan Schweinfest. (1994). "A System's Approach to National Accounts Compilation: UNSTAT's Experiences in Implementing the SNA." Paper submitted to the Twenty-third General Conference of the International Association for Research in Income and Wealth, St. Andrews, New Brunswick, Canada, August 21–27.

Young, Allan H., and Helen Stone Tice. (1985). "An Introduction to National Economic Accounting." *Survey of Current Business* (March), pp. 59–76.

DISCUSSION OF CHAPTER 2

Peter Hill

As a system, the *SNA* consists of a sequence of integrated economic accounts for each of the sectors that make up an economy. It can be envisaged as a matrix of accounts in which each row refers to a particular kind of account, while each column refers to the group of institutional units for which the account is compiled (see Table 1). In this scheme, each cell of the matrix contains a complete account. There are no empty cells. The five sectors together make up the total economy, which consists of the entire set of institutional units resident in the economy. The column of accounts referring to the total economy can legitimately be described as the *national* accounts. All the familiar macroeconomic aggregates such as GDP or net national income are embedded in the accounts for the total economy. However, in order to be able to analyze the working of an economy and the interactions between economic units on markets, the accounts must be compiled for individual sectors as well as the economy as a whole. In this way, information can be obtained about key variables such as household or government saving or their borrowing requirements.

Each of the accounts in the columns is connected directly or indirectly with the others. In principle, the number of accounts could be reduced by collapsing two or more accounts into a single account—for example, by

Table 3. Matrix of accounts in *SNA 1993*

	Sector					
Account	Nonfinancial corporations	Financial corporations	General government	Households	NPISHs	Total economy
Production						
Generation of income						
Primary distribution of income						
Secondary distribution of income						
Use of income						
Capital¹ account						
Financial account						
Other changes in assets						
Opening balance sheet						
Closing balance sheet						

integrating the income accounts—or increased by subdividing an account into two or more new accounts in order to identify new balancing items. Similarly, the sectors can be combined or subdivided as appropriate. A system of macroeconomic accounts such as *SNA 1993* is inherently flexible about the number of accounts and sectors separately distinguished.

The column of accounts for the total economy is shown in more detail in Table 1.3 of Carol Carson's paper. The complete set of accounts for both the individual sectors and the total economy is also shown in Table 2.5 of the paper. This table uses a succinct method of presentation extensively exploited in *SNA 1993* whereby the two sides of each account are shown on either side of a single central column in which all the entries for both sides of each account are listed. Such compact presentations of the detailed accounts may provide synoptic overviews of the entire system, but they are not easy to grasp without a good prior understanding of the individual accounts and their interrelationships. They are not for beginners.

As explained in Carol Carson's paper, the scheme outlined above is not a complete description of *SNA 1993*, even of its so-called central system. Resident units engage in transactions with nonresidents as well as with each other. The complete system has therefore to include an account in which these transactions are recorded from the viewpoint of the rest of the world. *SNA 1993* also includes supply and use tables in which flows of goods and services are cross classified by their origin (domestic or foreign) and by their type of use (intermediate or final). As explained by Carol Carson, the tables are compiled for industries—that is, groups of establishments—instead of sectors. They provide a convenient statistical and analytic framework for assembling and reconciling a great deal of detailed information drawn from a variety of different sources about flows of goods and services. Establishments and industries are only appropriate, however, for the analysis of flows directly connected with production. Establishments are production units that are capable of engaging in only a limited range of economic activities. Complete sets of accounts including income, capital, and financial accounts cannot be compiled for establishments.

The paper by Carol Carson provides a clear and concise description of the design and structure of the central system of *SNA 1993*. In the remainder of this note it is proposed to discuss an important feature of the structure of the accounts to which insufficient attention is paid in *SNA 1993*.

SNA 1993 recognizes that transactions among institutional units are not the only ways in which the values of the assets or liabilities held by units may change over time. The values of assets may change as a result of general inflation or specific price changes or as a result of changes in their quantities due to events such as their accidental destruction by disasters or wars. If, therefore, there is to be an exhaustive accounting for the difference between the opening and closing balance sheet values of assets and liabilities, changes in values due to these events have to be recorded as well as the changes resulting from the acquisitions or disposals of assets in transactions that are recorded in the capital and financial accounts. *SNA 1993* includes a new account—other changes in assets—for this purpose. It is grouped together with the capital and financial accounts under the general heading of accumulation accounts.

However, changes in assets due to transactions, especially changes in financial assets, are intrinsically different from other changes because they are related to changes taking place elsewhere in the overall system of accounts. Recording a market transaction involves quadruple-entry accounting. Following traditional double-entry bookkeeping, both parties to a transaction record credit and debit entries in their accounts giving rise to four equal entries in the system of accounts as a whole. For each party to a monetary transaction, the counterpart to the value of a use or resource recorded in the production, income, or capital accounts is some form of payable or receivable recorded in the financial account. The payables or receivable may lead to immediate changes in currency or deposits but may equally lead to the creation of short-term credits or debits.

If all monetary transactions for a group of institutional units are aggregated, the difference between the total values of the uses and resources recorded in their production, income, and capital accounts must be identical with the counterpart net change in their total financial assets and liabilities recorded in their financial accounts. The identity is not disturbed by the occurrence and recording of nonmonetary transactions, included imputed transactions, as these do not affect the financial accounts. The total values of the uses recorded for such transactions in the production, income, and capital accounts must balance the total values of resources recorded for them in the same accounts. Nor is the identity disturbed by purely financial transactions in which financial assets or liabilities are exchanged for each other.

The identity between the net flow of real resources recorded in the production, income and capital accounts and the counterpart net change in financial assets and liabilities is manifested in *SNA 1993* by the fact that the balancing item in the capital account, which measures net lending possibilities or net borrowing requirements, is, in principle, identical in value with the balancing item in the financial account, which records actual net lending or borrowing. The balancing item in the capital account assumes this critical role because the capital account is the last in the sequence of *integrated* accounts recording transactions involving the real activities of production, consumption, and capital formation. The integration is realized by carrying over the balancing item between uses and resources from one account to the opposite side of the next account in the *SNA*'s sequence of accounts. Of course, equality between the balancing items in the capital and financial accounts may be difficult to achieve in practice because of errors of measurement, but it serves as a useful statistical check.

The sequence of accounts covering transactions linked to the economic activities of production, income generation and distribution, consumption, and capital formation itself constitutes a self-contained system of accounts. The system is well defined as it relates to a general equilibrium system based on market transactions. In particular, the system provides insights into the interrelationships between financial markets, institutions, and instruments and the real economic activities with which they are linked. The coverage of this system of accounts is, of course, equivalent to that of *SNA 1968*, but its existence is not apparent in *SNA 1993*.

In *SNA 1993* prominence is given to the distinction between the current and accumulation accounts because *SNA 1993* provides a detailed and exhaustive set of accounts for changes in the values of assets over time. By defining a complete set of accumulation accounts, the capital and financial accounts become detached from the other accounts that record transactions and are presented as if their main purpose were to explain changes in the values of assets between the opening and closing balance sheets. While they obviously serve this purpose, the need to compile these two accounts for quite different, and economically compelling, reasons risks being overlooked. These accounts have to be compiled whether or not balance sheet data are available in order to have a complete accounting for economic activities and their associated transactions.

In a world of limited data and statistical resources, priorities may be influenced, even if unintentionally, by the way accounts are presented. The current accounts of the 1993 SNA may be seen as having first priority with the accumulation accounts being accorded lower priority if their main function is viewed as being the explanation of changes in frequently nonexistent balance sheet data. In practice, of course, it is essential to compile the capital and financial accounts in order to be able to observe and record all the activities and transactions taking place in an economy, irrespective of whether information is available on stocks of assets.

The inclusion for the first time of a full accounting for changes in assets in the *SNA 1993* marks a significant improvement over *SNA 1968*. However, this can be achieved without downplaying the special links that exist between the capital and financial accounts and the current accounts that together form their own separate and complete system of accounts.

3 EXPANSION OF BOUNDARIES AND SATELLITE ACCOUNTS

Robert Eisner

The national income and product accounts have been one of the most important contributions to economic understanding of this century—perhaps of any century. Now, joined with aggregated data on stocks or balance sheets and other accounts of financial flows in an updated and revised, internationally recommended, unified system of national accounts, they offer even more impressive tools and data for analysis. Yet more can be done.

More can be done in an enlarged framework of aggregate national accounts and in developing more or less detailed accounts for particular areas of economic activity. These satellite accounts can then feed in part into the conventional aggregate accounts and in part into the enlarged framework that they can help develop.

The national income and product accounts (NIPAs) of the U.S. Bureau of Economic Analysis (BEA) and the production and income accounts of the *System of National Accounts 1993* (*SNA 1993*) (United Nations, 1993), to which the BEA is moving in large part to conform, share the essential property of being market oriented. Their main focus is the measure of output produced for the market and the income earned from that product. Further, output is generally valued at market prices, exclusive of subsidies and the value of volunteered, donated, or nonmarket services.

The output to be measured is final product as opposed to all product including intermediate. In the *SNA 1993* terminology, *intermediate consumption* is netted out of production so that we are left with *value added* equal to domestic product. This definition is intended to avoid double counting: the coal used to produce the steel, the steel that goes into the car, and then the car itself. The definition is given practical force by the rule of counting purchases not resold (within the accounting period) as final.

There is the further effort to separate output into final consumption, which plays no part in future production, and investment, which adds to the capital used to provide for production in the future. This effort is implemented pragmatically in the BEA NIPAs by the definition of capital as residential and nonresidential structures and equipment owned by business and nonprofit institutions and inventories held by business. This follows from the definition of *product* as output of the market and the fact that it is these sectors that are producing for the market; goverment is not (although goverment enterprises are). Investment is then the acquisition of real, reproducible assets by these enterprises producing for the market. A major addition involves the inclusion of owner-occupied houses in the concept of capital and recognition of their acquisition as investment. For definitional consistency, homeowners are viewed as business enterprises in the business of renting housing units to themselves.

These measures have proved enormously useful but also leave enormous gaps in our measures of economic activity. The restriction of the measure of output to production for the market results in the exclusion of the great bulk of services produced in the household: child care, education of the young, marketing, cooking, cleaning, laundering, and more. Government output is valued only as the purchases of labor services, since these are the final purchases not resold; the value of the services of government capital is excluded.

3.1. Expansion and Alteration of Boundaries

A major extension of boundaries that would shed important information then would be one that included output that was not produced for the market or for sale. A major problem would relate to how to value such output.[1]

In the public sector we would be looking for a measure of the total value of the services of government. This would not be limited to the value of imputed output corresponding to the value of labor services sold to the government. An imputation for the value of the services of government capital, if output were to be continued to be measured by the value of input, would include the value of consumption of government capital. It would also include an imputed net return to capital. This might be the product of the value or current or replacement cost of government capital and rates of interest on government securities or, better, returns to capital in the private sector. Or we might turn to imputations of the value of output, as far as possible, on the basis of the prices of similar services that do flow through the mrket, as we do in estimating the value of rental services of owner-occupied housing. Perhaps we could value police services in terms of the prices for the services of private detectives or security guards!

The extension of boundaries would have its greatest impact in the household sector. Much nonmarket household output has market counterparts: provision of meals in restaurants, cleaning of clothes in laundries or laundermats, child care in nurseries or day-care centers. Most household services can be—and sometimes are—performed by paid domestic workers. Output may then be valued in terms of comparable output in the market. It may also be valued though in terms of the cost of its inputs. A woman's work at home—and it usually is a woman's work—may be valued by multiplying the number of hours put into the activity by the opportunity cost of her time, presumably what she could earn in market work. One difficulty with this is that since she is choosing to work at home we may presume either (1) that she values her work at home more highly than what she could earn in the office or factory or (2) that the work in the office or factory is not really available to her. Valuation may also depend, perhaps erratically, on who is performing the services. Is it the economist reading to his or her child at home or the supermarket clerk? And, of course, critical to input-based measures of nonmarket labor services would be time-use studies so that we might know how much time is being devoted to each activity.

There is further the question of just which nonmarket activities should be placed within our expanded boundaries. Should we count shaving or shampooing our hair? Presumably yes, since these activities have market counterparts at the hairdresser or barber. What about driving to the supermarket or driving our children to school. Should we value this at the cost of taxi services or bus rides? But then what about a drive in the country for pleasure or even driving to work? Havrylishyn (1977, p. 89), following Margaret Reid (1934) invokes a "third party critierion" to state that "economic services are then defined conceptually as those producing indirect utility, and identified in practice by reference to the criterion: is it conceivable to have third person (e.g. market) do it?" Kuznets (1941, pp. 6–7) would exclude as overly extensive "acts that might be called 'personal,' such as washing, shaving, and playing for amusement on the piano." (Quoted in Eisner, 1989a, p. 13, from Murphy, 1980, p. 7.) Output identical to the last obviously could not be provided by a third person, and it might well be argued that one's morning ablutions can reasonably be excluded on the third-person criterion as well. We could conceivably bring someone into our home every morning to wash and shave us, but it is hardly feasible.

Measures of market output will understate the value of production when they utilize productive services that are not paid for or not paid for fully. A conspicuous example of the former are the services of volunteers— in hospitals, schools, museums, churches, and elsewhere. With regard to the latter we may note particularly the services of conscripts and jurors in those years or nations where this is releveant. The market cost of military services would be far greater if conscripts had to be paid whatever wage were necessary to recruit them.[2] This might reflect the opportunity cost of their military service.

The notion of recognizing opportunity costs in nonmarket output arises in valuing education services. If a company sends its executive to a management training program and pays her salary while she participates, the cost and value of this education or training measured in the market includes both the tuition and fees for the program and the salary of the executive. How then should we value the output of educational services for those in schools, colleges, universities, or professional shcools? Should we not impute the opportunity cost of wages and salaries lost by students who could otherwise be working? This issue will become particularly relevant as we extend our boundaries of investment to include investment in the intangible capital of education.

The measure of investment in the income and product accounts offers a very incomplete view of the economic concept of provision for future production. In the U.S. BEA NIPAs, there is no government or public investment, no matter how much federal, state, and local governments acquire in the way of structures, equipment, and inventories, although it is to be expected that this will be changed as the BEA moves toward conformity with the *SNA*. There is also no investment by households other than the acquisition of new houses and the built-in equipment that comes with them. If a new automobile is purchased by Hertz or a leasing agency and then rented or leased to a household, the purchase is viewed as investment. If the household buys the car itself, it is counted as consumption. If it is purchased by a government agency, it is viewed, in the United States, as government purchases of goods and services and, implicitly, as public consumption. Yet in each case, regardless of its legal ownership, acquisition of the auto may properly be viewed as investment in a capital asset that will produce serives over a substantial period of time in the future.

Expanded boundaries for investment would then include the acquisition by households of consumer durables. These acquisitions would be excluded from consumption. We would substitute in consumption the value of the services of consumer goods.

The definition of *gross private domestic investment* in the U.S. NIPAs is critically narrow in other regards. It includes acquisition of structures and equipment by business (including "landlords" of owner-occupied houses) and nonprofit institutions and the additions to inventories by business. In addition to excluding tangible investment by government and households, this definition excludes all investment in intangible capital. Business spending for research and development (R&D), except for the physical equipment, is thus excluded despite the widespread view that R&D investment adds considerably more to future productivity than the tangible investment actually included. And, of course R&D spending by nonprofit institutions and by government is also excluded from the measure of investment. Gross fixed capital formation in *SNA 1993* is somewhat broader, including fixed investment by government and investment by enterprises in computer software, the latter a new revision, with software assets recognized as intangible fixed capital.

Perhaps the most important provision for the future in economies hoping to compete in a technologically advancing world is the education and training and retraining of its people. This might well be viewed as investment, but it is not in our central income and product accounts. Yet any government looking to the allocation of resources between consumption and investment in the future would be foolish indeed to ignore critical investment in education and in knowledge generally. Along with this should come a significant part of expenditures for health, which keep children in a position to learn and adults in a position to remain productive workers. We might well than extend the boundary of investment or capital formation to include all investment in all sectors— government and households as well as business and nonprofit institutions —in intangible or human capital as well in tangible, physical capital.

Boundaries between final and intermediate product also raise serious questions. Media services—of newspapers, television, and radio—are financed in large part in many countries by advertising. This means, for example, that the movie we see on television is not a final product. Its advertising content is a purchase by a sponsor from the TV network and an input into the final product—automobile, soap, or greeting cards—that the sponsor is selling. If the same movie is seen on public or government-owned television, its exhibition costs go into the GDP as government purchases of goods and services. They would also be included—as consumption—if the movie were on pay-for-view private television or, of course, were seen in a movie house.

Boundaries questionably located in the other direction are those relating to police and military services. Since these are generally provided by government, they are automatically classified as final. But are they final or, rather, intermediate inputs (presumably) necessary to the protection of our businesses and homes and our enjoyment of consumption? The anomaly may be noted by the fact that if a business arranged to provide for its own police protection in return for an abatement of its taxes, the GDP would go down by the amount of the government services turned over to private enterprise.

Similarly, we might recognize expenses related to work, such as commuting costs, as intermediate rather than final consumption. Currently, these expenses are so recognized if employers pay for them but not if they are paid for by employees out of their wages and salaries.

Many of these alternative definitions or boundaries would bring vast changes in the numbers. My estimate of total consumption in 1981, including nonmarket services produced in households, was 150 percent of essentially market-produced "personal consumption expenditures" in the BEA NIPAs (Eisner, 1989a, p. 235). Total gross domestic capital accumulation was no less than 413 percent of the BEA's gross private domestic investment. And total GNP was put at 157 percent of the official GNP figure.

These differences are important not only because of their magnitude but also because they may well fluctuate over time. As economies develop, production tends to move out of the household and into the market. Looking only at market production may yield a picture that exaggerates the growth in total output. The vast movement of women into the labor force in the United States in recent decades may also lead to an exaggeration of rates of growth of output if we take no note of the lost output of women at home, output for which TV dinners, restaurant meals, and nursery school child care are substituted.

Cyclical fluctuations in output may be exaggerated if we ignore increased work around the house by the unemployed. Policy measures to increase provision for the future may prove wide of the mark if they focus on gross private domestic investment, to the possible detriment of public and household investment and investment in research, education and training, and health. The economic welfare of a nation may be misjudged if its high GDP reflects a large amount of intermediate military output. The effects of increasing or decreasing resources devoted to the military may similarly be misjudged if they are viewed as producing final product. *SNA 1993* (United Nations, 1993, p. 227) recognizes this implicitly in part by excluding from public investment government expenditures for weapons.[3]

National income and product accounts constructed in accordance with the altered and generally expanded boundaries for output and capital formation I have been suggesting may be noted in Table 3.1. Adapted from Eisner (1985, 1989a), they incorporate market components from the conventional accounts for 1981 along with estimates of nonmarket output aggreated from individual sectors and various further adjustments for the altered boundaries.

3.2. Satellite Accounts

Expansion and alteration of boundaries for output and investment offer the prospect of vital new information on the position and progress of national economies and what can be done about them. Yet there is, understandably, substantial objection to wholesale modification of the central accounts that have long proved a mainstay of economic analysis and policy making. The new *System of National Accounts 1993* outlines the characteristics of "satellite accounts" that, "without overburdening or disrupting the central system," will permit "the use of complementary or alternative concepts . . . when needed to introduce additional dimensions to the conceptual frameword of national accounts" (Commission of the European Communities, 1993, p. 489).[4]

The satellite accounts will also offer "additional information on particular concerns of a functional or cross-sector nature." There might, for example, be an R&D account, which would group all R&D activities by government, business, and nonprofit institutions. There might be an education account that would pull together all educational activities, in public and private schools, in the workplace and at home, market and nonmarket. There might be a transportation account that would similarly bring together all transportation services, no matter how or where provided. There might be a tourism account, comprising all the various services of different industries on which tourists rely. *SNA 1993* indeed

Table 3.1. TISA: National Income and Product Accounts, 1981 (billions of dollars)

Debits		Credits	
1. Labor income	3,208.7	1. Consumption	2,856.0
2. Compensation of employees	1,769.2	2. Household expenditures for services and nondurables	1,044.2
3. Additional imputations	1,502.0		
4. Employee training	73.7	3. Expense account items of consumption	24.6
5. Expense account items of consumption	24.6	4. BEA imputations other than housing	44.5
6. Labor income of self-employed	138.8	5. Subsidies allocated to consumption	7.3
7. Opportunity costs of students	248.2	6. Transfers	280.1
8. Unpaid household work	980.7	7. Nonmarket services produced in households	1,455.4
9. Less: Expenses related to work	62.5		
10. Rental income owner-occupied nonfarm dwellings	9.3	8. Gross domestic capital accumulation	1,677.9
		9. Original cost	1,823.0
11. Capital income	369.8	10. Tangible	972.8
12. Interest paid	332.1	11. Structures & equipment and household durables and semidurables	953.8
13. Net imputed interest (excluding business)	11.8		
14. Net interest, rest of world	26.0	12. Business	344.5
15. Net operating surplus	247.7	13. Nonprofit institutions	10.3
16. Corporate profits	192.3	14. Government enterprises	22.3
17. Proprietors' capital income	−18.6	15. Government	102.7
18. Gross business investment in research and development	33.9	16. Households	444.3
		17. Fixed gross private domestic product reconciliation	19.1
19. Government enterprise surpluses	12.1		
20. Net rental income of persons	28.0	18. Government capital accumulation reconciliation	10.6
21. Net revaluations	−153.7		
22. Net surplus (15 + 21)	94.0		

23.	National income (1 + 10 + 11 + 22)	3,681.8
24.	*Less:* Intangible capital consumption	402.3
25.	Net national income (23–24)	3,279.5
26.	Business transfer payments	33.5
27.	Media support	15.8
28.	Health and safety	4.7
29.	Other	12.9
30.	Uncompensated factor services	18.7
31.	Net indirect business taxes	98.0
32.	Indirect business taxes	219.3
33.	*Less:* Intermediate product transferred from government	121.3
34.	Statistical discrepancy	−4.9
35.	Net national product (25 + 26 + 30 + 31 + 34)	3,424.7
36.	Capital consumption allowances	1,135.5
37.	Tangible	733.1
38.	Intangible	402.3
39.	Charges against gross national product (35 + 36)	4,560.1

19.	Change in inventories	19.0
20.	Intangible	850.2
21.	Research and development	68.5
22.	Education and training	640.1
23.	Health	141.6
24.	Subsidies and government enterprise transfers allocated to investment	8.5
25.	Net revaluations	−153.7
26.	Net exports	26.3
27.	Exports	368.8
28.	Imports	342.5
29.	Gross national product	4,560.1

Source: Abridged from Eisner (1985, pp. 36–37, table 1).
Note: The adjusted ENP estimate is 1,066 times the offical GNP estimate for 1981 of 4,277.7.

suggests satellite accounts in culture, education, health,[5] social protection, tourism, environmental protection, research and development, development aid, transportation, data processing, housing, and communications. Looming particularly large would be accounts for households, R&D, and the environment, into which considerable effort has already been invested.

Satellite accounts would not be bound by the conventions and boundaries of the central accounts but would be constructed in a fashion consistent with them. It would thus be generally possible to note the impact on the central accounts of consolidating them with one or more of their satellites. I would myself imagine the possibility of consolidating household and government satellite accounts with the existing central account. We could then get pictures of total output (market and nonmarket), total investment (public and private, tangible and intangible), and total capital (tangible and intangible), with balance sheets showing changes in valuation from year to year. And satellite accounts could also include large amounts of physical data regarding labor, capital, and output.

Satellite accounts could report all kinds of income, including transfers in cash and kind and imputations corresponding to nonmarket output. We might note, for example, the transfers of education services by the state to the household or of police services to business and to individuals. Following *SNA 1993* guidelines, satellite accounts would themselves offer internally consistent data on flows of income and product, balance sheets, and the flow of funds and financial claims. The functionally oriented accounts may, however, well overlap. Transportation services may appear in a tourism account as well as an account dedicated to transportation. Research on health may show up in a health account as well as an R&D account.

3.2.1. Household Accounts

We may see better the potential of satellite accounts, particularly in relation to changes and expansion of boundaries by considering a few of them in some detail. We may begin with a set that we might imagine constructing for households.[6] In Table 3.2 we may note numbers that I estimate for the income and product account component of such a set.

On the income side we might begin, in the category of labor income, with the relatively minuscule numbers for compensation of employees, essentially that for domestic help. There would then be major imputations, the largest for unpaid household work, which can be broken down

Table 3.2. Household Income and Product, 1981 (billions of dollars)

Debits		Credits	
1. Labor income	1,271.1	1. Consumption	1,511.1
2. Compensation of employees	7.0	2. Market (Labor services in households)	7.0
3. Imputations	1,265.0	3. Nonmarket	1,455.4
4. Employee training	0.1	4. Net space rent on owner-occupied nonfarm dwellings	178.9
5. Opportunity costs of students	284.2	5. BEA net space rent on owner-occupied nonfarm dwellings	178.6
6. Unpaid household work	980.7		
7. Less: Expenses related to work	1.0	6. Subsidies	0.2
8. Capital income	143.1	7. Capital services other than on owner-occupied dwellings	332.3
9. Owner-occupied housing	100.5		
10. Interest paid	87.2	8. Durables	209.5
11. Net imputed interest	4.1	9. Gross	237.0
12. Gross imputed interest	91.2	10. Less: Services allocated to investment	8.9
13. Land	21.1		
14. Owner-occupied dwellings	70.1	11. Less: Services to expenses related to work	18.6
15. Less: Interest paid	87.2		
16. Net rental income	9.3	12. Semidurables	122.0
17. Rental income on nonfarm own-occ. dwellings and land	13.3	13. Inventories	0.8
		14. Labor services	944.3
18. Less: Net imputed interest	4.1	15. Total imputed labor services	1,265.0
19. Consuumer goods	42.6	16. Less: Labor services allocated to investment	320.8
20. Consumer interest	54.3		
21. Net imputed interest	−11.6	17. Intermediate product of government to consumption	48.7
22. Gross imputed interest	42.6		
23. Durables	35.7	18. Capital accumulation	282.5
24. Semidurables	6.1		
25. Inventories	0.8		

Table 3.2. *Continued*

Debits			*Credits*		
26.	*Less:* Consumer interest	54.3	19.	Intangible at original cost	348.6
27.	Net revaluations	−66.0	20.	Education	335.5
28.	Land	−17.6	21.	Teaching children at home	26.8
29.	Owner-occupied dwellings	−13.7	22.	Opportunity cost of students	284.2
30.	Consumer goods	−34.7	23.	Durable services allocated to education	6.3
31.	Durables	−25.5			
32.	Semidurables	−9.4	24.	Intermediate product of government to education	18.2
33.	Inventories	0.2	25.	Health	13.0
34.	Income originating (1 + 8 + 27)	1,348.1	26.	Employee training	0.1
35.	*Less:* Intangible (human) capital consumption	351.1	27.	Net revaluations	−66.0
			28.	Services to expenses related to work	18.6
36.	Net income originating and charges against net household product (34−35)	997.0	29.	*Less:* Intermediate product transferred from government	102.5
37.	Capital consumption allowances	711.7	30.	*Less:* Expenses related to work	1.0
38.	Tangible (nonhuman)	360.6	31.	Gross household product	1,708.7
39.	Original cost	282.9			
40.	Revaluations	77.7			
41.	Intangible (human)	351.1			
42.	Original cost	176.8			
43.	Revaluations	174.3			
44.	Charges against gross household product (36 + 37)	1,708.7			

in considerable detail and evaluated by a variety of methods. An important component of labor income that we might add would be the opportunity costs of students—that is, what students could earn if they were working instead of attending school. There is also a tiny item of employee training, recognized as income to the workers who receive it. I would also subtract expenses—partcularly travel expenses—related to work.

Capital income accruing to households is the sum of (1) imputed interest and net rental income of owner-occupied housing and associated land and (2) imputed interest on consumer goods—durables, semidurables, and inventories. Revaluations of tangible household capital net of inflation may also be counted as income or may go into an accumulation account. Finally on the debits side of the account, we include capital consumption allowances for both intangible and tangible capital.

Consistent with the central accounts, a satellite account for households would have a credit side that allocated product to consumption and investment. Consumption would include, in addition again to the small item of market labor services, an overwhelming imputation of nonmarket services. Under this rubric we would have the value of rents on owner-occupied housing and services of consumer goods that were not allocated to investment. We also have a vast amount of labor services, even after netting out labor services (particularly those relating to education) that are allocated to investment. We also have a substantial, if minor, amount of intermediate product of government counted as consumption services transferred to households.

Household output going to *capital accumulation*—perhaps a more apt term than the usually more narrowly construed *investment*—relates largely to education: teaching children in the home, the opportunity costs of students old enough to work, and some services of durables. Other intangible capital accumulation of households includes that in health and employee training and the intermediate product of education transferred from government. Rounding out capital accumulation we have those *net* revaluations. In balance sheets for households in nominal dollars we will have to add back the changes in the value of capital corresponding to changes in the general price level.

In addition to the balance sheets to which we have alluded, we may wish to include a saving and investment account or a capital accumulation account for households. This would encompass all capital acquired by households and not only accumulation of capital produced in the household or transferred from government. They would include intangible as well as tangible capital, however, and could be consolidated with saving and investment or accumulation accounts for other sectors to yield corresponding accounts for the economy as a whole.

A set of household satellite accounts might also include a great deal of demographic data and information on physical assets. These would be consistent with the labor and capital income and output in value terms that go into the income and product accunts and balance sheets in value terms.

3.2.2. R&D Accounts

The BEA has been working on satellite accounts in the area of R&D.[7] They offer immediately a good example of boundary shifting with respect to investment and final product. In the conventional central accounts, all R&D expenditures for goods and services by government, including government research institutes and state universities, are treated as just that—government expenditures for goods and services—and hence included in GDP. R&D expenditures by business and by nonprofit institutions for tangible capital goods are included in gross private domestic investment and hence in GDP. Wages, salaries, and other current costs of R&D incurred by business are subsumed in whatever the business is producing; they are not final product. Thus, if business spends more on these items of current R&D cost, this merely reduces profits and has no effect on GDP, nominal or real. If it raises prices to cover these increased costs, nominal GDP rises but real GDP is unaffected. And to complicate the picture further, R&D current expenditures by nonprofit institutions are treated, like other nonprofit current expenditures as consumption. They enter GDP in personal consumption expenditures.

The central accounts might well be modified, as I have suggested, to capitalize all R&D expenditures, including them in a new expanded measure of gross investment, public and private. At least as starters, though, we might do so in a satellite account for R&D. We would distinguish R&D tangible investment in facilities and equipment and other R&D investment. We would then depreciate both at appropriate rates. If we did so, we would reduce personal consumption expenditures, which we might rename *personal current account expenditures* (Carson and Grimm, 1990) by the amount of the net nonprofit investment in R&D. We would take out of current consumption the nonprofit current R&D spending, which would now be designated investment, and put back the capital consumption of nonprofit R&D capital.

We would then have a new category of R&D investment going into the GDP: it would also include the business R&D current spending, which had previously been expensed, and the government R&D current spending, which had previously been part of government purchases. We would have a government current purchases account, which would include, however, the consumption of government R&D capital. GDP would thus be raised by the total of the new category of R&D investment minus the reduction of consumption by the substitution of capital consumption allowances for expenditures in nonprofit R&D and the reduction of government purchases by the substitution of capital consumption allowances for expenditures in government R&D.

This may be better followed by looking at some illustrative numbers and the corresponding Table 3.3, taken with slight modification from Carson and Grimm (1990). They show the effects on the national income and product account of reclassifying $130 billion of R&D expenditures as investment with corresponding capital consumption allowances (consumption of capital) of $95 billion distributed as follows:

Sector	R&D Investment	R&D Capital Consumption Allowances
Nonprofit institutions	$ 10 billion	$ 5 billion
Business	60	45
Government	60	45
Total	$130 billion	$95 billion

The satellite account might then offer a great deal of detail on R&D expenditures. It might break down and cross-classify R&D by sector of financing and sector performing—federal government, industry, universities and colleges, and other nonprofit institutions. It might break R&D down, by sector and subsector performing, into basic, applied, and development. It might include physical data as to full-time equivalents of scientists and engineers involved. And it might of course distinguish between current spending and spending for capital equipment and facilities used in R&D.

Corresponding to the accounts in nominal dollars would be product and investment accounts in constant dollars. If the value of R&D investment is, as I would propose, measured at cost, converting to constant dollars will raise serious questions of measurement of productivity. If productivity is increasing, all of the increases in costs of inputs should not be treated as inflation to be exorcised in conversion to constant dollars—a problem analogous to that faced and essentially ignored in accounting for government product.

Table 3.3.　The National Income and Product Accounts, without and with R&D capitalization (billions of dollars)

A. Without R&D Capitalization

Debits		Credits	
Compensation of employees	$3,150	Personal consumption expenditures	$3,400
Proprietors' income with IVA and CCAdj	350		
Rental Income of persons with CCAdj	10	Gross private domestic investment	800
Corporate profits with IVA and CCAdj	300	Fixed investment	750
Net interest	440	Inventory investment	50
National income	4,250	Net exports	−50
Business transfer payments	20	Government purchases	1,050
Indirect business tax and nontax liability	400		
Less: Subsidies less current surplus of government enterprises	20		
Net national product	4,650		
Consumption of fixed capital	550		
Charges against gross national product	5,200	Gross national product	5,200

B. With R&D Capitalization

Debits		Credits	
Compensation of employees	$3,150	Personal current account expenditures	$3,395
Proprietors' income with IVA and CCAdj	350		
Rental income of persons with CCAdj	10	Gross private domestic investment	800
Corporate profits with IVA and CCAdj	315	Fixed investment	750
Net interest	440	Inventory investment	50
National income	4,265	R&D investment	130
		Nonprofit institutions (households)	10
Business transfer payments	20	Business	60
Indirect business tax and nontax liability	400	Government	60
Less: Subsidies less current surplus of government enterprises	20	Net exports	−50
Net national product	4,665	Government current account purchases	1,035
Consumption of capital	645		
Fixed capital	550		
R&D capital	95		
Charges against gross national product	5,310	Gross national product	5,310

CCAdj   Capital consumption adjustment
IVA   Inventory valuation adjustment
R&D   Research and development

This leads us to the vexing problem of capital accounts and the attribution of depreciation to the stocks created by R&D spending. Physical R&D facilities can presumably be depreciated and stocks calculated in the same fashion as all other structures and equipment, utilizing similar given lengths of life and depreciation rates. These are in principle, however, consistent with rates that would be obtained by surveys of retirements and rather difficult calculations of declines of efficiency of assets over their lifetimes. The discount rate necessary to make the original present value of services equal to original cost or supply price can then be used to trace the declining present value of facilities over their lives and the consequent flow of depreciation charges.

The stream of services from intangible capital is even more difficult to measure, however. When is there a payoff to basic research? Once research does result in some useful discovery, does that remain permanently a part of research capital, so that there is no depreciation? Or is nothing permanent? How are we to handle increases in basic research capital resulting from work in the rest of the world?

One can make arbitrary assumptions as to lengths of life and depreciation rates for basic, applied, and development R&D capital: infinite life and zero depreciation for basic research or fifty-year life and straight-line depreciation, twenty-year life and straight-line depreciation for applied and development capital, or various rates of geometric (declining balance) depreciation for each. And we may estimate production and profit functions including R&D tangible and intangible investment and capital and derive depreciation rates from them. Nadiri and Prucha (1993) have recently estimated the geometric R&D intangible capital depreciation rate in manufacturing to be .12. A satellite account might present estimates of depreciation, net investment and capital stocks on the basis of a variety of assumptions.

3.2.3. Environmental Accounts

Other prime candidates for a satellite account are natural resources, including land, and the environment. Such an account would essentially include in the capital of the economy the eonomic value of its land, water, air and natural resources, whatever the titles to their ownership— or lack of rights to ownership. In the central SNAs, measures of capital formation are restricted to assets to which there are ownership rights. Ignoring ownership rights, additions to known reserves and growth of new forests would be treated as capital accumulation. Depletion of oil and timber or pollution or degradation of the environment would then be treated as negative accumulation. Expenditures to restore the land or environment would be treated as gross investment to be matched by depreciation or depletion. Might we treat increases in assets in the form of wild fish and uncultivated forests, along with those baffling increases in the stock of basic knowledge as a result of R&D in the rest of the world, as capital accumulation in assets with no (domestic) rights of ownership?

The new *System of National Accounts 1993* offers a detailed framework, in Chapter 21, for a satellite account for the environment that could be integrated with the central accounts.[8] It largely follows, as it points out, a system of environmental economic accounts (SEEA) presented in United Nations (1992). In the environmental accounts, "SNA aggregates are amended to treat natural resources as capital in the production of goods and services, to record the cost of using—i.e., depleting and degrading—those resources and to record the implicit transfers needed to account for the imputed cost and capital items" (United Nations, 1993, p. 508). They would thus account for "new scarcities of natural resources which threaten the sustained productivity of the economy and the degradation of environmental quality and consequential effects on human health and welfare."

Environmental cost and capital items can be included in physical and in monetary terms. The environmental accounts, of course, must give considerable attention to nonproduced assets. These can be depleted as their stocks, as in the case of oil reserves or virgin forests, are drawn down. Or they can be degraded, as soil erosion reduces the serviceability of land and as pollution reduces the serviceability of water and air. Provision is made for the transfer of natural assets to and between economic uses. Record is made of the "non-sustainable extraction of fishstock from oceans and rivers, extraction of firewood and lumber from tropical and other virgin forests or hunting of animals living in the wild and also the effects of emission of residuals on the quality of air, water, fishstocks, wild forests, and the effects of other economic activities (recreation, agriculture, transport, etc.) on eco-systems and species habitat" (United Nations, 1993, p. 512).

We thus replace net capital formation in the *SNA* with net accumulation in SEEA. The SEEA includes, in addition to the produced assets of the *SNA*, changes in nonproduced economic assets and in natural assets other than economic assets. For the former we have the "net effects of negative depletion and degradation and positive additions of natural assets that are transferred to economic uses." For the latter it is "the economic valuation of the impact of economic activities on the environment and it is the sum of negative depletion and degradation effects and negative effects of incorporating natural assets as economic assets." An environment domestic product (EDP) would differ from the conventional NDP by the difference between the SEEA net accumulation and the conventional *SNA* net capital formation.

The asset boundaries in the satellite environment account would thus be extended beyond economic assets, which are characterized as contributing benefits to their owners. They would include all known natural assets other than human capital. Subsoil assets, as in the central SNA, however, are limited to proven reserves. They would include our air and water, owned by no one but affecting and affected by economic activity. They "would, in principle, include all forests (including virgin forests), all fishstocks, and all animal herds whether they are controlled by human activities or not, as all can be affected by human activities" (United Nations, 1993, p. 513).

Depletion of nonproduced natural assets, even if owned by no one, might therefore be treated as a cost, if it can be evaluated, in the environmental accounts and as a reduction in inventories. Similarly, degradation of nonproduced, nonowned environmental assets might be treated as a cost or charge against production of those who create the degradation and hence as a reduction of net output, reducing environmental domestic product (EDP) in the satellite account as compared to the net domestic product (NDP) for corresponding activities in the central *SNA*.

The extended measure of accumulation then includes not only the capital formation entailed in changes in the stock of produced assets used in production but also changes in nonproduced natural assets that are used in production. It does not include natural growth of noncultivated biological resources included in net capital accumulation. These should show up though, like catastrophic losses, as changes in assets not related to accumulation.

3.3. Conclusion

Expansion and alteration of boundaries for income, product, assets, and accumulation offer the possibility of significant advances in our knowledge and understanding of the functioning of national economies. In some cases accounts with new boundaries might be substituted for the old ones. More likely, at least for the immediate future, modified accounts will be offered as supplements to the existing ones.

Satellite accounts offer the possibility of introdu g major boundary changes in particular sectors or areas of economic activity. The satellite accounts, following a basic methodology consistent with that employed in the central *SNA* (or U.S. NIPAs) can then readily be integrated with the central accounts to present varied pictures of the aggregates. They can also put together large bodies of data regarding particular functions and activities, both in physical terms and in the value measures of the *SNA*.

Expansion and modification of boundaries, without losing the enormous contributions of more narrowly constructed accounts, and the satellite accounts that facilitate this, may thus contribute in a major way to the continued development and improvement of economic national accounts in an ever-changing world.

Notes

1. Major expansion and modification of boundaries has been proposed and implemented by a number of economists, as discussed in Eisner (1988). See, in particular, Kendrick (1976, 1979), Nordhaus and Tobin (1972), and Eisner (1985, 1989a, 1989b, 1991, 1994).

2. An estimate of the value of military output, however, might take into account the saving in efficiency of paying optimal wages to recruit the most productive personnel and combining their services in optimal proportion with those of other factors of production.

3. *SNA 1993* distinguishes between destructive weapons that have no use in producing goods and services and other military equipment and structures that might have such use. The former are not recognized as fixed assets. I would treat the output of defense and police services as intermediate (see Eisner, 1989a, pp. 9–10) but would then count the equipment and structures that produce them as fixed assets just as steel mills that produce intermediate product are fixed assets. Production of more military equipment would then count as capital formation, no matter how destructive or useless.

4. General conceptual and illustrative treatment of satellite accounts may be found in Lemaire (1987) and Schäfer and Stahmer (1990).

5. Substantial proposals for the treatment of health expenditures are to be found in Foulon (1982) and Sunga and Swinamer (1986).

6. Satelliete accounts for households have been discussed and presented by numerous economists and statisticians, including Chadeau (1985), Lützel (1989), and Schäfer (1992).

7. See Carson and Grimm (1990, 1991) and internal memoranda of the BEA by Carol Evans and Bruce Grimm and Eisner. I am indebted to Evans for much of the bibliography at the end of this chapter. For a Japanese satellite account for R&D, see Kurabayashi and Matsuda (1989).

8. See Vanoli (1989) for what was an earlier draft of much of this chapter. See also Barelmus, Stahmer, and Van Tongeren (1989) and Gervais (1990).

References

Bartelmus, P., C. Stahmer, and J. van Tongeren. (1989). "SNA Framework for Integrated Environmental and Economic Accounting." International Association for Research in Income and Wealth.

Carson, C. (1989). "The United Nations System of National Accounts: A Revision for the Twenty-first Century." Paper presented to the American Economic Association, December 29, Atlanta.

Carson, C. and B. Grimm. (1990, 1991). "Satellite Accounts in a Modernized and Extended SNA." Washington, D.C.: Bureau of Economic Analysis, U.S. Department of Commerce.

Chadeau, A. (1985). "Measuring Household Activities: Some International Comparisons." *Review of Income and Wealth* 31(3): 237–253.

Eisner, R. (1985). "The Total Incomes System of Accounts." *Survey of Current Business* 65 (January): 24–48.

——.(1986). *How Real Is the Federal Deficit?* New York: Free Press.

——.(1988). "Extended Measures of National Income and Product." *Journal of Economic Literature* 26 (December): 1611–1684.

——.(1989a). *The Total Incomes System of Accounts.* Chicago: University of Chicago Press.

——.(1989b). "Divergences of Measurement and Theory and Some Implications for Economic Policy." *American Economic Review* 79 (March): 1–13.

——.(1991). "The Real Rate of U.S. National Saving." *Review of Income and Wealth* 37 (March): 13–32.

——.(1994). *The Misunderstood Economy: What Counts and How to Count It.* Boston: Harvard Business School Press.

Foulon, A. (1982). "Proposals for a Homogeneous Treatment of Health Expenditures in the National Accounts." *Review of Income and Wealth* 28(1) (March): 45–70.

Gervais, Y. (1990). "Some Issues in the Development of Natural Resources Satellite Accounts: Valuation of Non-Renewable Resources." Ottawa: Statistics Canada.

Havrylishyn, Oli. (1977). "Towards a Definition of Non-market Activities." *Review of Income and Wealth* 23(1): 79–96.

Kendrick, John W. (1976). *The Formation and Stocks of Total Capital.* New York: Columbia University Press for NBER.

——.1979. "Expanding Imputed Values in the National Income and Product Accounts." *Review of Income and Wealth* 25(4): 359–363.

Kurabayashi, Y. and Y. Matsuda. (1989). "A Satellite Account Approach Applied to Research and Development: Japanese Data." International Association for Research in Income and Wealth. Lahnstein, Germany.

Kuznets, Simon. (1941). *National Income and Its Composition, 1919–1938* (2 vols.). New York: NBER.

Lemaire, M. (1987). "Satellite Accounts: A Relevant Framework for Analysis in Social Fields." *Review of Income and Wealth* 33(3) (September): 305–325.

Lützel, H. (1989). "Household Production and National Accounts." *Statistical Journal of the United Nations* 6(4) (December): 337–348.

Minder, J.F., N. Rubel, and P. Müller. (1989). Le Compte De La Recherche. *INSEE Methodes*, Series No. 1.

Müller, P. (1990). L'Élargissement du Concept de FBCF et Ses Conséquences Pour Les Comptes Nationaux. Paris: INSEE.

Murphey, Martin. (1980). *The Measurement and Valuation of Household Nonmarket Time*. Washington, DC: BEA, U.S. Department of Commerce.

Nadiri, M.I. and I.R. Prucha. (1993). "Estimation of the Depreciation Rate of Physical and R&D Capital in the U.S. Total Manufacturing Sector." National Bureau of Economic Research Working Paper No. 4591. Cambridge. MA: NBER.

Nordhaus, William, and James Tobin. (1972). "Is Growth Obsolete?" *Economic Growth* (Vol. 5). New York: NBER.

Pommier, P. (1981). "Social Expenditure: Socialization of Expenditure? The French Experience of Satellite Accounts." *Review of Income and Wealth* 27(4) (December): pp. 373–386.

Reid, Margaret G. (1934). *The Economics of Household Production*. New York: Wiley.

Rostadsand, J.I. and E.J. Flottum. (1989). "Satellite and Adjunct Accounts in the National Accounts, Development of Health Accounts in Norway." International Association for Research in Income and Wealth. Lahnstein.

Schäfer, D. (1992). "Concepts and Plans for a Satellite System on Household Production." International Association for Research in Income and Wealth, Flims, Switzerland.

Schäfer, D. and C. Stahmer. (1990). "Conceptual Considerations on Satellite Systems." *Review of Income and Wealth* 36(2) (June): 167–176.

Smith, R. (1990). *An Annotated Bibliography of the Resource and Environmental Literature*. Ottawa: Statistics Canada.

Sunga, P. and J. Swinamer. (1986). "Health Care Accounts: A Conceptual Framework and an Illustrative Example." *Review of Income and Wealth* 32(3) (September): 277–298.

Teillet, P. (1988). "A Concept of Satellite Accounts in the Revised *SNA*." *Review of Income and Wealth* 34(4) (December): pp. 411–439.

Vanoli, A. (1989). "Satellite Accounts." SNA Expert Group Coordinating Meeting. New York: United Nations.

United Nations. (1992). "Intergrated Environmental and Economic Accounting: An Interim Report." New York: United Nations. Subsequently issued as a United Nations publication, Sales No. E.93.XVII.12.

United Nations, Commission of the European Communities, International Monetary Fund, Organization for Economic Co-operation and Development, United Nations and World Bank. (1993). *System of National Accounts 1993*. Brussels/Luxembourg, New York, Paris, Washington, DC: United Nations.

DISCUSSION OF CHAPTER 3

F. Graham Pyatt

Introduction

There used to be a time when lectures on national income accounting were a standard component of serious courses in economics. That is sadly not the case today, and, while most economists have been content to entrust the *System of National Accounts (SNA)* to statisticians, there remain a precious few who have retained an interest in the subject. Robert Eisner is, of course, one of these, and his contribution to this volume cites the work of others who have similarly maintained over the years that it matters a great deal not only for our understanding of the past but also in formulating policies for the future just what is and what is not included within the definition of GDP and the associated macroeconomic aggregates that are recognized in the *SNA*.

As one who has championed the case for extending the boundaries of the *SNA* and reclassifying particular categories of transactions, Robert Eisner might well be disappointed that *SNA 1993* does not represent a more substantial movement toward his position on such key issues as the location of the production boundary, the treatment of government expenditures, and the need for a more comprehensive measure of investment. Of course, there is some virtue in maintaining consistent definitions over time and Eisner recognises this point. In doing so, he makes great play of the fact that *SNA 1993* offers some hope of emancipation from the constraints of historical precedents. This is to be found in the active sponsorship within the *SNA* of satellite accounts for special topics. Professor Eisner devotes much of his present essay to a discussion of the potential for innovation that is offered by the satellite systems, focusing particularly on the household, R&D, and the environment as important cases in point.

I am not myself persuaded that it is an entirely adequate response by the authros of the new *SNA* to suggest that the concerns that Professor Eisner and kindred spirits have expressed over the years should be consigned to a variety of satellites that orbit around a refurbished central system any more than I am persuaded that the *SNA* should be promoted without reference to the macroeconomic models that it might be hoped to support. Some further comment on two of the main areas of concern that have been identified by Robert Eisner may therefore be useful—namely, the location of the production boundary and the treatment of government expenditures.

The Production Boundary

The case for maintaining a constant set of definitions for GDP and its main components rests essentially on the proposition that time-series data are more useful if they are consistent. In practice, however, this case has been undermined by the *SNA* itself in admitting a progressive movement of the production boundary through the sequence of 1953, 1968, and 1993 *SNA*s. As Professor Eisner explains in his paper, the boundary was drawn initially quite close to the *de facto* limits of the monetary economy. And now it is proposed to move to a new boundary so as to include all production of goods and housing services plus all production of services which are rendered outside the household. It follows that constant definitions have not, in fact, been maintained in the past and that there are more changes in store for the future. This is the first point. A second point is that constant boundaries could have been maintained without losing the advantages that follow from extending the coverage of the *SNA*. Monetary economics has no problem in recognizing an increasingly broad definition of money supply through a series of aggregates that are known as M_0, M_1, M_2, and so on. Why, then, should we not approach the measurement of GDP in the same spirit? Y_0 could measure the size of the monetized economy. Y_1 could then be the halfway house that is defined by *SNA 1968*. And Y_2 could be the measure that is now proposed—that is, the *1993 SNA* definition of GDP. This would then allow a future Y_3 corresponding to the potential limits of the monetised economy.

A somewhat separate question of some importance is whether the new Y_2 is going to prove an easy concept to work with. And an issue closely related to that is whether or not there now remains a case for further expansion of the boundary and, therefore, for going beyond Y_2.

In response to the first of these questions, it can be anticipated that there will be considerable pressure on statistical offices to move from present practice to the newly promoted Y_2 because an important part of the difference between Y_1 and Y_2 is attributable to a range of DIY activities that are typically undertaken by women as unpaid family workers. To this extent, therefore, the Y_1 concept is gender biased. This is of psychological and political importance: it is therefore not only of economic importance that the scale and content of DIY activity should be better understood in both developed and developing countries.

In turning to the second of the above questions, it should be noted that gender bias will not be removed by the adoption of Y_2 since the services which are rendered within the household are contributed predomniently by women of all ages. It is necessary accordingly to rethink what we mean by the domestic product if this and other fundamental difficulties are to be overcome.

Perhaps economic theory can be helpful at this point. All uses of time have an opportunity cost, and in its choice of relocation for the production boundary, the new SNA has ruled out of account not only the contribution made by leisure to welfare but also the time that is devoted to human capital formation, both time at school and the human resource costs of reproduction. So if we want to recognize human capital formation within the national accounts, then we have to go beyond Y_2 and value such uses of time at their opportunity cost. However, if we are to do this, then we should also recognize that the gross return to human capital is the total value of time, irrespective of how it is used. And to obtain the net return, which is the contribution to GDP, we must subtract from this total value those expenditures that are necessary for the maintenance of human capital—that is, that part of what is currently referred to as consumption that is necessary to provide an adequate diet, shelter, and clothing: what some people might refer to as basic needs. By the same token, time that is spent on personal maintenance—sleep, ablutions, and so on—should be netted out and therefore does not contribute to GDP. But leisure (or free time) does.

The Treatment of Government Expenditure

The capital expenditure of governments, whether on buildings or guns, results in the acquisition of assets that have a value. Such expenditure is therefore investment, says Eisner, despite what the new SNA might have to say about armaments. It is less easy, however, to be sure how current government expenditure should be treated, perhaps because there is no simple, single answer, the uniform treatment of all current expenditure in the SNA as final consumption expenditure notwithstanding.

While the DIY production of services rendered within the household is excluded from Y_2, as noted above, the SNA has always included an estimate (based on opportunity cost) of the value of output for those government activities that supply public goods. Those that give pleasure, such as public broadcasting, are correctly treated as contributing to final consumption only to the extent that they have to be paid for (to which should be added the opportunity cost of time spent enjoying such facilities if the notion of production is extended to include all time use). But for others, such as the maintenance of law and order, it is argued by Eisner that all their output is intermediate, not final, and this would indeed seem to be the most appropriate treatment, not just in these cases but for public administration in general and also for the law makers themselves, since their product is clearly facilitating and not an end in itself. In much the same vein it can be argued, as Eisner does, that current defense expenditure might well be justified as protecting life, real assets and property rights—that is, in contributing toward the maintenance of existing assets. It does not create any new assets (except, possibly, when defense leads to conquest) and is not, therefore, a part of capital formation.

Health and education expenditures present a somewhat different set of issues, the treatment of which must depend on whether human capital is recognized as such. If it is, then much preventive medicine, like education, should be a part of investment, along with the resource costs of reproduction and maternity services. Curative health services, on the other hand, are maintenance expenditures and therefore intermediate, as are some but not all expenditures on the services of public utilities: the consumption of gas, electricity, water, and sanitation services are final only to the extent that they are not necessary to maintain human capital.

An Integrated system

The model that is presented by the *1993 SNA* of a core system with surrounding satellites has much appeal, not least in encouraging the R&D effort that is needed to establish enviromental accounting and similar potential developments. But this particular way of structuring the *SNA* also has the considerable limitation of failing to show how Y_1 is nested within the Y_2 that is now proposed, and that Y_0 is nested within Y_1. Similarly, it fails to suggest that there need be no harm in going beyond Y_2 to a more sophisticated measure of product that incorporates the notion of human capital. *SNA 1993* could have been a nested system of related concepts within which individual countries would be encouraged to develop their capabilities, perhaps from small beginnings, by maintaining consistent series over time while simultaneously extending the coverage in line with increasing capabilities and resources. Of course, the presentation of the *SNA* in such a nested form would be greatly facilitated by retaining the matrix format that was the glory of the 1968 version. But that is another story. The one that can be concluded here is that a layered approach to the development of the *SNA* from Y_0 onward would do some belated justice to the valuable contributions that Robert Eisner and others have promoted over the years since 1968. It hardly seems enough to corral their innovations in a satellite system of household and other accounts. Perhaps at the next revision of the SNA there will be less preoccupation with what the GDP is. Instead, the accounts of a nation might be allowed to emerge as a record of monetized activity that is embodies within a comprehensive statement of the use of scarce resources, valued at their opportunity cost.

4 HOUSEHOLD SECTOR INCOME, CONSUMPTION, AND WEALTH

Heinrich Lützel

4.1. Households in national Accounts

National accounts are economic accounts. Economic units produce goods and services, finance or insure other units, distribute income, and use income for buying goods and services or for the formation of wealth.

There is nearly no room for private households in their more general capacities as families with children, school problems, sick persons, nice weekends, and holidays. In national accounts households are interesting only as providers of labor input to producers, as purchasers of goods and services for final consumption, as depositors of money that can be used to finance fixed capital formation of the economy, and to a small extent as producers of goods and services in their function as owners of unincorporated enterprises or as owners of rented or owner occupied dwellings.

Production in national accounts covers also the preparing of meals in restaurants, teaching of children in private or public schools, cleaning of rooms by paid domestic servants, and washing of clothes in laundries. However, unpaid household work is *not* included in the production boundary of national accounting: preparing meals for one's own family, teaching children by members of the family, cleaning rooms, and washing clothes without payment are activities not recorded in national accounts. Why is household production not recorded in national accounts? This is a serious question for which a precise answer cannot be given. When services are produced for the family, there are no interactions in a market. Everything is internal: producing goods and services, generating income, using (imputed) income, consuming the products.

All these procedures take place within the household and cannot be measured in monetary terms. What exactly has to be included in household work, how can it be measured, and how can it be valued? These are more questions that cannot be answered easily. It is obvious, however, that for individuals the activities of households are important and that for the nation unpaid household work is as important as any type of market production. It seems that statistical problems are the main reason for not including household production in national accounts. In Section 4.3 this question is brought up again.

The main focus of national accounts as prepared in nearly all countries according to the rules of the international systems is on market producers and on the general government. This is true for *A Standardised System of National Accounts* of the OEEC (1952) as well as for *A System of National Accounts* of the United Nations (*SNA 1968*) and for the *European System of Integrated Economic Accounts* (ESA) of the European Communities (1970). During the revision of *SNA 1968*, carried out by the expert group from 1986 to 1992, the questions of the production boundary and of the position that should be established for the sector of households were very important. For the household sector accounts, some progress was made, but household production is still outside the production boundary of the *SNA*.

4.2. Households in *SNA 1993*

The household sector in *SNA 1993* comprises persons living together, sharing (part of) their income and wealth, and consuming goods and services together. One person living alone can be a household, too. Included are institutional households with persons living permanently and for a long time in institutions like monasteries, retirement homes, or prisons.

SNA 1993 distinguishes sectors and industries.[1] The statistical units of sectors are institutional units with decision-making authority and a complete set of accounts. An institution should be entitled, in its own right, to own assets, incur liabilities, and engage in economic activities. The statistical units of industries are establishments. These are producing units comprising market as well as nonmarket producers. An establishment may coincide with an institutional unit like a corporation. But an establishment may also be part of an institutional unit. In this case it is not engaged in transactions on its own account, it cannot incur debts, and normally it does not have a complete set of accounts. But statistical information on the production account (output and inputs), the number of employees, and fixed capital formation should be available if an establishment is identified as a separate producing unit in the *SNA*.

A household as an institutional unit may comprise an unincorporated enterprise. But in the breakdown by industries these producers are treated like establishments and recorded as being part of the industry[2] that typically produces the goods or services in question. For private households with persons employed, only production by domestic servants is recorded. In the input-output framework of the *SNA* only industries are shown. So in this presentation of national accounts data no information is given on the production of the household sector.

But the *SNA 1993* includes production accounts also for institutional sectors. This is new as compared with *SNA 1968*. In these accounts the production of unincorporated enterprises is included in the household sector. So output, intermediate consumption, gross value added, fixed capital consumption, compensation of employees (paid), and the operating surplus (mixed income) in the production account and in the generation of income account concern unincorporated enterprises almost exclusively.

Also new in *SNA 1993* is the breakdown of output into market output, output for own final use, and other nonmarket output of general government and of nonprofit institutions serving households (NPISHs). For the household sector this is interesting because it shows to what extent the production of households for own final use is included in the production boundary of the *SNA*. In developed economies these mainly are services related to owner-occupied dwellings, domestic services, agricultural production for own household consumption, and own-account fixed capital formation in connection with the construction of dwellings or with major repairs of dwellings.

It should be mentioned that not all private unincorporated enterprises are part of the household sector. Quasi-corporations are included in the sectors of financial and nonfinancial corporations. Quasi-corporations are unincorporated enterprises that function as if they were corporations but do not have an independent legal status. A statistical requirement is that they keep a nearly complete set of accounts including information on the use (distribution) of the profit. These criteria are not very precise, and identifying quasi-corporations will depend on the situation in individual countries.

At the expert group meeting on the *SNA* revision there was a long discussion with changing majorities[3] concerning the question whether private nonprofit institutions serving households (NPISHs) should be included in the household sector or not. The final decision proposed a separate sector for these institutions. This was mainly recommended by representatives of developing countries. They argued that it is important to know the economic activities of NPISHs in their countries. At the moment the data available do not allow such an exclusion. However, if *SNA 1993* asks for such a sector split, it may become easier to obtain new statistics on the NPISHs.

Another difficult question concerned the proposed subsectoring of households and applying of criteria for this classification. *SNA 1993* proposes the following household subsectors: employers, own-account workers, employees, recipients of property income, recipients of pensions, recipients of other transfer incomes, and others. But this classification can be modified if countries consider other classifications to be more relevant to their situation.

Households should be allocated to subsectors according to the largest income category of the household as a whole. But in household surveys the reference person is often used for classifying households. This seems to be acceptable for national accounts purposes if the reference person contributes the largest part to the household income. Sometimes the reference person is the one listed at the top in household survey questionnaires. From an economic viewpoint this solution can be accepted only as a third-best criterion for grouping households.

The subsectoring of households is a good step in the right direction. Experience with German national accounts shows that the figures published on the household sector income were of interest only for the general public and for many special users when the Federal Statistical Office of Germany published income data by type of household (Spies, 1992). And here income per household as well as income per person or per consuming unit is of greatest interest. Many users of these data compare them with their own monthly wages or salaries and complain that the national accounts figures are much too high. They usually do not take into account that household income also covers the income of other members of the household, income paid only once a year, and imputed income for owner-occupied housing or imputed interest on insurance technical reserves attributed to the policy holders. In Germany this imputed interest amounts to about one-quarter of the total property income of households. It is important to explain all these details when national accounts figures are presented to users who are not familiar with national accounts concepts. A distinction between monetary and nonmonetary income would be useful for this purpose.

4.3. Production Boundary

The production boundary is in two respects important for national accounts: it defines income because in the system income can be generated only by production, and it defines household consumption because in the system only goods and services that have been produced can be consumed.

For households it is extremely important to decide to what extent the production of goods for own final use and services for own final use is in principle included in the production boundary. *SNA 1993* answers these questions rather clearly, though it is not always easy to understand why the decisions were taken the way they were.

The production of all goods by households is included in the production boundary of the *SNA*. A typical example is the production of agricultural products for final consumption in the own household. At the time when the production of goods takes place, it is not always clear whether part of the output will be sold or bartered on the market. This is the main reason that household production of goods is included in the *SNA* when it is significant at the national level. *SNA 1993* explains: "When the amount of a good produced within households is believed to be quantitatively important in relation to the total supply of that good in a country, its production should be recorded. Otherwise, it is not worthwhile trying to estimate it in practice" (*SNA 1993*, para. 6.25). It is very likely that in developing countries the importance of own-account production is much greater than in developed economies. In the European Union (EU), by convention, only own-account construction of dwellings and the production, storage, and processing of agricultural products is included. All other own-account production of goods by households is deemed to be insignificant for EU countries.

Within households mostly services are produced. *SNA 1993* states: "The production of domestic and personal services for consumption within the same household: the preparation of meals, care and training of children, cleaning, repairs, etc. . . . all of these activities are productive in an economic sense" (*SNA 1993*, para. 1.21). "In most countries a considerable amount of labor is devoted to the production of these domestic and personal services, while their consumption makes an important contribution to economic welfare. However, national accounts serve a variety of analytical and policy purposes and are not compiled simply to produce indicators of welfare. The reasons for not imputing values for unpaid domestic or personal services produced and consumed within households may be summarised as follows" (*SNA 1993*, para. 6.21):

- In contrast to goods it is typical for services that the decision on the consumption of the service must be taken at the moment when the service is produced. By definition it is not possible to produce a service and to decide afterward whether it should be sold on the market or consumed within the family. So in every case it is possible to decide whether a service is destined for the household or for the market. Only services for sale or barter on the market and—by convention—services of owner-occupied dwellings and services of paid domestic staff are included in the production boundary of the SNA.
- As household services are not typically produced for the market, there are no comparable market prices. So the problem of valuation is extremely difficult to solve, and because of the huge volume of these services—they can amount to up to 50 percent of gross domestic product (GDP)—the impact of these weak estimates on nearly all figures in the system is strong.
- For many analytical and political purposes for which national accounts data are used, imputed values are compared with market transactions of minor importance. As, for example, nearly all persons are more or less engaged in household production, there is no unemployment in a country. So for employment analysis this seems to be not suitable. Another example is the analysis of inflation for which market prices are needed.

There are at least two purposes for which the inclusion of household production is important: for welfare analysis the inclusion of total unpaid work (as well as of all impacts of the economy on the environment) is a must. The other important purpose is the analysis of the female contribution to the economic welfare of the nation. But these are not the main purposes of national accounts because the measurement of welfare is not possible with the existing tools of national accounts (*SNA 1993*, para. 1.82) and the impact on statistics of policy regarding women is not strong enough yet. For these reasons *SNA 1993* proposes to show the impact of total household production on the economy within a satellite system.

In Germany the demand for information on the contribution of women to the GDP, including unpaid work of households, was so enormous that the Federal Statistical Office received the financial resources to conduct a representative time-use survey and to prepare estimates of the value of household production. The survey covered 16,000 persons age twelve years and over, who kept detailed twenty-four-hour diaries for two days. On the basis of the time-use data of the total population, first estimates on the value of unpaid household work were published within a complete satellite system on household production (Schäfer and Schwarz, 1994). In this system productive activities are defined applying the third-person criterion. So all activities are included in household production that could be performed by other persons on a paid basis, too.

The main finding regarding the German estimates is that the wage rate chosen for valuing the unpaid time worked is most important for the value added and the output of household production. Three factors are essential for the valuation basis (see Table 4.1):

- *Gross or net wages*: Gross wages also include income tax as well as employers' and employees' social security contributions. In

Table 4.1. Working time and income in national accounts and in household production, former territory of the Federal Republic of Germany, 1992

Total Hours Worked	*Billions of Hours*
All activities in national accounts	47.7
Employees	41.4
Self-employed persons	6.3
Unpaid work in household production	76.5[a]

Income Per Hour Worked	*DM per hour*
In national accounts	
Net value added at factor costs	44.40
Compensation of employees	36.80
Net[b] wages and salaries	19.80
In household production, imputed	
Compensation of housekeepers	25.00
Net[b] wages of housekeepers	
Per hour actually worked	14.70
Per hour of normal working time	11.70

a. Of which 0.5 billions of hours spent on own-account production included in national accounts.

b. Net of income taxes and social contributions of employers and employees.

Germany these elements amount to about 45 percent of the compensation of all employees and 41 percent of the compensation of housekeepers.

- *Wages paid per normal working time or per actual working time*: Because of free days (holidays, leave, or sickness), the monthly wages per hour worked are about 25 percent higher than the wages per hour of paid normal working time.
- *Comparable market wages chosen*: In Germany the wages of housekeepers are about 30 percent lower than the average wages and salaries of all employees.

Table 4.2 shows the output and value added in 1992 of all households in the territory of Germany before the unification using different wage rates for the valuation of unpaid household work. The consumption of fixed capital is calculated for consumer durables used in the production process and for owner-occupied dwellings. Goods and services used up in the production process are recorded as intermediate consumption, though in national accounts they are included in the final consumption of households. The ouput of household production is calculated as the sum of production costs. Household production, as shown in Table 4.2, includes also goods and services for own final use that are recorded within the production boundary of national accounts. In Germany these concern services related to owner-occupied dwellings and of paid domestic staff, agricultural products, and own-account construction of dwellings. The valuation alternative of using net wages of housekeepers per hour actually worked seems to be most adequate for the valuation principles of national accounts.

4.4. Final Consumption of Households

In *SNA 1993* only those goods and services can be consumed by households that are recorded within the production boundary. So services produced for consumption in the own household—except services related to owner-occupied housing and of paid domestic servants—are not included. Table 4.3 shows an estimate of these services as recorded in the German satellite system on household production. The value of these services is higher than the total amount of final consumption expenditure as recorded in *SNA 1993*.

As households can own unincorporated enterprises, it is necessary to distinguish between final consumption on the one hand and intermediate

Table 4.2. Production accounts including household production, former territory of the Federal Republic of Germany, 1992 (Billions of DM)

Aggregate	National Accounts		Household Production at Wage Rates of housekeepers		
			Per Hour Worked		Per Normal
	Total Economy	Own-Account of Households[a]	Gross	Net	Working Time, net
Output	6,739	150	2,462	1,675	1,447
Intermediate consumption	4,164	32	396	396	396
Gross value added	2,575	118	2,066	1,279	1,051
Consumption of fixed capital	359	41	80	80	80
Taxes on production less subsidies	98	2	6	6	6
Net value added at factor cost	2,118	75	1,980	1,193	965
Compensation of employees	1,523	3	3	3	3
Operating surplus/mixed income	594	72	1,977	1,190	962

a. Services related to owner-occupied housing and of paid domestic staff, agricultural products for own final consumption, and own-account fixed capital formation in connection with dwellings are included in national accounts as well as in household production.

consumption or the formation of fixed capital on the other hand. In this connection it is important that durables purchased by households that are not used to produce other goods and services within the production boundary of the *SNA* are not recorded as investment goods but as consumer durables. They are treated as being totally consumed in the period in which they are purchased. Only in the satellite system on household production is household expenditure on consumer durables reclassified from final consumption to fixed capital formation, as is shown in Table 4.3.

For households owning an unincorporated enterprise, all goods and services purchased that are used up for the production of output are recorded as intermediate consumption, and expenditures on durables used for production purposes are treated as fixed capital formation. If durables, like vehicles, are used for production as well as for private purposes, a split must be estimated for the part recorded as fixed capital formation and the part included in final consumption. The first part is consumed during the lifetime of the asset via depreciation (consumption of fixed capital), and the second part is treated as if it were consumed immediately.

Purchases of dwellings and major renovations and repairs of dwellings

Table 4.3. Final consumption of households, former territory of the Federal Republic of Germany, 1992

Aggregate	Billions of DM
In *SNA 1993*:	
Final consumption expenditure of households	1,471
+ Individual consumption expenditure of general government[a]	300
+ Final consumption expenditure of NPISHs	39
= Actual individual consumption of households	1,810
In the satellite system:	
− Expenditure on consumer durables	193
− Expenditure on intermediate consumption	364
= Direct individual consumption of households	1,253
+ Consumption of consumer durables[b]	106
+ Output of household production[c]	1.525
= Total final consumption of households	2.884

a. Rough estimates.
b. Depreciation on consumer durables not used in household production.
c. As far as not included in national accounts.

are always recorded as fixed capital formation. Expenditure of the owners of rental dwellings for current repairs and maintenance are included in intermediate consumption. But expenditure for repair and maintenance of owner-occupied dwellings commonly carried out by tenants is included in the final consumption of households. Services related to owner-occupied dwellings are part of final consumption. The value should be estimated with reference to rentals that would be paid on the market for dwellings of the same size, quality, and type.

Households employing paid domestic staff produce services for own final consumption. The value of these services, by convention, equals simply the compensation paid in cash and in kind (*SNA 1993*, para. 9.52). So the foodstuffs purchased by a household for the preparation of a meal by a paid cook are not recorded as intermediate consumption. Only in the satellite system on household production those goods and services that are transformed to other goods and services are treated as intermediate consumption, as is shown in Table 4.3.

New in *SNA 1993*, as compared with *SNA 1968*, is the treatment of valuables purchased by households. They are no longer included in final consumption but in fixed capital formation of households: "Valuables are expensive durable goods that do not deteriorate over time, are not used up in consumption or production, and are acquired primarily as stores of value. They consist mainly of works of art, precious stones and metals and jewellery fashioned out of such stones and metals. Valuables are held in the expectation that their prices, relative to those of other goods and services, will tend to increase over time, or at least not decline. Although the owners of valuables may derive satisfaction from possessing them, they are not used up in the way that household consumption goods, including consumer durables, are used up over time" (*SNA 1993*, para. 9.45). This idea is good, but how to implement it is another question.

Another important change versus *SNA 1968* is the proposal to allocate the imputed service charge for banking services—called "Financial Intermediation Services Indirectly Measured" (FISIM) in *SNA 1993*—to the users of these services (*SNA 1993*, paras. 6.124–6.131, and annex III). For this allocation a reference rate of interest can be applied: "The type of rate chosen as the reference rate may differ from country to country but the inter-bank lending rate would be a suitable choice" (*SNA 1993*, para. 6.128). The difference between the reference rate and the interest receivable on savings of households and the interest payable to banks on consumer debt are recorded as banking services purchased by households for final consumption. If, for example, household A owns DM 10,000 in savings with an interest rate of 3 percent, household B has a consumer debt of DM 5,000 with an interest rate of 9 percent, and the reference rate chosen is 7 percent, for household A the final consumption of FISIM amounts to DM 400 and for household B to DM 100.

But *SNA 1993* also offers as an alternative method the recording of FISIM as global intermediate consumption of the whole economy, like in *SNA 1968*. Unfortunately in this case the GDP is lower than with allocating FISIM to users. The second alternative was adopted only in the final decision of the Statistical Commission of the United Nations at its twenty-seventh session, held in New York from February 22, to March 3, 1993. On this point the positions of the members of the Statistical Commission differed so markedly that the adoption of the revised *SNA* as a whole was jeopardized. But, nevertheless, offering two alternative methods of recording FISIM is a bad compromise because the level of GDP is affected by the decision a country takes.

Household consumption is presented in *SNA 1993* according to the expenditure concept (as in *SNA 1968*) and according to the consumption concept, called household actual final consumption. According to this concept also those goods and services produced by the general government or by NPISHs that can be allocated to single persons (like public health services) or to special groups of persons (like education services) are reclassified via a social transfer in kind from the final consumption expenditure of general government and of NPISHs to the actual final consumption of households as shown in Table 4.3. In actual final consumption of general government only collective services are recorded. With reference to the classification of the functions of government (COFOG), *SNA 1993* explains:

> By convention, all government final consumption expenditure under each of the following headings should be treated as expenditure on individual services except for expenditures on general administration, regulation, research, etc.:
> 04   Education
> 05   Health
> 06   Social Security and Welfare
> 08.01 Sport and recreation
> 08.02 Culture.
>
> In addition, expenditures under the following sub-heads should be treated as individual when they are important:
> 07.11 part of the provision of housing
> 07.31 part of the collection of household refuse
> 12.12 part of the operation of transport system. (*SNA 1993*, para. 9.87).

And in addition "all the services provided by NPISHs are by convention treated as individual" (*SNA 1993*, para. 9.85). So in *SNA 1993* it is important to know which concept is chosen for the presentation of final consumption. Only the allocation of final consumption to sectors is concerned. For the entire economy, final consumption expenditure and actual final consumption result in the same amount. This concept does not concern consumer durables. In actual final consumption they are also treated as if they were totally consumed in the period in which they are purchased.

4.5. Income of Households

The 1968 *SNA* does not explicity define income. In defining disposable income, *SNA 1993* makes reference to the definition of Hicks (1950, p. 172): "we ought to define a man's income as the maximum value which can be consumed during a week, and still expect to be as well off at the end of the week as he was at the beginning." The 1993 *SNA* explains this as follows: "From a theoretical point of view, income is often defined as the maximum amount that a household, or other unit, can consume without reducing its real net worth" (*SNA 1993*, para. 8.15). This is a very wide income concept. In principle it includes income from all sources in cash and in kind, transfers received in cash and in kind, as well as other changes in real net worth after deduction of any income or transfer paid to other units. But *SNA 1993* does not include all receipts and changes affecting real net worth. Excluded are capital transfers, real holding gains or losses on assets and liabilities, and the effects of natural disasters or of war on assets.

Some experts in the *SNA* revision group questioned the distinction between current transfers and capital transfers. But it was stated by other experts that this distinction is "fundamental" to the system. And if something is fundamental no further discussion will be possible. So—and from the view of the author of this article this was unfortunate—the distinction between current transfers and capital transfers was maintained in the *SNA*.

A long discussion in the expert group meetings concerned the question whether real holding gains and losses should be included in disposable income or not. Real holding gains accrue when the prices of assets increase more than the general price level or when the prices of liabilities increase less than the general price level. Assuming that a household owns shares with a market value of DM 100,000 at the beginning of the year and DM 110,000 at the end of the year and savings of DM 5,000 and liabilities of DM 20,000 at the beginning as well as at the end of the year.

Furthermore, it is assumed that during the year there are no transactions in assets and liabilities and that the general price level—represented by the price index of final domestic use of goods and services—is 4 percent higher at the end of the year than at the beginning of the year. In this example the real holding gains on shares amount to DM 6,000 and on liabilities to DM 800, whereas on the savings there is a real holding loss of DM 200. The holding gain on the net worth amounts to DM 6,600. In the terminology of *SNA 1993*, real holding gains may be obtained by subtracting neutral holding gains (0.04 · 100,000 on shares in the example) from nominal holding gains (DM 10,000 on shares and DM 0 on savings and liabilities). In the final decision of the expert group, real holding gains were not included in income because this would have been a serious change in the traditional income concept. Furthermore, the statistical realization would be impossible for most countries in the foreseeable future because full sectoral balance sheets are necessary for the estimation of nominal, neutral, and real holding gains. But *SNA 1993* shows the real holding gains in the accounts "III. 3.2.2 Real holding gains/losses account," included in the revaluation accounts connecting the transaction accounts with the balance sheets. So those users who want to include real holding gains in disposable income can do so if balance sheet data are available.

Income comprises monetary income, like wages and salaries in cash, and income in kind, like (1) wages and salaries in kind, (2) operating surplus (mixed income) in connection with own-account production, and (3) social transfers in kind.

Wages and salaries in kind equal the value of goods and services provided by employers to their employees as part of the remuneration. This may concern output given for free or at nominal prices to the employees, as well as free meals or housing services, the private use of vehicles owned by the producer, transportation to and from the workplace or car parking (*SNA 1993*, para. 7.40). On the production side these goods and services are included in output, and on the use side they belong to the final consumption of households. At the same time wages and slaries are recorded that are used for the "purchase" of these goods and services.

The generation of income in kind (operating surplus/mixed income) in connection with own-account production equals the value of these goods and services (the output) after deducation of the production costs (intermediate consumption, compensation of employees, production taxes/less subsidies, and consumption of fixed capital). For this type of income it is important that household production is not covered by the production boundary of the system. Table 4.4 shows that the disposable income of

Table 4.4. Diposable income of households former territory of the Federal Republic of Germany, 1992

Aggregate	Billions of DM
In *SNA 1993*:	
Operating surplus/mixed income	450
+ Compensation of employees[a]	1,448
+ Property income[b]	155
+ Current transfer income	544
= Income received	2,597
− Current taxes on income, wealth, etc.	296
− Employers' social security contributions	287
− Employees' social security contributions	244
− Other current transfers paid	88
= Disposable income	1,682
+ Social transfers in kind	339
= Adjusted disposable income	2,021
In the satellite system:	
+ Net value added of hosuehold production[c]	1,118
= Total disposable income	3,139

a. Net of income paid to other households.
b. Net of interest on consumer debts.
c. As far as not included in national accounts.

households in Germany would increase by 66 percent if unpaid work in households were valued and included in production.

The recording of social transfers in kind is new in *SNA 1993* versus *SNA 1968*. This income transfer is the counterpart to the goods and services provided for free to households by the general government and NPISHs as explained in the previous chapter. In Germany the adjusted disposable income of households including social transfers in kind is about 20 percent higher than the disposable income according to the expenditure concept. So in *SNA 1993* it is important to know if the disposable income of sectors or the adjusted disposable income is presented. For the total economy there is no difference between the amount of disposable income on the one hand and the amount of adjusted disposable income on the other hand.

In households owning an unincorporated enterprise, the owner and other members of his family usually work in this enterprise without receiving any compensation on a contractual basis. Their remuneration is included in the operating surplus. Because of statistical problems, unfortunately it is not possible to divide the operating surplus into a part representing remuneration for work done and the surplus accruing from production. For many purposes as well as for a correct interpretation of the data on operating surplus, a breakdown into labor income and capital income would be extremely useful, but there is no statistical information for the preparation of reliable estimates. So the new term *mixed income* was chosen to make clear that the operating surplus of unincorporated enterprises usually reflects remuneration for the work done by the owner and his family as well as a return to entrepreneurship: "Operating surplus and mixed income are two alternative names for the same balancing item" (*SNA 1993*, para. 7.80). "Mixed income is the term reserved for the balancing item of the generation of income account of unincorporated enterprises owned by members of households . . . except owner-occupiers in their capacity of producers of housing services for own final consumption and hoseholds employing paid domestic staff, an activity that generates no surplus" (*SNA 1993*, para. 7.81).

The presentation of income in the sequence of accounts of *SNA 1993* is more detailed compared with *SNA 1968*. The full sequence of accounts for households comprises

I   Production account with gross and net value added as balancing items,

II.1.1   Generation of income account with operating surplus and mixed income as balancing items,

II.1.2   Allocation of primary income account with balance of primary incomes as balancing item and with the entrepreneurial income account and allocation of other primary income account as subaccounts,

II.2   Secondary distribution of income account with disposable income as balancing item,

II.3   Redistribution of income in kind account with adjusted disposable income as balancing item,

II.4.1   Use of disposable income account with saving as balancing item, and

II.4.2   Use of adjusted disposable income account with the above saving as balancing item.

These accounts are followed by the accumulation accounts, the other changes in assets accounts, and the balance sheets.

4.6. Wealth of Households

The wealth of sectors is presented in balance sheets at the beginning as well as at the end of the year. On the asset side they include the market value of tangible, intangible, and financial assets, and on the opposite side they show liabilities and net worth as the balancing item. The 1968 *SNA* did not comprise a well-developed system of wealth accounts, so it was up to *SNA 1993* to fill this gap in the system of national accounts. In addition to the balance sheets, *SNA 1993* introduces accounts for the revaluation of assets and liabilities due to price changes and for other changes in the volume of assets and liabilities not included in the normal flow accounts.

The revaluation accounts show the nominal holding gains, which are subdivided into neutral holding gains and real holding gains. Nominal holding gains represent the change in the values of assets and liabilities during a year due to changes of the market prices (or the replacement costs) of the assets and liabilities. The neutral holding gains are analytical constructs showing the changes in the value of all items in balance sheets that would be necessary to compensate for the loss of purchasing power of money. So neutral holding gains are needed to keep the real value of assets, liabilities, and net worth intact. The real holding gains or losses show to what extent the real purchasing power of the assets and liabilities has been increased or decreased during a year valued at the prices of the year. They may be obtained as the difference between the nominal and the neutral holding gains.

The other changes in the volume of assets accounts record those changes in assets and liabilities during a year that are not recorded in the transaction accounts or in the revaluation accounts. Examples are the economic appearance of nonproduced assets (like changes in proven reserves of subsoil assets or the purchase of goodwill), the economic appearance of produced assets (like first recording of antiques as valuables), catastrophic losses, uncompensated seizures, or changes in the classifications (like the change of monetary gold into commodity gold or the reclassification of an institutional unit from one sector to another). All these elements affecting balance sheet items are not recorded as transactions in the flow accounts.

In the balance sheet of the household sector, produced assets comprise only those tangible and intangible assets that are recorded as fixed capital formation. New is the inclusion of valuables, as explained in section 4.4 of this chapter. Nonproduced assets mostly comprise the value of land owned by households. Shares and other equity are included in the

Table 4.5. Fixed assets and consumption of fixed capital, former territory of the Federal Republic of Germany, 1992 at current replacement costs (billions of DM)

| | Opening assets | | Consumption |
Assets	Gross	Net	of Fixed Capital
Tangible fixed assets[a]	11,891	7,638	360
Machinery and equipment	2,557	1,394	200
Dwellings[b]	5,293	3,634	77
Other buildings and structures[a]	4,041	2,610	83
Consumer durables[c]	1,931	1,087	145

a. As recorded in national accounts. Public roads, dams, bridges—gross 1,354 billions of DM—not included.
b. Of which about 55 percent owner-occupied.
c. Of which about one quarter used in household production.

financial assets of households and in the liabilities of corporations and quasi-corporations.

Consumer durables of households used for household production or for direct final use are not included in the balance sheet but should be presented as a memorandum item. The value of these assets can be important, as shown in Table 4.5. In Germany the value of consumer durables amounts to 75 percent of the value of all machinery and equipment as recorded in national accounts (Schäfer and Bollayer, 1993). But for a realistic presentation of the wealth status, the value of consumer durables should be included in the balance sheet of the household sector and in national wealth.

Acknowledgments

The author acknowledges the collaboration of his colleagues Ms. Hannappee, Ms. Raimers, and Mr. Bleses.

Notes

1. The same is true for *SNA 1968*. In the SNA 1993 industries also include nonmarket producers, which in the SNA 1968 were called "other producers."
2. The industries are classified by the "International Standard Industrial Classification of all Economic Activities (ISIC), Rev. 3."

3. From 1986 to 1992 there were about two expert meetings on the revision of the 1968 SNA per year, each lasting about two weeks. There were some core experts who participated in all meetings as well as changing special experts. At a meetng the experts had to make clear proposals, if necessary with majority votes. But it was up to the next expert group to decide whether to tackle the problem again and to reach new decisions.

References

Hicks, John R. (1950). *Value and Capital*. Oxford Oxford University Press.

Schäfer, Dieter, and Rita Bollayer. (1993). Gebrauchsvermogen privater Hauschalte (Value of consumer durables). *Wirtschaft und Statistik* 8.

Schäter, Dieter, and Norbert Schwarz. (1994). Wert der Haushaltsproduktion 1992 (Value of household production in 1992). *Wirtschaft und Statistik* 8.

Spies, Veronica. (1992). Verfügbares Einkommen nach Haushaltsgruppen (Disposable income by groups of households). *Wirtschaft und Statistik* 7.

DISCUSSION OF CHAPTER 4
Luisella Goldschmidt-Clermont

This commentary will concentrate on household production for own consumption and particularly on the part of this production that is outside the *SNA* boundary. In constructing the first satellite account of household production, Heinrich Lützel and his team at the German Federal Statistical Office performed the most thorough exercise ever accomplished on the measurement of nonmarket household production. It is therefore a pleasure to comment on this subject with concrete data at hand.

Household Production for Own Consumption:
SNA 1968 and *SNA 1993*

In the six years during which the revision of the *SNA* was carried through, a small revolution was occurring in the conceptual understanding of what had been named, perhaps one century earlier, "housewives' services." Originally these services were seen as women's contribution to family welfare, a domain of private life, a matter of social value. The gradual recognition of these services as production had sporadically led national accountants to make estimates of their economic value. However, when the Nairobi Forward Looking Strategies (United Nations, 1986) endorsed by the United Nations Economic and Social Council requested that the value of these services be included in GNP, trouble started. The experts, at work with the enormous task of revising the whole of *SNA*, had with respect to household production to face conflicting requirements: preserving the well-established uses of the national accounts, while admitting the newly recognized member of the economic family. Somehow they were asked to codify a revolution while it was going on, a revolution they were part of themselves, some experts being more progressive than others. In such circumstances, some incoherences are unavoidable. The door, however, is opened to what appears as a realistic compromise between the advantages of tradition and the adaptation of national accounting to new economic, social, and political requirements: to resort to the satellite account solution.

The 1993 *SNA* introduces a few modifications and innovations on the subject of household production for own consumption:

- Inclusion, within the production boundary, of all goods produced by households for own consumption (para. 6.24). The 1968 *SNA* already included, under restrictive conditions, part of the goods produced by households. Now the rule is simpler and easier to apply and the inclusion of the additional goods is not likely to generate any major quantitative difference in the *SNA* aggregates.
- Inclusion, within the boundary, of water carrying (para. 6.24b). Although introduced to meet a situation prevalent in some developing countries, households in some areas of the developed countries will be pleased to learn that part of the statistically unrecorded service they provide by transporting heavy weekly loads of groceries is now admitted: the transportation of bottled water which is rapidly gaining ground because of the deteriorating quality of tap water.
- Explicit recognition of household production for own consumption (goods and services) as an economic activity (para. 1.21). This point is fundamental. It breaks away from a relatively recent tradition that recognized as economic almost exclusively the monetized activities; paragraph 1.21 restores the household's etymological citizenship in economics.
- Domestic services remain outside the production boundary, but the 1993 SNA recommends including them in a special satellite account covering the entire household production for own consumption (para. 2.247). Its multiple advantages are illustrated by the

German satellite account, of which extracts are presented in Lützel's chapter.

But why then, having at hand the possibility of including all of households' production for own consumption in a satellite account, did *SNA 1993* bother to include a few additional goods and water carrying within the central framework? Why not leave them out with the bulk of production for own consumption.?

There Are Good Reasons for Keeping Household Production for Own Consumption Out of the Central Framework

Against the introduction of domestic services in the central framework, it has often been argued that national accounts are not designed for measuring economic welfare. It should be noted here that this argument is irrelevant. Household production accounting does not claim to measure welfare: like *SNA 1993* (para. 1.82), its purpose is to measure production (the unrecorded part) and consumption (the unrecorded part), in order to provide more comprehensive tools for economic analysis, decision making, and policy making.

The most solid argument offered against the inclusion of domestic services in the central framework is that the many purposes that the national accounts have served so far, would be hindered if this large nonmarket element was mingled with market production in the accounts. It is desirable not only to avoid introducing a high proportion of imputations but also to maintain the stability of the time series.

With such valid reasons at hand, why does *SNA 1993* indulge in further argumentation? Why wrap up a realistic approach in a debatable dress of rationality? The distinction between goods and services is weak and not operational in the perspective of households' productive activities. For instance, one may prepare, in one single operation, a larger amount of food than what will be consumed at the next meal, with the intention to freeze part for delayed consumption. Is this activity the production of a service or of a good? Or is it a processing of agricultural products? Is the processing of agricultural goods included within the boundary only if they were initially "produced by households . . . an extension of the goods-producing process" (para. 6.24), thus excluding the same processing operation by households who buy the agricultural goods on the market? We are not opening here a modern variation of the quarrel on the sex of angels. All we are trying to say is that these refined distinctions not only are not operational but they also are not necessary. The first set of arguments is strong and convincing enough: domestic services produced by households for own consumption should not be included in the central framework.

The flexibility of the satellite system answers the needs of household production accounting. It includes all production, either for the benefit of other units or for own consumption—the part that is included in the central framework and the part that lies outside the *SNA* production boundary. The latter, it should be mentioned, extends beyond "housewives' domestic services" to all household members' contribution, male or female, employed or not employed, and to all non-*SNA* activities (domestic and related, including, for instance, maintenance and small repairs of dwelling and equipment). The satellite account thus offers a comprehensive picture of household production, without being constrained by the rigidities the central framework inherited from its historical background. In addition, it presents the labor inputs required for production.

Methodology

In order to establish the distinction between economic activities (*SNA* and non-*SNA*) and noneconomic activities, *SNA 1993* paraphrases the "third-person" criterion applied in time-use research: "activities that are not productive in an economic sense include basic human activities such as eating, drinking, sleeping, taking exercise, etc., that it is impossible for one person to obtain another person to perform instead" (para. 6.16) or "that cannot be produced by one person for the benefit of another" (para. 1.75). According to this criterion, "studying and learning do not qualify as production. . . . Pupils and students are consumers of the educational services produced by teachers and educational establishments" (para. 1.75). This consumption results in investments in human capital that may be profitable for economic and non-economic activities, thus "improving the general quality of life of those consuming [the educational services]" (para. 1.53).

Data on the volume of labor inputs measured in time units are available for many countries, globally for *SNA* activities and in detailed categories for non-*SNA* activities. Time-use studies cover the twenty-four hours day; they steer clear of *a priori* exclusions. They can therefore assist national accountants to set aside their beliefs in deciding whether an activity is quantitatively important and worthwhile estimating (para.

6.25); activities believed to be important mostly in some developing countries (paras. 6.23, 6.24) may prove to also be non negligible in developed countries, particularly in the rural areas. The difference between these countries is that, in the latter, household production for own consumption is a contribution to a higher level of consumption, while, in the former, it may be a matter of survival.

The monetary valuation of households' production for own consumption raises questions as to the appropriate method for imputing a monetary value to activities that are not the object of monetary transactions. The German satellite account uses an input-based approach: household production is valued at the costs of production, qualified by *SNA 1993* as "a second best procedure" (para. 6.85). The major input, unpaid labor, requires an imputation. It is valued at the market value of labor that could, in the household, replace unpaid labor; this imputation is the only appropriate one for national accounting purposes.

However, in the same satellite account, there are items borrowed from the central framework: services of owner-occupied dwellings, own-account fixed capital formation, agricultural production for own consumption, other goods produced for own consumption such as cloth, clothing, furniture, and so on. The value of these items is imputed on the basis of the prices of similar goods and services sold on the market (paras. 2.68 and 4.147); this is an output-based approach.

In order to be compatible with the other items included in the satellite account, the output of domestic and related activities should also be valued at the price of similar goods and services sold on the market. This valuation method requires the measurement of the physical quantities produced by households. These quantities (goods and services) have been estimated in several studies, both in industrialized and in other countries, for some activities. Only once has the measurement of household output been performed, at the macroeconomic level, for the whole range of activities (Finland Ministry of Social Affairs and Health, 1980–1986). However, in no country have the price imputations been done yet to the physical outputs. Such imputations, after deduction of households' intermediate consumption and of fixed capital consumption, would permit the calculation of the mixed income derived from household production.

Measurements

Lützel's Table 4.1 shows that, in the former territory of the Federal Republic of Germany, in 1992, all *SNA* activities required 47.7 billion hours of work, while unpaid work in household production required 76.5

billion hours. "Extended" labor (*SNA* plus non-*SNA*) thus amounted to 124.2 billion hours. In other words, the exclusion of households' unpaid work for own consumption from labor statistics hides 62 percent of actual human labor.

In the face of such figures, it might be wise to reconsider terminology and to acknowledge as economically active those who contribute to extended labor, even if a large part of the adult population would fall under this heading. If this is a fact, there is no point in concealing it under misleading terminology. The concept of "population not currently active" (Hussmanns, Mehran, and Verma, 1990, p. 43) is misleading when applied to persons "engaged in household duties" because it confuses our image of how humans achieve their standard of living and, as a result, because it induces unrealistic labor and social policies. The ILO definitions of *employment* and *unemployment* are appropriate for SNA activities; these terms should not be applied to non-*SNA* labor (para. 1.22).

When the contribution of household production to total ("extended") final consumption of households is compared, in the satellite account, to the contribution of *SNA* activities (Table 4.3), one cannot help but being taken aback. In as industrialized a country as 1992 Germany (the data refer to the former territory of the FRG), the activities excluded from *SNA* contribute more than half of what households actually consume. The contribution of household production adds more than half to adjusted disposable income (Table 4.4).

Looking Ahead: The Research Agenda

Under this title, *SNA 1993* briefly discusses or just cites some twelve topics the Inter-Secretariat Working Group recommended to place on the research agenda (*SNA 1993*, pp. xliii–xlv). "The 1993 *SNA*, like its predecessors, represents a stage in the evolution of national accounting. To continue that evolution, further research will need to be carried out. Consensus must be reached on certain topics before they can be incorporated into international guidelines and standards." The environmental satellite account appears among the seven priority topics. "Output of services, including services produced within households" is merely cited among the five other topics.

The inclusion of a topic on the agenda is determined by the frequency at which the Statistical Commission experts expressed interest for it. It is not surprising therefore that traditional *SNA* topics are predominant on the research agenda. The understandable desire to further improve the handling of traditional topics should however not prevent the development of new topics: staff, expertise, and financial resources are limited, in national accounting as in other areas.

Given the measurements presented by Lützel, it may seem appropriate to reconsider the research agenda criteria and to include, not only household services but the entire household production satellite account among the priorities. Sixty percent of actual human labor, more than fifty percent of actual household consumption, are no minor statistical gaps; they need to be filled.

The German Federal Statistical Office produced the first satellite account of household production, and other statistical offices are working on the subject. It is urgent to maximize the results of these endeavours and to preserve for the future the international comparability of results by confronting experiences and by adopting, as much as possible, coordinated methodologies. Selection of imputed wages, price determination, delimitation of intermediate consumption, definition of capital consumption, and so on are topics that national accountants can handle without much difficulty. Other topics, such as the measurement of labor inputs and the measurement of household output, require collaborations with other fields of research.

The strong social and political wave that resulted in the Nairobi forward-looking strategies and in the financing of the German satellite account shares the view that the national accounts serve "to facilitate analysis of the economy and decision-making. The *SNA*, through its structure and definitions, not only determines the kind of analysis that can be carried out but also influences the way economic and social issues are considered" (*SNA 1993*, pp. xliii–xliv).

References

Finland Ministry of Social Affairs and Health. (1980–1986). *Housework Study*. Helsinki: Official Statistics of Finland, Special Social Studies.

Hussmanns, Ralf, Farhad Mehran, and Vijay Verma. (1990). *Surveys of Economically Active Population, Employment, Unemployment and Underemployment: An ILO Manual on Concepts and Methods*. Geneva: International Labour Office.

United Nations. (1986). *The Nairobi Forward-Looking Strategies for the Advancement of Women*. Adopted by the World Conference to Review and Appraise the Achievements of the United Nations Decade for Women: Equality, Development and Peace, Nairobi, July 15–26, 1985. New York: United Nations.

5 CAPITAL AND WEALTH IN THE REVISED *SNA*

Charles R. Hulten

5.1. Introduction

Hicks (1981) was surely right when he observed that "the measurement of capital is one of the nastiest jobs that economists have set to statisticians." Capital, in one form or another, touches almost every aspect of economic activity, and each aspect must be accounted for in a complete system of national economic statistics. A well-designed accounting system therefore must include the division of income between consumption and saving, the linkage between saving and investment and the corresponding linkage between capital stocks and wealth, the contribution of capital services to the production of output, and, finally, the allocation of total income between capital and labor. These various aspects of capital are interdependent and must be treated in a consistent way if the accounts are to provide an accurate picture of current and future economic welfare.

While there are many practical difficulties involved in building a comprehensive and internally consistent set of accounts, such of the past nastiness of the job has been the fault of economic theorists, who have failed to provide a clear blueprint for the work to be done. Discussions of capital theory have often bogged down in doctrinal disputes over the

nature of capital—"What is capital, really?"—and the competing para-
digms imply very different accounting systems (cf Harcourt, 1972). Even
within the market-oriented neoclassical paradigm, the same terminology
and definitions are often used for very different concepts, leading to
inconsistent procedures and seemingly endless debates over appropriate
methodology (Triplett, 1992).[1] Many practical problems have their origin
in these theoretical and terminological confusions.

Given this history of ambiguity, the recently revised *System of National
Accounts, 1993* (*SNA 1993*) must be applauded as a major advance. *SNA
1993* provides an internally coherent set of guidelines based on (or, at
least, consistent with) the neoclassical model of consumption and production. Countries that correctly implement this blueprint will not only have
a set of national accounts that are, for the most part, consistent *inter alia*
but also a set that is linked to the key concepts of "standard" economic
theory and is therefore internally consistent. This is a great advantage for
those who study the causes of economic growth from the standpoint of
formal theory.

Since standard economic theory is the essential foundation on which
the *SNA* accounts are erected, the main goal of this chapter is to expand
the exposition of the main linkages between capital theory and the accounting conventions recommended by the *SNA* guidelines. This is not a
trivial objective. The *SNA* is a lengthy and complex document, and the
unwary reader may thus fall prey to the confusions and errors of interpretation that have haunted wealth accounting in the past. Only if a
consistent conceptual framework is imposed on the accounts will their full
value be realized. A secondary purpose is to discuss some of the practical
problems that may be encountered when actually trying to implement the
SNA guidelines. This discussion will necessarily be limited, since "the
devil is in the detail" and an entire volume would be needed to do justice
to the main issues.

5.2. Accounting for Capital: The Conceptual Framework

5.2.1. The Capital Account

Two economic decisions are fundamental to the capital accounting "problem": saving and investment. The decision to save is a decision to defer
current *consumption* in order to increase consumption in the future. The
decision to invest, on the other hand, involves the diversion of resources
from the *production* of consumption goods in order to increase the stock

of capital goods and is usually made by different economic agents. The two are, however, linked: on the one hand, the diversion of resources from the production of durable goods is possible only to the extent that consumers are willing to defer consumption; on the other hand, saving will increase future consumption in the aggregate only if future productive capacity is expanded through additions to the stock of capital goods.

The saving-investment accounting identity enters the SNA through the capital account in account III.1. This table presents investment (gross fixed capital formation), net of economic depreciation, and balances it against net saving and net lending from external sources. Data are presented at the aggregate level of detail and for the five *SNA* sectors. Transfers of capital among sectors are also shown in account III.1.

The sectoral structure of the *SNAs* is one of the features that most clearly differentiates it from the consumption-production dichotomy of the conventional "circular flow" approach to national income accounting. In a pure circular-flow model, all saving is attributed to the consumption sector regardless of whether the decision to save is actually made by businesses, households, or governments; investment, on the other hand, is located entirely in the production sector, even though it includes the direct nonmarket investments of households. In contrast, the SNA takes the position that each sector is a decision-making entity that both saves and invests. The advantage of this convention is that it accounts for flow in the sector in which the decisions are made. The problem is that, in so doing, this approach loses sight of the clear division in economic theory between consumption and production.

Moreover, while the *SNA* disaggregates investment by sector, it does not disaggregate investment by type of capital—by machine tools, autos, office buildings, and so on. This is due, in part, to the difficulty in accounting for the intersectoral flows of a large number of capital goods. But since there are significant differences in the economic and technical characteristics of different types of capital, a disaggregation of the latter sort is an important adjunct to the accounts. This is not explicitly provided for in the main accounts but could be presented as a satellite account of the input-output section of the SNA accounts.

5.2.2. The Perpetual Inventory Method

The stock of durable capital is not a single physical entity but rather a collection of durable goods from different vintages.[2] Letting I_s denote the quantity of durable goods produced in year s, the collection of vintage durables (or "assets") available for production in any year t can be represented by the vector $[I_{t-1}, I_{t-2}, \ldots, I_{t-T}]$, where T is the age of the oldest surviving vintage. A set of accounts could be constructed that preserves vintage detail (see Hulten, 1978), but the SNA does not take this approach: neither the capital accounts, production account, nor balance sheets present data on separate vintages of investment. Instead, the vintages are summed to a total and only the aggregate amount—the "stock"—is reported.

This method of aggregation is termed the "perpetual inventory method" and is described in Section 6.189 of *SNA 1993*. The basic assumption of the perpetual inventory method is that the "quantity" of durable goods in each vintage can be expressed as some fraction of the capital in the newest vintage, regardless of how the characteristics of the capital goods have changed over time. Given this assumption, past vintages of capital can be added up to get the total amount of "capital stock," in the productivity sense of the term:

$$K_t = \phi_0 I_{t-1} + \phi_1 I_{t-2} + \ldots + \phi_T I_{t-T-1}. \qquad (5.1)$$

The weights, ϕ_i, express the productive capacity (actually, the marginal productivity) of an s-year-old asset as a fraction of the productive capacity of a newly produced asset. The ϕ's are thus indexes of a relative efficiency in which the $\phi_0 = 1$.[3]

A lot more will be said about the exact form of the ϕ sequence in subsequent sections, since its measurement is the main practical obstacle to using the perpetual inventory method to measure capital. It is sufficient for now to point out a key implication of the perpetual inventory approach: since one unit of vintage v capital is treated as the equivalent of only ϕ_{t-v} units of new capital, and stock K defined in this way is equivalent to the amount of new investment needed to equal the productive capacity of all of the surviving past investments. Thus, the perpetual inventory method defines the capital stock in efficiency units.

5.2.3. The Valuation of Capital Stock

One of the enduring issues in national income accounting concerns what method should be used to value the vintages that comprise the perpetual inventory capital aggregate. *SNA 1993* recommends the "remaining present value" approach as the basis for asset valuation: in Section 6.182, it is stated that "the value of a fixed asset to its owner at any point in time is determined by the present value of the future rentals (i.e., the sum of the discounted values of the stream of future rentals)" (p. 147), and in Section 10.118 "The value of a fixed asset depends upon the benefits that can be expected from using it in production over the remainder of its useful life. This value is given by the present discounted value, calculated at the average prices of the period, of the stream of rentals that the owner of a fixed asset could expect if it were rented out to producers over the remainder of its service life" (p. 233). This is the method recommended by the neoclassical paradigm of capital valuation put forth by Irving Fisher (1930), John Hicks (1946), Dale Jorgenson (1963), and many others. It runs counter to those who want to use a "consumption-foregone" approach to valuation or a naive resource cost standard.[4]

The remaining present value concept can be illustrated by the following example of a new machine that is expected to last three years before being retired from service. Assume that the machine is expected to earn $P_{t,3}^K$ dollars in gross rental income at the end of year t, $P_{t+1,4}^K$ in the following year, and $P_{t+2,5}^K$ in the year before retirement.[5] With a discount rate r, the present (or capitalized) value of this rental stream at the start of year t, $P_{t,3}^I$, is then

$$P_{t,3}^I = \frac{P_{t,3}^K}{(1+r)} + \frac{P_{t+1,4}^K}{(1+r)^2} + \frac{P_{t+2,5}^K}{(1+r)^3}. \tag{5.2}$$

In a fully arbitraged market for capital, $P_{t,3}^I$ is also the price that a rational investor would pay for a three-year-old asset in year t—that is, the left side of (5.2) can be interpreted as the cost of acquiring the asset, and the right hand side as the associated benefit.

At the end of one year of use, the same asset is worth less (in real terms) because one year's rental income has been subtracted from the stream. Thus, a rational investor with a discount rate r would then be willing to pay

$$P_{t+1,4}^I = \frac{P_{t+1,4}^K}{(1+r)} + \frac{P_{t+2,5}^K}{(1+r)^2} \tag{5.3}$$

to acquire the asset. This is the remaining present value of the asset in the following year when it is one year older. Note that rental prices P^K may have increased because of price inflation or revaluation.

The general expression for the remaining present value of an s-year old asset is

$$P_{t,s}^I = \sum_{\tau=0}^{T} \frac{P_{t+\tau,s+\tau}^K}{(1+r)^{s+1}}, \tag{5.4}$$

where, again, we have assumed for simplicity that discount rate is constant over time.

Each vintage of investment in the collection $[I_{t-1}, I_{t-2}, \ldots, I_{t-T}]$ that makes up the aggregate K_t has its own remaining present value $P^I_{t,s}$, and the total value of the collection is therefore

$$V^K_t \equiv P^I_{t,0}I_{t-1} + P^I_{t,1}I_{t-2} + \ldots + P^I_{t,T-1}I_{t-T}. \tag{5.5}$$

This is the valuation concept implied by *SNA 1993* with its endorsement of the remaining present value standard. It is the amount that an investor would be willing to pay for the whole collection of assets $[I_{t-1}, I_{t-2}, \ldots, I_{t-T}]$. Moreover, it is the amount that a bank would use in determining collateral value for a loan.[6]

The symmetry between the value of capital above and gross property income, defined as the income obtained from renting each piece of capital in the collection $[I_{t-1}, I_{t-2}, \ldots, I_{t-T}]$, is worth noting. This is product of the rental $P^K_{t,s}$, and the quantity I_{t-s}, summed over the active vintages

$$\pi^K_t \equiv P^K_{t,0}I_{t-1} + P^K_{t,1}I_{t-2} + \ldots + P^K_{t,T-1}I_{t-T}. \tag{5.6}$$

In other words, property income is the sum of past investments valued using vintage rental prices, while the value of capital stock is the sum value at vintage asset prices.

One final implication of the valuation equation (5.5) should be mentioned. The valuation procedure implied by (5.5) involves the following steps: estimate the quantity of surviving investment in each vintage; then, estimate the corresponding remaining present values and use the result to value the corresponding investment goods; finally, sum to get the total value V^K_t. This procedure must be implemented for every type of capital asset used in the production of current or future consumption. It thus comprises the fixed capital used in households and government as well as by businesses, but goes far beyond fixed capital to include intangible assets (such as patented knowledge and computer programs), human capital, and environmental assets, and natural resources. In principle, any capital that has a positive shadow price should be included in the valuation process that leads to a complete set of national balance sheets. In practice, it is hard to include all assets that meet this criterion and boundaries must be established. A discussion of these boundaries is deferred to a subsequent section.

5.2.4. Asset Valuation and Depreciation

The value of capital can be established directly using the procedure described by equation (5.5). This is, however, *not* the approach recommended in *SNA 1993* because it is not feasible to estimate a remaining present value for each vintage of each type of capital in each year. Instead, *SNA 1993* advocates the conventional procedure of revaluation and depreciation, which is based on the identity relating the price of an asset in one year and its price in the following year:

$$P^I_{t+1,s+1} = (1 + \rho_{t+1,s+1})(1 - \delta_{t,s})P^I_{t,s}. \tag{5.7}$$

ρ is the rate of change of asset price purely because of the passage of time (that is, asset *revaluation*), and δ is the rate of change of asset price because of *economic depreciation.*[7] This identity indicates that the price of an $s + 1$-year-old asset in year $t + 1$ (for example, a ten-year-old asset in 1994) is equal to its price in the preceding year (in 1993 when it was nine years old) increased by the rate of revaluation and decreased by the rate of depreciation. The revaluation term in (5.7) is equal to the percentage difference between the price of two identical assets of the *same age* in successive years and can be expressed as

$$\rho_{t,s} = \frac{P^I_{t+1,s+1}}{P^I_{t,s+1}} - 1. \tag{5.8}$$

The depreciation term, on the other hand, is the percentage difference in price of capital between two successive ages in the *same year* and can be expressed as

$$\delta_{t,s} = 1 - \frac{P^I_{t,s+1}}{P^I_{t,s}}. \tag{5.9}$$

This is the erosion of capital value due to the process of aging. It is also the Hotelling-Hicks definition of economic depreciation: the amount of capital value that must be "put back" in order to keep the real value of the wealth intact.[8]

    This identity provides a useful alternative to the procedure of estimating the remaining present value of each vintage in each year. This alternative can be implemented by estimating the average rates of revaluation ρ and depreciation δ for all vintages and applying (5.7) recursively: the remaining present value of a one-year-old asset is estimated by grossing up the price of a new asset by the revaluation term and then writing down the result by the depreciation rate δ; the remaining present value of a two-year-old asset is then estimated by grossing up the estimated price of the one-year-old asset by the revaluation term and then depreciating the result, and so on. This alternative approach can be implemented with estimates of new asset prices, average revaluation, and average depreciation.

The estimation of the average total rate of revaluation is apparently easier to accomplish than the estimation of the rate of depreciation. The change in the price of new assets is the result of three factors: a change in the general price level because of inflation, the change in the relative price of assets because of shifts in supply and demand, and changes in asset quality embodied in the design of capital. These factors influence the price of assets of all ages, and while the effects are not necessarily proportional across ages, the change in the price of new assets is a reasonable proxy for the revaluation of assets of all ages (provided quality adjustments are done correctly which is very problematic (Hulten, 1995)). The price of new assets are commonly collected as part of the national income accounting process and can be used in constructing the revaluation account, Table III.3.2 of the SNA framework, and in the valuation of assets in the balance sheets.

Estimating the rate of depreciation is more complicated. In Section 6.198, SNA 1993 recommends two methods of implementing the approach of the preceding paragraph: "The value of the capital consumption on a fixed asset may be estimated by applying either the linear or geometric depreciation formula to the actual or estimated current purchaser's price of a new asset of the same type" (p. 150). There are many practical considerations and problems involved in choosing the appropriate method of depreciation—straight-line, geometric, or other. These practical considerations have many complicated nuances and will be given a section of their own below. We turn first to consider the overarching issue on which all other considerations depend: the method of depreciation cannot be selected independently of the relative efficiency sequence used in the perpetual inventory method estimate of the capital stock.

5.2.5. Efficiency and Depreciation

One of the most commendable aspects of SNA 1993, from the standpoint of capital accounting, is the distinction that is made between the quantity of capital and the value of capital, and the corresponding distinction between the decline in asset afficiency and economic depreciation. The key statement appears in Section 6.193 (p. 149):

Consumption of fixed capital is proportional to the reduction in the present value of the remaining rentals. . . . This reduction, and the rate at which it takes place over time [i.e., the rate of depreciation], must be clearly distinguished from the decline in the efficiency of capital assets themselves [i.e., the ϕ's]. The distinction is most obvious [in the case of constant and undiminished efficiency up to the point of retirement from service]. Although the efficiency, and hence the renal, of an asset may remain constant from period to period until it disintegrates, the capital consumption is not constant.

This point is clearly of crucial importance for the construction of a set of capital accounts for, once the efficiency sequence $\{\phi\}$ has been selected, the method of depreciation cannot be chosen independently. This point has often been ignored in the construction of capital accounts.

The exact link between the efficiency sequence and the method of economic depreciation was developed by Jorgenson (1973), based on the aggregate production function as represented by

$$Q_t = A_t F(L_t, K_t) = A_t F(L_t, [\phi_0 I_{t-1} + \phi_1 I_{t-2} + \ldots + \phi_T I_{t-T-1}]).$$
(5.10)

The concept of capital stock K_t in this expression is identical to that used in the valuation equation (5.5). By implication, any attempt to estimate the parameters of (5.10) or calculate a total factor productivity residual will therefore involve exactly the same data as those needed to construct the capital stock side of the balance sheet.

The marginal product of any vintage s of investment in the production function (5.10) can be represented as

$$\partial Q_t / \partial I_{t-s} = \phi_s \, \partial Q_t / \partial K_t,$$
(5.11)

from which it follows immediately that the efficiency index ϕ_s is really nothing more than the ratio of the marginal product of an s-year-old asset to the marginal product of a new asset. (As an aside, the Leontief (1947) aggregation theorem states that capital can be aggregated using the perpetual inventory method 5.1 if, and only if, this ratio (i.e., ϕ) is a constant number; in other words, aggregation can proceed only when the relative efficiency of assets of different vintages is a constant.)

The next step in linking the asset efficiency and economic depreciation is the assumption that rental prices are equal to marginal products. In light of the preceding expression for the marginal product of vintage capital, this assumption implies that

$$\frac{P_{t,s}^K}{P_t^Q} = \partial Q_t / \partial I_{t-s} = \phi_s \, \partial Q_t / \partial K_t.$$
(5.12)

Comparing this marginal product to that of new assets then gives the fundamental equation linking prices and quantities:

$$\frac{P^K_{t,s}}{P^K_{t,0}} = \frac{\partial Q/\partial I_{t-s-1}}{\partial Q/\partial I_{t-1}} = \phi_s \qquad (5.13)$$

(note that this formulation implies that $\phi_0 = 1$). This equation is the formal expression of the statement in Section 6.192 (p. 149) of *SNA 1993* that "The amounts of rentals which users are prepared to pay will be proportional to the relative efficiencies of the assets."

The expression relating asset efficiency and depreciation can be obtained by inserting the expression above into the general present value formula of the first section. The result is a formulation that expresses the remaining present value of an asset in terms of the rental price of a new asset

$$P^I_{t,s} = \sum_{\tau=0}^{T} \frac{\phi_{s+\tau} P^K_{t+\tau,0}}{(1 + r)^{s+1}}. \qquad (5.14)$$

This expression provides an important insight into the link between the production and valuation sides of the national accounts. In view of (5.12) and (5.13), the marginal product of capital could be inserted into (5.14) in place of ϕ, in which case it becomes clear that the value of the stock of capital derives from its productivity in generating future output.

Equation (5.14) also provides a fundamental insight into the nature of economic depreciation. This expression can be made to yield

$$\delta_{t,s} P^I_{t,s} = P^I_{t,s} - P^I_{t,s+1} = \sum_{\tau=0}^{T} \frac{(\phi_{s+\tau} - \phi_{s+\tau+1}) P^K_{t+\tau,0}}{(1 + r)^{s+1}}. \qquad (5.15)$$

In view of the definition of the rate of depreciation above, this equation links the amount of money that must be "put back" in order to keep capital value intact (economic depreciation) to the present value of the *shift* in asset efficiency from one age to the next. In other words, when an asset is used in the production of output over the course of a year, it is the erosion of current *and future* productive capacity ($\phi_{s+t} - \phi_{s+t+1}$) that causes the erosion of asset value ($P^I_{t,s} - P^I_{t,s+1}$).[9]

This expression also is important for the debate over the appropriate method of depreciation to be used in calculating wealth. It clearly indicates that the method of depreciation cannot be selected independently of the method assumed for the measurement of capital stocks: indeed, the depreciation pattern on the right side of (5.15) is uniquely determined by the rental price and the discount rate. Thus, if the efficiency pattern has the straight-line form, economic depreciation will not (in general) follow the straight-line pattern.

5.2.6. The Income and Production Accounts

Issues of asset measurement and valuation are important for the income and product sides as well, since the production account is logically based on the existence of an aggregate production function in which capital is combined with other inputs to produce consumption and more capital (equation (5.10)). Under the assumption that inputs are paid the values of their marginal products and that production takes place under constant returns to scale, the value of output at the aggregate is equal to the value of inputs: property income (5.6), labor, and intermediate inputs

$$P_t^Q Q_t = \pi_t^K + P_t^L L_t + P_t^M M_t \qquad (5.16)$$

with output allocated among the its various uses according to

$$P_t^Q Q_t = P_t^C C_t + P_t^I I_t + P_t^D D_t. \qquad (5.17)$$

Gross value added is defined as the sum of the payments to labor and capital, $P^L L + \pi^K$, so (5.17) represents the division of gross output into its value added and intermediate input components. This division parallels the allocation that appears in the Production Accounts I in *SNA 1993*. The Goods and Services Account 0 gives the allocation of output to deliveries of intermediate consumption, $P^D D$, consumption, $P^C C$, and capital formation, $P^I I$.

The allocation of gross value added between the compensation of labor and gross property income does not appear in the production account, but rather in the primary distribution of income accounts II.1.1 and II.1.2. While this is certainly not incorrect, it obscures the fact that capital and labor income originate from the production of goods and services— that is, that the value added terms in (5.16), $P^L L + \pi^K$, are as much a part of the production account as the intermediate input term. This, in turn encourages the view that property income is nothing more than a residual category, "operating surplus", and thence to the problematic conclusion, expressed in Section 16.146, that "the net operating surplus is an accounting residual which does not possess quantity and price dimensions of its own. It may also be negative, of course. It is not possible, therefore, to decompose the net operating surplus into its own price and volume components." The problem with this statement is that, in view of (5.16), operating surplus and depreciation is equal to the rentals paid to capital, π^K, and, in view of (5.6), this can indeed be separated into price and quantity components, $P_{t,s}^K$ and I_{t-s}. There may, of course, be other rent components associated with non-constant returns to scale, monopoly, uncertainty, and so on, but these additional factors are also part of the rental price. However, to lose sight of the rental price in the production account is to lose sight of the connection between capital as an input (with its own marginal product) and the value of the capital asset (which is based on the income generated by that marginal product).[10]

This connection can be made even more intuitive by introducing the Hall-Jorgenson (1967) rental price (or "user cost") into the discussion. The expression for Hall-Jorgenson rental price is given by

$$P_{t,s}^K = [r - \rho_{t,s} + (1 + \rho_{t,s})\delta_{t,s}] P_{t,s}^I. \tag{5.18}$$

This follows from the fact that the remaining present value equation (5.4) can be inverted to yield an expression for the rental price. Equation (5.18) has a straightforward interpretation: the equilibrium rental cost of an asset equals *ex post* return to the money invested in the asset r (adjusted for asset revaluation, ρ), plus the cost of economic depreciation. In this formulation, the rate of return, r, is measured on an *ex post* basis and thus includes may excess returns or rents accruing to the asset (or any deficits). Berndt and Fuss (1986) show that the *ex post* rental price, so defined, equals the marginal product of capital. Moreover, this formulation is consistent with the asset valuation equation (5.14) under rational expectations about future returns, and with property income (5.6).

The income account logically is derived from the product account by extracting valude added from the latter and then deducting economic depreciation from gross property income (to arrive at net income). The appropriate measure of depreciation for this purpose is exactly the same as the measure discussed above in the valuation of capital. This can shown by inserting (5.18) into the expression for gross value added, which gives (in the expositionally simple case of geometric depreciation)

$$VA_t = P_t^L L_t + r P_t^I K_t - \rho P_t^I K_t + \delta P_t^I K_t. \tag{5.19}$$

This expression, in combination with equation (5.17), leads directly to the result that consumption plus change in net worth (the Haig Simons definition of income, $P^C C + P^I I + \rho P^I K - \delta P^I K$) is equal to factor income, $P^L L + r P^I K$. This is also Hicksian income—the largest sum that could be spent on consumption while maintaining future consumption (wealth) intact.

One final point: the concept of income differs from the notion of net product. The subtraction of economic depreciation from gross product to arrive at Hicksian income makes intuitive sense, as a measure of sustainable consumption. On the other hand, the separate notion of "net national product" defined as product less the cost of the physical capital exhausted in production (see note 8), makes little intuitive sense: there is no such thing as a physical "net auto"—that is, an auto less the capital stock used up in its production—and there is no natural units in which physical "net" product can be measured.

5.2.7. Wealth, Capital, and the Balance Sheet

Balance sheets are constructed from estimates of the value of capital goods and wealth. The distinction between these two concepts is, however, one of the greatest sources of confusion in the field of income and wealth accounting. The term *capital* is sometimes used as a synonym for wealth, as in the old capital stock studies carried out by the U.S. Bureau of Economic Analysis. In other cases, such as in most studies of productivity and economic growth, the term is used to denote the cumulated stock of durable goods used as an input to production. This ambiguity has led to many misunderstandings, including the confusion between depreciation (the loss of asset value) and the loss of productive capacity, $\phi_s - \phi_{s+1}$ (Triplett, 1992). It also encourages the erroneous view that there is one definition of capital that is suitable for wealth accounting purposes and a different definition that is suitable for production functions.

Wealth is, indeed, conceptually different from the stock of capital goods, in exactly the same way that saving is different from investment. In standard Fisherian capital theory, the stock of wealth is defined as the present value of future consumption, discounted at a rate of interest that reflects the subjective rate of time preference. This is not a directly observable magnitude, but it is reflected in the value of the financial claims created by saving. On the other hand, the stock of capital is a collection of productive investment goods acquired over a span of many years. Its quantity is measured by the amount of investment in each vintage $[I_{t-1}, I_{t-2}, \ldots, I_{t-T}]$, and thus (5.1), and its value by V^K in (5.5).

But while V^K is different from Fisherian wealth, the two are linked through the fundamental equation of wealth accounting, which relates Fisherian wealth, defined as the present value of future consumption expenditures, to the present value of labor income *plus* the value of capital stock defined by (5.5):

$$\sum_{s=0}^{\infty} \frac{P_{t+s}^C C_{t+s}}{(1 + r)^{s+1}} = V_t^K + \sum_{s=0}^{\infty} \frac{P_{t+s}^L L_{t+s}}{(1 + r)^{s+1}}. \qquad (5.20)$$

This expression defines the consumption paths that are possible given the current stock of capital and the future flows of labor input and is thus essentially an intertemporal "budget constraint." Once labor is paid its wages in terms of consumption, the residual consumption goes to capital. The current value of physical capital stock (as defined in (5.5)) is thus equal to capital's share of future consumption and can be thought of as the current net worth of the economy at any point in time.

The intertemporal identity (5.20) has two important implications for the *SNA*. First, it demonstrates that the remaining present value procedure advocated by the *SNA* for the measurement of capital is the appropriate concept for wealth accounting. This identity implies that a complete systems of national accounts should present independently measured estimates of wealth, built up from financial claims reflecting the ownership of the capital stock (stocks, bonds, pension, and so on), and the value of the capital stock measured from the produtivity side as per (5.5). A reconciliation of these two stocks occurs in the balance sheet statement of assets and liabilities (account IV of the *SNA*).

Moreover, equation (5.20) again shows that the concept of "capital" as a productive input is not a separate concept from the "capital" whose value enters the national balance sheet. This can be demonstrated directly in the special case of geometric depreciation, though it is true more generally. Under geometric depreciation, the price of an *s*-year-old asset is equal to the price of a new asset weighted by the efficiency index for vintage assets: that is, $P^I_{t,s} = \phi_s P^I_{t,0}$, where the ϕ's have the form shown below in (5.23). The valuation equation (5.5) may then be expressed as

$$V^K_t \equiv P^I_{t,0}[\phi_0 I_{t-1} + \phi_1 I_{t-2} + \ldots + \phi_{T-1} I_{t-T}] = P^I_{t,0} K_t. \quad (5.5')$$

We have already seen that the ϕ's are marginal products, so (5.5') implies that the ϕ's used in computing capital stocks as inputs of the production function enter directly into the computation of net worth as per (5.20). Thus, only one concept of capital, that embodied in the perpetual inventory equation (5.1), is required for an internally consistent set of income, product, and wealth accounts constructed using the framework developed in this section.

5.3. Practical Issues of Implementation

5.3.1. Admissible Efficiency and Depreciation Patterns

The productive efficiency of some types of capital is inherent in the nature of that capital. The radioactivity of a uranium rod, for example, will tend to decay at a constant, so that older "vintage" rods are proportionately less productive than new rods. In this case, the relative efficiencies ϕ (that is, relative marginal products) are technological constants that decline geometrically, and the productive capacity of the stock of uranium rods is the sum of the individual rods weighted by the efficiency index. A similar situation prevails with light bulbs, since older bulbs provide basically the same light as new ones until they fail, and the capital stock can be constructed by assigning the ϕ-index a value of one for all surviving vintages and adding up surviving investments.

However, the efficiency of most types of capital is not a technological given but depends, instead, on technical and economic choices about initial durability, the pattern of use, and the amount of maintenance. Since the implied ϕ's are defined as the ratios of marginal products, they are endogenous variables that will, in principle, vary from asset to asset (even for otherwise idential assets owned by the same firm). A completely accurate account of the productive capital in any economy would thus have to measure the ϕ index of every piece of capital in that economy.

This is clearly not practical. Even if the ϕ's could be observed directly, there are simply too many assets for this to be computationally tractable. And any attempt to measure the ϕ's—directly or indirectly—must take into account the fact that the marginal products of most types of vintage capital vary with economic circumstances, so the corresponding ϕ's are generally not constant parameters whose values can be estimated by statistical methods. A realistic set of capital accounts must recognize these problems and abandon the hope of exact measurement. Instead, a viable set of capital accounts must resort to generalizations and approximations of the efficiency sequence.

This is the approach taken in *SNA 1993*, which recommends three generic efficiency patterns in Section 6.190. The constant efficiency pattern, also known as the one-hoss-shay pattern, has the form

$$\phi_0 = \phi_1 = \ldots = \phi_{T-1} = 1, \quad \phi_{T+\tau} = 0 \quad \tau = 0, 1, 2, \ldots \quad (5.21)$$

In the one-hoss-shay form, assets retain full efficiency until they completely fall apart. In this form, the efficiency sequence is completely characterized by the service life T, and the measurement problem reduces to the problem of estimating T.

The straight-line efficiency pattern is the second form recommended by *SNA 1993*. Under straight-line, the efficiency falls off linearly until the date of retirement:

$$\phi_0 = 1, \phi_1 = 1 - (1/T), \phi_2 = 1 - (2/T), \ldots, \phi_{T-1} = 1 - ((T-1)/T)$$
$$\phi_{T-\tau} = 0 \quad \tau = 0, 1, 2, \ldots \quad (5.22)$$

In this form, efficiency decays in equal increments every year—that is, $\phi_{\tau-1} - \phi_\tau = 1/T$. As with one-hoss-shay, T completely determines the efficiency pattern.

Geometric decay is the third pattern mentioned in Section 6.190. This is the uranium rod case considered above, in which the productive capacity of an asset decays at a constant rate $\delta = (\phi_{\tau-1} - \phi_\tau)/\phi_{\tau-1}$. This gives the efficiency sequence

$$\phi_0 = 1, \ \phi_1 = (1 - \delta), \ \phi_2 = (1 - \delta)^2, \ldots, \phi_\tau = (1 - \delta)^\tau, \ldots$$
$$(5.23)$$

This form is characterized by a single parameter like the preceding cases, but the parameter is now the rate δ rather than the service life T. However, the two are related by "declining balance" formula $\delta = X/T$. Under "double declining balance" form, $X = 2$. It is sometimes maintained that the case $X = 1$ is equivalent to straight-line depreciation, but a comparison of (5.22) and (5.23) shows that this is only true for the first year (as the *SNA 1993* observes) and only approximately true for later years.

These three patterns refer to relative asset efficiency and, in view of equation (5.15), they must be distinguished from the corresponding depreciation patterns. *SNA 1993* is careful to do this and notes in Section 6.195 that the geometric pattern is the only one that is self-dual. That is, it is the only case in which the efficiency sequence has exactly the same form as the depreciation pattern. This property is shown in Figure 5.1 as the fact that both relative efficiency and normalized asset price decline along the same path AC—that is, both decline at the rate δ. Neither the one-hoss-shay nor straight-line patterns have this property. The one-hoss-shay form is represented in Figure 5.1 by the line segment AB, and the associated path of the remaining present value (as in equation (5.4)) will have a concave form like the dashed line from A to T in Figure 5.1 (except, that is, when the discount rate is zero, in which case the remaining present value has the straight-line form). The pattern of depreciation is low in the early years of asset life and accelerates with age. The straight-line efficiency sequence, on the other hand, follows the line pattern. In this form, depreciation accelerates with age, as with one-hoss-shay, but at a more rapid rate in the early years of asset life.

The self-dual property of the geometric form makes it the most attractive *a priori* choice among the three patterns. When the geometric pattern is selected for a given type of asset, the same number δ that is used for the perpetual inventory method can be used in computing asset values and

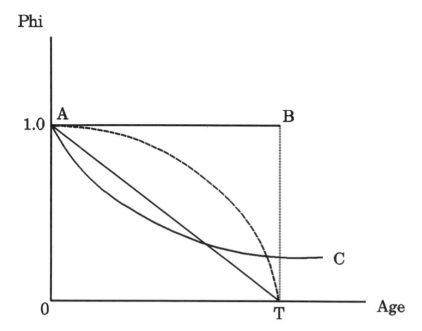

Figure 5.1. The One-Hoss-Shay, Straight-line, and Geometric Efficiency (ϕ) Patterns

capital consumption allowances. Moreover, it is not necessary to keep track of the individual vintages of past investment. In any other form, like straight-line or one-hoss-shay, the computation is much more complicated. If straight-line efficiency is assumed, depreciation is not straight-line but depends in a complicated way on the rate of discount, and timing of past investments matters (that is, how much investment is in each vintage). If straight-line depreciation is assumed, then the efficiency sequence is a complicated nonlinear function. The same holds true for the one-hoss-shay form or for the combination of the two forms discussed in Sections 6.193 and 6.194.

Geometric depreciation thus scores a clear victory over its competitors on pragmatic grounds. However, there is also the important question of which pattern most nearly fits the evidence on economic depreciation and asset efficiency. We turn to this below, after considering two important issues on which the *SNA* is largely silent: obsolescence and retirement from service.

5.3.2. Quality Change and Obsolescence

The decision by the Bureau of Economic Analysis to adjust computer prices for changes in quality (Cartwright, 1986) triggered an active controversy in national acounting circles. This decision was prompted by the study of Cole et al. (1986), which found that the dramatic increase in the computing power over the few decades was not reflected in the conventional procedures for measuring the price of computers. When the price statistics were corrected for the improvement in computing power embodied in successive generations (vintages) of computers, the quality-corrected price of computers was found to fall at double-digit rates (in the range of 10 to 20 percent) rather than rise as the uncorrected estimates indicated. The decision by BEA to switch over to the falling quality-corrected measure of computer prices has the effect of increasing the implied "quantity" of investment.

The main issues involved in the adjustment of capital prices for quality change can be illustrated by the following example. Suppose that technological innovation in the design of personal computers (PCs) led to an 10 percent increase in the marginal product of a particular type of PC produced in 1994 relative to a PC made in the preceding year. Suppose, also, that the price of new PCs was $1,000 in 1993 and that this price rose to $1,100 in 1994 because the improvement in efficiency cost more to produce. Procedures that ignore quality change would assign the $100 increase in price to revaluation and assert that there was no change in quantity between the two years. With an adjustment for quality, the price of the 1994 computer would be recorded as $1,000 and quantity would be increased by 10 percent.

This example is a special case of a more general procedure in which quality change is expressed as an increase in the relative efficiency of new capital, ϕ_0, from year to year. In our example, the 10 percent increase in the marginal product of a new computers from 1993 to 1994 implies that the latter might be assigned an efficiency index of $\phi_0 = 1.1$ if the former is given an index of $\phi_0 = 1$ (note that this corresponds to an outward shift in the efficiency profiles of Figure 5.1). Under this convention, quality change embodied in the design of capital is expressed as an equivalent increase in quantity of capital—that is, *better* is translated as "more." This convention follows from the Leontief aggregation theorem (Fisher, 1965) and is consistent with the interpretation of the perpetual inventory method measure of capital, (5.1), as the equivalent to the amount of new investment needed to equal the productive capacity of the surviving past investments. From a computational standpoint, (5.1) continues to be the basic equation of capital stock measurement, with an upward adjustment in the ϕ assigned to new assets to allow for embodied improvements in quality.[11]

Following this convention, the efficiency function is adjusted upward for quality change while the corresponding asset price is adjusted downward by a proportionate amount. The total value, P^I_I, is thus left unchanged: in the case of a PC that costs $1,000 and whose quality has doubled, the quality-adjusted quantity is two units and the quality-adjusted price is $500, leaving total value equal to $1,000. This invariance property hold regardless of whether it is costly or costless (Triplett, 1992).

However, while these quality adjustments on the input side do not depend on whether quality change is costly or costless, the costliness of quality change does have important implications for the revaluation of new investment goods and of used assets but not for depreciation (Hulten, 1995). For example, in the case in which changes in quality require a proportional change in cost, investment in better quality *is exactly like* investment in more quantity. Thus, the renal price, $P^K_{t,s}$, of older assets *per unit of efficiency* ϕ is exactly the same as the rental on a new asset per unit of efficiency, and the remaining present value equation (5.4) indicates that the price of older assets, $P^I_{t,s}$, does not change. In otherwords, there is no obsolescence term in the revaluation of the used capital good.

An additional effect is, however, present when quality change is *costless*. The appearance of technically superior (more efficient) new assets forces down the rent on older, less efficient, assets until the rent per unit of efficiency is equalized. As the rent on older assets falls, so does the remaining present value. The change in the price of older assets from one year to the next thus has an additional component associated with the fact that it becomes increasingly obsolete over time.[12] But in neither case does the cost of quality change in asset price affect economic depreciation; it only affects revaluation (Hulten, 1995).

Though obsolescence is mentioned only with reference to the distinction between expected and unexpected obsolescence, *SNA 1993* deals with the issue of quality change extensively in Sections 16.105 through 16.129. Four options are listed, two ignoring quality change and two involving alternative methods of making quality adjustments. *SNA 1993* rejects the former and endorses the latter but notes that quality adjustment may be difficult to implement in practice (the use of price-hedonic methods is mentioned in this regard). The SNA thus sides with those who advocate making quality adjustments, and the pure resource-cost approach to asset valuation is rejected.

5.3.3. Retirement from Service

We have thus far treated capital as though it were retired from service at a single point in time, T (some assets like land may not be retired from service, in which case T is infinity). When capital goods are grouped for purposes of measurement, as they inevitably must be, the assumption of a single retirement date is not appropriate. Some of the capital goods within any collection are virtually certain to be taken out of service before other members of the same collection because of breakage, different intensity of use or maintenance, or varying economic circumstances. Some early retirements may be unexpected—as when a building burns—but, when dealing with groups of assets, even catastrophic losses are statistically predictable. The assumption of a single retirement date is therefore unrealistic and must be replaced by a more appropriate assumption about the distribution of retirement dates.

There are two ways that the distribution of retirements can be introduced into the efficiency-function framework described in preceding sections. First, a groups of assets (such as all IBM PCs put into service in 1993) can be broken into cohorts according to the date of expected retirement, as determined by some estimate of the expected retirement distribution. Suppose, for example, that the average useful life of IBM PCs is three years, with 25 percent of the 1993 PCs lasting two years, 50 percent lasting three years, and 25 percent lasting four years. In this case, three retirement cohorts would be defined, with service lives of two, three, and four years, respectively. An efficiency sequence—such as the straight-line pattern—would then be determined for each cohort using the appropriate cohort life. This is essentially the method used by the Bureau of Economic Analysis (U.S. Department of Commerce, 1987) to measure depreciation.

Alternatively, the efficiency sequence could be treated as an average value for the group assets as a whole. In this interpretation, the ϕ measures the relative efficiency of an asset drawn at random from a group of assets. This is essentially the procedure used by Hulten and Wykoff (1981a, 1981b) in their studies of economic depreciation. Hulten (1990) shows that the efficiency sequence defined in this way is directly related to the ϕ's used in the BEA approach, and the choice of approaches is, to a large extent, a matter of empirical convenience. However, it should be emphasized that whatever the convention adopted, the assumptions about retirement should be internally consistent: a retirement distribution applied directly to perpetual inventory method (5.1) will have implications for the asset valuation equation (5.4), and vice versa.

SNA 1993 does not provide much guidance on the subject of retirements. If does, however, stress the distinction between expected and catastrophic losses. Section 6.187 states that "losses of fixed assets due to normal accidental damage are also included under the consumption of fixed capital; that is, damage caused to assets used in production resulting from their exposure to the risk of fire, storms, accidents due to human errors, etc. When these kinds of accidents occur with predictable regularity they are taken into account in calculating the average service lives of the goods in question." This could be interpreted as discounting the importance of the retirement distribution, but since unforeseen retirements may affect more than the average service life, this is not an appropriate interpretation. *SNA 1993* recommends in Sections 12.35 through 12.48 that unforeseen losses due to damage or obsolescence should be recorded in the "other changes in assets account" (Account III.3.1). It is recognized there that unforeseen changes may exceed or fall short of expected changes in any year, implying that it is the difference between the two (not the whole unforeseen amount) that enters the "other changes" account. This, in turn, implies the existence of an underlying distribution of expected retirements, though there is no explicit discussion, much less recommendation, about the appropriate methodology.[13]

5.3.4. Implementation Issues I

The "devil in the detail" becomes apparent when one attempts to implement the accounting theory of the *SNA*. The form of the perpetual inventory method is simple enough in principle, but it requires a number of crucial decisions to put into practice. First, the boundary between capital and intermediate consumption of inputs must be defined. *SNA 1993* expands the boundaries of the preceding guidelines to include some intangible assets but stops short of the "total capital" concepts developed in Kendrick (1976) or Eisner (1985). *SNA 1993* treats consumers durables as an intermediate good, not as capital, and the stock of human capital is largely ignored. This is a potentially important omission, since Kendrick estimates that human capital accounted for 53 percent of the 1969 total stock of capital ($5 trillion in 1958 dollars). The methods used by Jorgenson and Fraumeni (1990) suggest an even larger role for human capital.

Any asset that enters the production function of an economy, or whose use subtracts from the utility of consumers, should, in principle, be included in a complete system of national income accounts. In practice, however, the attempt to draw boundaries involves arbitrary judgments. Expanding the boundaries of the national accounts usually moves the accounts farther away from the use of market-transaction data toward increased use of imputations. This process increases the ratio of assumption to fact and reduces one's comfort in the reliability of the data. Different imputation procedures may give very different results, and large error may be introduced by any particular method. For example, the use of expenditure data to measure the stock of self-constructed assets (such as many household assets, assets used by the informal sector of developing economies, or R&D "knowledge" capital) will understate the size of the stock if increases in productivity of the self-construction process are ignored.

On the other hand, to ignore such assets altogether is to assign a zero weight to them. This, in turn, may introduce a systematic bias in comparing developing and industrialized nations and comparing the growth of capital over time in any country. The solution to this dilemma advocated by *SNA 1993* is to place those categories of capital that are thought to involve such problems (such as R&D capital) into satellite accounts.

There are, however, problems even within the hospitable boundaries of fixed capital assets with clearly defined market transactions. As noted above, the heterogeneity of fixed assets is so great that they must be grouped for purposes of measurement. The assets within a group are treated as though they were homogenous and assigned the same efficiency sequence ϕ so the way assets are grouped matters. If the grouping procedure brings together assets of distinctly different characteristics, substantial error may result. The fifty types of producers' durable equipment and nonresidential structures listed in the U.S. national accounts provide a good example of this problem. This is clearly a very detailed and disaggregated taxonomy of fixed business capital—too detailed, in fact, to be useful in many statistical analyses. There is, however, enormous heterogeneity within the individual classes: the metalworking machinery class, for example, comprises assets with very short service lives, like grinders, and assets with very long lives, like metal presses.

One solution is to expand the number of classes, but this soon leads to an intractable number of asset classes. Another is to use hedonic techniques to take into account differences in the characteristics of assets. This approach has been used successfully to account for differences in the characteristics of buildings. However, it is also true that variations in the survey procedures used in such studies can lead to very different results— such as different degrees of sample coverage with respect to small enterprises. Moreover, the sample may have a time dimension that is too short for the perpetual inventory method. According to equation (5.1), the capital stock at time t is the efficiency-weighted sum of past investments, going back to the oldest surviving vintage T. For some structures, T may be as large as several hundred years.

Data series of this length may not be available in many countries, in which case the perpetual inventory method would have to be estimated using a benchmark to fix the stock of capital for some year in the investment sample period. If, for example, there are only ten years of data on investment and these start in 1970, the perpetual inventory estimate of the stock in 1980s would be

$$K_{1980} = \phi_0 I_{1979} + \phi_1 I_{1978} + \ldots + \phi_9 I_{1970} + K_{1970}. \qquad (5.24)$$

If surveys methods are used to construct the 1970 benchmark, detailed estimates of the various component vintages must be obtained and weighted by the relevant ϕ values. The construction of a benchmark can serve as a check on the accuracy of the perpetual inventory method even when investment data are available over a long period of time. Since the accuracy of historical estimates is likely to decline as the investment data series are extended backward in thime, the national wealth survey benchmark is likely to be a valuable complement to any program of capital measurement (a point noted in Kendrick et al., 1964).

5.3.5. Implementation Issues II

Data on investment expenditures, appropriately deflated and grouped into categories, are converted to a stock of capital via the perpetual inventory method. This step requires an estimate of the efficiency sequence and, as the *SNA 1993* puts it in Section 6.202 (p. 150), "It is clear from the preceding sections that the consumption of fixed capital is one of the most difficult items in the accounts to measure and estimate. . . . Consumption of fixed capital does not represent the aggregate value of a set of transactions. It is an imputed value whose economic significance is different from entries in the accounts based mainly on market transactions." Imputations can be based on any of the three methods identified above, but in Section 6.197 (p. 150), *SNA* guidelines opt for just two: "Both the linear and the geometric, or declining-balance, methods are easiest to apply. The choice between them depends on knowledge, or assumptions, about the implied profiles of rentals which underlie them. It is not possible on a priori grounds to recommend the use of one in preference to the other in all circumstances. It is possible, for example, that linear depreciation may be realistic in the case of structures, while geometric depreciation is more realistic in the case of machinery or equipment. In practice, the choice of formula seems to rest between one or the other of these two methods, and there seems little justification for the use of more complex formulas."[14] The question of whether straight-line depreciation is more realistic than the geometric form is a matter of greater controversy (see, for example, the debate between Feldstein and Rothschild, 1974, and Jorgenson, 1973, and the surveys by Hulten and Wykoff, 1981b, and Triplett, 1992).

The case for straight-line depreciation and the combination of one-hoss-shay and straight-line efficiency loss mentioned by the *SNA* in Section 6 rests mainly on intuition. Casual experience with commonly used assets suggests that most assets have pretty much the same level of efficiency regardless of their age—a one-year-old hammer does the same job as a ten-year-old hammer. The popularity of the straight-line depreciation pattern also reflects the widely used convention, borrowed from depreciation accounting, that assets should be amortized in equal increments over a useful service life. The geometric form, on the other hand, is often regarded as empirically implausible because of the rapid loss of efficiency in the early years of asset life (for example, 34 percent of an asset's productivity is lost over four years with a 10 percent rate of depreciation). Moreover, assets are never completely retired in the geometric form, implying the service life in infinite.

A test of this intuition can be developed from the remaining present value equation (5.4). If economic depreciation has the straight-line form, the inflation-adjusted remaining present value of an asset should decline linearly with age; if it has the geometric form, it should decline geometrically. Thus, if capital assets sold in second-hand markets command a price that is equal to the remaining present value, the observed price of used capital should indicate which form is appropriate. Hulten and Wykoff use this approach to study the depreciation patterns of a variety of fixed business assets in the United States—machine tools, construction equipment, autos and trucks, office equipment, office buildings, factories, warehouses, and other buildings. The straight-line and concave patterns (represented in Figure 5.1 by the lines between *A* and *T*) are strongly rejected; geometric is also rejected, but the estimated patterns are extremely close (though steeper than) to the geometric form, even for structures. Although it is rejected statistically, the geometric pattern is closer by far to the estimated pattern than either of the other two candidates.

The use of second-hand price data has been criticized on a variety of grounds, but other than intuition, there is little systematic evidence to support any of the alternatives, including the straight-line form. And the intuition that rejects geometric depreciation may be faulty on two accounts. First, while it may well be true a one-year-old hammer does the same job as a ten-year-old hammer, not all hammers reach an age of ten. Thus, the collection of hammers that were new in 1980 may experience a loss in aggregate efficiency and value due to retirement from service, even though the assets that did survive to age ten retained their full productive capacity. It is not hard to show that a normally distributed pattern of retirements can lead to an accelerated pattern of efficiency and value decline *for a collection of assets as a whole*, even though the pattern for each individual asset is decelerated with respect to the straight-line pattern.

Second, the intuition that rejects geometric depreciation may fail because of obsolescence. As our example of IBM PCs illustrates, capital may experience a repid decline in value in the early years of its life even though the efficiency pattern is close to being one-hoss-shay. A constant rate of obsolescence can, by itself, yield a depreciation pattern that is close to the geometric pattern.

The second-hand market analysis of Hulten and Wykoff takes both of these effects into account. Second-hand market prices necessarily refer to assets that have survived long enough to enter the market, and they are thus not representative of the whole population of assets put into service in the initial year of the cohort's existence. This can lead to a form of censored-sample bias if not corrected. The Hulten and Wykoff studies correct for this bias using a procedure that weights the observed prices of surviving assets by the probability of survival. The resulting estimates of the rate of depreciation thus refer to the average decline in value of an entire vintage of assets, and a direct correction for retirement, such as the procedure used by BEA, is not needed.

The obsolescence component of depreciation is automatically taken into account in the used-price approach of Hulten and Wykoff. The used-price approach estimates the decline in price with age and thus includes both the pure deterioration effect arising movements along the ϕ profiles of Figure 5.1 and the obsolescence effect arising from the shift in the ϕ function.

A summary version of the Hulten-Wykoff depreciation rates is shown in Table 5.1. These rates are approximations derived from the more detailed asset classification of the earlier studies.[15] As a rough rule of thumb, a depreciation rate of 15 percent can be used for producers'

Table 5.1. Rates of economic depreciation (δ)

Asset class	Approximate depreciation rate
Producers' durable equipment:	
Furniture and fixtures	12%
Agricultural machinery	12
Industrial machinery and equipment	12
Construction tractors and equipment	18
Farm tractors	18
Service industry equipment	18
Electrical equipment	18
Aircraft	18
Trucks and autos	30
Office and computing equipment	30
Nonresidential structures	3

Source: Based on detailed estimates by Hulten and Wykoff (1981b), revised and updated.

durable equipment other that motor vehicles and computing machinery, and 30 percent can be used for the latter. For nonresidential structures, an approximate rate of 3 percent is appropriate. Estimates of δ for a more detailed list of assets is available in the orginal Hulten-Wykoff study (1981b).

It is important to stress, again, that these estimates can be used to compute *both* the stock of capital, using the perpetual inventory method (5.1), and the estimate of economic depreciation used in moving from gross to net value added (or national income) and in computing the Hall-Jorgenson user cost (5.18). In implementing the perpetual inventory method using Table 5.1, the ϕ function for new capital, ϕ_0, must first be increased by an estimate of embodied quality change (obtained, perhaps, using price hedonics); then, starting from the initial value for ϕ_0, the rest of the ϕ sequence is computed from the δ's in Table 5.1 using equation (5.23). Since the retirement of assets is already embodied in the estimates of Table 5.1, no separate adjustment of the capital stock for retirement is needed, but the δ's should be adjusted downward to strip out quality change, which has already been accounted for.

The accounting book value of assets offers one alternative to the use of second-hand market prices, but as the *SNA* observes in Section 3.77 (p.

78), "business accounting often adopts valuations that are not appropriate for national accounts. Similarly, accounting for tax purposes often serve objectives that differ from those of macroeconomic analysis. For example, the depreciation methods favored in business accounting and those prescribed by tax authorities almost invariably deviate from the concept of consumption of fixed capital employed in the System." National wealth surveys that reflect the definitions and requirements of the *SNA* framework are perhaps the most important supplement to data on used asset prices (Kendrick, 1964). If such surveys are conducted at regular intervals, not only is the perpetual inventory method made more accurate, but a part of the rate of depreciation can be inferred: if the efficiency sequence in equation (5.24) has the geometric form so that $\phi_s = (1 - \delta)^s$ (recall equation (5.23)), benchmark estimates of K_{1980} and K_{1970}, plus estimates of the intervening investment $[I_{1979}, I_{1978}, \ldots, I_{1970}]$ give a polynomial expression in the δ's, which can be solved to obtain an implicit estimate. This procedure does not, of course, include obsolescence, but the estimated rate of obsolescence could be added to the polynomial estimate to get the total rate of depreciation. This is another good reason to carry out periodic national wealth surveys.[16]

5.4. Conclusion

The reader should be persuaded by now that the measurement of capital is, indeed, a nasty job. However, the nastiness of the undertaking makes the success of the outcome even more commendable. The success of the *SNA 1993* guidelines stems, in no small part, from the merger of economics and statistics. For measurement that is not linked to theory is arbitrary, and theory that is not linked to measurement is empty. The greatest praise that can be given to the *SNA* guidelines is that they recognize this fundamental dualism.

There are, of course, still many points of controversy. For example, *SNA 1993* (p. 146) argues that "the actual use of destructive weapons can scarcely be treated as an input into an economic process of production" and concludes that single-use munitions and military equipment should not be treated as fixed assets. This position fails to recognize that one "output" of the military production function is deterrence and that the stock of weapons contributes to this output. Beyond this, much of the rest of government capital input is not valued using the rental price imputation implied by equation (5.18). The treatment of consumers' durables and intangible and environmental assets is also likely to provoke controversy, and there is too much reliance on the "Other Changes in Assets" account. However, the 1993 document itself recognizes that the *SNA* is evolving over time and there are research issues that remain unresolved (p. xliii). The point, however, is not how far the SNA needs to go in the future but how far it has already come and how much has been achieved.

Acknowledgments

I would like to thank Dale Jorgenson, Jack Triplett, and Frank C. Wykoff, as well as my editor, John Kendrick, and my discussant, Derek Blades, for valuable comments on an earlier draft. Remaining interpretations, and errors, are my own responsibility.

Notes

1. As an indication of this confusion, Denison (1989) concluded that his view of capital was really close to the Harrodian consumption-forgone approach of T.K. Rymes (1971), while other observers have generally seen the famous Jorgenson-Griliches (1967, 1972)-Denison (1972) debate as a controversy over the right way to measure shifts in the production function.

2. A "vintage" of capital comprises all the capital goods of a given type put into service in a given year. For example, machine tools constructed during the year 1985 belong to the 1985 vintage, and the "age" of the machine tool is simply the number of years that have elapsed since the vintage was new; thus, machine tools from the 1985 vintage are nine years old as of 1994.

3. The ϕ indexes are often thought of as declining over time. However, new assets may require a "shake down" period in order to reach peak efficiency. In this case, the ϕ's can be represented as increasing at first, before declining.

4. Space limitations prevent a full discussion of alternative valuation procedures, like that proposed by Cas and Rymes (1991). Cas and Rymes advocate dividing the growth rate of capital by the Harrodian rate of technical change in order to express each vintage of capital on an equal basis in terms of foregone consumption. Technical change in the production of capital means that less saving—and therefore less foregone consumption—is needed to sustain a given quantity of capital. The reader is referred to Hulten (1992a) for a more detailed discussion of this point, and we will observe here only that it is not necessary for a reasonable accounting system nor is it consistent with the standard "year-by-year" view of standard theory.

5. The term P^K has been given many names in the literature on applied capital theory: the rental price of capital, the service price, the user cost, and the quasi-rent. Under any name, it is the price associated with using a piece of capital for one time period. When the asset is rented, it is the rental price. When the asset is owner-utilized, it is the implicit rent that the owner would charge himself in order to reflect the opportunity cost of the capital. Thus, it is simultaneously a cost and a source of income. The first subscript denotes the year

the flow of cost (gross income) is realized, and the second denotes the age of the asset generating the flow (this allows for the possibility that older assets generate less income than their newer counterparts). The superscript K distinguishes this one-period user cost from the cost of purchasing the asset, P^I.

6. It is important to note that the remaining present values used in the valuation of assets in (5.5) are equivalent to the price that vintage assets would command in a competitive second-hand market. This is very different from valuing the same asset in terms of *new* assets—that is, using the price of new assets $P^I_{t,0}$. This alternative approach treats productive capacity as an inventory of efficiency units that are literally used up in the production of output (like an intermediate input). In this view, the value of a piece of capital of vintage s at any point, t, in time is the value of the remaining inventory of efficiency units, $P^I_{t,0}\phi_s$. For all vintage assets combined, this notion of asset valuation replacement cost leads to

$$P^I_{t,0}K_t = P^I_{t,0}\phi_0 I_{t-1} + P^I_{t,0}\phi_1 I_{t-2} + \ldots + P^I_{t,0}\phi_T I_{t-T-1}. \tag{5.5*}$$

This expression can also be interpreted as the cost of replacing the efficiency units embodied in the existing collection of capital goods with the equivalent "amount" of new capital.

A comparison of this expression with the remaining present value definition (5.5) reveals a significant difference. The replacement cost of s-year-old assets, $P^I_{t,0}\phi_s$, is not equal to the remaining present value, $P^I_{t,s}$, except for special cases (see, for a further discussion of this point, equations (5.15) and (5.5′) and the associated text). This implies that (5.5*) is not consistent with the rest of the production theoretic framework of capital measurement implicit in the *SNA*. It also leads to a notion of depreciation that is inconsistent with the standard Hicksian concept.

7. *SNA 1993* recommends the term *capital consumption allowance* instead of *depreciation* on the grounds that depreciation is a concept used in business and tax accounting. The SNA is certainly correct in arguing that financial and tax depreciation is usually different from true or "economic" depreciation. But the term *capital consumption allowance* is itself subject to misinterpretation because it seems to suggest that capital itself is being consumed, not the *value* of capital (recall note 6). To avoid such confusions, we will stick with the term *economic depreciation* or *depreciation* in this chapter.

8. There are other formulations of depreciation besides the Hicksian definition. The replacement cost discussed in note 6 leads to a concept in which depreciation is the cost of replacing the efficiency units used up in production during the year: $P^I_{t,0}(\phi_s - \phi_{s+1})$. Yet another definition is based on the amount of capital exhausted in production. As Triplett (1992) has observed, exhaustion occurs because each year that passes makes an asset less productive in that year *and* in each remaining year of useful life. That is, the productive capacity of an asset that is exhausted in a given year is not limited to the contemporaneous loss in productive efficiency, $(\phi_s - \phi_{s+1})$ but also includes the efficiency losses in all subsequent years of service. These subsequent efficiency losses occur because the whole life-cycle productivity profile has been shifted by one year's use (that is, the asset has one year's less productive capacity in every year of its remaining useful life). The concept of exhaustion is meant to capture the whole vector of current and future efficiency loss, $[\phi_s - \phi_{s+1}]$. This leads to an alternative concept of depreciation based on the cost of replacing the units of capital exhausted in each year—that is, $\Sigma_s\, P^I_{t,0}(\phi_s - \phi_{s+1}) = P^I_{t,0}\phi_T$ with a zero discount rate. In other words, the sum of money needed in order to replace the exhausted capital is equal to the cost of replacing the last year's efficiency loss. Triplett (1992) provides a detailed discussion of this alternative concept of depreciation and its antecedents.

It is important to stress that these alternative definitions of "depreciation" are not the same as the Hicksian definition—the amount of capital *value* that must be "put back" in order to keep the real value of the investment intact—except in special cases (such as geometric depreciation). Indeed, the alternative views can be thought of as the value of the amount of capital that must be "put back" in order to keep the real quantity of the investment intact. This is one basis for the notion of "capital consumption allowance."

9. Specifically, asset values depreciate because each year that the asset is used to produce rental income means that it is one year older (and thus potentially less productive) in every future year and *also* one year closer to retirement. Thus, depreciation occurs because asset efficiency may decline with asset age and because assets have finite service lives. We will also see, below, that the introduction of new technology may cause older assets to lose value because they become obsolete (for example, newer computers are technically superior to their older counterparts and the introduction of each new model drives down the price of existing computers).

10. One "fix" for this problem is to combine the Production and Income Accounts in the *SNA*. However, a better solution is to construct the Production Account so as to reconcile the value of output (revenues) with the value of inputs (cost) and then formulate a separate Income Account which reconciles the value of inputs (the demand side of the factor market) with income received (the supply side of the factor market).

11. This treatment of quality change has led to a wave of criticism on both theoretical and practical grounds. Some analysts, including Denison (1989), would prefer to use a measure of capital that is not adjusted for quality change, when it is costless to achieve. This leads to a situation in which improvements in quality are assigned to aggregate total factor productivity and not to capital. In the case of industries, quality change is assigned to total factor productivity in the industry using computers, in this alternative view, while it is assigned to the computer producing industry in the efficiency-based view. Hulten (1992b) provides the exact relationship linking the two approaches.

12. Suppose that revaluation, depreciation, and embodied changes in quality all proceed at constant rates over time (p, δ', and γ, respectively). Following Hall (1968 and 1971), the price of an asset of age s in year to the next is $\exp[pt - \delta's + \gamma(t - s)]$. The term $t - s$ represents the vintage (or year placed in service) and $\exp[.]$ is the exponential operator. These terms can be rewritten as $\exp[(p + \gamma)t - (\delta' + \gamma)s]$. In view of the definition of depreciation in (5.9), this way of expressing the asset price indicates that the depreciation effect is the sum of two terms, one due to wear, tear, and retirement and the other to obsolescence of older assets.

13. The existence of unforeseen retirements may complicate an already complicated model. In principle, the conditional retirement distribution must be revised every time an unforeseen retirement occurs. This revision causes the remaining present value to changes and thus affects depreciation rates.

14. This remark comes dangerously close to confusing efficiency and depreciation. The statement that the choice between linear and geometric profiles depends on the rentals that underlie them suggests, in view of equation (5.13), that the profiles in question are *efficiency* profiles (that is, ϕ functions). Taken at face value, this is not consistent with the remainder of the quote, which refers to linear and geometric *depreciation*. However, it is certainly true that once the efficiency profile has been chosen, by whatever means, including observation of the rentals, the depreciation pattern is fixed by equation (5.15). If the pattern of rentals suggest a linear efficiency pattern, the corresponding depreciation pattern is not linear.

15. If the only information available is on the average service life, T, the rate of depreciation can be estimated using the formula $\delta = X/T$ discussed in connection with equation (5.23). In the Hulten-Wykoff studies, the average value of X for producers' durable equipment was found to be 1.65 (later revised to 1.86). For nonresidential structures, X was found to be 0.91.

16. There are other ways to approach the measurement of depreciation and efficiency decay besides the use of second-hand market prices or book values. One possibility is to estimate the rate of depreciation as a parameter of the production process (for example, Epstein and Denny, 1980). However, this approach yields estimates only for a highly aggregated definition of capital (all producers' durable equipment) and makes construction of capital stocks the outcome of econometric analysis and not an input into that analysis. Data on insurance appraisals and tax assessment valuation of assets can also be useful, but are not comprehensive and may be somewhat arbitrary.

References

Berndt, Ernst R., and Melvyn A. Fuss. (1986). "Productivity Measurement with Adjustments for Variations in Capacity Utilization, and Other Forms of Temporary Equilibrium." *Journal of Econometrics* 33: 7–29.

Cartwright, David W. (1986). "Improved Deflation of Purchases of Computers." *Survey of Current Business* 66(3) (March): 7–9.

Cas, Alexandra, and Thomas K. Rymes. (1991). *On Concepts of Multifactor Productivity*. New York: Cambridge University Press.

Cole, Rosanne, Y.C. Chen, J.A. Barquin-Stolleman, E. Dullberger, N. Helvacian, and J.H. Hodge. (1986). "Quality-Adjusted Price Indexes for Computer Processors and Selected Peripheral Equipment." *Survey of Current Business* 66 (January): 41–50.

Denison, Edward F. (1972). "Some Major Issues in Productivity Analysis: An Examination of the Estimates by Jorgenson and Griliches." *Survey of Current Business* 49 (5, pt. 2): 1–27.

Denison, Edward F. (1989). *Estimates of Productivity Change by Industry: An Evaluation and an Alternative*. Washington, DC: Brookings Institution.

Eisner, Robert. (1985). "The Total System of National Accounts." *Survey of Current Business* 65(1) (January): 24–48.

Epstein, L., and M. Denny. (1980). "Endogenous Capital Utilization in a Short-Run Production Model (Theory and an Empirical Application)." *Journal of Econometrics* 12: 189–207.

Feldstein, Martin S., and Michael Rothschild. (1974). "Towards an Economic Theory of Replacement Investment." *Econometrica* 42 (May): 393–423.

Fisher, Franklin. (1965). "Embodied Technical Change and the Existence of an Aggregate Capital Stock." *Review of Economic Studies*: 326–388.

Fisher, I. (1930). *The Theory of Interest*. New York: Macmillan.

Hall, Robert E. (1968). "Technical Change and Capital from the Point of View of the Dual." *Review of Economic Studies* 35: 34–46.

Hall, Robert E. (1971). "The Measurement of Quality Change From Vintage Price Data." In Zvi Griliches (ed.), *Price Indexes and Quality Change*. Cambridge, MA: Harvard University Press.

Hall, Robert E., and Dale W. Jorgenson. (1967). "Tax Policy and Investment Behavior." *American Economic Review* 57: 391–414.

Harcourt, G.C. (1972). *Some Cambridge Controversies in the Theory of Capital.* Cambridge: Cambridge University Press.

Hicks, John. (1946). *Value and Capital.* London: Oxford University Press.

Hicks, John. (1981). *Wealth and Welfare: Collected Essays in Economic Theory.* Cambridge, MA: Harvard University Press.

Hulten, Charles R. (1978). "Growth Accounting with Intermediate Inputs." *Review of Economic Studies* 45 (October): 511–518.

Hulten, Charles R. (1990). "The Measurement of Capital." In Ernst R. Berndt and Jack E. Triplett (eds.), *Fifty Years of Economic Measurement.* Studies in Income and Wealth (Vol. 54) (pp. 119–152). Chicago: Chicago University Press for the National Bureau of Economic Research.

Hulten, Charles R. (1992a). "Accounting for the Wealth of Nations: The Net versus Gross Output Controversy and Its Ramifications." *Scandinavian Journal of Economics* 94 (suppl.): S9–S24.

Hulten, Charles R. (1992b). "Growth Accounting when Technical Change Is Embodied in Capital." *American Economic Review* 82(4) (September): 964–980.

Hulten, Charles R., "Endogenous Growth and the Cost of Quality Change in Capital Goods," Paper Presented at the 1995 Summer Institute, National Burean of Economic Research, Cambridge MA (July 1995).

Hulten, Charles R., and Frank C. Wykoff. (1981a). "The Estimation of Economic Depreciation Using Vintage Asset Prices." *Journal of Econometrics* 15: 367–396.

Hulten, Charles R. and Frank C. Wykoff. (1981b). "The Masurement of Economic Depreciation." In Charles R. Hulten (ed.), *Depreciation, Inflation, and the Taxation of Income from Capital* (pp. 81–125). Washington, DC: Urban Institute Press.

Jorgenson, Dale W. (1963). "Capital Theory and Investment Behavior." *American Economic Review* 53(2) (May): 247–259.

Jorgenson, Dale W. (1973). "The Economic Theory of Replacement and Depreciation." In W. Sellykaerts (ed.), *Econometrics and Economic Theory.* New York: MacMillan.

Jorgenson, Dale W., and Barbara M. Fraumeni. (1990). "The Accumulation of Human and Nonhuman Capital, 1948–84." In Robert E. Lipsey and Helen Stone Tice (eds.), *The Measurement of Saving, Investment, and Wealth*, Studies in Income and Wealth (Vol. 52) (Chicago: pp. 119–152). Chicago University Press for the National Bureau of Economic Research.

Jorgenson, Dale W., and Zvi Griliches. (1967). "The Explanation of productivity Change." *Review of Economic Studies* 34 (July): 349–383.

Jorgenson, Dale W., and Zvi Griliches. (1972). "Issues in Growth Accounting: A Reply to Edward F. Denison." *Survey of Current Business* 52: 65–94.

Kendrick, John W., David Hyams, and Joel Popkin, (eds.). (1964). *Measuring the Nation's Wealth.* Report of the Wealth Inventory Planning Study. Washington, DC: J.E.C.

Kendrick, John W. (1976). *The Formation and Stocks of Total Capital.* New York: National Bureau of Economic Research.

Leontief, W.W. (1947). "Introduction to a Theory of the Internal Structure of Functional Relationships." *Econometrica* 15 (October): 361–373.

Rymes, Thomas K. (1971). *On Concepts of Capital and Technical Change.* Cambridge: Cambridge University Press.

Triplett, Jack E. (1987). "Hedonic Functions and Hedonic Indexes." In John Eatwell, Murray Milgate and Peter Newman (eds.), *The New Palgrave Dictionary of Economics* (Vol. 2) (pp. 630–634). New York: Macmillan.

U.S. Department of Commerce, Bureau of Economic Analysis. (1987). *Fixed Reproducible Tangible Wealth in the United States, 1925–85.* Washington DC: USGPO.

DISCUSSION OF CHAPTER 5

Derek W. Blades

Professor Hulten is to be congratulated. Not only has he digested the 700-odd pages of the *System of National Accounts 1993* and identified the portions relevant to investment and wealth, but he has written a cogent and insightful analysis of the theoretical underpinnings of *SNA*'s *1993* treatment of this complex area. In what follows, I have tried to bring some further thoughts—strictly of a nontheoretical nature—to complement his chapter.

Sector Accounts and Consolidated Accounts

As Professor Hulten notes, *SNA 1993* puts much emphasis on deconsolidation of the accounts in order to highlight transactions between the sectors—financial and nonfinancial corporations, government, households and private nonprofit institutions serving households. While recognizing the advantages of the sectoral approach, Hulten regrets that it "loses sight of the clear division in economic theory between consumption and production." The 1993 system does, however, provide for consolidated accounts and, in practice, they will remain the core of the system. Many countries will not find it practical or useful to advance beyond the consolidated accounts for some years to come, and for the relatively few countries that can move to a full sectoring of the accounts, consolidated accounts will continue to show the simple division between consumption and production and between saving and investment. Whether this is an advantage or an oversimplification is a question addressed at the end of this note.

Disaggregation of Investment

Another small confusion relates to the degree of commodity detail called for in *SNA 1993*. Professor Hulten writes that the *SNA* "does not disaggregate investment by type of capital—that is, by machine tools, autos, office buildings, and so on." While it is a minor complaint on Hulten's part, I mention it because it illustrates an important feature about the 1993 *System*. Early on in the revision process, it was agreed that the new version, unlike its 1953 and 1968 predecessors, would include *accounts* but not *tables*. The former *define* the system while the latter provide guidance on how to *implement* it. Classifications by kinds of activity, by product, and by function are summarized in an annex to *SNA 1993*, and it is expected that countries will make use of these in drawing up their own national accounts tables. Tables using these standard classifications will also form part of the international questionnaire, and, based on past experience, many countries will take these as models for their own national publications.

Capital Stocks: Gross or Net?

This important distinction is fundamental to any discussion of the stock of capital. The *gross* capital stock is the value of capital assets at the prices they would command if they were still new; the *net* capital stock is the value of the same assets at the prices they would command if they were put on the market in their present condition.

Capital stock estimates on a gross basis are most often used in studies of production, productivity, and industrial capacity. This is because throughout their entire service lives, most assets carry on producing nearly as well as they did when they were first acquired. It makes more sense, therefore, to value them at the as-new prices used for gross stock estimates than at the written-down values required for the net stock figures. However, while the gross estimates are most commonly used in economic analysis, they have no formal place in the *System of National Accounts*. Gross capital stock is mentioned in *SNA 1993* but only because it is the usual starting point in estimating two important items that do feature in the system—namely, net capital stocks and consumption of fixed capital. (I say the "usual" starting point because these two items could also be measured directly—a point I will come back to later.)

The net capital stock is one of the main entries in the balance sheets, which are designed to show the wealth of the various sectors or of the nation as a whole. Since they are here being considered as a component of wealth, they must be valued at their current market prices or, which is the same thing, as the "sum of the discounted values of future rentals" to use *SNA 1993* terminology. Professor Hulten is quite correct in saying that the *SNA* recommends that capital stocks be valued at "remaining present value," but it is important to emphasize that this is because *SNA 1993* deals only with capital stocks as a form of wealth. The system has nothing to say about what is, for many purposes, the more mportant issue of valuing the capital stock as an input into production.

Perpetual Inventory Method

SNA 1993 describes the perpetual inventory method (PIM) as the standard procedure for obtaining the capital stock and capital consumption statistics required in the system. It is certainly the case that the vast majority of countries that publish these statistics—perhaps twenty-five countries in total—use the PIM, but a few words of caution are in order.

First, the PIM requires information about the service lives of assets that has proved difficult to obtain by empirical methods. What are the average lifetimes for different kinds of asset? What is the dispersion of deaths around the average? Are there secular or cyclical variations in service lives? A recent OECD study (OECD, 1993) has shown that in the absence of firm information on these questions, statisticians in individual countries have come up with very different answers. PIM estimates have a high guess component—almost certainly higher than for most official statistics. For this reason statistical offices in several countries are looking at other ways to estimate capital stocks.

The obvious way to proceed is through direct surveys of companies. These have been tried by several countries—Japan in 1960, Taiwan in the 1980s, South Korea, at ten-year intervals since 1960, and, more recently but on a more limited scale, the Netherlands and Canada. To estimate the net value of the capital stock, the question to be asked is deceptively simple: what is the market value of your fixed assets? In practice, respondents almost never know the answer because they have rarely contemplated selling their stock of assets; moreover company balance sheets almost always value fixed assets at acquisiton costs and not at replacement costs (which would give stock estimates on a gross basis) or at current market values (which would give stock estimates in net terms).[1] Consequently, surveys require skilled interviewers to visit a sample of enterprises and conduct detailed, on-the-spot investigations. For this reason they are expensive operations, but some countries have nevertheless thought it worthwhile to carry them out simply because of doubts about the validity of the pperpetual inventory method. Ann alternative, and potentially much cheaper, approach is desscribed by Jaffey (1990), wwho has shown how, despitee their shortcomings, company accounts can be exploited to provide valid estimates at economically meaningful values.

None of this is to say that the PIM should be discarded, but it is clear that in devoting space to the PIM, the authors of the *SNA 1993* and did not intend to give it their seal of approval or suggest that it is the preferred method. It is rather a recognition that at the present time the PIM is probably the only method that is feasible for most countries.

Consumption of Fixed Capital

This remains a murky area at least at the practical level even though, as Professor Hulten acknowledges, the discussion of the topic in *SNA 1993* is clear and helpful. There is no dispute about the general definition of consumption of fixed capital. *SNA 1993* defines it as "the decline during the course of the accounting period in the current value of the stock of fixed assets owned and used by a producer as a result of physical deterioration, normal obsolescence and normal damage" (paragraph 6.179). The problem at the practical level is that, as noted above, the current values of capital stocks are not generally known by the owners of assets and company accounts use inappropriate valuation methods.

Hulten and Wykoff (1981) have carried out one of the few empirical studies on how asset prices decline by examining the prices of second-hand assets of differing vintages. Professor Hulten reports their conclusion that "the evidence from the second-hand market [in the United States] strongly supports the geometric pattern." This contrasts with the more agnostic approach of *SNA 1993*, which considers that both straight-line and geometric consumption patterns may be appropriate for different kinds of assets; it suggests that geometric may be better for machinery and equipment while straight-line better for buildings. In particular, the authors note that straight-line depreciation will closely approximate the decline in the market price of an asset whose efficiency (measured by its contribution to value-added) declines by approximately equal amounts each year and that is discarded before efficiency declines to zero. Buildings are commonly thought to fall into this class of assets, so it is surprising to find that the Hulten and Wykoff study found geometric depreciation applicable to buildings as well as machinery. A possible explanation is that buildings in North America contain a higher proportion of machines— heating, air-conditioning, and lifting devices, for example—than are incorporated into buildings in more user-friendly climates.

Perhaps the safest conclusion is that no single pattern—either straight-line or geometric—is appropriate for all assets and for all countries. Investigations into second-hand asset prices of the kind conducted by Hulten and Wykoff could usefully be carried out in other countries to bring some empiricism to what is currently an area of sheer conjecture.

Before leaving this topic, a minor quibble. Professor Hulten argues that simplicity of application gives the geometric consumption pattern the edge over straight-line. One problem with geometric depreciation is that the value never declines to zero, and countries that use the geometric pattern have to add a rule to retire assets when the remaining value declines below some arbitrary threshold, such as 5 or 10 percent of original value. But logically, this information—that the asset will be retired after a certain number of years—should be incorporated into the depreciation rate applied each year from the year of installation. If this is done, the depreciation rate stops being a simple geometric rate and may be no easier to apply than the straight-line method.

Accounting for Quality Changes in Assets

SNA 1993 is quite clear on the question of quality change. When producers improve their products, the improvement represents higher quantity. In this context, an improvement means higher marginal utility in the case of products purchased for final consumption and higher marginal productivity in the case of goods purchased by producers, whether for intermediate consumption or for capital formation. I believe this has been the accepted wisdom among national accounts compilers since constant price estimates were first invented, and the recommendations in *SNA 1993* are fully in line with this approach. Non-U.S. readers may be surprised that Professor Hulten devotes so much space to the "debate over the desirability of making quality adjustments." They will be relieved though, that both Professor Hulten and the U.S. Bureau of Economic Analysis come down on the right side of the argument.

Among the various methods used to quantify changes in quality, "hedonic regression" is potentially one of the most powerful. And it also has the advantage that it can be used to quantify "costless" quality changes—those that are not accompanied by price increases. Costless quality changes are thought to be particularly frequent in the area of informatics, and it was presumably for this reason that the Bureau of Economic Analysis decided to adopt hedonic methods in constructing deflators for computers. The point that should be stressed here is that this decision in no way represented a change in the Bureau's underlying philosophy. Like statistical offices in every other market economy, they had always been trying to quantify improvements in computer hardware, but the techniques they had been using—essentially comparing the price movements of unchanged models—were simply not capable of capturing the very dramatic technical improvements that have occurred in the last two decades.

Professor Hulten explains that the "heart of the debate over the desirability of making quality changes [is that] when quality improvements are costless . . . , *the quantity of capital is no longer related to the resources used to produce the new capital.*" The philosophy of those who have opposed quality change adjustments seems similar to that underlying the old Material Product System. Left-footed boots, inoperable machines, and defective equipment of all kinds were recorded as output alongside products that actually served some useful purpose simply because they had all absorbed resources in their production.

Definition of Capital

In the course of the revision, many hours of deliberation were devoted to the question of the *asset boundary*: exactly what kinds of outlays were to be regarded as capital formation? In particular, a long list of expenditures by producers was reviewed to identify possible candidates for reclassification from intermediate consumption to capital formation. These included expenditures on research and development, professional and technical training, computer software, and mineral prospecting.

One problem that soon became apparent is that while it is rather simple to reclassify a given type of expenditure as a capital outlay and rework a few basic tables using the new definitions, it becomes far more complicated when the new definitions have to be fitted into a comprehensive framework such as *SNA 1993*. Research and development expenditures illustrate the problem. It is easy enough to transfer these expenditures from intermediate to final output in tables showing final expenditures on the GDP or value added by industry, but *SNA 1993* requires that these expenditures also be included in the net capital stock in the opening and closing balance sheets. This requires agreement on how capital consumption is to be calulated, and this in turn needs an estimate of average service lives. R&D projects—like the one that resulted in the invention of the wheel—may have an infinite service life, while others may remain commercially exploitable for only a few years or even months.

The basic difficulty was identified by the main author of *SNA 1993*—Peter Hill. There are many kinds of expenditures that are unambiguously capital in nature, such as the purchase of a machine tool or the construction of a bridge; there are equally many kinds of expenditures that are just as clearly current in nature, such as the purchase of a sandwich or the costs of running a vehicle. But a number of forward-looking expenditures that producers incur are similar to capital outlays in that they are aimed at increasing future incomes but are not at all like conventional capital expenditures either because they have no physical embodiment or because their future outcome is much less predictable.

The conventions of national accounts, which are determined by standard economic theory, require that all expenditures be placed in either the capital or current box. Professor Hulten is not alone in appreciating the clear two-dimensional picture presented by national accounts, but perhaps what is needed is for some unconventional member of the economics profession to devise theories that recognize the three-dimensional nature of the real world.

Acknowledgments

The author works at the OECD in Paris and participated in many of the expert groups that worked on the 1993 SNA. The opinions expressed in this note are his alone and not those of the OECD.

Notes

1. One notable exception is provided by the United Kingdom in the early 1980s. As a result of inflation following the first oil shock, the United Kingdom's Accounting Standards Committee drew up recommendations for a system of "current cost accounting." These were promulgated in 1980 and were applied, on a voluntary basis, by a substantial number of large companies in the years 1981 to 1984. A.D. Smith used these data to make partial estimates of the gross capital stock for the corporate sector for the year 1983 (see Smith, 1987).

References

Hulten, Charles R., and Frank C. Wykoff. (1981). "The Estimation of Economic Depreciation Using Vintage Asset Prices." *Journal of Econometrics* 15, pp. 367–396.

Jaffey, Michael. (1990). "The Measurement of Capital Through a Fixed Asset Accounting Simulation Model." *Review of Income and Wealth* (March), pp. 95–110.

OECD. (1993). *Methods Used by OECD Countries to Measure Stocks of Fixed Capital.* Paris: OECD.

Smith, A.D. (1987). "A Current Cost Accounting Measure of Britain's Stock of Equipment." *National Institute Economic Review* (May), pp. 42–57.

6 GOVERNMENT IN THE 1993 *SYSTEM OF NATIONAL ACCOUNTS*

Jonathan Levin

6.1. Introduction

National accounts, as the *System of National Accounts 1993* (*SNA 1993*) explains, "provide a comprehensive and detailed record of the complex economic activities taking place within an economy and of the interaction between the different economic agents, and groups of agents, that takes place on markets or elsewhere. . . . They [the national accounts] usually do this by recording the values of the goods, services or assets involved in the transactions between individual units that are associated with these activities rather than by trying to measure the physical process [of production, consumption, and accumulation of assets] directly" (paras. 1.1, 1.12).[1]

Fitting into this framework the activities of government and its interaction with other economic agents poses a series of challenges. These are discussed in the following sections, which focus on valuation, allocation of consumption, distinguishing market from nonmarket production, sectorization, subsectorization, distinguishing current from capital expenditures, revenue classification, and facilitating public finance analysis.

6.2. Valuation

A government's purchases of inputs, its lending and distribution of un-requited transfers, and its borrowing and compulsory exactions from the rest of the economy to pay for them take place through record-able transactions. But the government's principal activity—its output of nonmarket goods and services provided to the rest of the economy—does not come through transactions that can be recorded at some value with identifiable recipient institutional units. What is needed, therefore, is some means of measuring government production other than by recording the value of goods and services the government provides in transactions with other institutional units and some means of establishing who receives and consumes this nonmarket production other than by identifying the other transactor.

The solution chosen by *SNA 1993*, following the practice of its prede-cessor, *SNA 1968*, is to record government output of nonmarket goods and services as equal in value to the cost of government inputs—the sum of intermediate consumption (that is, the purchase of goods and services from others) plus the compensation of employees, the consump-tion of fixed capital, and any taxes (less subsidies) on production the government pays other than taxes or subsidies on products (para. 6.219). The alternative—valuing government nonmarket output by the price of comparable goods and services on the market—has faced the problem of noncomparability of many government services with services sold on the market. The *SNA* recommends that production by institutions other than government or nonnprofit institutions that is not sold be valued at the market price of comparable goods and services, when available, but this solution is not provided for government output. A step in this direction, the valuation of one input—rent on buildings owned and occupied by government—at comparable market prices rather than at depreciation of the buildings' costs, was considered at one stage in the preparation of *SNA 1993* but was deleted in the final version (p. xliii).

One result of valuing government output by the cost of government inputs is to omit the residual "net operating surplus," which in the case of market production remains after the subtraction of input costs from sales proceeds to cover the cost of capital—interest and dividends. Government output is thus undervalued in comparison to market output by the cost of capital. This may be illustrated by the *SNA* value recorded in the case of a downtown bus service provided free by government with the proceeds of taxes. The *SNA* value for this bus service would fall short of the value of a comparable service provided by a private bus company charging fares that also would have to cover the cost of capital, though government may have had to borrow an equal amount to cover the cost of capital. Though both bus systems would have to cover depreciation—that is, consumption of capital over the time of its use—*SNA* valuation of the free, nonmarket service as the cost of the inputs would not include the cost of borrowing the capital.

The problem of choosing a suitable mark-up of costs to include the cost of capital (that is, a net operating surplus) in the valuation of outputs for which no sales price is available is surmounted in the case of other producers—for example, in the acquisition of unfinished structures (para. 10.76), own-account construction costs (para. 10.78), work-in-progress costs (paras. 10.104, 13.48), and cultivated asset work-in-progress costs (para. 10.107)—but not for government. Some means of including a comprehensive measure of capital costs as an input in the valuation of government output, therefore, remains a subject for future research (p. xliii).

The absence of transactions by which government provides its output to recipients makes it impossible to identify the destination of government output, as would be the case, for example, if government services were purchased as a business's intermediate consumption or a household's final consumption. In lieu of institutions or groups of institutions identifiable as consumers of government output, *SNA 1968* and, following in its footsteps, *SNA 1993* attribute to government itself, as a surrogate for the entire community, the consumption expenditure for the government's entire nonmarket output minus any part of it for which payment is made. By this convention, all government nonmarket production, other than any amount paid for through sales, becomes own-account production. For the valuation of production that is not sold in the market, the *SNA* nevertheless distinguishes own-account production from other nonmarket production. It prescribes valuation at the average price of similar products traded on the market for own-account production, which is restricted to producers other that government or nonprofit institutions, but input-cost valuation for other nonmarket production (paras. 6.219, A.1.49).

Reflecting dissatisfaction with the declining share of household consumption registered under *SNA 1968* in countries with growing government nonmarket production—and hence government consumption expenditures—*SNA 1993* has introduced a new, approximate, split in the total of government consumption expenditures. This is a distinction between individual goods and services (such as health and education services), which could be provided to individual households for sale under other conceivable circumstance, and collective services (such as defense), which are automatically acquired and consumed by all members of the community or group without any action on their part (paras. 9.42, 9.43). Since there is no direct measure of the value of government services provided, either individual or collective, the distinction is drawn between government expenditures for the inputs devoted to the production of such services, on the basis of the classification of government expenditures by functions, contained in the Classification of the Functions of Government (COFOG) (para. 18.2). Individual consumption of government nonmarket goods and services is defined to include education, health, social security and welfare, sport and recreation, culture, and parts of housing, household refuse, and transportation (para. 9.87).

To carry out this separation of individual from collective consumption, *SNA 1993* distinguishes from the concept of final consumption expenditures a new concept, called actual final consumption, covering goods and services actually received regardless of who ultimately bears the expense (paras. 9.22, A.1.55). Government final consumption expenditures classified as providing for individual consumption, along with all final consumption expenditures of nonprofit institutions serving households (para. 8.23), are classified as current social transfers in kind to households, which are added to households' own final consumption expenditures to derive households' actual final consumption (paras. 8.38–8.40). Government's actual final consumption is thus restricted to its final consumption expenditures for collective consumption, benefitting society as a whole (paras. 9.91, A.1.56). The imputed social transfers in kind are used also to derive a concept of adjusted disposable income, through addition to households' disposable income and subtraction from government's disposable income (para. 8.25).

The labeling of government final consumption expenditures devoted to individual consumption as social transfers in kind, and the account in which the adjustment for such consumption is made as the Redistribution of Income in Kind Account, has necessitated a number of previously unnecessary counter-factual conventions. Thus, *SNA 1993* finds it necessary to specify that private transfers in kind (paras. 8.79, 8.80), private social insurance benefits in kind (para. 8.7), social transfers in kind from nonresidents (para. 8.16), intergovernmental transfers in kind (para. 9.32), and technical assistance in kind (para. 14.18) are all to be treated as cash transfers, a distinction that would be unnecessary had the provision of nonmarket individual services been labeled something other than social transfers in kind and the account showing their provision something other than the Radistribution of Income in Kind Account.

6.3. Distinguishing Market from Nonmarket Production

Given the fundamental differences in the valuation of output and in the identification of who consumes it, the dividing line between market and nonmarket production has important implications for both sectoral and economywide aggregates. The 1993 *SNA* departs from the 1968 *SNA* in its definition of this dividing line. It replaces the 1968 distinction between industries—selling goods and services that are normally intended for sale on the market at a price that covers their cost of production or providing goods and services that are of a kind which are often provided by business establishments (*SNA 1968*, paras. 1.46, 5.12)—and other producers with a distinction between market and nonmarket output. Market output is defined as output that is sold at prices that are economically significant in that they have a significant influence on the amounts producers are willing to supply and on the amounts that purchasers wish to buy (paras. 6.45, A.1.52, A.1.53). While more specific than the previous criterion of a business-like output, the criterion of an economically significant price permits greater flexibility than the requirement of a price covering at least half of production costs, which was considered at one stage in the preparation of *SNA 1993*.

Most market production, as noted below, is classified outside government. Market output that remains in government, by unincorporated enterprises that do not have full accounts (paras. 4.113, 5.36), as secondary activities of units or as services provided for fees is valued not by the cost of inputs buy by the sale price. While output sold by government units at less than significant prices is valued at the cost of inputs, the sales proceeds received are subtracted so that government consumption expenditures are valued at input costs minus sales proceeds (paras. 2.127, 9.78).

6.4. Sectorization

While the market-nonmarket distinction is fundamental to how output is valued and to whom its consumption expenditures are attributed, equally basic is the *SNA*'s grouping together of institutional units—economic entities capable in their own right of owning assets, incurring liabilitie and engaging in economic activities and in transactions with other entities—into sectors. The sectors—nonfinancial corporations, financial corporations, nonprofit institutions serving households, general government, and households—are intrinsically different from each other in their economic objectives, functions, and behavior (para. 4.17). Government units are described as unique kinds of legal entities established by political processes that have legislative, judicial, or executive authority over other institutional units within a given area and whose principal functions are to assume responsibility for the provision of goods and services to the community or to individual households and to finance their provision out of taxation or other incomes, to redistribute income and wealth by means of transfers, and to engage in nonmarket production (para. 4.104).

It is on the basis of these characteristics that entities are classified in the general—that is, overall—government sector. Some activities more characteristic of other sectors—producing for the market like a nonfinancial corporation or providing financial intermediation like a financial corporation—may nonetheless be classified within government if they are not the primary activities of entities qualifying as separate institutional units. To keep the government as homogeneously nonmarket as possible, however, the 1993 *SNA* goes further than the 1968 SNA in encouraging the exclusion from the government sector of all institutional units primarily engaged in market output, even though not incorporated, so long as they have complete sets of accounts, including information on withdrawals of entrepreneurial income (paras. 4.107, 5.36, A.1.13). The 1968 provision retaining in government unincorporated public units that primarily sell goods and services to the public but do not operate on a large scale (*SNA 1968*, Table 5.13) caused considerable confusion in its implementation and was deleted by *SNA 1993*. Regardless of scale of operations, therefore, market-producing institutional units with complete accounts are excluded from government and classified in the nonfinancial corporations sector.

Institutional units engaged in market production that are excluded from government and included in the nonfinancial corporations sector are classified as public nonfinancial corporations if they are majority owned by government, either directly or through another public corporation—clarifying the *SNA 1968* provision—or are controlled by government by some other means, "control over a corporation being defined as the ability to determine general corporate policy by choosing appropriate directors, if necessary" (paras. 4.72, A.1.17).

In the financial area, however, the stress on institutional rather than functional integrity can leave significant nongovernmental functions within the government sector. The issue arises in a number of countries where some monetary authority functions, such as management of foreign exchange and gold reserves and dealings with the International

Monetary Fund, are carried out not by the central bank but by parts of the government that do not qualify as separate institutional units. To maintain the functional integrity—that is, the analytical homogeneity—of the data presented for the monetary authorities and for the government, the IMF's statistical presentations for money and banking, government finance, and the balance of payments have for some time grouped the monetary authority functions carried out by government with those of the central bank in a combined monetary authorities subsector forming part of the financial institutions (now financial corporations) sector. Government operations involving management of foreign exchange or gold reserves or transactions with the IMF were shown as transactions between the government and the monetary authorities, who in turn dealt with the other transactors. Such transactions could be thought of as being rerouted through the financial corporations sector, much as employer social security contributions are rerouted through employees (paras 7.44, 8.67) or the salary payments to long-time resident foreign employees from nonresident enterprises are routed through fictitious resident quasi-corporations (para. 14.18).

The *SNA 1993*, like the *SNA 1968*, assigns such monetary authority functions of government only to the government sector, separate from the financial corporations sector (para. 4.87). It recommends that separate supplementary data be compiled for such government performance of monetary authority functions for comparability with IMF data (para. 4.121). It is not entirely clear, however, whether references to monetary authorities in various parts of *SNA 1993*, particularly in the chapter on the financial accounts and the annex on the balance of payments, refer to the central bank alone or to similar operations carried out by the government as well (paras. 11.64, 12.50, 12.61, A.1.83, A.2.13).

A useful clarification of the dividing line between the government sector and the financial corporations sector is provided by *SNA 1993* with regard to government employee pension funds. Under the *SNA 1968*, pension funds whose reserves were invested entirely with the employer were presumed to be under employer control rather than independent control and were classified in the sector of the employer rather than in the insurance corporations and pension funds subsector of the financial institutions sector (*SNA 1968*, para. 5.57). This was not a valid presumption for government employee pension funds invested entirely with securities of the employer government, however, since this could be done for reasons of prudence. In *SNA 1993*, consequently, government employee pension funds that are separate institutional units are classified not in government but in the financial corporations sector even if they are invested primarily or entirely in securities of the employer government (paras. 4.98, A.1.26).

The dividing line between government and nonprofit institutions serving households remains unchanged in *SNA 1993*. Nonprofit institutions that are both primarily financed and controlled by government are classified in the government sector, leaving in the nonprofit institutions sector those institutions that may or may not receive most of their financing from government but are independently controlled and those that may be government controlled but receive most of their financing from outside government. This is a different standard from that applied to determining whether corporations are public or private, for which either control or majority ownership, not financing, results in classification as public.

6.5. Subsectorization

Within the general government sector, institutional units in turn fall into more homogeneous groupings, sometimes with significant variations between countries. To recognize these variations, two changes in the subsectorization of the general government sector are contained in *SNA 1993*. In the first of these changes, an additional breakdown for state government is introduced between central government and local government—the two levels of government recognized by *SNA 1968*—to be applied in those countries where it is meaningful, in federal countries, for example (paras. 4.123–4.127, A.1.28).

The second, and perhaps more far-reaching, subsectoring change departs from the previous requirement that social security funds be grouped separately from central and local governments in a subsector containing only social security funds. This requirement reflected primarily European experience with social security funds that had developed more independently of other government institutions, sometimes for different occupational groups, and had retained a separate, though perhaps diminishing, identity, particularly in the perception of their participants. In other countries, however, where social security funds represented clear government initiatives and served as an integral tool of overall fiscal prolicy, the concept of central government excluding social security fund operations would present a partial, and possibly misleading, picture of central government performance.

To accommodate these different circumstances and perceptions, *SNA 1993* recommends two possible ways of subsectoring general government: one with social security funds as a subsector separate from the other operations of all levels of government, as in *SNA 1968*, and the other with social security funds as a part of each level of government at which they operate. Though parts of *SNA 1993* stress that equal priority is to be assigned to each of the two possible choices (para. A.1.27), elsewhere treatment is less even-handed, with the newly introduced choice referred to as "the alternative" (paras. 4.122, 4.131). In both variations, separate subsubsector accounts are to be compiled for social security funds operating at each level of government.

6.6. Classification of Transactions

Across the dividing lines separating government from the rest of the economy, a multitude of transactions take place, though not for the provision of most nonmarket services, as noted above. Because government is so large, carries out transactions with so many parts of the economy, and, for purposes of budgetary control and accountability, keeps more complete and accessible accounts of these transactions than many other transactors, government plays a large and special role in the national accounts. Government serves as a kind of calibrated mirror, in which some operations of other sectors are revealed and measured. There are several problems with this government role as a calibrated mirror, however. These involve the character of government data, the difficulty of applying to government the principles of classification appropriate for other sectors, and instances of asymmetry between the nature of a transaction for government and for the other transactor.

6.7. Data

Government accounts register most transactions on a cash basis—that is, when actual payments are made or received. This can differ both in timing, in magnitude, and even in whether a transaction is to be recorded, from the accrual basis data utilized by the *SNA* to measure economic activity when it takes place rather than when it is paid for. Government accounts can register a business's tax liability not when it accrues, as a result of sales or income, for example, but only when it is declared, assessed, or paid.

In contrast to *SNA's 1968* requirement that taxes be recorded as of the date they are due to be paid without penalty, with supplementary income tax data on when the income was earned (*SNA 1968*, paras. 7.27, 7.62),

SNA 1993 requires that taxes be recorded at the time the liability arises, so as to coincide with the underlying economic activity giving rise to the liability (para. 8.49). The amount recorded, however, is to reflect the amount of the subsequent assessment (paras. 3.99, 7.59).

Because the timing of tax recording may thus differ between the accrual accounts of taxpayers and the assessment or actual cash receipt accounts of the government, adjustment of government data is necessary for measuring the many areas of economic activity where data from the other transactors are not available. This is true also of data for government expenditures, which most frequently records cash payments, or authorization of cash payment, rather than accrual of the liability. While they generally provide the broadest continuous reflection of activities in much of the economy, therefore, the data recorded for the government's own purposes require adjustments when applied both to the rest of the economy and to the national accounts for the government itself.

6.8. Distinguishing Current from Capital Expenditures

The difficulty of applying to government the principles of classification utilized for other sectors is illustrated by several of the changes introduced by *SNA 1993* affecting the distinction between current and capital expenditures. Prominent among them is the decision to classify as fixed capital formation—that is, usable for productive purposes for a period greater than one year—not only the military expenditure for dependents housing, so recorded in *SNA 1968*, but all military expenditures on machinery and equipment other than those for destructive weapons and the vehicles and equipment that can be used only to release such weapons. Two reasons are presented for classifying weapons and their delivery systems as current: first, that, though durable, weapons are single-use goods, and second, that the actual use of such weapons in combat to destroy lives or property cannot be construed as the production of goods or services, so that, by extension, neither can vehicles and equipment delivering them (paras. 6.167–6.172, 10.65–10.68, A.1.70).

So long as military expenditures are counted in the government's product, however, the decision to classify them as production of goods and services has already been taken. Most military expenditures, moreover, are not used in combat but to exercise deterrence until they become obsolete, so that they provide security as a continuous collective service to the community. Application of the current-capital distinction to military expenditures, therefore, might more appropriately classify as capital those expenditures that serve to provide defense for more than one year, with the exception of those that because of their small magnitude and frequency fall into the current category, like small tools.

Another change in the current-capital dividing line that raises difficulties is the *SNA 1993* decision to include in government inventories not only strategic materials, grains, and other commodities of special importance to the nation, so treated in *SNA 1968*, but all goods held by the government, in a manner symmetrical with the treatment of goods stored by market producers (13.Annex.Inventories, para. A.1.74). Aside from the practical difficulties arising from the general absence of government accounting for supplies, other than strategic stocks, awaiting use, the measurement of government inventories faces conceptual difficulties. Unlike most producers, for whom the timing of inputs and outputs is established by explicit, recorded transactions, government has no time of production, separate from input, identified by transactions. The consumption of capital usable over several years determines the timing of one set of inputs and the accrual of liabilities for the delivery of goods and services and for the compensation of employees establishes the timing of other inputs. Government output is identified with government inputs, however, and there is no intervening period of production as there would be in the preparation of market production for sale. The government's intermediate consumption and compensation of employees are used to value government production in the period in which they are acquired. The interjection of inventories in this process, either as materials and supplies, work-in-progress, or finished goods awaiting shipment, raises difficulties *SNA 1993* does not explore.

A *SNA 1993* decision that should raise no difficulties is the requirement that allowances for the consumption of capital be applied for such structures as roads, bridges, and dams with long service lives that *SNA 1968* had assumed could be infinite with the proper maintenance and repair and would require no capital consumption allowances (paras. 6.186, 10.72, A.1.81). While this brings no change in the current versus capital classification of expenditures for such structures, the addition of capital consumption to government inputs during their long service lives results in increasing the magnitude of government product, and hence national product.

6.9. Revenue Classification

In practice, all but earmarked government revenues generally go into a single pot to be used fungibly to cover all government outlays. To maintain the *SNA* as a comprehensive, integrated system of accounts, however, transactions must be classified identically for both transactors (para. 8.33). In the *SNA*, therefore, government revenues are recorded in three separate accounts, reflecting the stages in the process of production, primary or secondary distribution of income, and capital acquisition from which they are derived. Taxes on products—that is, on the outputs of production or imports (termed commodity taxes in *SNA 1968*)—along with other taxes on production, levied on the inputs of production or on the production process (previously called other indirect taxes), are recorded in the primary distribution of income account (paras. 7.2, 7.54, 15.45–15.47). Taxes on income, wealth, and so on (previously called direct taxes), along with social contributions (distinguished from taxes and routed through employee incomes even if paid by employers (paras. 7.44, 8.67) are presumed to derive from production income already distributed and are recorded in the secondary distribution of income account (paras. 8.6, 8.7). Taxes on inheritances, on other capital transfers, or levied at irregular intervals on capital (previously referred to only as capital transfers) are recorded as capital taxes in the government's capital account (para. 8.31). The previous direct-indirect tax terminology, based on the idea that indirect taxes could be passed on to the purchasers by including them in prices while direct taxes come out of the incomes of those who pay them—an assumption now not readily accepted—is no longer used in the *System* (paras. 7.51, A.1.46, A.1.47).

Continuing the practice of the previous *SNA*, subsidies are treated as negative taxes on products or negative taxes on production, so that taxes on products as well as other taxes on production are recorded net of subsidies—that is, current government transfers to enterprises (paras. 7.71–7.79, 15.52, 15.53). Explicit recommendations are provided for the treatment of value added taxes (VAT), which have gained prominence since *SNA 1968*. The net system of recording VAT is recommended, which calls for excluding VAT invoiced by the producer from both the producers' price and the basic price, which excludes also net taxes on products (para. 7.6), and excluding VAT from the value of imports (paras. 7.6, 15.29, 15.49–15.51, A.1.42–A.1.45).

An inheritance tax is classified as a capital tax because it may be regarded as a transfer of capital by the taxpayer, who may not pay the entire amount out of income, though it is regarded as a current receipt by government because it receives many such transfers. A transfer should be classified as capital for both parties, *SNA 1993* explains, even if it involves the acquisition or disposal of an asset by only one of the transactors (paras. 8.31, 8.33, 10.133, 10.136). For government, as a result, the financing of current expenditures with the proceeds of inheritance taxes is recorded as dissaving. By this principle, should the government decide to finance capital expenditures by earmarking for this purpose an existing tax, it would presumably be classified as a capital tax, with increased saving shown as coming from the taxpayer.

Within the framework of taxes on products, other taxes on production, taxes on income and wealth, social contributions, and capital taxes, *SNA 1993* generally follows the classifications tied to the base or trigger of each tax developed over the past two decades by the IMF's 1986 *A Manual on Government Finance Statistics* (GFS) and the Organization for Economic Cooperation and Development's *Revenue Statistics* (OECD) (paras. 7.56, A.1.48). The *SNA* classification, however, is affected by the circumstances in which the taxes are paid and by the institutional units paying the tax. Taxes paid in the process of production are classified by the *SNA* as taxes on production (para. 8.53). Similarly, while the OECD-GFS import tax category is restricted to taxes levied solely because a product enters the country, the *SNA* import tax category adds to this any domestic taxes on goods and services paid on imports so as to separate the impact on imports from the impact on domestic production (paras. 7.57, 7.58). Unlike *SNA 1968*, however, in *SNA 1993* the distinction between tax revenue—unrequited and compulsory—and nontax revenue—paid in exchange for goods or services or assets—is not affected by whether or not payment is made in the process of production. For the grey area in which it is unclear whether or not license fees are paid in exchange for a service, *SNA 1993* adopts the OECD-GFS convention, which follows the specified majority practice among countries (paras. 8.54c, 9.62).

6.10. Public Finance Analysis

To facilitate the application of national accounts to areas of particular interest for public finance analysis, in addition to the national accounts' contribution to analysis of the economy as a whole, a number of changes are added to *SNA 1993*.

To permit the compilation of a total for taxes and social contributions parallel to the OECD-GFS total for all taxes, which includes compulsory social security contributions as taxes but excludes voluntary social contributions, *SNA 1993* requires that voluntary social contributions be shown separately (paras. 8.61, A.1.48). It does not discuss, however, a total for taxes and social contributions, which has been compiled in OECD and GFS data presentations and is of some importance to a number of countries. This is the total tax burden including not only taxes paid to general government but also taxes paid to supranational authorities, notably the European Community.

SNA 1993 notes in its text the correspondence between each of its tax categories and those of the OECD-GFS, so as to facilitate reference to the more detailed descriptions provided by the OECD and GFS. It does not contain, however, a comprehensive analysis of the relationship between the *SNA* and GFS classifications, like that relating the *SNA*'s rest of the world account and the IMF's balance of payments accounts in the *SNA's 1993* Annex 2. To fill a part of this gap, two graphic bridge tables showing in matrix format the correspondence between *SNA* and GFS classifications of government transactions are provided in Tables 6.1 and 6.2.

Table 6.1 covers nonrepayable receipts constituting revenue and grants received in GFS, and Table 6.2 covers payments and repayable receipts comprising expenditure, lending minus repayments and financing in GFS. In each chart, GFS classifications are arrayed down the side and *SNA* classifications across the top. A cell is completely filled in when a GFS category corresponds to a single *SNA* category and is partially filled in when a GFS category corresponds partially to each of several *SNA* categories. Footnotes indicate categories requiring subdivision for cross-classification or additional adjustments other than the difference between cash and accrual recording. The penultimate columns and rows cover elements that are not covered by corresponding classifications in the same table, in some cases because of classification as negative receipts or negative payments.

SNA 1993 recommends the compilation of accounts also for the overall public sector, including the subsectors of general government and the public subsectors of nonfinancial and financial corporations. This is intended to portray the role of the public authorities in supplying goods and services to the economy and the demands made on the resources for production by the public authorities. Such accounts are also meant to delineate the means of financing production, consumption, and capital formation by the public sector, its contribution to inflationary or deflationary pressures and to the external surplus or deficit and external debt (para. 19.37). *SNA 1993* recommends also the compilation of consolidated capital and financial accounts for narrower concepts of the public sector: the nonfinancial public sector—consisting of general government plus public nonfinancial corporations—and the nonmonetary public sector—consisting of the nonfinancial public sector plus public financial corporations except the central bank and other depository corporations (paras. 19.42, A.1.29). Compilation of consolidated accounts separate from

Table 6.1. GFS-*SNA* bridge table revenue and grants

Chart 1

GFS-SNA Bridge Table
Revenue and Grants

■ GFS correspondence with single SNA category

◢ GFS partial correspondence with several SNA categories

	GFS \ SNA	Markt Outpt		Taxes on products								Other current transfers						Capital transfrs					
		Market producers	Nonmarket producers	VAT-type taxes (c)	Import duties	Taxes on imports excl VAT & duties (c,d)	Export taxes (c)	Taxes on prod excl VAT,imp,exp dut (c,d)	Other taxes on production (a)	Taxes on income	Other current taxes (a)	Compulsory social contributions (g,h)	Voluntary social contributions	Non-life insurance claims (c))	Current transfers within general govt.	Current international cooperation	Miscellaneous current transfers (c)	Capital taxes (b)	Investment grants (i)	Other capital transfers (i,j)	Property income	GFS items not incl. in SNA items shown (e,f)	Total
REVENUE – CURRENT – TAX	1.1 Taxes on income, individual									■													
	1.2 Taxes on income, corporate									■													
	1.3 Taxes on income, unallocated									■													
	2.1 Social security contributions, employee											■											
	2.2 Social security contributions, employer											■											
	2.3 Social security contributions, self-emp.											■											
	2.4 Social security contributions, unallocated											■											
	3 Taxes on payroll, work force								■														
	4.1 Recurrent taxes on immovable property (a)								◢		◢												
	4.2.1 Recurrent taxes on net wealth, indiv.										■												
	4.2.2 Recurrent taxes on net wealth, corp.										■												
	4.3 Estate, inheritance, & gift taxes (b)																	■					
	4.4 Taxes on financial & capital transactions										■												
	4.5 Nonrecurrent taxes on property (b)																	■					
	4.6 Other recurrent taxes on property (a)								◢		◢												
	5.1 Gen. sales, turnover, value-added taxes (c)			◢		◢		◢															
	5.2 Excises (d)					◢		◢															
	5.3 Profits of fiscal monopolies							■															
	5.4 Taxes on specific services (d)					◢		◢															
	5.5.1 Business & professional licenses								■														
	5.5.2 Motor vehicle taxes (a)								◢		◢												
	5.5.3 Other taxes on use, etc. (a)								◢		◢												
	5.6 Other taxes on goods & services (a)								◢		◢												
	6.1 Import duties				■																		
	6.2 Export duties						■																
	6.3 Profits of export or import monopolies (c)					◢	◢																
	6.4 Exchange profits								■														
	6.5 Exchange taxes								■														
	6.6 Other taxes on internat'l trade, transact. (a)								◢		◢												
	7.1 Poll taxes										■												
	7.2 Stamp taxes (a)								◢		◢												
	7.3 Other taxes not elsewhere classified (a)								◢		◢												
REVENUE – CURRENT – NONTAX	8.1 Surpluses of departmental enterprises (e)	◢																			◢	◢	
	8.2 Property income from public enterprises																				■		
	8.3 Other property income																				■		
	9 Admin. fees, charges, nonindustrial sales		■																				
	10 Fines and forfeits																■						
	12 Other nontax revenue (f)												◢	◢			◢					◢	
REVENUE – CAPITAL	13 Sales of fixed capital assets (f)																					■	
	14 Sales of stocks (f)																					■	
	15 Sales of land & intangible assets (f)																					■	
	16.1 Capital transfers from nongov. resdnts																			■			
	16.2 Capital transfers from nongov. abroad																			■			
GRANTS	17.1 Current grants from abroad															■							
	17.2 Capital grants from abroad																		■				
	18.1 Current grants from other levls of gov.														■								
	18.2 Capital grants from other levls of gov.																		■				
	19.1 Current grants from supran'l authorits.															■							
	19.2 Capital grants from supran'l authorits.																		■				
	SNA items not in GFS items above (g,h,i)	■	■									■			■	■	■		■	■			
	Total																						

(a) Paid by business vs. nonbusiness. (b) Differing current-capital distinction. (c) Detail of breakdown.
(d) Paid on imports vs. domestic products. (e) Gross in SNA. (f) Includes receipts shown as negative payments in SNA.
(g) Includes imputations. (h) Consolidation differences. (i) In-kind transactions. (j) Includes cancellation of debt.

Table 6.2.   GFS-*SNA* bridge table expenditure, lending minus repayments, financing

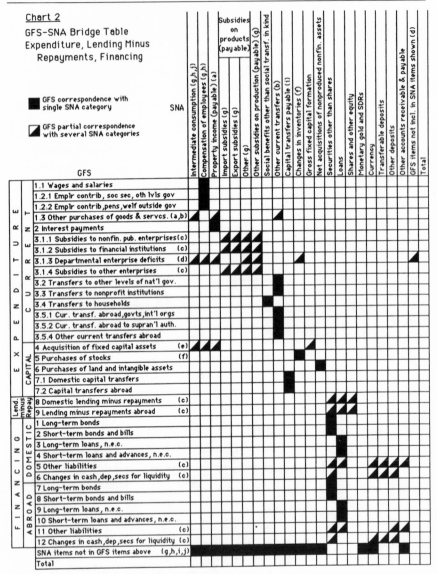

(a) Includes rent on leased or rental lands. (b) Includes net casualty insurance premiums. (c) Detail of breakdown.
(d) Shown gross in SNA. (e) Includes own-account capital formation. (f) Shown net in SNA. (g) Includes transactions in kind.
(h) Includes imputations. (i) Includes assumption and cancellation of debt. (j) Reflects receipts shown as negative payments.

the central bank and other depository corporations should reveal a key financial indicator: the central bank's and other banks' lending to the government and to other public sector institutions, which can be an important source of inflationary pressures. In consolidated accounts for the entire public sector such lending would be eliminated in consolidation.

SNA 1993 does not discuss, however, the relationship between national accounts concepts and the most widely watched indicator of government performance: the overall deficit or surplus. This indicator measures the extent to which revenue and grants received cover not only expenditures but also the considerable volume of lending some governments undertake in addition to expenditures. Though a significant element in a number of countries, government lending is not discussed other than in the general classification of financial assets and liabilities for all sectors. An approximate measure of a government's overall deficit or surplus can be derived from the SNA financial account by subtracting from the government's net incurrence of liabilities its net acquisition of monetary gold and SDRs, currency and deposits, and other accounts receivable.

6.11. Conclusion

Economists too frequently take for granted the ingenuity and persistence that have gone into measuring government in the alien framework of market-priced, transaction-based production, and consumption while keeping, or indeed shaping, a relationship with the popular conception of what government does. SNA 1993 has carried these efforts further. It has refined the fine lines distinguishing units carrying out business-like activities from units carrying out government-like activities. It has provided the extra flexibility to accommodate appropriate groupings of units within government. It has incorporated in its tax classifications the categories widely used in public finance analysis and has provided added flexibility to meet other needs of public finance analysis.

Some issues, such as valuation, remain for future research, and the usefulness and feasibility of the SNA 1993's innovations will be demonstrated only in their implementation. The bringing together of these changes, while maintaining the integral position of government in the overall national accounts, however, must be viewed as a considerable achievement.

Notes

1. Source references are to paragraphs in *SNA 1993* unless otherwise indicated. References beginning with *A* are to annexes.

DISCUSSION OF CHAPTER 6

Utz-Peter Reich

Given the enormous volume of *SNA 1993*, it will be difficult to convince the ordinary statistician of the need to take the time off his daily duties and work his way through it. Levin's paper offers a useful summary for those who work on the government sector. Statistical offices are generally not organized by the different types of accounts defined in the system but follow rather the structure of the economy providing the data for them. In this way there will usually be one department responsible for all accounts of the government sector, which requires that the recommendations pertaining to the work of this group are consolidated from all over the 700 pages of the new book. Levin has done the job of collecting this information for the professional user of the *SNA* in a specific area, an effort that will enhance the application of the new system.

Levin has placed less effort on a critical evaluation of what has been achieved in the domain. Such evaluation is necessarily subjective, but it can also help the user to come to grips with the manual because the points raised may be of general interest, and controversial discussion is the first step toward refinement. To take up this part of a reviewing process will be the task of the following pages. In doing so we will keep to the order of affairs set out in Levin's paper, reserving the right to curtail the argument at some point or to introduce new ones where necessary.

The first point addressed is valuation. Valuing an output that has no value in the strict market sense of the term is a theoretical paradox deeply engraved in our system of national accounts. As economists we are trained to believe that there is only one mechanism for determining value and that this is the market. In this context the value of government output is zero. Government output is a free good. As statisticians we are forced to assign a value to government output, and we resort to the notion of cost. As a consequence domestic product at market prices includes government output valued at cost, a clear logical inconsistency. The new *SNA* has inherited it from the old one in all its bluntness.

One consequence of this situation is the need to address a challenge to traditional value theory. Under the assumption that the force driving the statistician into a logical contradiction is not virtual but corresponds to a necessity caused by the rules in which modern economies are organized— namely, the principles of a mixed economy—one wonders how value theory can ignore this fact and continue to define value year after year as an operation only of markets. The theory of value must be revised if a matching between it, the national accounts, and their object (the total economy) is to be attained. This, however, is not a task of the *SNA*, and we pass over the issue here.

More of a problem of the system is contained in the list of nonmarket items named by Levin where valuation is oriented toward market price, as opposed to cost: the acquisition of unfinished structures, own-account construction costs, work-in-progress costs, and cultivated asset work-in-progress costs. Levin draws attention to the existence of these two valuation procedures, side by side, and implicitly lets us know that the reason that some items are valued this way and some the other way has not been worked out very well but has been left "to future research." Generally, in the system, output produced for final use is nonmarket but should be valued at market prices of comparable goods; all other non-market output should be valued at cost. The latter includes government output. As a result, Levin says—government output is undervalued be-cause it omits the difference between price and cost—namely, net operating surplus. This conclusion is not convincing, for it entails a systematic contradiction.

As pointed out above, the national accounts employ two concepts of value. The problem is to keep them apart from each other and consistent within each of their spheres of application. If, on the one hand, value is defined by markets, it includes net operating surplus but excludes all nonmarket output (or includes it at a value of zero). Thus, under the definition of market value, cost valuation of nonmarket output is too high. If, on the other hand, value is defined as the sum of costs, market prices are too high. The concept of cost is applicable equally to nonmarket and to market output. If as an ingenious device we measure nonmarket output by basing it on the concept of value at cost, no theoretical reason prevents us from being consistent and valuing all production on this base. This is not done in practice, of course, but it would be a theoretically consistent solution of the valuation problem. It is realized partially in the national accounts within the concept of national product at factor cost, which is used within the production approach but not the expenditure approach. If it were, it would mean consistent valuation across the board. And in it the valuation of government at cost is just right, as it would be for all market output. There is still a small difference. In its present definition the concept of factor cost includes operating surplus of market production, but if the meaning of the term cost were realized, it would exclude it, at least in as much as pure profit—that is, income not attributable to a factor is concerned. Thus what one can criticize about the system is that the concepts of market value and of factor cost have not been worked out in their last consequence and distinction, but the statement that cost value is too low is shortsighted in respect of the implications of a rule of valuation for the economic circuit as a whole.

Levin's example of the bus service, focusing on the cost of capital, is misleading. Interest is not a cost in the national accounts. It is a distributive transaction that distributes value added between owners, but there is no product corresponding to it. If there were, interest payments could be treated as sales and all FISIM problems would disappear. In economic theory, that is true: interest is a cost, but again the discrepencay between this and the national accounts' view of the matter should be reflected in the first before compatibility can be hoped for. In addition, the example does not even hold for the private sector. Not all companies borrow their capital; many run without the imputed interest that would have to be placed on the equity capital of the business owner, in theory, and to assume that all capital has the interest rate that is actually borne only by borrowed capital is not the statistician's business.

Turning from production to use, Mr. Levin takes up the new distinction between individual and collective services provided by government as his second point. The idea is beautiful and simple and solves an old controversy that has been with the national accounts ever since the introduction of the government sector, best known as the *Economica* debate between Kuznets and Hicks. However, speaking as one of the authors from whose research the operationalization of the idea was generated originally (Reich, 1986, table 3), one can only express disappointment at the manner in which it has been executed in the revision. Due to a dogmatic misunderstanding of the rule that income must always be equal to consumption and saving, the development of the consumption concept was misused to develop new income concepts without reflecting or being scared away by the consequences this has on many a traditional concept of the system. Levin's remark that this artificial balancing has "necessitated a number of previously unnecessary counterfactual conventions" is a comment in this direction made by an impartial observer.

It was at Gouvieux in France where a truly Cartesian discovery caught the minds of the participants of the Seventeenth IARIW General Conference—namely, the distinction between consumption and consumption expenditures. Simple as it was, all of a sudden, it made "les choses claires et distinctes." Jean Pêtre (1982) presented the idea in a careful and thorough paper on "the treament in the national accounts of goods and services for individual consumption produced, distributed or paid for by government." Cumbersome as its title was, it nevertheless separated three kinds of government outlays that can clearly be distinguished theoretically and in practice. The paper was accepted at once by the public. It did not say that because of this distinction income concepts would have to be revised. It did, however, include ameliorations of which not a trace is found in the SNA. It proved that government purchases must be separated into goods distributed and those used for intermediate consumption so that the traditional equalization of purchases with intermediate consumption is wrong not only for the reason of changes in stocks. And it made the point that some of government output might be input in other sectors of the economy and thus not part of final consumption at all. This, too, has not been answered in the SNA. Thus in the SNA 1993 distinction of individual consumption only half of the fruits of the discussion that led to the revision of this variable have been reaped. The revising took so long that the public forgot.

The distinction between industries and other producers being replaced by the more pertinent distinction between market and nonmarket producers, based on the flexible notion of an economically significant selling price, is supported by Levin, and I agree. The point serves conceptual clarification. In a similar way, the exclusion from government of market-producing institutional units with complete accounts, and their classification in the nonfinancial corporations sector as public nonfinancial corporations refines the distinction between these two fundamental categories of producers.

According to Mr. Levin, the separation of government and monetary functions has come out in the new system, while the treatment of government employee pension funds has improved. Providing for two possible ways of classifying social security funds—one inside and one outside the general government—makes the system adaptive to different countries' conditions.

A possibly controversial issue is introduced by Levin's assessment of the treatment of transactions. The remark that "government serves as a kind of calibrated mirror, in which some operations of other sectors are revealed and measured" is a nice and pointed statement of the role of government in our economy. But the asymmetries noted in respect of this relationship are not perfectly analyzed. Levin goes over the different stages at which a transaction may be recorded and with some regret expects incompatibilities between government statistics, on the one hand, and the national accounts requirements, on the other, which will create a need of possibly severe adjustments. This deserves a broader comment.

In the course of the revision debate it has been recognized that the statistical substance of the national accounts are transactions. Consequently, an extra chapter about "flows, stocks and accounting rules" has been incorporated in the publication as a theoretical guideline for what is to follow. A subchapter of it is devoted to the time of recording. This text is not without flaws. Given the diversity of times of recording found in the statistical material, it is first of all necessary to define a theoretical landmark, irrespective of its eventual realization. This geometrical point should have one quality—precision. Unfortunately, this has not been achieved. Read the text: "Distributive transactions are recorded at the moment the related claims arise. As a result, for example, compensation of employees, interest, rent on land, social contributions and benefits are all registered in the period during which the amounts payable are built up" (para. 3.99). Two times of recording have been lumped together in this statement.

There is one stage when a claim comes into existence. This is the moment at which the creditor obtains a legal obligation of the debtor, on the basis of which he can sue if needed. In practice, this is when the bill is written and received by the debtor with a warning to pay within fourteen days of notice or similarly. In *SNA 1968* the claim is due without penalty, which describes this stage very well. The other time of recording is when the economic value from which the claim is to be satisfied "accrues" or "is built up." This, as the slight slip in language shows, is not a definite point in time but is some small period that is not easily quantified. It is of analytical interest, of course, to find out the activity that is behind a certain claim, but it is not precisely measurable. Leaving aside, for the moment, the issue of whether the change from the old *SNA* point of view of the legal time to the new point of view of the economic time was wise, it must be must be pointed out that in the statement quoted above the two have not clearly been distentangled. This blurs the concept of transaction and will undoubtedly lead to a multitude of different times of recording being pursued in constructing the accounts and to corresponding discrepancies.

It may be said in defense of the quoted text that the small obliqueness in expression is overruled by the general recommendation found in the chapter to value all transactions at the time of accrual (para. 3.91). This is a significant change from the old system that has not been discussed in public. Let it at least be argued now. It is at variance with other chapters of the system. Thus, in the chapter on the production account, the old point of view is stated. "The times at which sales are to be recorded are when the receivables and payables are created: that is when the ownership of the goods passes from the producer to the purchaser or when the services are provided to the purchaser" (para. 6.54). Again we find a mix of criteria here because the creation of a receivable is not identical to the change of ownership in the corresponding good or to the time of the provision of the service, but we take it that the first criterion is the dominant one, at least in respect of transactions as a legal phenomenon. In any case, nothing is said here about accrual.

The argument that only the time the claim arises legally is the correct time of recording of transactions is actually quite simple. It is a direct consequence of their definition. A transaction we know is given when a claim and a liability are created between two institutional units. Nothing is more natural than to record the time of this creation as the time of the transaction. This was the early naive approach to national accounting, stemming from the rules of business accounting, and it still is the best rule. A derivative and more complex argument runs as follows. We have the distinction between distributive and financial transactions. Distributive transactions create claims; financial transactions create, and in paying debts, extinguish claims. A clear distinction between these two types of transaction requires the coming into existence of the claim being taken as the time of recording. Otherwise the two types could not be clearly distinguished.

Financial transactions are characterized by the fact that they leave net worth intact. They exchange a claim against another claim (for example, when buying or selling a financial asset against cash) or create a claim and a liability on both sides of the balance sheet (such as increase bank deposits by way of credit). In this way, the payment of a tax in cash reduces the cash on the equity side (claims), and it extinguishes the tax liability on the liability side of the balance sheet of the tax payer, mirrored in a complementary change in values on the government's balance sheet. Distributive (or income) transactions, in contrast, change net worth. At the time the tax falls due, the arising liability simultaneously diminishes the net worth of the citizen and increases the net wealth of the government. The ensuing payment is a financial transaction that does not touch on the initial net worth effect created by the income transaction between the two balance sheet holders. All this has nothing to do, yet, with production or other material economic activity and thus nothing with accrual. It is simply the consistent application of the rules that define a transaction in the legal sphere.

The point is explained in Table 1. A transaction takes place when the claim is due. From that date on it exists, and its value is registered in the balance sheets of owners. The tax is a distributive transaction, changing net worth at the date its claim arises (a). Its payment is a financial transaction leaving net worth unchanged and keeping the balance between currency assets and payable liabilities (b). It should be noted that for balance sheets *SNA 1993* rules: payables and receivables "should be valued for both creditors and debtors at the amount of principal the debtors are contractually obliged to pay the creditors when the obligation is extinguished" (para. 13.81). Again a hint toward maturity as the correct time of recording, and here it is for a third reason. Only at the time the claim is due is its value equal for both sides. One day later the creditor may already classify it as a bad debt if he has relevant information and write off a portion asymmetrically. The time when the claim falls due is the only time when the value of the business transaction is the same for both parties in their accounts.

Relating the tax to a corresponding economic activity is a second step that comes after the correct and consistent treatment of all property transactions in the accounts. It is highly desirable, of course, to find out from what economic activity a certain value transaction has been taken,

Table 1.   Observation of Transactions in the Balance Sheet

(a) Distributive Transaction		(b) Financial Transaction			
Payables	100	Currency	−100	Payables	−100
Change in net worth	−100			Change in net worth	0

but this date is not a certain one. It is not at all obvious, for example, whether the economic activity that relates to a tax assessed for year 1 in year 2, called for in year 3, and finally paid in year 4 is any one of theses years. It is precisely because distributive transactions—in contrast to transactions in goods and services (sales and purchases, to be precise)—are not connected directly to a specific item of production that they are difficult to relate to such activity. If we follow the principle of maturity for all transactions alike, we can at least say that the taxes of this year (in terms of claims arising) are paid from the primary income of this year (again in terms of claims arising) derived from production of this year. The interpretation is not without sense. It says that claims to the production of this year originating from production in this year (income) have been ceded to others by redistribution, all times referring to one and the same period. But if for each transaction a different time of reference is recorded—namely, when it accrued by whatever hypothesis—no reliable link can be established between them any more. The error implied in the accrual hypothesis is the idea that it may be a task to establish a cause-and-effect relationship between transactions and economic activity in the accounts. This, however, is not possible. All we can measure is temporal (and spatial) coincidence. The rest is inference and interpretation. This elaboration has broadened the issue referred to by Mr. Levin, but it explains a reason for his voiced uneasiness.

I will make a last comment in this respect. In the chapter, flows and transactions have been put under the same roof. More precisely, the distinction between consumption expenditure and consumption or between ourput sales and output production has not been carried out neatly. If it were, one would have noticed that the two types of economic flows—namely, production and consumption, on the one hand, reflecting the transformation of matter, and the legal transaction of values, on the other hand—require two different times of recording: accrual for the first, maturity for the second, their difference being reconciled in the reconciliation account.

Time of recording is also behind a point when Mr. Levin speaks about the decision of *SNA 1993* to include in government inventories all goods held by the government, in a manner symmetrical with the treatment of goods stored by the market producers. Levin feels that this innovation raises difficulties that are not explored in *SNA 1993*. The latter is true. Very little is said about it, and the reference given in A.1.74 of paragraph 6.106 does not seem to be the correct one. But the problem is not as severe as Mr. Levin makes us feel. He is afraid that the inclusion of inventories blurs the definition of the moment of time at which production is recorded. In principle this is when the activity takes place measured by compensation of employees in the government sector. A full account of inventories might be used to get away from the principle that purchases equal intermediate consumption in the government sector, and then Mr. Levin's fears might play a role, but this has not been envisaged. As it stands, *SNA 1993* includes inventories on the balance sheet, and this does not interfere with the traditional, although unsatisfactory, compilation of government production.

Concerning tax revenue classification, Mr. Levin notes the discontinued use of the term *direct-indirect tax*, with seeming indifference. A comment not on this but on the general treatment of the topic may be of interest here. It has been argued that an indirect tax is defined as one that can be passed on to other institutional units by increasing the prices of goods or services sold. This is not completely true. The distinction between direct and indirect taxes is older than the value theory explaining it in terms of price behavior (Musgrave). Its roots are in the German system of accounts, for example, where indirect taxes are defined as those that are deductible before profit. Direct taxes, by inference, are nondeductible. They are paid out of profit. In this old, prebehavioristic interpretation, the distinction between direct and indirect taxes is no less well founded than the distinction between taxes on products and on production. The criterion is what the corresponding tax law defines as the basis of proration.

That subsidies are treated as negative flows is a tradition of the *SNA*. Levin does not argue it, but it is arguable because it contradicts the principle of gross accounting. Negative flows are not real. And the reason for treating them this way is not explained. If this were correct, one might also balance social contributions against social benefits, insurance preminums against insurance claims, intermediate consumption as negative production. In short, the tradition is neither well founded nor consistently applied.

Mr. Levin closes his presentation by adding a table bridging the *SNA* and GFA, which will help the national accountant a great deal in the data transfer. It is a pity that the accompanying verbal comments have been cut short. The entries are not all self-explicative, and a memo for using the table would have greatly increased its applicability.

Mr. Levin's final assessment that *SNA 1993* will demonstrate its usefulnes in its application will find general agreement. Like its predecessor, it can be sure of its success in that it has brought together and merged an enormous amount of knowledge, skills, and last but not least, politics, and it will serve as the point of orientation for all national accounting debates to come. This applies also to the government sector.

References

Pètre, J. (1982). *The Treatment in the National Accounts of Good and Services for Individual Consumption Produced, Distributed or Paid for by Government.* Luxembourg.

Reich, U.P. (1986). "Treatment of Government Activity on the Production account". *Review of Income and Wealth* 32: 69–86.

7 FINANCIAL INTERMEDIATION AND FINANCIAL ACCOUNTS

Albert M. Teplin

This chapter describes broad-based developments in financial intermediation and the problems these developments have represented for aggregate financial accounts, and comments on the ability of the new *System of National Accounts 1993* (*SNA 1993*) (United Nations, 1993) to deal with such problems. The continued growth and greater degree of complexity of financial activity in the United States and elsewhere have been accompanied by an increase in institutions and types of transactions, which have blurred traditional classification schemes. Such changes call for continual flexibility in compiling national financial accounts. The outline for financial accounts in the new *SNA* appears to be broad enough to encompass most situations. A number of sound recommendations are made for handling specific types of financial activities. However, compilers must be careful not to make their accounts so general that much of the information useful for analysis and international comparisons will be hidden within large categories of transactions of a few large sectors.

7.1. Evolution of Financial Intermediation

The concept of financial intermediation is rather simple. It is the process of channeling funds from economic units or sectors that save to sectors in need of funds to finance their desired level of outlays. In the *System of National Accounts 1993*, financial intermediaries are described as having "as their special function the creation of a financial market that indirectly links lenders and borrowers by incurring liabilities to net lenders through taking deposits or issuing securities and providing the financial resources thus mobilized to borrowers" (para. 11.6, p. 243).

This straightforward definition is sufficient to cover the institutions and transactions in financial markets in a modern economy. Traditionally, broad studies and accounts have focused on depositories and insurance companies as intermediaries and on deposits, loans, mortgages, short-term paper, bonds, and equities as types of transactions.

The activities of depositories and insurance companies have been and continue to be captured fairly well in most national financial account. Their intermediary functions are widely understood, and the information on the financial flows through them is readily available, in large part because the institutions are monitored by government authorities; detailed statistics on assets and liabilities are usually a by-product of reports filed with regulators.

In the United States, depository institutions, in general, and commercial banks, in particular, have long been a dominant form of financial intermediary. As suggested by the definition in *SNA 1993*, these institutions typically convert deposits and funds obtained through other sources to make loans or purchase securities that finance outlays of governments and businesses. The *SNA 1993* definition of an intermediary readily incorporates specialized depositories that finance home purchases or consumer lending; such institutions in the United States exist in the form of savings and loan associations, mutual savings banks, and credit unions. Life insurance companies, another traditional type of financial intermediary, carry out a similar function, although their assets typically are bonds, mortgages, and equities of business, and their liabilities are reserves and other obligations incurred to meet the costs of payouts to policy holders.

In recent years, however, the proportion of intermediation carried out by these traditional lenders has declined. In the United States, banks now supply about 20 percent of credit market funds,[1] compared with nearly 30 percent in the 1970s. The thrift industry, which supplied close to half of all home mortgages in the 1970s, now accounts for only 15 percent of that total. Altogether, depository institutions' share of credit market funds supplied has dropped by more than fifteen percentage points over the past two decades (Figure 7.1). The proportion supplied by life insurance companies has also fallen, although by only a few percentage points.

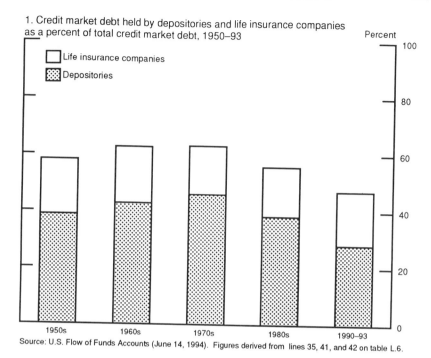

1. Credit market debt held by depositories and life insurance companies as a percent of total credit market debt, 1950–93

Source: U.S. Flow of Funds Accounts (June 14, 1994). Figures derived from lines 35, 41, and 42 on table L.6.

Figure 7.1. Credit Market Debt Held by Depositories and Life Insurance Companies as a Percent of Total Credit Market Debt, 1950–1993
Source: U.S. Flow of Funds Accounts (June 14, 1994) (figures derived from lines 35, 41, and 42 on table L.6).

The decline in the relative importance of traditional intermediaries has occurred despite a remarkable increase in the volume of financial intermediation itself. The nature of that increase can be seen by examining the ratio of total credit market assets held by all financial institutions to the total of credit market debt owed by domestic nonfinancial sectors (Figure 7.2). By this measure, financial intermediation has trended upward over most of the postwar period. At the beginning of the period the ratio was about 0.65, meaning that financial institutions held roughly sixty-five cents of credit market instruments (including those owed by financial institutions) for each dollar owed by the domestic nonfinancial sectors. Debt was also held directly by households, businesses, and governments. Foreigners, as one would expect, were not significant lenders to U.S. borrowers in the early postwar years. In the 1970s the ratio had reached about 0.9, and most recently the financial intermediaries' holdings of

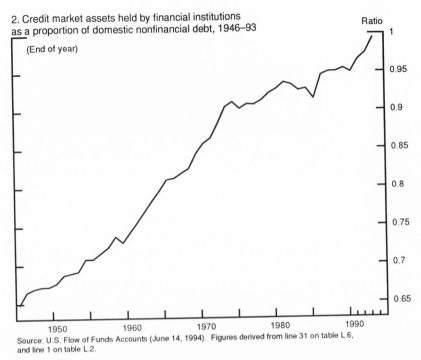

2. Credit market assets held by financial institutions
as a proportion of domestic nonfinancial debt, 1946–93

Source: U.S. Flow of Funds Accounts (June 14, 1994). Figures derived from line 31 on table L.6,
and line 1 on table L.2.

Figure 7.2.   Credit Market Assets Held by Financial Institutions as a Proportion
of Domestic Nonfinancial Debt, 1946–1993
Source: U.S. Flow of Funds Accounts (June 14, 1994) (figures derived from line 31 on table
L.6, and line 1 on table L.2).

credit market instruments has risen to close to 1.0; that is, it now about
matches the debt owed by the domestic nonfinancial sectors.[2]

Thus, compilers of financial accounts have been faced with the problem of constructing accounts with sector groupings that are inclusive of
institutions and transaction categories that intermediate outside the traditional structure. In practice this means that accounts must remain flexible
in the way sectors (or subsectors) and transaction categories are defined.
New subsectors will appear from time to time, and these may evolve into
major suppliers of credit market debt or equity capital, while the role of
other sectors will dissipate. At times, channels for financing may make it
difficult to define a sector that a new transaction flows through because
some markets do not have a well-defined intermediator. In these cases,
national accounting methods are likely to be difficult to apply.

7.2. Alternative Intermediaries and Transaction Categories

A description of financial market growth in two particular areas provides examples of the type of detail and flexibility required in the accounts. Indeed, it is the case that detail is an important element for future flexibility. The two examples that tested the comprehensiveness of the U.S. accounts were the rapid movement of funds out of deposits and into mutual funds and a stream of innovations in markets that securitized financial assets.

7.2.1. Mutual Funds

Mutual funds are open-ended investment companies that issue shares representing an interest in a portfolio of financial assets, such as stocks of other corporations, bonds, and government securities. The funds continuously issue and redeem shares, and the prices of shares fluctuate with the market value of the underlying assets. From the standpoint of financial intermediation, mutual fund shares provide households and other investors with a direct substitute for deposits (as well as for direct holdings of the instruments held by the funds), albeit with different risk and liquidity characteristics. Although mutual funds are not a new investment vehichle—they have been offered in the United States since the 1920s—their popularity increased substantially in the 1980s. Mutual fund holdings of credit market debt rose from less than 0.4 percent of the total outstanding in 1979 to 2.6 percent by 1990. Growth of the funds jumped further over the 1991 to 1993 period, and mutual funds came to hold nearly 5 percent of credit market assets before growth slowed in 1994. Even more dramatic growth has occurred in the proportion of the total value of corporate equities held by mutual funds, from 3 percent in 1979 to 12 percent by early 1994.

The underlying economic causes and possible implications for the increased role of mutual funds as intermediaries are discussed elsewhere (see Mack, 1993; Investment Company Institute, 1994). The lesson of this rapid rise for aggregate financial accounts is the need for clear distinctions to be made among nontraditional financial intermediaries and likewise for distinctions to be made within certain transaction categories—in this case, equity shares. Moreover, because much of the increase in shares has come from deposit accounts, a sector that was once of minor importance has begun to loom large for analysis of the growth of money. Also, the emergence of mutual funds poses risks to households from changes in value of their financial holdings, complicates the process of financing business investment, and raises questions about coordinating the increased availability of a larger pool of savers for cross-sector investment. The rapid change in the intermediation process can be captured only if the structure contains sufficient detail. If the accounts combine several small institutions into larger groups, or combine equity shares held by mutual funds into a broader overall equity asset category, the accounts likely will be less useful for analysis.

Some expansion of this latter point may be in order. Shares issued by mutual funds are equity investments, and, as noted, their return is determined by the performance of the portfolio of financial assets acquired by the fund. Since mutual funds invest proceeds of share issuance in equity issues of other corporations as well as corporate and government bonds, the account must be sufficiently detailed to permit disentanglement of these collective investments. Otherwise, all equity shares of mutual funds would have to be combined with all other equities, with the combination representing some double counting. If the equities of the funds are excluded, there would be some undercounting of total equity investments undertaken. Knowing the mutual fund portfolio investments in stocks as distinct from bonds allows for estimating and correcting for over- or undercounting of financial transactions in the aggregate system.

7.2.2. Securitization of Assets

As to the second area of change in financial markets, the development of securitized financial instruments—that is, transactions in securities backed by pools of other financial instruments—provides an example of the increased complexity of the intermediation process and consequent difficulty for presentation in national economic accounts. An early manifestation of the securitization process occurred in the U.S. mortgage markets. As noted earlier, in the 1970s most home mortgages were held by thrift institutions, a form of depository. Banks and insurance companies accounted for a large proportion of the remainder. Over the 1970s, a secondary market for mortgage assets was fostered by the creation of two corporations chartered by the federal government—the Federal National Mortgage Association (FNMA) and the Federal Home Loan Mortgage Corporation (FHMLC). FNMA, which raises funds in both credit and equity markets, was initially little more than a buyer of loans originated by traditional intermediaries and mortgage companies, but both FNMA and FHMLC later experimented with repackaging the mortgage assets, making them attractive to a wide variety of investors. Also important for the development of the secondary market was the issuance of mortgage securities, whose principal and interest payments were guaranteed by an agency of the federal government. The Government National Mortgage Association (GNMA) mortgage-backed security (MBS) program began in 1969 and was a forerunner to similar security issuance by FNMA, FHMLC, and several other institutions.

Accounting for the growth of the secondary mortgage market created a number of problems for the U.S. financial accounts. Although it was a simple matter to add a subsector to record the holdings of FNMA and FHMLC, accounting for MBSs was more problematic. MBSs have many characteristics of federal government securities (through their explicit or implicit guarantee), but they are not a direct liability of the federal government or of any clearly defined financial institution.[3] Also, the mortgages underlying the securities were removed from the books of the originators, typically depository institutions or mortgage bankers, once the securities were issued. Somewhat amorphous institutional structures—special-purpose trusts that administered the securities—were now the holders.

To record the activity, the U.S. financial flow accounts were changed to carry a "sector" called "federally related mortgage pools." Creation of this new sector, whose liabilities are mortgage pool securities, has allowed analysts to trace the growth of the secondary market, although information on origination of the underlying mortgages is not in the accounts.

In more recent years, further layers of securitization, both inside and outside the mortgage market, have developed. Mortgage pools themselves are now securitized and derivative instruments backed by a portion of the pools are sold as bonds. There has been securitization of credit card receivables, business trade credit, business loans, and even student loans. As a result, U.S. financial accounts were changed again in the late 1980s to add another sector, now called issuers of asset-backed securities (ABS), to record the flows into and out of these newer derivative instruments. The dollar volume of financial intermediation occurring through the federally related mortgage pool and ABS sectors grew from virtually nothing a decade ago to nearly a quarter of all domestic nonfinancial borrowing by the end of 1993. The important role they play in home mortgage lending is shown in Figure 7.3. Although flows have fluctuated in recent years, the amounts have remained a large part of total activity. In terms of growth of intermediation discussed earlier in the chapter, all types of credit market assets held by this rather loose set of institutional

3. Home mortgage lending, 1970–93

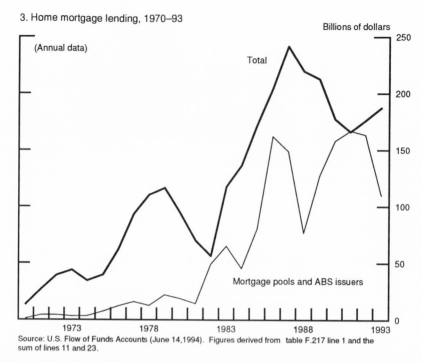

Source: U.S. Flow of Funds Accounts (June 14,1994). Figures derived from table F.217 line 1 and the sum of lines 11 and 23.

Figure 7.3.   Home Mortgage Lending, 1970–1993
Source: U.S. Flow of Funds Accounts (June 14, 1994) (figures derived from table F.217 line 1 and the sum of lines 11 and 23).

structures—federally related mortgage pools and the ABS—are now about 15 percent of domestic nonfinancial debt, accounting for a large portion of the rise in the ratio shown in Figure 7.2.

7.3. *SNA 1993* Financial Account and the Treatment of Financial Evolution

SNA 1993 describes the financial account in Chapter 11 (pp. 142–261). A general discussion of the role of financial transactions within the total accounting framework is provided, noting that many transactions recorded in this account take place "entirely within the financial account" in large part because of exchanges of one type of asset (or liability) for another. Most of the relevant material on sectorization for the financial accounts appears earlier in Chapter 4, Section D. In that chapter, *SNA 1993* lists a wide variety of possible institutional arrangements; the generality of the descriptions allow for considerable flexibility.

Importantly, the financial account chapter notes that changes in volume and value that do not involve a transaction between financial units are recorded outside the financial account, in accounts that reconcile balance sheet changes due to prices and changes due to other factors. In theory, this designation is commendable. However, in practice, separating such information from available data is difficult. Many financial flows are estimated from reported changes in institutional balance sheets, and only through indirect measurement, such as the application of price indexes or off-balance sheet information, can a separation of the type indicated be made. *SNA 1993* provides little guidance on how one would implement the called for separation of flows.

On the other hand, *SNA 1993* clarifies and makes recommendations for several practices that have posed problems for compilers and users in recent years and frequently create inconsistences in international comparisons. Particularly noteworthy are the following two:

- *Defeasance*, a practice in which a debtor matches a liability with an asset and then removes both from the balance sheet, should not result in a reduction in a reduction in assets and liabilities in the aggregate financial account. In practice such actions may be difficult to capture, but the principle in *SNA 1993* is sound because assets and liabilities may not match across sectors. Frequently, the recognition that defeasance is a common activity for a subsector will help the compiler resolve discrepancies in asset and liability flows for a particular set of transactions.
- *Financial leases*, in general, are to be treated as financial claims. Leasing activity has grown as a substitute for collateralized loans in recent years. *SNA 1993* appears to follow the practice most common among compilers by treating the lease as a loan asset or liability for the relevant sector. The only problem here is that combining leases and loans may lose a detail of interest. But the important part of the recommendation is that leases belong in the financial account.

SNA 1993 is a bit thin on guidance for treatment of the newer complex financial arrangements presented by asset-backed securities, although the *SNA* clearly recognizes such securities. It states that "the new assets should be classified as securities other than shares. The previously existing assets will continue to be reported on the balance sheet of the institutional units that hold them" (para. 11.75, p. 254). The latter part of this statement is unclear for two reasons. First, as noted above, the original assets are removed from the balance sheet of the originator, and it is unclear what the "continue to be reported" refers to here. The interpretation should be that the assets belong with the issuer of the new asset-backed security. Second, the *SNA* gives no guidance on what to do in the cases noted above where the securitized assets are frequently not held by a clearly defined institutional unit.

More generally, the discussion of transaction categories in *SNA 1993* notes that maturity should be deemphasized as a basis for classification and that one should not rely on functional categories. We are then left with a description of seven main categories. These categories are broad enough to incorporate what is currently enumerated in most financial accounts, but one is left with a feeling that the list lacks a theory. Some categories are very specific ("monetary gold and SDRs"), while others are general ("securities other than shares"). No doubt the *SNA 1993* authors felt the same frustration as compilers concerning categorization of the growing variety of financial instruments.

On balance, *SNA 1993* does recognize the importance of change in financial markets; as the preface to the document notes, "It establishes criteria for the delineation of the financial corporate sector and for the classification of financial instruments in light of the many innovations in this field" (p. xxxiii). Moreover, in its introductory chapter, *SNA 1993* states, "Only by disaggregation into sectors and sub-sectors is it possible to observe the interactions between the different parts of the economy that need to be measured and analyzed for purposes of policy-making" (para. 1.13, p. 3). These statements at the outset of the document clearly were in focus for the description of the financial account in Chapter 11. However, the generality of the transaction categories and the problem areas dealt with in the chapter can leave the reader with a feeling that specificity is not as essential as form. But in the end, the practitioner is left with a valuable framework that has the potential of flexibility and analytical usefulness.

Acknowledgments

The author wishes to thank Elizabeth M. Fogler and Robert L. Rewald for their comments and insights. The analyses and conclusions set forth are those of the author and do not necessarily indicate concurrence by the

Board of Governors, the Federal Reserve Banks, or members of their staffs.

Notes

1. Figures cited in this chapter are taken from the U.S. Flow of Funds Accounts, Board of Governors of the Federal Reserve System, Z.1 quarterly statistical release, June 14, 1994. A detailed description of these accounts is found in Board of Governors of the Federal Reserve System (1993).
   Credit market funds include eight broad categories of financial instruments: U.S. government securities, tax-exempt (municipal) securities, corporate and foreign bonds, mortgages, consumer credit, bank loans (other than mortgages and consumer credit), open market paper, and other loans. It excludes equities and mutual fund shares.

2. In 1993, the ratio of credit market debt outstanding to *all* sector holdings was about 1.29. At first blush, a ratio greater than one may seem incongruous. However, a ratio larger than one is indicative of the added complexity of the intermediation process, and particularly of the growth of securitization that is discussed later in this chapter and the increase in debt issued by financial and foreign institutions in the United States.

3. Indeed, financial institutions typically reported MBS holdings as federal government securities. It has only been in recent years that U.S. accounts have been able to separate these holdings from U.S. Treasury securities.

DISCUSSION OF CHAPTER 7

John C. Dawson

I wish to comment on three aspects of the treatment of finance in *SNA 1993* and Albert Teplin's paper. The first is a general comment on the importance of finance in *SNA 1993* relative to its predecessors. The second and third deal with analytical problems raised by the evolutionary developments Teplin lays out and by the financial transaction classifications in Chapter 11.

Finance in *SNA 1993*

My sense is that finance has finally arrived with *SNA 1993*.

Looking back over the SNA development we can recall that *SNA 1953* contained little in the way of finance. Its standard accounts had no finance sector; its net borrowing concept was undefined. Domestic borrowing and lending were essentially consolidated out of the system, and we were left only with the ultimate "finance" of sector saving.

SNA 1968 made major strides in the incorporation of finance. The deconsolidation of the national income and outlay and national capital finance accounts each included a separate financial institutions account.

And the sector capital finance accounts each detailed the sector's net lending into changes in the various financial assets and liabilities. Furthermore, these claims were defined and classified. In effect the set of capital finance accounts built the flow-of-funds matrix into the system.

Nevertheless, finance remained very much in the background. The *SNA 1968* text was focused on the system as a basis for input-output analysis and quantity-price comparisons. The system as a basis for financial analysis was simply not discussed. Even the basic description of the capital finance accounts was cursory, occupying only a few paragraphs.

In *SNA 1993* finance is moved considerably back toward the center of analysis. The integrated economic accounts—the core system—contain a full set of sector accounts and these include a separate sector for financial corporations (see Table 2.8). The sector capital finance accounts also appear in this core system, each divided into a capital account and a financial account. So these parts of *SNA 1968* are here made more central and financial intermediation is explicitly presented in the accounts. In *SNA 1993*, furthermore, the core system continues on with an analysis of nontransaction changes in all balance sheet items to provide a complete analysis of the movement from opening to closing balance sheets. So balance sheets are now an integral part of the system. It should be added that parallel to the expansion of this system toward input-output analysis is a further detailed financial analysis.[1]

The text of *SNA 1993* also deals more extensively with finance, providing chapters on the financial account and the balance sheet. The functions of finance, especially financial intermediation, are made explicit. And the nature and uses of financial analysis are suggested.

In my view these changes provide *SNA 1993* with a much improved balance in its treatment of finance relative to the other major aspects of national accounting.

Financial Intermediation and Financial Layering

Teplin's charts document a situation in the Unites States where (1) the absorption of claims by the financial sectors is growing faster than the issue of claims by the nonfinancial sectors and (2) the traditional financial institutions (banks, thrifts, insurance and pension funds) are absorbing a declining share of the claims acquired by all financial institutions, being replaced by the innovating finance n.e.c., sector. And because the borrowing of the newer nontraditional financial institutions uses the same types of credit instruments as do the nonfinancial sectors, the financial sector as a whole has become a major borrower alongside the nonfinancial sectors in the main credit market arena.

Teplin's discussion of the examples of this evolution is an instructive one, suggesting how little guidance in these matters is provided by the SNA. I find the adaptations made in the U.S. accounts fully satisfactory.[2] However, as an analyst I find this evolution troublesome with respect to the concept of intermediation used both by Teplin and SNA 1993.

In simpler times when only the traditional intermediaries existed, the claims issue of the financial sector consisted of instruments that were specialized to these intermediaries (currency, deposits, insurance, and pension reserves) and that were entirely taken up by the nonfinancial sectors as ultimate lenders. In this case we could infer that financial-sector lending necessarily was headed to the ultimate borrowing of the nonfinancial sectors alongside the direct flow from ultimate lenders. The total acquisition of financial assets by the finance sector was an unambiguous measure of the volume of intermediation.

Today, however, much of the credit advanced by the financial sector is going to finance the financial sector itself. The extent of the problem can be illustrated with U.S. flow data for Teplin's financial market group, credit market funds. In 1993 credit market borrowing by the nonfinancial sectors (including rest-of-world) was $640 billion. The financial sectors advanced 832 into this market but also obtained 240 from it, a net advance of 592. The remainder of the lending was the 47 of the nonfinancial sectors.[3] So how much intermediation took place? Teplin and SNA 1993 would say that the 832 increase in the credit market assets of the financial sectors all represented intermediation. But clearly not all the 832 went to finance ultimate borrowing, which in this market was 640. Much of the 832 was financing the 240 that came back to the financial sector itself. But intermediation implies obtaining funds from ultimate lenders and providing funds to ultimate borrowers. Our unambiguous measure of intermediation has disappeared.

It is true that as a financial system develops we can expect to see debt layering in the intermediary process. Teplin's cases are examples: issuers of asset-backed securities may acquire home mortgages from households and issue corporate bonds that are then taken up by other financial institutions. And we can envision mutual funds replacing households as the immediate buyers of corporate equities and in turn issuing mutual fund shares to them. Adding stages to the intermediary process adds layers of financial assets and liabilities to the financial sector. But, as perhaps in these cases, the layering may not add to the volume of funds advanced to ultimate borrowing.

Intermediation is not an end in itself. Its purpose is to serve the legitimate needs of ultimate borrowers and ultimate lenders. We need to know how much of the rapid growth of the financial sectors—the "intermediation" of *SNA 1993*—actually does these things and how much is a mere churning of claims or worse. Is some of our new "intermediation" simply adding profitable layers of unhealthy speculation to the financial system? To make such distinctions we will need some new measurement conventions for intermediation.

Sector-Oriented Transaction Tyes

Section F in Chapter 11 asserts that a sector's financial account (see Table 11.1) with net lending and borrowing analyzed into the standard types of transaction (see Table 11.2) does not in general tell us *who* is financing the sector or *who* is being financed by it. Section F also seems to imply that the to whom/from whom facts will be available if we estimate the "detailed flow-of-funds" of Tables 11.3a and 11.3b. In my view these two propositions are substantially misleading.

It is true that finding out who is financing whom is a central task of financial analysis. To see what is involved consider the situation when Sector B finances Sector A. What we observe statistically is, for example, A's increased liability for some type of transaction (such as securities) and B's increased financial asset holding for the same type. If this type of claim is only issued by A and only acquired by B, we can infer that B financed A. But if several sectors issue this type of claim and several sectors acquire it, we often cannot infer from the data that B was financing A. If in addition this claim has a secondary market, the inference is even more difficult. In fact the analyst faces a spectrum of cases lying between these extremes in which we may or may not be able to infer the to whom/from whom identification. Our techniques remain ad hoc.

Our best aid for intersectoral financial tracing is the existence of what I will call *sector-oriented transaction types*. These are transaction types defined with a sector connection so that they are issued by only one or two sectors or are acquired by only one or two sectors. This type of transaction is very common in existing flow-of-funds systems. In the U.S. accounts, for example, we have had for many years U.S. government securities, state and local government securities, home mortgages, consumer credit, and bank loans, n.e.c. In the areas discussed by Teplin we now find mutual fund shares and government-sponsored agency issues. None of these transaction types appear in the standard classification table

(Table 11.2), and so we have to view these as subtypes under Securities (F.3) or Loans (F.4).[4] The liberal presence of such sector oriented transaction types enables the analyst to accomplish a good deal of to whom/from whom identification *with the standard classification scheme of Table 11.2*. However, as a principal of transaction type classification, sector identification is not mentioned in Section E of Chapter 11.

Let us now consider what is added if we have available the detailed flow-of-funds data of Tables 11.3a and 11.3b. In the simple example above we would now know that sector B's new security asset is a debt of sector A and that A's increased security liability is owed to sector B. Even if other sectors issued or acquired these securities, we could now infer that B had financed A, provided there was no secondary market in the securities. If there was a secondary market and, for example, sector C had liquidated its holdings to sector B, our previous to whom/from whom identification would be in error.

Although the creditor-debtor identification of the detailed tables would no doubt help us with sector-to-sector tracing, the estimation of Tables 11.3a and 11.3b might well be very difficult. What needs to be seen is that sector-oriented transaction types perform essentially the same service. If the transaction type in the above example were U.S. government securities, we would know that the U.S. government was the creditor for every asset holder of this type and financial tracing of who finances the government might well be feasible. Similarly, an examination of bank loan, n.e.c. liabilities can reveal whom the banks are financing. Since such sector-oriented transaction types can be extensively used within the standard scheme of transaction types, to whom/from whom financial tracing is far more feasible than Chapter 11 suggests.

Notes

1. This cross-classification of financial transaction types by creditor-debtor sector first appeared as Table 24 in *SNA 1968*. I believe we owe this table to Stan Sigel.

2. It is illustrative of the problem to find in Teplin's Figure 7.3 analysis of the home mortgage market that one of his intermediaries is sectored in finance (the ABS sector) and the other is not (federally related mortgage pools).

3. The data are all from Board of Governors of the Federal Reserve System, Z.1 quarterly statistical release, June 14, 1994 (Table F.6, lines 2 plus 10, line 11, line 31, and lines 24 plus 29 plus 30).

4. Table 11.2 does contain currency, transferable deposits, and net equity of households in life insurance reserves and pension funds, all of which have sector connections.

8 PRICE AND VOLUME MEASURES IN THE *SYSTEM OF NATIONAL ACCOUNTS*

W.E. Diewert

8.1. Introduction

This paper is a review of Chapter 16 in the *System of National Accounts, 1993* entitled "Price and Volume Measures," which was written by Peter Hill (1993). Sections 8.2 to 8.11 below will provide a brief review of the major topics that were covered in Chapter 16 along with some references to the literature. A decision was made not to include references in the new *System of National Accounts*, but this is rather unfair to the reader who may want to explore a particular topic at greater length. Thus we hope that this paper will serve as a useful supplement to Chapter 16.

Topics that were not discussed in Chapter 16 are discussed in Section 8.12 and 8.13. Section 12 below provides an introduction to the recent literature on sources of bias in consumer price indexes, while Section 13 lists a number of price measurement and index number problems that were not considered in Chapter 16. Section 14 concludes.

We complete this section by listing some important books and surveys on index number theory. General works on index number theory include Lowe (1823), Frisch (1936), Stone (1956), Hill (1988), Turvey (1989), and Diewert (1981, 1987, 1993a). There are two main approaches to index

number theory: the test approach and the economic approach. References
to the test approach include Walsh (1901, 1921a, 1921b, 1924), Fisher
(1911, 1921, 1922), Eichhorn (1976, 1978), Eichhorn and Voeller (1976),
Balk (1992), Dalén (1992), and Diewert (1992a). References to the
economic approach to index number theory include Konüs (1924), Konüs
and Byushgens (1926), Hicks (1940, 1981), Samuelson (1947, pp. 146–
163), Allen (1949, 1975), Malmquist (1953), Pollak (1971, 1989), Afriat
(1972, 1977), Fisher and Shell (1972), Samuelson and Swamy (1974), and
Diewert (1976, 1978, 1980, 1983a, 1983b).

8.2. Values, Prices, and Quantities

In this section, we discuss Hill's definitions of price and volume indexes.
However, first we introduce some notation.[1] Suppose that the task at
hand is to construct price and volume indexes for N commodities over
$T + 1$ periods. The base period is period 0. The price, quantity, and
value of commodity i in period t is p_i^t, q_i^t, and $v_i^t \equiv p_i^t q_i^t$, respectively, for
$i = 1, \ldots, N$ and $t = 0, \ldots, T$. Hill (1993, p. 381) defined a price
(volume) index as a weighted average of the proportional changes in the
prices p_i^t/p_i^0 (quantities q_i^t/q_i^0) of a specified set of goods and services
between two periods of time. Later, Hill (1993, p. 382) regarded the price
and volume indexes between periods 0 and t as functions of the $4N$ prices
and quantities that pertain to the two periods under consideration. Thus
defining the period t vectors of prices and quantities by $p^t \equiv [p_1^t, \ldots, p_N^t]$
and $q^t \equiv [q_1^t, \ldots, q_N^t]$ for $t = 0, 1, \ldots, T$, we denote a generic price
index as $P(p^0, p^t, q^0, q^t)$ and a generic volume or quantity index as
$Q(p^0, p^t, q^0, q^t)$. It is also evident that Hill (1993, p. 382) assumed that
the price and volume indexes should satisfy the following conservation of
value equation:[2]

$$P(p^0, p^t, q^0, q^t)Q(p^0, p^t, q^0, q^t) = p^t \cdot q^t / p^0 \cdot q^0. \qquad (8.1)$$

By inspecting equation (8.1), we see that the price and volume indexes,
P and Q, represent decompositions of the value change between periods
0 and t, $p^t \cdot q^t / p^0 \cdot q^0$, into a price change component P and a quantity
change component Q.

Hill (1993, p. 381) introduced the rather odd term *volume index* in
place of the more usual term *quantity index* to distinguish his definition of
a volume index (as a weighted average of quantity relatives) from the sum
of the quantities, $\Sigma_{i=1}^N q_i^t$. It appears that Hill wanted to distinguish what is
normally called a *bilateral quantity index* $Q(p^0, p^t, q^0, q^t)$ from what

Eichhorn (1978, pp. 140–146) called a *quantity level*, which is a function $Q^*(p^t, q^t)$ that simply aggregates the quantities $q^t \equiv [q^t_1, \ldots, q^t_N]$ that pertain to a single period t.

We turn now to Hill's discussion of bilateral price and volume indexes in the time-series context.

8.3. Intertemporal Index Numbers of Prices and Volumes

In this section, Hill (1993, pp. 381–384) discussed the problems involved in choosing functional forms for the price and volume indexes P and Q in the context of aggregating up the microeconomic price and quantity information that pertains to a subset of the economy under consideration for time periods 0 and t. Hill noted that the most commonly used price indexes are the Laspeyres (1871) and Paasche (1874) price indexes defined as follows:

$$P_L(p^0, p^t, q^0, q^t) \equiv p^t \cdot q^0 / p^0 \cdot q^0 = \Sigma^N_{i=1} s^0_i(p^t_i/p^0_i), \qquad (8.2)$$

$$P_P(p^0, p^t, q^0, q^t) \equiv p^t \cdot q^t / p^0 \cdot q^t = [\Sigma^N_{i=1} s^t_i(p^t_i/p^0_i)^{-1}]^{-1}, \qquad (8.3)$$

where $s^t_i \equiv p^t_i q^t_i / p^t \cdot q^t$ is the share of commodity i in period t expenditure on the commodities. Notice that the price indexes defined by (8.2) and (8.3) can be viewed as expenditure share weighed arithmetic and harmonic averages of the price ratios p^t_i/p^0_i, facts first demonstrated by Walsh (1901, p. 559) and Fisher (1911, pp. 397–398, 1922, p. 60). Hill also noted that the two most commonly used quantity or volume indexes are the Paasche and Laspeyres quantity indexes defined by

$$Q_P(p^0, p^t, q^0, q^t) \equiv p^t \cdot q^t / p^t \cdot q^0 = [\Sigma^N_{i=1} s^t_i(q^t_i/q^0_i)^{-1}]^{-1}, \qquad (8.4)$$

$$Q_L(p^0, p^t, q^0, q^t) \equiv p^0 \cdot q^t / p^0 \cdot q^0 = \Sigma^N_{i=1} s^0_i(q^t_i/q^0_i). \qquad (8.5)$$

Note that the indexes defined by (8.4) and (8.5) can be viewed as weighted harmonic and arithmetic averages of the quantity ratios q^t_i/q^0_i, $i = 1, \ldots, N$.

Hill (1993, p. 382) observed that the product of the Laspeyres price index and the Paasche quantity index and the product of the Paasche price index and the Laspeyres quantity index satisfied the product test (8.1)—that is, we have

$$P_L(p^0, p^t, q^0, q^t)Q_P(p^0, p^t, q^0, q^t) = p^t \cdot q^t / p^0 \cdot q^0, \qquad (8.6)$$

$$P_P(p^0, p^t, q^0, q^t)Q_L(p^0, p^t, q^0, q^t) = p^t \cdot q^t / p^0 \cdot q^0. \qquad (8.7)$$

Hill (1993, p. 383) indicated that whenever the price and quantity relatives or ratios, p_i^t/p_i^0 and q_i^t/q_i^0, were negatively correlated (the usual case), then the Laspeyres price index would be above the Paasche price index (and vice versa for quantity indexes)—that is, we would have[3]

$$P_P(p^0, p^t, q^0, q^t) < P_L(p^0, p^t, q^0, q^t). \tag{8.8}$$

At this point, Hill (1993, p. 383) introduced the economic approach to index number theory: "From the point of view of economic theory, the observed quantities may be assumed to be functions of the prices, as specified in some utility or production function. Assuming that a consumer's expenditures are related to an underlying utility function, a cost of living index may then be defined as the ratio of the minimum expenditures required to enable a consumer to attain the same level of utility under the two sets of prices."

The above verbal definition of a cost of living index may be put into a more concrete form as follows. Let the consumer's utility function (or the producer's production function) be denoted by $f(q_1, \ldots, q_N) \equiv f(q)$. Define the consumer's *expenditure* (or the producer's *cost*) *function* C as the solution to the following cost minimization problem:

$$C(u, p) \equiv \min_q\{p \cdot q : f(q) \geq u\}, \tag{8.9}$$

where $p \equiv (p_1, \ldots, p_N)$ is a vector of positive commodity prices that the consumer (or producer) faces and u is a reference utility (or output) level that must be attained. The Konüs (1924) *price index* between periods 0 and t for reference utility (or output) level u is then defined as

$$P_K(p^0, p^t, u) \equiv C(u, p^t)/C(u, p^0). \tag{8.10}$$

Hill (1993, p. 383) went on to state that the Laspeyres price index P_L defined earlier by (8.2) provides an upper bound to the unobservable theoretical Konüs price index when the reference utility level is chosen to be the consumer's base period utility $u^0 \equiv f(q^0)$ and the Paasche price index P_P defined by (8.3) provides a lower bound to the Konüs price index when the reference utility level is chosen to be the consumer's period t level of utility $u^t \equiv f(q^t)$—that is, we have the following bounds, due originally to Konüs (1924, pp. 17–19):

$$P_K(p^0, p^t, u^0) \leq P_L(p^0, p^t, q^0, q^t), \tag{8.11}$$

$$P_K(p^0, p^t, u_t) \geq P_P(p^0, p^t, q^0, q^t). \tag{8.12}$$

Hill further noted that if preferences are homothetic (that is, the under-lying utility or aggregator[4] function is a monotonic transform of a linearly homogeneous function), then the Konüs price index $P_K(p^0, p^t, u)$ is independent of u and hence P_L and P_P will provide bounds to the underlying unobservable Konüs price index.[5]

At this point, Hill (1993, p. 384) introduced Irving Fisher's (1921, 1922) ideal price and quantity indexes, P_F and Q_F, which are the geometric means of the corresponding Paasche and Laspeyres price and quantity indexes:

$$P_F(p^0, p^t, q^0, q^t) \equiv [P_L(p^0, p^t, q^0, q^t)P_P(q^0, p^t, q^0, q^t)]^{1/2}, \quad (8.13)$$

$$Q_F(p^0, p^t, q^0, q^t) \equiv [Q_L(p^0, p^t, q^0, q^t)Q_P(p^0, p^t, q^0, q^t)]^{1/2}. \quad (8.14)$$

Hill noted that Fisher (1922, p. 63) advocated the use of (8.13) and (8.14) because he initially thought[6] that they were the only pair of indexes that satisfied Fisher's *three reversal* (or symmetry) *tests*: (1) *commodity reversal* (the indexes are invariant to the ordering of the commodities), (2) *time reversal* (the index numbers going from period t to 0 are the reciprocals of the index numbers going from period 0 to t), and (3) *factor reversal* (the functional form for the quantity index is the same as the functional form for the price index except that the roles of prices and quantities are reversed[7]).

Hill (1933, p. 384) also looked favorably on the Törnqvist (1936) or translog price and volume indexes, P_T and Q_T, defined as follows:

$$P_T(p^0, p^t, q^0, q^t) \equiv \Pi_{i=1}^{N}(p_i^t/p_i^0)^{(1/2)(s_i^0+s_i^t)}, \quad (8.15)$$

$$Q_T(p^0, p^t, q^0, q^t) \equiv \Pi_{i=1}^{N}(q_i^t/q_i^0)^{(1/2)(s_i^0+s_i^t)}, \quad (8.16)$$

where, as usual, $s_i^t \equiv p_i^t q_i^t/p^t \cdot q^t$ is the expenditure share of good i in period t.

Hill (1993, pp. 383–384) identified the Fisher and Törnqvist indexes as being *exact* indexes. Thus if the consumer's utility function is a homogeneous quadratic function, say $f(q) = (q \cdot Aq)^{1/2}$ where A is a symmetric matrix of constants, or if the consumer's unit cost function is a homogeneous quadratic function, say $c(p) \equiv C(1, p) \equiv (p \cdot Bp)^{1/2}$ where B is a symmetric matrix of constants, then under the assumption of optimizing behavior in periods 0 and t (and the absence of corner solutions), we obtain

$$Q_F(p^0, p^t, q^0, q^t) = f(q^t)/f(q^0), \quad (8.17)$$

$$P_F(p^0, p^t, q^0, q^t) = c(p^t)/c(p^0). \quad (8.18)$$

Thus the observable Fisher price and quantity indexes, P_F and Q_F, are *exactly* equal to the theoretical Konüs price index $c(p^t)/c(p^0)$ (the ratio of unit costs) and to the theoretical quantity index $f(q^t)/f(q^0)$ (the ratio of utilities or outputs) respectively. The result (8.17) is originally due to the Russian mathematician Byushgens (1925); see also Konüs and Byushgens (1926) who started the systematic study of exact indexes as well as Frisch (1936, p. 30), Wald (1939, p. 331), Samuelson (1947, p. 155), Afriat (1972, p. 45), Pollak (1971, p. 49) and Diewert (1976, p. 132). Result (8.18) is due to Diewert (1976, p. 132). Similarly, Diewert (1976, p. 122) showed that the Törnqvist price index P_T is *exactly* equal to the Konüs theoretical price index, provided that the consumer's cost function is translog[8] and that the reference level of utility u^* is chosen to be the geometric mean of the period 0 and t levels of utility, u^0 and u^t—that is, we have

$$P_T(p^0, p^t, q^0, q^t) = P_K(p^0, p^t, u^*), \qquad (8.19)$$

where $u^* \equiv (u^0 u^t)^{1/2}$. Diewert (1976, p. 120) also showed that the Törnqvist quantity index Q_T is *exactly* equal to the theoretical quantity index $f(q^t)/f(q^0)$ provided that the consumer is optimizing in both periods and that f is a homogeneous translog aggregator function.[9]

What is the importance of the results (8.17) through (8.19)? Consider the following quotation: "When the production possibilities being analyzed can be represented by a homogeneous translog production function, it can be shown that the Törnqvist index provides an exact measure of the underlying theoretic volume index. Thus the Törnqvist index, like the Firsher index, provides an exact measure under certain very specific circumstances. Both indices are examples of 'superlative' indices: i.e., indices that provide exact measures for some underlying functional form that is 'flexible,' the homogeneous quadratic and homogeneous translog functions being particular examples of such flexible functional forms" (Hill, 1993, p. 384).

Diewert (1974, p. 113) defined a *flexible* functional form as one that can provide a second order approximaton to an arbitrary function (in the class of functions being considered). Diewert (1976, p. 117) defined a quantity index $Q(p^0, p^t, q^0, q^t)$ to be *superlative* if it is exact for a flexible linearly homogeneous aggregator function $f(q)$—that is, we have $Q(p^0, p^t, q^0, q^t) = f(q^t)/f(q^0)$ where f is flexible. Diewert (1976, p. 134) also defined a price index $P(p^0, p^t, q^0, q^t)$ to be *superlative* if it is exact for a flexible unit cost function $c(p)$—that is, we have $P(p^0, p^t, q^0, q^t) = c(p^t)/c(p^0)$ where c is flexible. The importance of superlative index number formulae is that (1) they can be evaluated knowing only prices and quantities pertaining to the two periods under consideration (thus no econometric estimation is required) and (2) they are likely to approximate underlying (unobservable) economic indexes rather well.

Hill (1993, p. 384) went on to suggest that the use of a superlative index number formula has some practical and conceptual disadvantages, the two most mportant being the following: (1) microeconomic prices and quantities for both periods under consideration are required to evaluate superlative indexes, whereas the Laspeyres price index requires both price vectors and only base period quantities[10]; (2) the Fisher and Törnqvist quantity indexes are not *additively consistent*—that is, they cannot be used to create an additive set of "constant price" subaggregates.

Hill's first criticism of superlative price indexes is undoubtedly valid in many situations where timeliness is required. However, several statistical agencies have managed to calculate Fisher or Törnqvist indexes. Examples include the following agencies: the Customs and Tariff Bureau of the Ministry of Finance in Japan has calculated Fisher ideal price and quantity indexes for Japanese exports and imports since 1955; the U.S. Bureau of Labor Statistics (1983, 1993) has used Törnqvist quantity indexes since 1983 to aggregate inputs and outputs in its measures of multifactor productivity for the U.S. economy; the U.S. Bureau of Economic Analysis has recently calculated Fisher ideal indexes for the years 1959 through 1990 for the major components of U.S. gross domestic product (see Triplett, 1992; and Young, 1992).

Hill addressed the problem of the lack of additive consistency of superlative quantity indexes in his discussion of chain indexes, so we defer discussion of this issue until the following section.

Hill concluded his discussion of bilateral index number theory with the following words: "Thus economic theory suggests that, in general, a symmetric index that assigns equal weight to the two situations being compared is to be preferred to either the Laspeyres or Paasche indices on their own. The precise choice of superlative index—whether Fisher, Törnqvist or other superlative index—may be of only secondary importance as all the symmetric indices are likely to approximate each other, and the underlying theoretic index, fairly closely, at least when the index number spread between the Laspeyres and Paasche is not very great" (Hill, 1993, p. 384).

In order to explain more precisely the meaning of the above quotation, it will be useful to list all of the known superlative indexes.

In addition to the superlative price and quantity indexes defined by (8.13) through (8.16) above, the following families of index number formulae have been shown to be superlative:

$$Q_r(p^0, p^t, q^0, q^t) \equiv [\Sigma_{i=1}^N s_i^0 (q_i^t/q_i^0)^{r/2}]^{1/r} [\Sigma_{n=1}^N s_n^t (q_n^t/q_n^0)^{-r/2}]^{-1/r}, \quad (8.20)$$

$$P_r(p^0, p^t, q^0, q^t) \equiv [\Sigma_{i=1}^N s_i^0 (p_i^t/p_i^0)^{r/2}]^{1/r} [\Sigma_{n=1}^N s_n^t (p_n^t/p_n^0)^{-r/2}]^{-1/r}, \quad (8.21)$$

$$Q_\alpha(p^0, p^t, q^0, q^t) \equiv [p^0 \cdot \alpha p^t \cdot q^t + p^t \cdot \alpha p^0 \cdot q^t]/$$
$$[p^0 \cdot \alpha p^t \cdot q^0 + p^t \cdot \alpha p^0 \cdot q^0], \quad (8.22)$$

where $s_i^t \equiv p_i^t q_i^t / p^t \cdot q^t$. The indexes Q_r and P_r defined by (8.20) and (8.21) are defined for each scalar parameter $r \neq 0$; the index Q_α defined by (8.22) is defined for each nonnegative (and nonzero) vector of parameters $\alpha \equiv (\alpha_1, \ldots, \alpha_N)$. Q_r is the *quadratic mean of order r quantity index*, which is exact for the quadratic mean of order r aggregator function $f(q) \equiv [\Sigma_{i=1}^N \Sigma_{j=1}^N a_{ij} q_i^{r/2} q_j^{r/2}]^{1/r}$ (Diewert (1976, pp. 129–132)); P_r is the *quadratic mean of order r price index*, which is exact for the quadratic mean of order r unit cost function $c(p) \equiv [\Sigma_{i=1}^N \Sigma_{j=1}^N b_{ij} p_i^{r/2} p_j^{r/2}]^{1/r}$ (Diewert (1976, pp. 130–134)); and Q_α is the *normalized quadratic quantity index* (with quantity weights vector α) whose price index $P_\alpha(p^0, p^t, q^0, q^t) \equiv p^t \cdot q^t/p^0 \cdot q^0 \times Q_\alpha(p^0, p^t, q^0, q^t)$ is exact for the normalized quadratic unit cost function[11] $c(p) \equiv [b \cdot p + (1/2)(p \cdot \alpha)^{-1} p \cdot Ap]$, where b is a parameter vector and A is a symmetric matrix of parameters (Diewert (1992b, pp. 575–576)). Diewert (1992b, p. 577) also showed that if we set $\alpha = q^0$ or q^t, then Q_α defined by (8.22) reduces to the following more recognizable indexes:[12]

$$Q_{q^0}(p^0, p^t, q^0, q^t) = (1/2)Q_L + (1/2)Q_P, \quad (8.23)$$

$$Q_{q^t}(p^0, p^t, q^0, q^t) = [(1/2)Q_L^{-1} + (1/2)Q_P^{-1}]^{-1}, \quad (8.24)$$

where $Q_L \equiv Q_L(p^0, p^t, q^0, q^t)$ and $Q_P \equiv (p^0, p^t, q^0, q^t)$ are the familiar Laspeyres and Paasche quantity indexes defined by (8.5) and (8.4) above. Thus using (8.23), (8.13), and (8.24), we see that the arithmetic, geometric and harmonic means of the Laspeyres and Paasche quantity indexes are all superlative indexes.

By inspecting (8.13) through (8.16) and (8.20) through (8.22), we see that all superlative index number formulae do treat the data pertaining to the two periods in a symmetric fasion in the sense that Walsh's (1901, p. 389, 1921a, p. 108, 1921b, p. 540, 1924, p. 506) time reversal test[13] is satisfied by these indexes—that is, we have

$$P(p^t, p^0, q^t, q^0) = 1/P(p^0, p^t, q^0, q^t), \quad (8.25)$$

$$Q(p^t, p^0, q^t, q^0) = 1/P(p^0, p^t, q^0, q^t), \quad (8.26)$$

if P and Q are superlative.[14] However, the weighting of the quantity ratios q_i^t/q_i^0 in (8.20) and of the price ratios p_i^t/p_i^0 in (8.21) is quite complex. Moreover, the family of superlative quantity indexes Q_α defined by (8.22) cannot even be written as simple functions of the quantity ratios q_i^t/q_i^0.[15]

Even though the above superlative index number formulaes look quite different, it can be shown that they approximate each other to the second order around any point where the two price vectors are proportional and the two quantity vectors are proportional (see Diewert, 1978, p. 888, 1992b, pp. 577–578). Thus the actual choice of a superlative index is relatively unimportant numerically, as Hill suggested in the last quotation above.

Finally, Diewert (1978, p. 888) defined an index number formula to be *pseudo-superlative* if its second order Taylor series approximation around an equal price and quantity point (that is, $p^0 = p^t$ and $q^0 = q^t$) coincided with the corresponding second-order Taylor series approximation to a superlative index. Thus pseudo-superlative index numbers will be numerically close to superlative index numbers, at least in the time series context where prices and quantities typically change slowly over time. Diewert (1978, p. 897) showed that any symmetric mean[16] of the Paasche and Laspeyres price (quantity) indexes is a pseudo-superlative price (quantity) index.[17]

We turn now to Hill's discussion of chain indexes.

8.4. Chain Indexes

In this section,[18] Hill (1993, pp. 385–390) contrasted the common statistical agency practice of constructing fixed-base Laspeyres volume indexes using the formula (8.5) with the use of chain indexes.[19] The chain system measures the change in output going from one period to a subsequent period using a bilateral index number formula involving the prices and quantities pertaining to the two adjacent periods. These one-period rates of change are then cumulated to yield the relative levels of output over the entire period under consideration. Thus if the bilateral quantity index is Q, the chain system generates the following pattern of relative aggregate quantities for the first three periods:

$$1, \; Q(p^0, p^1, q^0, q^1), \; Q(p^0, p^1, q^0, q^1)Q(p^1, p^2, q^1, q^2). \quad (8.27)$$

Thus the output growth rate going from period t and $t + 1$ is always defined by $Q(p^t, p^{t+1}, q^t, q^{t+1})$ in the chain system.

Comparing the fixed base system (8.5) with the chain system (8.27), Hill noted that the chain system will not preserve the additivity of the components of the index whereas the fixed base Laspeyres quantity index (8.5) will. Since many users of the national accounts find it extremely convenient to have additive real components for their aggregate of interest, this lack of additivity makes the chain system less desirable.

However, the fixed base Laspeyres quantity index (8.5) cannot be used forever: eventually, the base period prices $p^0 \equiv [p_1^0, \ldots, p_N^0]$ are so far removed from the current period prices $p^t \equiv [p_1^t, \ldots, p_N^t]$ that the base must be changed.[20] As soon as the base is changed, Hill (1993, p. 385) pointed out that additivity is lost. Thus as a practical matter, additivity of components of a volume index cannot be maintained for long periods of time.

Hill (1993, pp. 387–388) noted the main advantage of the chain system: under normal conditions, chaining will reduce the spread between the Paasche and Laspeyres indexes, and hence the use of either a chained Paasche or Laspeyres index should more closely approximate a superlative index like the Fisher ideal and hence approximate the underlying economic index.[21]

Hill (1993, p. 388), drawing on the earlier research of Szulc (1983) and Hill (1988, pp. 136–137), also noted that it is not appropriate to use the chain system when prices oscillate (or "bounce," to use Szulc's (1983, p. 548) term). This phenomenon can occur in the context of regular seasonal fluctuatons or in the context of price wars. However, in the context of roughly monotonically changing prices and quantities, Hill (1993, p. 389) recommended the use of chained Fisher or Törnqvist indexes.

We conclude this section with an observation about superlative indexes and aditivity[22]: there are superlative quantity indexes which preserve additivity for two periods (but only two periods). Examination of (8.22) shows that for any nonnegative, nonzero vector of quantity weights $\alpha \equiv [\alpha_1, \ldots, \alpha_N]$, the normalized quadratic quantity index with weights α, Q_α, is additive over its components for periods 0 and t. The ith constant price is $(\Sigma_{n=1}^N p_n^0 \alpha_n) p_i^t + (\Sigma_{n=1}^N p_n^t \alpha_n) p_i^0$.

There is one other superlative index number formula that preserves additivity over two periods. Recall the quadratic mean of order r price index P_r defined by (8.21) above. If we set $r = 1$ and divide the value ratio $p^t \cdot q^t / p^0 \cdot q^0$ by $P_1(p^0, p^t, q^0, q^t)$, we obtain the following quantity index due to Walsh (1901, p. 105, 1921a, p. 101):

$$Q_W(p^0, p^t, q^0, q^t) \equiv \Sigma_{i=1}^N (p_i^0 p_i^t)^{1/2} q_i^t / \Sigma_{n=1}^N (p_n^0 p_n^t)^{1/2} q_n^0. \qquad (8.28)$$

The above Walsh quantity index preserves additivity over periods 0 and t. The ith constant price is $(p_i^0 p_i^t)^{1/2}$, the square root of the product of the period 0 and period t prices for commodity i. Thus if statistical agencies wanted to provide superlative indexes for their users that were additive over the current period t and the previous period, the use of the rather simple Walsh quantity index $Q_W(p^{t-1}, p^t, q^{t-1}, q^t)$ is recommended over the somewhat more complex normalized quadratic quantity index $Q_a(p^{t-1}, p^t, q^{t-1}, q^t)$.[23]

8.5. Volume Measures for Gross Value Added and GDP

The material Hill (1993, pp. 390–393) presented in this section extended his analysis of the previous section to the situation where some commodities are outputs and others are (intermediate) inputs. Intermediate inputs must be distinguished from primary inputs, which are labor, capital, land, and natural resources. Intermediate inputs are (nondurable) inputs that were initially provided by other domestic or foreign producers. The nominal *gross value added* for an establishment, enterprise, industry, or sector is defined to be the value of outputs produced minus intermediate inputs used by the production unit during the time period under consideration. Hill (1993, p. 391) defined a *volume index for value added* (real value added in standard terminology) using a quantity index such as the Paasche or Laspeyres quantity index defined by (8.4) or (8.5) above, except that in the present situation, the quantities of intermediate inputs used during the two periods under consideration have negative signs attached to them.[24]

Hill revisited the analysis of the previous section, which presented the tradeoff between chaining and additivity. However, in the present context, Hill (1993, pp. 390, 393) was even more emphatic on the need for chaining as the following quotations indicate:

> If relative prices change, relative quantities will be adjusted in response. A process of production which is efficient at one set of prices may not be very efficient at another set of relative prices. If the other set of prices is very different the inefficiency of the process may reveal itself in a very conspicuous form, namely negative gross value added.

> Sooner or later the base year for fixed weight Laspeyres volume indices and their associated constant price series has to updated because the prices of the base year become increasingly irrelevant. When the base year is updated, series on the old base have to be linked to those on the new base. Thus, sooner or later additivity is lost as a result of linkage (assuming the rebasing is not carried backwards). Long runs of data, therefore, almost inevitably involve some form of chain indices. Annual chaining is simply the limiting case in which rebasing is carried out each year instead of every five or ten years.

To minimize the problem of meaningless or negative real value added, Hill (1993, p. 392) recommended the use of Fisher ideal chained volume indexes (or chained Laspeyres volume indexes as an acceptable alternative), with the proviso that the chain indexes be used to measure only year to year movements and not quarter to quarter movements. To meet the needs of additivity users, Hill (1993, p. 393) also recommended that disaggregated constant price series should be published in addition to the chain indexes for the main aggregates. However, if users demand additivity, then it may be better to use the Walsh quantity index $Q_W(p^{t-1}$, p^t, q^{t-1}, $q^t)$ (recall (8.28) above) as the linking superlative index number formula since this index will preserve the additivity of its components over periods $t - 1$ and t.

Elsewhere in the *System of National Accounts, 1993* (United Nations, 1993, p. 127), Hill stated that intermediate inputs are normally valued at purchasers' prices and outputs at basic prices, which are prices before taxes on outputs are added and subsidies on products are subtracted— that is, a basic output price represents the revenue from selling one unit of a product that the producer actually receives. This is the correct treatment of prices from the viewpoint of the economic theory of the producer. However, the existence of specific taxes on intermediate inputs (such as the former Canadian manufacturers sales tax) as well as the existence of complex systems of value-added taxation make the calculation of value added very complicated. These indirect taxes mean that in general the output price for a commodity will not equal the corresponding intermediate input price; taxes will create wedges between these two prices. It is important for economic analysts to have information on the commodity incidence of these indirect taxes that fall within the confines of the production sector so that their effects on production efficiency can be determined. The identification and appropriate treatment of taxes is a topic that deserves high priority in the next revision of the system of national accounts.

References to the literature on output indexes and the deflation of value added include Bowley (1921), Malmquist (1953), Stone (1956), Arrow (1974), Samuelson and Swamy (1974, pp. 588–592), Sato (1976; p. 438), Archibald (1977), Diewert (1980, pp. 455–464, 1983b, pp. 1054–1077) and Caves, Christensen, and Diewert (1982a, 1982b).

8.6. Internation Price and Volume Indexes

Hill (1993, pp. 393–397) drew on his earlier work (Hill, 1982, 1984) on international comparisons in writing an excellent summary of the current state of thought on how to make international (and interregional) comparisons.

Hill (1993, p. 393) started his exposition by noting that bilateral index number theory can be used to compare price and volume levels between countries: "It is possible to compare prices and volumes between countries using the same general methodology as for intertemporal comparisons within a single country. International volume indices are needed in order to compare levels of productivity or standards of living in different countries, while comparisons of prices can be used to measure purchasing power parities between different currencies."

Hill (1993, pp. 393–395) went on to note that international (or multilateral) comparisons differ from intertemporal (or bilateral) comparisons for at least five reasons:

- There can be large differences in the size of countries being compared.[25] This makes it more difficult to apply the economic approach to index number theory, which relies on assumptions about the homogeneity of tastes or technology.
- Countries are modifiable units. They can be partitioned into smaller countries or they can be merged into larger blocks. This raises issues of *weighting*. For example, comparing Canadian output with Mexican output in a North American multilateral framework should (perhaps) be invariant to whether the United States is treated as a single country or fifty states.
- Price and quantity movements tend to be gradual in the intertemporal context (and this makes the application of the chain method attractive). This is not the case in the international context. Therefore, the choice of index number formula will matter more in the multilateral context. Hill (1993, p. 393) also pointed out that there is no natural counterpart to the chain principle in the multilateral context.[26]
- Hill (1993, p. 394) noted that it is more difficult to collect price information in the multilateral context. In the intertemporal context, the price of commodity n in period t, p_n^t, can be in any unit of measurement, as long as that unit is not changed over time. In the multilateral context, the international prices for commodity n, p_n^i, must be measured in *exactly* the same physical units across countries i. This harmonization of units of measurements may be very difficult to do across country statistical agencies. Moreover, the list of commodities to be sampled at the elementary level[27] should be exactly the same across countries. This requirement for a standard

list of representative commodities to be priced by all statistical
agencies in the block of countries under consideration is impossible
to meet if the countries are diverse.

- Finally, Hill (1993, p. 395) noted that price or volume indexes in
  the multilateral context typically are required to be *transitive*—that
  is, if we compare countries i and j directly, this comparison should
  be the same as if we were to compare i with k and then k with j.
  Put another way, no single country should play an asymmetric role
  in forming the system of multilateral indexes. Hill (1993, p. 395)
  explained the difference between the intertemporal and multilateral
  situations as follows: "Transitivity is not important in a time series
  context because time periods from an ordered sequence. For this
  reason, there is little interest in direct comparisons between all
  possible pairs of time periods. Direct comparisons tend to be
  confined either to comparisons with a selected base period, typically
  the first period in the sequence (leading to fixed base Laspeyres or
  Paasche indices) or to comparisons between consecutive time
  periods (leading to chain indices). Comparisons between other
  possible pairs of periods are not usually needed or undertaken."

From the above list of difficulties, it can be seen that the choice of an
appropriate multilateral index number formula is not a trivial problem.

Hill (1993, pp. 395–397) finished his exposition of multiateral index
number theory by listing two broad approaches to the choice of functional
forms: (1) the *block approach* (or the *average prices approach*) and (2)
the *binary approach*. We will distinguish a third broad approach, which is
dual to the first approach: (3) the *average quantities approach*. In order to
explain these approaches, we need to introduce a bit of notation.

Suppose that we want to form price and quantity aggregates for N
commodities over J countries. Denote the price and quantity vectors for
country j by $p^j \equiv [p_1^j, \ldots, p_N^j]$ and $q^j \equiv [q_1^j, \ldots, q_J^N]$ for $j = 1, \ldots, J$.
Denote a multilateral price index between countries i and j (j relative to i)
by P^{ij} and the corresponding multilateral quantity index by Q^{ij}. In general,
these indexes will be functions of all block prices and quantities, $p^1, \ldots,$
p^J and $q^1, \ldots, q^J$. We assume that the P^{ij} and Q^{ij} satisfy the following
counterpart to the product test (8.1):

$$P^{ij}Q^{ij} = p^j \cdot q^j / p^i \cdot q^i, \quad 1 \leqslant i, j \leqslant J. \qquad (8.29)$$

Thus if P^{ij} is defined, then (8.29) can be utilized to define Q^{ij} and
vice versa.

In the *average prices method* for making multilateral comparisons, a vector of world average prices $\bar{p} \equiv [\bar{p}^1, \ldots, \bar{p}_N]$ must be defined. Once $\bar{p}$ is defined, Q^{ij} is defined for all $1 \leq i, j \leq J$ as follows:

$$Q^{ij}(\bar{p}, q^i, q^j) \equiv \bar{p} \cdot q^j / \bar{p} \cdot q^i. \tag{8.30}$$

Note that $Q^{ij} = Q^j / Q^i$ where $Q^i \equiv \bar{p} \cdot q^i$ and $Q^j \equiv \bar{p} \cdot q^j$. These latter two indexes are additive across commodities, which explains the attractiveness of this class of indexes.

Various choices for $\bar{p}$ have been suggested over the years, including the arithmetic means of country prices defined by

$$\bar{p}_n \equiv \Sigma_{j=1}^J (1/J) p_n^j, \quad n = 1, \ldots, N, \tag{8.31}$$

and the geometric means of country prices defined by

$$\bar{p}_n \equiv [\Pi_{j=1}^J p_n^j]^{1/J}, \quad n = 1, \ldots, N. \tag{8.32}$$

The use of (8.32) was advocated by Walsh (1901, p. 398) (his double weighting method) and by Gerardi (1982, p. 403). The use of (8.31) is an example of Fisher's (1992, p. 367) broadened base system.

Another more complex average prices method is the Geary-Khamis (Geary, 1958; Khamis, 1970, 1972) method. The nth average price is defined by

$$\bar{p}_n \equiv \Sigma_{j=1}^J (q_n^j / \Sigma_{k=1}^J q_n^k)(p_n^j / P^j), \quad n = 1, \ldots, N, \tag{8.33}$$

where the country j purchasing power parity P^j is defined as

$$P^j \equiv p^j \cdot q^j / \bar{p} \cdot q^j, \quad j = 1, \ldots, J. \tag{8.34}$$

Equations (8.33) and (8.34) can be regarded as $N + J$ simultaneous equations (one equation is dependent) in the N components of $\bar{p}$ and the $P^j, j = 1, \ldots, J$. We need one additional normalization (such as $P^1 = 1$) to solve the system. Khamis (1970, 1972) showed that a unique solution always exists if prices and quantities are positive. Note that $\bar{p}_n$ can be regarded as a *weighted arithmetic mean* of the purchasing power parity adjusted prices for commodity n, p_n^j / P^j, across countries where the country j weight is its share of world output for commodity n.

The *average quantities method* reverses the role of prices and quantities in the above method. Thus we now define a vector of block average quantities $\bar{q} \equiv [\bar{q}_1, \ldots, \bar{q}_N]$ and the price indexes P^{ij} are defined in terms of $\bar{q}$ as follows:

$$P^{ij}(\bar{q}, p^i, p^j) \equiv p^j \cdot \bar{q} / p^i \cdot \bar{q}, \quad 1 \leq i, j \leq J. \tag{8.35}$$

Once the P^{ij} are defined, the volume indexes Q^{ij} can be defined residually using (8.29). Obvious choices for $\bar{q}$ are the arithmetic and geometric means of block quantities:

$$\bar{q}_n \equiv \Sigma_{j=1}^{J}(1/J)q_n^j; \quad n = 1, \ldots, N; \tag{8.36}$$

$$\bar{q}_n \equiv [\Pi_{j=1}^{J} q_n^j]^{1/J}; \quad n = 1, \ldots, N. \tag{8.37}$$

The use of (8.36) was first suggested by Walsh (1901, p. 431), who called it Scrope's method with arithmetic weights. This method was also described by Ruggles (1967, p. 81), who called it the market basket method. The use of (8.37) was advocated by Walsh (1901, pp. 398–399), who called it Scrope's method with geometric weights. The quantity indexes Q^{ij} defined by (8.35) through (8.37) and (8.29) are not additive across commodities.

The final class of multilateral methods that we consider is that Hill (1993, p. 396) called the *binary approach*. Using each country as the base country, bilateral indexes are used to provide alternative price and quantity aggregates for all countries in the block. These J sets of parties are then averaged (or blended to use Fisher's, 1992, p. 305, term) to form an invariant set of multilateral indexes. Fisher (1992, p. 305) used an arithmetic average of the country specific parities, while Gini (1931, p. 12) used a geometric average. Both of these authors used the bilateral Fisher ideal indexes defined by (8.13) and (8.14) above as their basic bilateral formulae. It should be noted that Eltetö and Köves (1964) and Szulc (1964) also derived Gini's multilateral method using a least-squares approach, which we explain below.

Write the multilateral price indexes P^{ij} as $P^{ij} = P^j/P^i$ for some price levels P^j, $j = 1, \ldots, J$, and rewrite the multilateral quantity indexes Q^{ij} as $Q^{ij} = Q^j/Q^i$ for some quantity levels Q^j, $j = 1, \ldots, J$. We now assume that the price and quantity levels satisfy the following adding up conditions:

$$P^j Q^j = p^j \cdot q^j, \quad j = 1, \ldots, J. \tag{8.38}$$

The economic statistician now picks the "best" bilateral price and quantity indexes, $P(p^i, p^j, q^i, q^j)$ and $Q(p^i, p^j, q^i, q^j)$, that satisfy the product test (8.1). Country price levels P^j may now be found by solving the following least-squares problem:

$$\min_{P^1, \ldots, P^J} \Sigma_{i=1}^{J}\Sigma_{j=1}^{J}\{\ln[(P^i/P^j)P(p^i, p^j, q^i, q^j)]\}^2 \tag{8.39}$$

$$= \min_{P^1, \ldots, P^J} \Sigma_{i=1}^{J}\Sigma_{j=1}^{J}\{\ln[(P^i/P^j)p^j \cdot q^j/p^i \cdot q^i Q(p^i, p^j, q^i, q^j)]\}^2$$
using (8.1)

$$= \min_{Q^1, \ldots, Q^J} \Sigma_{i=1}^{J}\Sigma_{j=1}^{J}\{\ln[Q^i/Q^i Q(p^i, p^j, q^i, q^j)]\}^2 \text{ using}$$
(8.38)

$$= \min_{Q^1, \ldots, Q^J} \Sigma_{i=1}^{J}\Sigma_{j=1}^{J}\{\ln[Q^j/Q^i)Q(p^j, p^i, q^j, q^i)]\}^2, \tag{8.40}$$

where (8.40) follows from the line above if Q satisfies the time reversal test. In order to solve (8.39), a normalization on the P^j (such as $P^1 = 1$) is required and in order to solve (8.40), a normalization on the Q^j (such as $Q^1 = p^1 \cdot q^1$) is required. If the P^j are determined by solving (8.39), then the corresponding Q^j can be obtained by solving (8.38). If the Q^j are determined by solving (8.40), then the corresponding P^j can be obtained by solving (8.38). The equality between (8.39) and (8.40) shows that if the bilateral price or quantity index satisfies the time reversal test, then it does not matter whether we solve a least-squares problem involving the P^j or an analogous problem involving the Q^j: the same system of price and quantity levels will be obtained that satisfies the product test relations (8.38). Elteö and Köves (1964) and Szulc (1964) used the least-squares problem (8.39) with the bilateral formula P chosen to be the Fisher ideal P_F defined by (8.13) to derive the EKS purchasing power parities P^j. Van Ijzeren (1987, pp. 62–65) showed that one also obtained the Gini-EKS parities if either P_F, P_L, or P_P (recall (8.13), (8.2), and (8.3), above) were used as the bilateral index number formula P in (8.39) or if Q_F, Q_L, or Q_P (recall (8.14), (8.5), and (8.4) above) were used as the bilateral index number formula Q in (8.40). Hill (1993, p. 396) concluded his discussion of the EKS multilateral system by observing that the EKS quantity levels Q^j are not additively consistent across commodities.

Hill (1993, p. 397) concluded his discussion of multilateral indexes by recommending that statistical agencies compile both Geary-Khamis indexes (because they are additively consistent) as well as Gini-EKS indexes because they are based on bilateral Fisher ideal indexes, which have a better justification from the viewpoint of economic theory (recall our discussion of superlative indexes in Section 8.3, above).

In the context of bilateral index number theory, we saw that the requirement that a quantity index be additive in its quantity components was not inconsistent with the index being superlative if we were making comparisons over only two periods. Unfortunately, in the multilateral context, if there are more than three countries in the block, then it appears to be impossible to achieve both additivity and superlativeness. Let me try to explain why this is so.

Assume optimizing behavior on the part of economic agents in each country—that is, assume consumers in country i are maximizing a non-negative, linearly homogeneous, increasing and concave utility function $f(q)$ subject to the country i budget constraint, $p^i \cdot q = p^i \cdot q^i$ for $i = 1, 2, \ldots, J$.[28] We shall assume strictly positive prices and quantities in all countries to simplify our proofs. The assumption of optimizing behavior plus the linear homogeneity of the aggreagtor function f implies that

$$p^i \cdot q^i = c(p^i)f(q^i), \quad i = 1, 2, \ldots, J, \tag{8.41}$$

where $c(p)$ is the unit cost function dual to the aggregator function f—that is, $c(p) \equiv C(1, p)$ where the (total) cost function C was defined earlier by (8.9). Finally, we introduce the notation e_i and u_i for country i's unit cost and utility level respectively—that is, define

$$u_i \equiv f(q^i), \quad i = 1, \ldots, J, \tag{8.42}$$
$$e_i \equiv c(p^i), \quad i = 1, \ldots, J. \tag{8.43}$$

If the unit cost function c is differentiable, then by Shephard's (1953, p. 11) lemma (see also Diewert, 1993c, p. 117), we can obtain quantities q^i as functions of the prices p^i and utility levels u_i as follows:

$$q^i = \nabla c(p^i)u_i, \quad i = 1, \ldots, J, \tag{8.44}$$

where $\nabla c(p^i)u_i \equiv [c_1(p^i), \ldots, c_N(p^i)]$ is the vector of first order partial derivatives of $c(p^i)$ with respect to its price components.

If the aggregator function f is differentiable, then we can obtain prices p^i as functions of the quantities q^i and the unit cost levels e_i as follows:[29]

$$p^i = \nabla f(q^i)e_i, \quad i = 1, \ldots, J. \tag{8.45}$$

We now want to determine under what conditions on f or c, the additive quantity index defined by (8.30) is *exactly* equal to the economic index, $f(q^j)/f(q^i) = u_j/u_i$, for all i and j. In order to allow for more general average prices $\bar{p}_n$ other than those defined by (8.31) and (8.32), we replace $\bar{p}_n$ by $m(p_n^1, p_n^2, \ldots, p_n^J)$ for $n = 1, 2, \ldots, N$ where m is a homogeneous symmetric mean.[30]

Equating the right side of (8.30) to the aggregate quantity ratio $f(q^j)/f(q^i)$ and replacing each $\bar{p}_n$ by the general mean $m(p_n^1, \ldots, p_n^J)$ of the country prices for commodity n leads to the following system of functional equations that f or c must satisfy for all prices and quantities $p^1, \ldots, p^J$ and $q^1, \ldots, q^J$ that satisfy (8.41) through (8.45):

$$\Sigma_{n=1}^N m(p_n^1, \ldots, p_n^J)q_n^j / \Sigma_{n=1}^N m(p_n^1, \ldots, p_n^J)q_n^i = f(q^j)/f(q^i),$$
$$1 \leq i, j \leq J. \tag{8.46}$$

We first consider the case where the unit cost function c is once differentiable. In this case, we can eliminate the q^i in (8.46) by substituting (8.42) and (8.44) into (8.46). After simplifying, the resulting equations are

$$\Sigma_{n=1}^N m(p_n^1, \ldots, p_n^J)[c_n(p^j) - c_n(p^i)] = 0; \quad 1 \leq i, j \leq J. \tag{8.47}$$

Fix i and j. If $J \geq 3$, there exists a country k not equal to i or j. Choose a set of N p^k vectors—say, p^{kr} for $r = 1, \ldots, N$—such that the N vectors, $[m(p_1^1, \ldots, p_1^{kr}, \ldots, p_1^J), m(p_2^1, \ldots, p_2^{kr}, \ldots, p_2^J), \ldots, m(p_N^1, \ldots, p_N^{kr}, \ldots, p_N^J)]$ for $r = 1, \ldots, N$, are linearly independent.[31] Inserting the prices $[p^1, \ldots, p^{kr}, \ldots, p^J]$ for $r = 1, \ldots, N$ into (8.47) in place of $[p^1, \ldots, p^k, \ldots, p^J]$ leads to N linearly independent equations in the variables $[c_n(p^j) - c_n(p^i)]$ and hence we conclude that

$$c_n(p^j) - c_n(p^i) = 0 \quad \text{for } n = 1, \ldots, N \text{ and } 1 \leq i, j \leq J. \quad (8.48)$$

Equations (8.48) imply that the first-order partial derivatives of $c(p)$ are constants—b_n, say—and thus $c(p)$ must be the following linear function of prices:[32]

$$c(p_1, \ldots, p_N) = \Sigma_{n=1}^N b_n p_n. \quad (8.49)$$

Equation (8.49) tells us that the unit cost function is the Leontief unit cost function, which is dual to the zero substitutability Leontief aggregator function $f(q_1, \ldots, q_N) = \min_n \{q_n/b_n : n = 1, \ldots, N\}$.

We now consider the case where the aggregator funcion f is once differentiable. In this case, we eliminate the p^i in (8.46) by using equations (8.45). After simplifying, equations (8.46) become

$$\Sigma_{n=1}^N m[e_1 f_n(q^1), \ldots, e_J f_n(q^J)][\{q_n^j/f(q^j)\} - \{q_n^i/f(q^i)\}] = 0, \\ 1 \leq i, j \leq J. \quad (8.50)$$

Let f be a linear aggregator function—that is, suppose that there exist constants a_n such that

$$f(q_1, \ldots, q_N) \equiv \Sigma_{n=1}^N a_n q_n. \quad (8.51)$$

Substituting the partial derivatives of the f defined by (8.51) into the left side of (8.50) yields

$$\Sigma_{n=1}^N m[e_1 a_n, \ldots, e_J a_n][\{q_n^j/f(q^j)\} - \{q_n^i/f(q^i)\}]$$
$$= \Sigma_{n=1}^N a_n m[e_1, \ldots, e_J][\{q_n^j/f(q^j)\} - \{q_n^i/f(q^i)\}]$$

using the linear homogeneity property of m

$$= m[e_1, \ldots, e_J][\{f(q^j)/f(q^j)\} - \{f(q^i)/f(q^i)\}]$$

using (8.51) twice

$$= 0.$$

Thus if the aggregator function f is linear, then the functional equation (8.50) is satisfied. We now show that if $J \geq 3$, then (8.51) is the *only* differentiable linearly homogenous aggregator function that satisfies (8.50).[33]

Suppose that f satisfied (8.50) and the first-order partial derivatives of f are not all constant. Then we can find two quantity vectors—$q^{(1)}$ and $q^{(2)}$, say—such that for some commodities r and s, we have

$$f_r(q^{(1)}) < f_r(q^{(2)}),$$ (8.52)

$$f_s(q^{(1)}) \geq f_s(q^{(2)}).$$ (8.53)

Fix $i \neq j$ and choose $q_n^i = q_n^j$ for all n except when $n = r$ or s. For these two components, choose q_r^i, q_s^i, q_r^j, q_s^j such that

$$\{q_r^j/f(q^j)\} - \{q_r^i/f(q^i)\} \equiv z_r > 0,$$ (8.54)

$$\{q_s^j/f(q^j)\} - \{q_s^i/f(q^i)\} \equiv z_s \leq 0.$$ (8.55)

Substitute these choices for q^i and q^j into (8.50) to obtain

$$m[e_1 f_r(q^1), \ldots, e_k f_r(q^k), \ldots, e_J f_r(q^J)]z_r$$
$$+ m[e_1 f_s(q^1), \ldots, e_k f_s(q^k), \ldots, e_J f_s(q^J)]z_s = 0.$$ (8.56)

Since $J \geq 3$, there exists a country k not equal to i or j. Now replace q^k in (8.56) by $q^{(1)}$ and then $q^{(2)}$. Rewrite the resulting two equations as

$$x_{11} z_r + x_{12} z_s = 0, \quad x_{21} z_r + x_{22} z_s = 0.$$ (8.57)

The inequalities (8.52) and (8.53) plus the assumption that m is increasing in its arguments imply that the two equations in (8.57) are linearly independent. Hence the only solution is $z_r = z_s = 0$, which contradicts (8.54) and (8.55). Hence our *supposition* is false, and we conclude that the linear aggregator function defined by (8.51) is the only differentiable linearly homogeneous function that can be exact for additive indexes of the form defined by the left side of (8.46).

Putting this result together with our earlier unit cost function result, we see that essentially the only functional forms for an underlying homogeneous aggregator function that are exact for additive quantity indexes of the type defined by the left side of (8.46) are the *zero substitutability* Leontief aggregator and the *perfect substitutability* linear aggregator functions. Thus, although additivity may be very convenient for users, its economic foundations are rather weak.[34]

The economic foundations for the average quantities approach can be shown to be similarly weak. Allow the average quantities $\bar{q}_n$ that appear in (8.35) to be homogeneous symmetric means of the country quantities for commodity n—that is, assume

$$\bar{q}_n = m(q_n^1, \ldots, q_n^J), \quad n = 1, \ldots, N. \tag{8.58}$$

Now equate the right side of (8.35) to the correct theoretical economic price index $c(p^j)/c(p^i)$. The counterparts to equations (8.46) now become

$$\Sigma_{n=1}^N m(q_n^1, \ldots, q_n^J) p_n^j / \Sigma_{n=1}^N m(q_n^1, \ldots, q_n^J) p_n^i = c(p^j)/c(p^i),$$
$$1 \leqslant i, j \leqslant J. \tag{8.59}$$

First consider the case where the unit cost function $c(p)$ is once differentiable. Eliminate the q^i in (8.59) by using (8.44). After simplification, (8.59) becomes for $1 \leqslant i, j \leqslant J$:

$$\Sigma_{n=1}^N m[u_1 c(p^1), \ldots, u_J c(p^J)][\{p_n^j / c(p^j)\} - \{p_n^i / c(p^i)\}] = 0, \tag{5.60}$$

which is exactly analogous to (8.50). Applying the previous analysis, we conclude that unit cost function must be linear—that is, (8.49) is the only differentiable unit cost function solution to (8.59) if $J \geqslant 3$.

Consider next the case where the aggregator function f is once differentiable. Eliminate the p^i in (59) by substituting in equations (8.45). Using also (8.43), (8.59) becomes

$$\Sigma_{n=1}^N m(q_n^1, \ldots, q_n^J)[f_n(q^j) - f_n(q^i)] = 0, \quad 1 \leqslant i, j \leqslant J, \tag{8.61}$$

which is exactly analogous to (8.47). Applying our previous analysis, we conclude that the aggregator function must be linear in this case.

Consolidating the above results, we see that the only functional forms for an underlying unit cost function that are consistent with the additive price indexes defined by the left side of (8.59) are the unit cost functions that are dual to the linear and Leontief aggregator functions.

The above results on the exactness of the average prices and average quantities methods for making multilateral comparisons can be generalized to more complex formulas for the average prices $m(p_n^1, \ldots, p_n^J)$ that appear in (8.46) or for the average quantitities $m(q_n^1, \ldots, q_n^J)$ that appear in (8.59). In particular, under conditions that guarantee the existence and uniqueness of the Geary-Khamis indexes, it can be shown that the linear and Leontief aggregator functions are the only functions that are exact for the Geary-Khamis parities.

Recently, Dikhanov (1994) has revisited the problem of obtaining additive quantity indexes in the multilateral context. Dikhanov noticed that the Iklé (1972, p. 203) method for making multilateral comparisons is an average prices method which is analogous to the Geary-Khamis method[35] except that the average price for commodity n is defined as follows:

$$\bar{p}_n \equiv [\Sigma_{j=1}^J (\delta_n^j / \Sigma_{k=1}^J \delta_n^k)(p_n^j / P^j)^{-1}]^{-1}, \quad n = 1, \ldots, N, \tag{8.62}$$

where $\delta_n^j \equiv p_n^j q_n^j / p^j \cdot q^j$ is the expenditure share of commodity n in country j and P^j is the country j purchasing power parity defined by (8.14). Thus as in the GK system, the $\bar{p}_n$ and P^j are determined simult-aneously by (8.14) and (8.62).[36] Note that the Iklé $\bar{p}_n$ is a weighted harmonic mean of the country j PPP adjusted prices of commodity n, p_n^j / P^j, where the (normalized) country j expenditure shares for commodity n, δ_n^j, are used as weights. The reader should compare the Iklé $\bar{p}_n$ defined by (8.62) with the Geary-Khamis $\bar{p}_n$ defined earlier by (8.33). The in-teresting property of the Iklé multilateral system of indexes is that their quantity levels Q^j are additive over commodity components, and Dikhanov (1994) shows using World Bank data that the Iklé Q^j are numerically fairly close to the Gini-EKS Q^j.

It is straightforward to show that the linear and Leontief aggregator functions are exact for the Iklé system of indexes. I suspect that these are the only aggregator functional forms that are exact, but due to the complexity of (8.62), I have not been able to formally prove this.

In general, I am skeptical that additive multilateral quantity indexes of the type defined by (8.30) will be exact for flexible functional forms for the aggregator function if the number of countries (or time periods) exceeds two. This position seems to be in general agreement with that of Van Ijzeren (1987, pp. 91–92) as the following quotation indicates: "Instead of additivity, another central idea has to be accepted, namely, that every subaggregate, just like every individual product, should have a complete set of prices and quantities. To get some value for a subaggregate it is not sufficient to add the corresponding values of its component products. On the contrary, a set of consistent prices and quantities should be constructed for the subaggregate, thus making it, formally, [equivalent] to a novel, solitary product."

We conclude this section with a few more references to the literature. Economic approaches to multilateral indexes have been considered by Caves, Christensen, Diewert (1982a, 1982b) and Diewert (1986). Test approaches to multilateral indexes have been considered by Gerardi (1982), Hill (1982), Kravis, Summers, and Heston (1982), Diewert (1986, 1988), and Balk (1993). Other important works on multilateral methods not yet mentioned include Van Yzeren (Ijzeren)(1956, 1988), Drechsler (1973), Kravis (1984), Szilágyi (1986), Eurostat (1988), Summers and Heston (1988, 1991), Balk (1989), and Robert Hill (1994b). The early history of multilateral methods is reviewed by Diewert (1993a, pp. 52–58).

8.7. The Treatment of Differences and Changes in Quality

Hill (1993, pp. 397–398) opened up his discussion of quality differences by discussing alternative criteria for *classifying* or distinguishing commodities. Commodities can be different due to (1) differences in the physical characteristics of the good or differences in the delivery of services, (2) different conditions of sale (that is, inclusion or exclusion of transportation costs or warranties), (3) different levels of customer service or different environments where sales take place (such as fancy versus plain restaurants), (4) different locations or outlets where sales take place, and (5) different times of the day or season when sales are made.

Differences 1 and 2 listed above are relatively uncontroversial. The differences in 4 mean that commodities should be distinguished by region and thus the national accounts of a country should in principle be constructed on a regional basis rather than on a national basis. Taking a national basis means that commodities that are homogeneous on the basis of physical and economic characteristics (recall 1 and 2 above) could be aggregated together at the lowest level of aggregation. Taking a regional basis would mean that the same physical commodity produced in different locations would be treated as separate outputs in the system of national accounts (which is the correct treatment). However, it is not clear whether commodities should be distinguished not only by their region or market area, but also by their establishment or outlet (or point of sale or purchase). If commodities are distinguished by outlet, then shifts in purchases by consumers from high priced outlets to discount outlets will not show up as price declines in the national accounts.

With respect to classification criterion 5, Hill (1993, p. 398) was quite explicit in recommending that peak-load or time-of-day commodities should be distinguished as separate commodities as should seasonal commodities: "For example, electricity or transport provided at peak times must be treated as being of higher quality than the same amount of electricity or transport provided at off-peak times. The fact that peaks exist shows that purchasers or users attach greater utility to the services at these times, while the marginal costs of production are usually higher at peak times. The different prices or rates charged at peak and off-peak times provide measures of these differences in quality. Similarly, fruit and vegetables supplied out of season must be treated as higher qualities than the same fruit and vegetables in season which are cheaper to produce and of which consumers may be satiated."

In the context of quarterly national accounts, Hill's proposed treatment of time-of-day commodities does not propose any conceptual problems:

instead of being a homogeneous single commodity—say, electricity consumption by an economic unit over a quarter—we simply disaggregate
the consumption into peak and off-peak components, with separate prices
and quantities for each component. However, the treatment of seasonal
commodities in subannual accounts is much more difficult from a conceptual point of view. If we are constructing annual accounts, then
following Hill's advice, we can disaggregate the annual transactions involving a seasonal commodity into price and quantity components
distinguished by season. Then annual price and volume indexes can be
constructed in the usual fashion, treating transactions for the commodity
that take place in different seasons as separate commodities. Thus
seasonal sales in the month of December will be compared with sales in
the December of the base year. This is Stone's (1956, p. 75) solution to
the treatment of seasonal commodities in the context of *annual* accounts.
However, when constructing quarterly or monthly accounts, this strategy
breaks down.[37] Hill did not offer any advice on what to do in
this situation.

Hill (1993, p. 398) made some very perceptive comments on the
interpretation of price differences between commodities that are physically
idential or very similar: "In economic theory it is generally assumed that
whenever a difference in price is found between two goods and services
which appear to be physically identical there must be some other factor,
such as location, timing, conditions of sale, etc., which is introducing a
difference in quality. Otherwise, it can be argued that the difference
could not persist, as rational purchasers would always buy lower priced
items and no sales would take place at higher prices. In most cases,
therefore, differences in prices at the same moment of time must be taken
as prima facie evidence that the goods or services concerned represent
different qualities of the same general kind of good or service."

Hill noted that an implication of the above traditional view of price
differences is that a shift toward higher-priced varieties of the same
physical commodity will lead to an increase in aggregate quantity rather
than price; conversely, a shift toward lower-priced varieties will lead to a
decrease in aggregate quantity. If high and low prices remain the same in
the two periods under consideration, then the above traditional view of
price differences will imply to change in aggregate price no matter what
shifts in demand occur. However, Hill (1993, p. 398) went on to question
the assumption that the existence of different prices during the same time
period *always* reflects differences in the qualities of the goods or services
sold: "Nevertheless, it must be questioned whether the existence of
observed price differences always implies corresponding differences in
quality. There are strong assumptions underlying the standard argument

which are seldom made explicit and are often not satisfied in practice: for example, that purchasers are well informed and that they are free to choose between goods and services offered at different prices."

Hill (1993, pp. 398–399) observed that the traditional view of price differences reflecting quality differences could be wrong for three reasons: (1) consumers may lack information on where the lowest price is to be found (they may have to search for the lowest price, and search is costly),[38] (2) price discrimination may exist, particularly for government supplied goods, and (3) rationing of commodities sold at below normal prices may occur (put another way, many firms have "sales").

The importance of Hill's discussion on the traditional view of price differences reflecting quality differences will become evident when Hill discusses methods for dealing with quality changes.

Another preliminary topic that Hill discussed very ably is the problem of price variation within the period for a homogeneous commodity—that is, the sales of a particular commodity at a particular outlet over the accounting period of time will typically *not* take place at the same price. However, bilateral index number theory requires that all of this micro variation in prices and quantities during a period be aggregated into single price and quantity measures that will be inputs into the appropriate index number formula. How should this micro aggregation be accomplished? According to Hill (1993, p. 399), "When there is price variation for the same quality of good or service, the price relatives used for index number calculation should be defined as the ratio of the weighted average price of that good or service in the two periods, the weights being the relative quantities sold at each price. Suppose, for example, that a certain quantity of a particular good or service is sold at a lower price to a particular category of purchaser without any difference whatsoever in the nature of the good or service offered, location, timing or conditions of sale, or other factors. A subsequent decrease in the proportion sold at the lower price raises the average price paid by purchasers for quantities of a good or service whose quality is the same and remains unchanged, by assumption. It also raises the average price received by the seller without any change in quality. This must be recorded as a price and not a volume increase."

Thus Hill recommended the use of the commodity's *unit value* and the *total quantity transacted* as the theoretically correct price and quantity numbers that summarize the individual transactions involving the commodity over the accounting period under consideration. This treatment of commodity aggregation at the lowest level dates back to Walsh (1990, p. 96, 1921a, p. 88) and Davies (1924, p. 187, 1932, p. 59).[39]

The use of unit values as the theoretically "correct" prices at the lowest level of aggregation has some rather strong implications for current statistical agency practices: instead of collecting price quotations from establishments or outlets that pertain to a single point of time within the accounting period,[40] the total value of transactions and the total quantities transacted by the establishment during the accounting period should be collected. As more firms electronically record data on their transactions and as the costs of storing and transmitting information fall, this unit value approach to pricing becomes more feasible.

Hill (1993, p. 399) noted that the above contrasting views on the significance of different prices for the same commodity lead to difficult problems of judgment for statistical agencies: if the price differences are superficial and do not really reflect differences in quality, then unit values should be constructed that aggregate over all transactions involving these superficially different commodities to get the "correct" measure of average price that would be inserted into an index number formula. On the other hand, if the price differences are real, then the commodity transactions should be disaggregated into quality constant groups of transactions and be treated as separate goods. If there is doubt as to whether the price differences are superficial or real, then Hill (1993, p. 399) recommended that the statistical agency assume that the price differences reflect real quality differences.

After completing the above introduction, Hill (1993, pp. 399–401) went on to discuss four possible ways of incorporating quality change into price and quantity indexes: (1) ignore the fact that a new "package" for an old good has appeared and simply treat the new good as being equivalent to the old good; (2) omit the new good in the price index in the period when the new good first appears; (3) adjust the new good's price for the change in quality (that is, use a hedonic regression procedure), or (4) use the method of overlapping price quotations. Hill (1993, p. 399) did not favor the use of alternatives (1) and (2).

The overlapping price quotes method relies on the old and new variety being available on the market simultaneously for at least one period. For example, consider the following three-period situation: in period 0, the price and quantity transacted of the old good are p_1^0 and q_1^0, respectively; in period 1, the price and quantity of the old good are p_1^1 and q_1^1 and the price and quantity of the new good are p_2^1 and q_2^1, respectively; in period 2, the old good has disappeared and the price and quantity transacted of the new good are p_2^2 and q_2^2. Treating period 0 as the base period, the overlapping price quotes method treats the period 1 price index for the commodity group as the old goods price ratio, p_1^1/p_1^0. The price index going from period 1 to period 2 is taken to be the new goods price ratio

p_2^2/p_2^1. The overall sequence of price indexes for the three periods is assumed to be

$$1, p_1^1/p_1^0, (p_1^1/p_1^0)(p_2^2/p_2^1). \tag{8.63}$$

Dividing the above price indexes into the value ratios gives us the following sequence of quantity indexes for the overlapping quotes method:

$$1, (p_1^1/q_1^0) + (p_2^1/p_1^1)(q_2^1/q_1^0), (p_2^1/p_1^1)(q_2^2/q_1^0) \tag{8.64}$$

Thus the overlapping price quotes method assumes that one unit of the new good is equivalent in terms of final use utility to p_2^1/p_1^1 units of the old good. This method relies heavily on the assumption that the observed prices of both varieties in period 1 reflect 1 reflect real quality differences. Note that the goods are assumed to be perfect substitutes using the linear conversion factor, p_2^1/p_1^1.

Let us now follow the example of Hill and assume that (1) the new and old goods are denominated in the same effective final use units (for example, when comparing a new computer with an old one that differs in only one characteristic–say, speed–we denominate the prices of the two computers in dollars per unit of speed) and (2) the price differences in period 1 reflect only transitory differences and hence the correct price for the computer aggregate in period 1 is the unit value $[p_1^1 q_1^1 + p_2^1 q_2^1]/[q_1^1 + q_2^1]$. Under these assumptions, the correct sequence of price indexes for the three periods would be

$$1, (p_1^1/p_1^0)[q_1^1/(q_1^1 + q_2^1)] + (p_2^1/p_1^0)[q_2^1(q_1^1 + q_2^1)], p_2^2/p_1^0. \tag{8.65}$$

Typically, the old good will be overpriced compared to the new good when prices are measured in efficiency units–that is, we will typically have $p_1^1 > p_2^1$. Under these conditions, it can be verified that the period 1 and period 2 prices in the unit value sequence of prices (8.65) will be *lower* than the corresponding period 1 and 2 overlapping quotes prices in (8.63)—that is, under the above conditions, the traditional method will have an *upward* bias.[41]

We could take the point of view that is the opposite of the above unit value approach and assume that the new variety is a genuine new good that cannot be aggregated with the old good using a linear conversion factor as in (8.64). In this situation, we can apply the theoretical approach of Hicks (1940, p. 114) and assume that there exists a period 0 reservation price, p_2^{0*}, that would just equate demand for the new good to zero in period 0. We also assume the existence of a period 2 reservation price, p_1^{2*}, that equates demand for the disappearing old good equal to zero in period 2. Unfortunately, these reservation prices are unobservable and hence econometric estimation to determine them must be undertaken[42] or various conventional guesses for them must be made (see Diewert, 1980, pp. 498–501). We assume that the quantity of the new good in period 0 is zero ($q_2^0 \equiv 0$) and the quantity of the disappearing old good in period 2 is zero ($q_1^2 \equiv 0$). With these assumptions, we can evaluate the three period sequence of fixed base Laspeyres and Paasche price indexes, which turn out to be

$$P_L(P^0, p^t, q^0, q^t) = 1, \qquad\qquad p_1^1/p_1^0, \qquad\qquad p_1^{2*}/p_1^0, \quad (8.66)$$

$$P_P(P^0, p^t, q^0, q^t) = 1, [p_1^1 q_1^1 + p_2^1 q_2^1]/[p_1^0 q_1^1 + p_2^{0*} q_2^1], p_2^2/p_2^{0*}. \quad (8.67)$$

For successful new varieties that cause the demand for the old varieties to decrease dramatically, we can conjecture that the period 0 reservation price for the new variety, p_2^{0*}, is considerably higher than its period 1 price p_2^1, adjusted for inflation between periods 0 and 1, using p_1^0/p_1^1 as the inflation adjustment. Thus for successful new varieties, we will normally have

$$p_2^{0*} > p_2^1(p_1^0/p_1^1). \tag{8.68}$$

As for the disappearing variety, if we were to assume that the reservation price for good 1 in period 2 were simply its period 1 price p_1^1, adjusted for inflation between periods 1 and 2 using p_2^2/p_2^1 as the escalator, producers would probably be supplying the old good in period 2. Since there is no demand for the old good in period 2, it is probable that the old good reservation price lies below $p_1^1(p_2^2/p_2^1)$—that is, we will usually have

$$p_1^{2*} < p_1^1(p_2^2/p_2^1). \tag{8.69}$$

If we substitute (8.69) into (8.66) and (8.68) into (8.67), we find that

$$P_L(p^0, p^2, q^0, q^2) < (p_1^1/p_1^0)(p_2^2/p_2^1), \tag{8.70}$$

$$P_P(p^0, p^2, q^0, q^2) < (p_1^1/p_1^0)(p_2^2/p_2^1), \tag{8.71}$$

Thus under the above hypotheses, in period 2, both the fixed base Laspeyres and Paasche price indexes will be less than the corresponding price obtained by the traditional overlapping price method (recall the last entry in (8.63)).

The above analysis indicates that from both the unit value perspective and the new good perspective, the traditional overlapping price quotes method for dealing with quality change is likely to impart an upward bias to price indexes in many situations. With the growth in international trade and the proliferation of new products that has taken place over the past two decades, there is a need for statistical agencies to carefully examine their procedures for dealing with new products.[43]

The hedonic method for adjusting price indexes for changes in the quality of goods was introduced by Court (1939, p. 107) in order to deal with situations where the new varieties involved changes in more than one important characteristic: "Price per unit is a satisfactory procedure where the useful and desirable qualities of an article can be roughly summarized in terms of a single specification. Passenger cars serve so many diverse purposes that such a single, most important specification can not be found (like rated tonnage in the case of trucks). The simple method is inapplicable, but why not combine several specifications to from a single composite measure? The Hedonic suggestions are addressed to this problem of establishing an objective measure of usefulness and desirability in terms of which prices of products of complex function can be compared. In the case of passenger cars, if the relative immportance to the customer of horsepower, braking capacity, window area, seat width, tire size, etc., could be established, the data reflecting these characteristics could be combined into an index of usefulness and desirability. Prices per vehicle divided by this index of Hedonic content would yield valid comparisons in the face of changing specifications."

Court (1939, pp. 109–110) went on to set up essentially the modern hedonic regression framework: the logarithm of an auto price was regressed on a linear function of automobile characteristics (weight, wheelbase, and horsepower) plus some time dummies (which were later converted into annual price indexes for autos).

Hill (1993, p. 401) made the following observations on the applicability of the hedonic method: "The hedonic hypothesis may be used for any goods or services whose prices depend mainly on a few basic characteristics and for which sufficient numbers of different models, or qualities, are on sale on the market at the same time."

For a sampling of the vast literature on the hedonic approach to adjusting for quality change, see Stone (1956, pp. 47–60), Griliches (1961, 1971), Diewert (1980, pp. 503–505), Triplett (1986, 1987, 1989), Dulberger (1989), Gordon (1989, 1990), Berndt (1991), and Berndt and Griliches (1993).

For general discussions of quality change issues, see Court (1939, pp. 103–105), Hofsten (1952), Fisher and Shell (1972), Gordon (1990, 1992) and Baldwin, Després, Nakamura, and Nakamura (1994).

8.8. Choice Between Direct and Indirect Measurement of Prices and Volumes

When comprehensive price and quantity data are both available, Hill (1993, p. 401) noted that it is not necessary to calculate both the price and quantity indexes, since given one of the indexes, the product test, equation (8.1), can be used to generate the other index.

However, in a sampling context when complete price and quantity information is not available, Hill recommended that the price index be calculated directly (from the sample information) and the quantity index be calculated indirectly using (8.1), (assuming that the value ratio $p^t \cdot q^t / p^0 \cdot q^0$ can be calculated using other non sample information). Hill (1993, p. 401) gave two reasons for calculating the price index rather than the volume index form the sample information: "There are two reasons for this: first, it is usually necessary to estimate the average price or volume change from a selection or sample, of goods and services, and price relatives tend to have a smaller variance than the corresponding quantity relatives. Thus, the sampling error for a price index tends to be smaller than for a volume index. Secondly, the volume changes associated with new and disappearing products are properly reflected when current values are deflated by price indices."

Hill's first reason for preferring to construct the price index directly rather than indirectly is certainly valid from an empirical point of view.[44] However, we must be a bit cautious in accepting his second argument without some qualification. Hill esssentially advocated what Keynes (1930, p. 94) called the *highest common factor method* for dealing with the new goods problem: simply ignore any new or disappearing goods in the two time periods under consideration and calculate the price index on the basis of the goods that are common to the two situations. This is essentially equivalent to the overlapping price quotes method for dealing with new goods. As we saw in the previous section, this method is likely to impart an upward bias to the price index in many situations.[45] Although it is not practical to ask statistical agencies to estimate reservation prices for new and disappearing goods, it seems practical to ask them to utilize the overlapping unit values method (8.65) if the new good differs from an existing good in only one important characteristic.

8.9. Nonmarket Goods and Services

What should national income accountants do when there are no market prices for an output (or "unreasonable" market prices)? Hill (1993, p.

402) suggested the following strategy: (1) set the value of the output equal to the cost of producing it, and (2) calculate some sort of quantity indicator for the output. Now use (1) for values and (2) for quantities, and prices can be calculated by dividing values by quantities. Once prices and quantities have been obtained, normal index number theory can be applied. This is a very sensible strategy and can be implemented with a bit of work.[46]

Hill (1993, pp. 402–403) recommended that the "full" cost of production be used when calculating costs for government subsidized outputs and be included in this cost—labour costs, intermediate input costs, depreciation of capital inputs, and input taxes—but there was no mention of interest cost, since interest is treated as a transfer in the *System of National Accounts* and *not* as a productive output. This treatment of interest seems to us to be incorrect.

8.10. The Scope of Price and Volume Measures in the System

Hill (1993, p. 403) noted that his discussion of price and volume measures up to this point related mostly to the flows of goods and services production sector and utilized by the household sector. Hill further observed that some components of input cost could also be decomposed into price and volume components, including labor compensation, consumption of fixed capital (depreciation), and taxes and subsidies on products (values are total tax payments pertaining to the commodity and the corresponding prices are taxes paid per unit of the commodity). The fourth component of input cost is operating surplus. Hill (1993, p. 403) did not recommend that operating surplus be decomposed into price and volume components: "The net operating surplus is an accounting residual which does not possess quantity and price dimensions of its own. It may also be negative, of course. It is not possible, therefore, to decompose the net operating surplus into its own price and volume components."

Here again we see a deficiency in the national income accounting framework due to the treatment of interest as being unproductive. If interest (including imputed interest on equity capital) were treated as a productive factor of production and *user costs*[47] for the capital components of cost were calculated, then the interest and depreciation components of user cost would lead to a greatly diminished[48] "operating surplus." This diminished operating surplus would be approximately equal to the economist's notion of "pure profits" and would typically be very small.

Hence the fact that pure profits could not be decomposed into price and quantity components would not matter very much due to their small size.

8.11. Measures of Real Income for the Total Economy

Hill (1993, pp. 403–405) considered two substantive topics in this section: how can the real income of an economy be defined, and how can gross domestic product be adjusted for changes in the economy's terms of trade?

On the first question, Hill did not make any specific recommendations. Typically, a consumer price index or a producer price index is used to deflate household nominal income into a "real" income.[49]

On the second question, Hill (1993, p. 404) noted that a rise in the price of a country's exports relative to the price of its imports has an effect that is similar to a productivity gain: the economy can provide domestic final demanders with more outputs for the same amounts of domestic inputs supplied to the prouction sector of the economy.

General references to the adjusting for changes in the terms of trade literature include Nicholson (1960), Bjerke (1968), Kurabayashi (1971), Hamada and Iwata (1984), and Silver and Mahdavy (1989). For an approach that is more explicitly based on producer theory and exact index numbers, see Diewert (1983b, pp. 1083–1100), Diewert and Morrison (1986, 1990) and Kohli (1990, 1993).

8.12. Sources of Bias in Consumer Price Indexes

It may be useful to alert national income accountants to the recent literature on sources of bias in consumer price indexes. Many of these sources of bias are also present in producer price indexes. Recent surveys on this topic include Gordon (1993), Fixler (1993), Crawford (1993), Wynne and Sigalla (1994), and Diewert (1995a).

Of course, bias can only be defined relative to the "correct" underlying theoretical concept. In what follows, the "correct" concept is taken to be the Konüs (1924) price index, generalized to groups of consumers.[50]

As least five sources of bias have been distinguished in the literature: elementary price index bias, commodity substitution bias, outlet substitution bias, overlapping price quotes bias, and new goods bias.

Elementary price index bias results from the use of an inappropriate index number formula to aggregate up prices at the very lowest level of aggregation. This source of bias added approximately 0.5 percent per year to the U.S. consumer price index for the years 1987–1994 (see Moulton, 1993; Reinsdorf and Moulton, 1994; Armknecht, Moulton, and Stewart, 1994). Recent papers dealing with this type of bias include Szulc (1989), Dalén (1992), Balk (1994a), Schultz (1994), and Diewert (1995a).

Commodity substitution bias is the bias which results from the use of Laspeyres or Paasche price indexes, which are exact only for preferences that exhibit no substitution (see Pollak, 1989, p. 14).[51] This source of bias can be avoided by the use of superlative price indexes. The work of Manser and McDonald (1988), Balk (1990, p. 82) and Aizcorbe and Jackman (1993) indicates that this source of bias adds about 0.2 to 0.3 percent per year to a typical consumer price index (CPI).

Outlet substitution bias is the bias that results from inappropriately treating purchases from high and low cost outlets as separate goods; recall Hill's discussion on the validity of regarding price differences as evidence of quality differences in Section 8.7 above. The estimates of Reinsdorf (1993) and Saglio (1994) suggest that this bias might add something like 0.25 percent to 0.4 percent per year to a typical CPI in recent years.

Griliches (1979, p. 79) and Gordon (1981, 1990, 1993) emphasized the source of bias that results when the *overlapping price quotes* method of adjusting for quality change is used.[52] Gordon (1990) estimated that the durables component of the U.S. CPI was biased upward by about 1.5 percent per year during the period 1947–1983 due to this source of bias.

Our final source of bias is the *new goods bias* that results from an expansion in consumers' choice sets.[53] Hill (1988, p. 138) explicitly recognized this source of bias in an earlier paper, but he did not suggest a method for dealing with the problem. Diewert (1987, p. 779, 1993a, pp. 59–63), following Marshall's (1887, p. 373) analysis of product cycle pricing, suggested that this bias could be substantially reduced by simply introducing new goods into the pricing basket in a timely fashion.[54] Triplett (1993, p. 200) termed the subset of the new goods bias caused by delays in introducing new products into the index the *new introductions bias*. Empirical evidence on the possible magnitude of the new goods bias can be found in Berndt, Griliches and Rosett (1993), Griliches and Cockburn (1994), and Hausman (1994).

Of all the sources of bias listed above, I believe that the biases associated with the introduction of new goods are the most significant. In the past fifteen years, we have seen a proliferation of new goods and services. Traditional economics, rooted in models that have only a fixed number of commodities, has, by and large, missed the significance of this phenomenon of an increasing dimension for the commodity space.[55] Thus productivity improvements are no longer taking place only by production units achieving economics of scale but also by the application of science and technology through the creation of new products and new processes. It seems likely that statistical agencies have simply missed the improvements in our standard of living that are due to the increased number of commodities that consumers now have in their choice sets.

8.13. Omitted Topics

A number of additional topics could be discussed in the context of constructing price and volume indexes. We list a few of them below:

- The current *System of Accounts* has no role for productivity accounts.[56] The reason for this omission can be traced to the *System*'s treatment of interest; recall our discussion of this topic in Section 8.10 above.
- The current *System of Accounts* has an inconsistent treatment of durables in consumer price and volume indexes: housing is treated appropriately as a flow of consumption services but for other consumer durables, only additions to household stocks count. Again, there is a reluctance on the part of national income accountants to embrace the user cost concept. In order to improve the international (and intertemporal) comparability of consumption and savings statistics, consumption flows should be modelled rather than additions to stocks (see Eisner, 1989; Johal, 1991).
- The reluctance of the *System* to impute a productive role for interest leads to rather strange measures of output for most financial industries as well as for distributive industries where inventory holdings are large. Again, a user cost approach would lead to straightforward measures of inputs and outputs (Hancock, 1985; Barnett, 1987; Fixler and Zieschang, 1991, 1992; Diewert and Smith, 1995).
- There are major conceptual problems involved in measuring the outputs of industries where risk or uncertainty is associated with the outputs sold, such as insurance, gambling, and financial options. This is an area for future research (Diewert, 1995b).

We conclude this section by providing a few references to the vast literature on seasonal adjustment (recall Hill's discussion of seasonal commodities in Section 8.7 above). References that take primarily economic approaches to seasonal adjustment include Turvey (1979), Balk (1980a, 1980b), Diewert (1983c), and Baldwin (1985). References that take primarily statistical approaches include Cleveland (1983), Bell and Hillmer (1984), and Hylleberg (1992).

8.14. Conclusion

Peter Hill has written a masterful survey of modern index number theory and practice. Chapter 16 of the *System of National Accounts 1993* will be an invaluable reference for not only national accounting specialists but also for students and practitioners of economics in general. In twenty-seven pages, Hill has managed to accurately summarize a vast literature in an elegant and readable fashion—a splendid accomplishment.

Acknowledgments

This research was supported by a Strategic Grant from the Social Sciences and Humanities Research Council of Canada. Discussions with Peter Hill and Jack Triplett were very helpful. Thanks are due as well to Alice Nakamura and also to Louise Hebert and Keltie Stearman for typing a difficult manuscript.

Notes

1. Rather than use Hill's notation for prices and quantities, which involved double subscripts, we use a more standard notation where the superscript denotes the time period and the subscript denotes the commodity. We change Hill's notation in other ways as well.

2. Define the inner product of the vectors p^t and q^t as $p^t \cdot q^t \equiv \Sigma_{i=1}^N p_i^t q_i^t$. Frisch (1930, p. 399) called (8.1) the product test, while Samuelson and Swamy (1974, p. 572) called it the weak factor reversal test. The originator of the test was Irving Fisher (1911, p. 403).

3. This point was originally made by Bortkiewicz (1923, p. 377).

4. Diewert (1976, p. 115) introduced this term to cover both the consumer and production theory contexts.

5. This result seems to have been obtained first by Frisch (1936, p. 24); for a modern proof, see Pollak (1971, p. 65). Hill did not mention another result due to Konüs (1924, pp. 20–21) that does not require the assumption of homotheticity: there exists a utility level between u^0 and u^t, u^* say, such that $P_k(p^0, p^t, u^*)$ lies between P_L and P_p. See Diewert (1981, p. 185) for a modern proof of this result.

6. Walsh (1921b) showed Fisher (1921) how to "rectify" any index number formula to make it consistent with the time reversal test, a fact that Fisher (1922) neglected to mention in his book.

7. Moreover, the product of the price and quantity indexes must equal the appropriate value ratio—that is, (8.1) must be satisfied. Diewert (1992a) showed that the Fisher ideal indexes satisfy more sensible tests than any of the other bilateral indexes commonly used.

8. Christensen, Jorgenson, and Lau (1973) introduced the translog functional form into the economics literature.

9. Diewert (1976, pp. 123–124) also showed that Q_T is exact for a general nonhomothetic aggregator function provided that the Malmquist (1953) quantity index is used as the underlying theoretical construct.

10. This problem was stressed by Turvey (1989, p. 1). It was also mentioned by Arthur Bowley in his response to Fisher (1923, p. 252) as the following quotation indicates: "The trouble is that we only infrequently have the data for double weighting, and it is therefore important to examine carefully the criticisms and tests applied to formulae in actual use."

11. Diewert and Wales (1987, p. 54) established the flexibility of this functional form.

12. Sidgewick (1883, p. 68) and Bowley (1901, p. 227) first proposed the use of (8.23) applied to price indexes; Fisher (1922, p. 487) listed the price index counterparts to (8.23) and (8.24) as his formulas 8053 and 8054.

13. Walsh (1921, p. 108) called his test the circular test while Diewert (1993a, p. 40) called it a multiperiod identity test. Fisher (1922, p. 64) specialized Walsh's test to two periods and called it the time reversal test.

14. The indexes defined by (8.23) and (8.24) also satisfy the time reversal test in the sense that $Q_{q^0}(p^0, p^t, q^0, q^t)Q_{q^0}(p^t, p^0, q^t, q^0) = 1$ and $Q_{q^1}(p^0, p^t, q^0, q^1)Q_{q^1}(p^t, p^0, q^t, q^0) = 1$.

15. However, if we treat α as a fixed quantity vector q, then $Q_\alpha(p^0, p^t, q^0, q^t) = [(p^t \cdot q^t/p^t \cdot q) + (p^0 \cdot q^t/p^0 \cdot q)]/[(p^t \cdot q^0/p^t \cdot q) + (p^0 \cdot q^0/p^0 \cdot q)] = \Sigma_{n=1}^N[s_n^{0*} + s_n^{t*}][q_n^t/q_n]/\Sigma_{i=1}^N[s_i^{0*} + s_i^{t*}][q_i^0/q_i]$, where $s_i^{0*} \equiv p_i^0 q_i/p^0 \cdot q$ and $s_i^{t*} \equiv p_i^t q_i/p^t \cdot q$ for $i = 1, \ldots, N$. Thus when $\alpha = q$, the numerator of Q_α can be rewritten as a share weighted sum of the quantity relatives q_i^t/q_i and the denominator as a share weighted sum of the quantity relatives q_i^0/q_i.

16. A symmetric mean of two numbers x and y—$m(x, y)$, say—has at least the following two properties: (1) it is symmetric—that is, $m(x, y) = m(y, x)$ and (2) it has the mean property—that is, $m(x, x) = x$. For further properties of symmetric means, see Diewert (1993b).

17. Samuelson and Swamy (1974, p. 582) have a related result.

18. This section is based on Hill (1988, pp. 135–145).

19. The chain principle was introduced independently into the economics literature by Lehr (1885, pp. 45–46) and Marshall (1887, p. 373). Both authors observed that the chain system would mitigate the difficulties due to the introduction of new commodities into the economy, a point also mentioned by Hill (1993, p. 388). Fisher (1911, p. 203) introduced the term "chain system."

20. If the p^t are approximately proportional to the base period price vector p^0, there will be no major problems with the use of (8.5). However, in recent years, computers have become a large component of investment expenditures and their prices have been dropping dramatically year after year; see Dulberger (1989) and Triplett (1989, 1993). As Young (1992, p. 33) notes: "changes in the prices and quantities of computers have been large enough to make the measurement of the change in real GDP quite sensitive to the choice of price weights." Thus the United States has given up on providing constant price indexes for the components of GDP back to 1926.

21. These points were made earlier by Diewert (1978, p. 895).

22. This point emerged from discussions with Jack Triplett.

23. If Q_α were to be used, there is the awkward problem of choosing α.

24. Initially, Hill (1993, pp. 390–391) assumed that the dimensionality of the commodity space was 2N—that is, each commodity was allowed to be either an input or output or both. He also initially assumed that the price vector for outputs was equal to the price vector for intermediate inputs. Hill (1993, p. 392) later recognized that at the economy wide level, changes in the volume of GDP may be calculated using data on total final expenditures and imports—that is, at the total economy level, intermediate inputs become imports and hence will have different prices than the components of final demand. Note that this treatment of imports assumes that they flow through the producer sector of an economy initially, a treatment pioneered by Kohli (1978, 1991).

25. "It is as though a volume comparison were to be made between a complete decade and a single year" (Hill, 1993, p. 392).

26. Actually counterparts to the chain principle can be found in the multilateral context. Gerardi (1982, p. 399) and Robert Hill (1994a) suggested the use of multilateral chain systems where the links would be forged by minimizing some distance function depending on the prices and quantities of the two countries in that link. Hill suggested $\ln[\max\{P_L^{ij}, P_P^{ij}\}/\min\{P_L^{ij}, P_P^{ij}\}]$ (where P_L^{ij} and $\{P_P^{ij}$ are the Laspeyres and Paasche price indexes between countries i and j) as a suitable distance measure. For other distance functions, see Allen and Diewert (1981, p. 433) and Martini (1992, p. 369). Fisher (1922, p. 272) in his discussion of comparisons between Egypt, Georgia, and Norway explicitly ruled out the use of a multilateral chain principle as the following quotation indicates: "But evidently, if we are intent on getting the very best comparison between Norway and Egypt, we should not go to Georgia for our weights."

27. Turvey (1989, ch. 3) defined the elementary level as the lowest level of aggregation.

28. Alternatively, assume that producers in country i are maximizing revenue $p^t \cdot q$ subject to a nonnegative, linearly homogeneous, increasing and convex factor requirements function $f(q) = u_i$ where $u_i > 0$ is the quantity of input available. See Diewert (1974) for the duality between factor requirements functions and revenue functions.

29. To derive this, use Wold's (1944, pp. 69–71) identity plus the linear homogeneity of f, which implies $q^i \cdot \Delta f(q^i) = f(q^i) = u_i$. See Diewert (1993c, p. 135).

30. Diewert (1993b, p. 361) defined a symmetric mean $m(x_1, \ldots, x_N)$ to be a continuous, symmetric and increasing function of its arguments, which has the mean value property: $m(\lambda, \ldots, \lambda) = \lambda$ for all λ in the domain of definition. For a homogeneous symmetric mean, add the linear homogeneity property: $m(\lambda x_1, \ldots, \lambda x_N) = \lambda m(x_1, \ldots, x_N)$ for all $\lambda > 0$ and all $(x_1, \ldots, x_N)$ in the domain of definition.

31. Since m is strictly increasing in each of its arguments, this can always be done.

32. Since unit cost functions must be linearly homogeneous, there is no constant term on the right side of (8.49). See Diewert (1993c, p. 122) for the properties of unit cost functions.

33. We are assuming that $N \geq 2$—that is, that there is more than one commodity. There is no index number problem if $N = 1$.

34. For the case of a Leontief aggregator function, quantity vectors must be proportional across countries; for the case of a linear aggregator function, price vectors must be proportional across countries.

35. This fact was noted by Van Ijzeren (1983, p. 42) but he did not obtain the elegant formula (8.62) due to Dikhanov (1994).

36. Van Ijzeren (1983, p. 53) provided an elegant proof of the existence of a solution for the case of two countries. There does not appear to be a proof of existence in the general J case.

37. Turvey (1979) showed that statistical agency practices differed enormously in this situation and that very different subannual indexes resulted from the same seasonal data set

that he sent to statistical agencies.

38. For papers that incorporate consumer search into cost of living indexes, see Anglin and Baye (1987) and Reinsdorf (1993).

39. See Diewert (1995a) for references to the literature on aggregation at the lowest level. Fisher (1922, p. 318) casually endorsed the use of total quantities and unit values as the following quotation indicates: "On what principle should this average be constructed? The *practical* answer is *any* kind of average since, ordinarily, the variations during a year, so far, at least, as prices are concerned, are too little to make any perceptible difference in the result, whatever kind of average is used. Otherwise, there would be ground for subdividing the year into quarters or months until we reach a small enough period to be considered practically a point. The quantities sold will, of course, vary widely. What is needed is their sum for the year. . . . In short, the simple arithmetic average, both of prices and of quantities, may be used. Or, if it is worth while to put any finer point on it, we may take the weighted arithmetic average for the prices, the weights being the quantities sold." What Fisher failed to emphasize is if the sum of quantities transacted is used as the quantity concept, then the unit value *must* be taken as the corresponding price concept in order to preserve the value of transactions within the period. Note that Fisher, like Hicks (1946, p. 122), defined the appropriate time period to be a time period during which variations in price can be neglected.

40. This is the current statistical agency approach (see Turvey, 1989, p. 50). The price quotes that are collected are regarded as being representative of all transaction prices for the commodity in the period under consideration.

41. Gordon (1990, 1992, pp. 9–10), Griliches and Cockburn (1993) and Nordhaus (1994) discussed this type of bias and provided estimates of it in various situations. Diewert (1995a, p. 33) called this type of bias the "linking bias."

42. Hausman (1944) did this for new breakfast cereals.

43. Baldwin, Després, Nakamura, and Nakamura (1994) survey how new goods are introduced into the producer price indexes of Canada and Japan. These authors also make the important point that a new good does not have to be new in the sense that the good did not exist anywhere in the world in the previous period but rather a new good is one which was not available in the local market in the previous period. This observation which dates back to Marshall (1887, p. 374) greatly widens the scope of the new goods problem and the possibility of bias in official indexes.

44. Allen and Diewert (1981, pp. 432–433) justify Hill's preference from a slightly different point of view: if price relatives have a small variance, then the conditions for Hicks' (1946, pp. 312–313) composite commodity theorm are approximately fulfilled and the price index should be constructed directly. On the other hand, if quantity relatives have a small variance, then the conditions for Leontief's (1936, pp. 54–57) aggregation theorem are approximately satisfied and the quantity index should be constructed directly.

45. Diewert (1980, p. 501) made this point in the context of evaluating the highest common factor method using the Hicksian (1940) reservation price methodology.

46. Denis Lawrence has used the above strategy quite successfully in Australia in comparing the productivity performance of government market oriented enterprises with each other and comparable best practice enterprises overseas (see Lawrence, 1992; Industry Commission, 1993).

47. See Jorgenson and Griliches (1967) and Christensen and Jorgenson (1970) for examples of how user costs can be calculated in a national income accounting framework. The user cost concept dates back to Walras (1874, p. 269) at least. See Jorgenson (1963, 1989), Diewert (1980, pp. 475–486) and Griliches (1988) for more recent discussions of user costs. For a treatment of inventory user costs, see Diewert and Smith (1994).

48. The interest component of user cost could be treated in a manner analogous to Hill's proposed treatment of the depreciation component or the two components could be combined as in the Jorgenson and Griliches (1967) treatment of user cost.

49. For a theory of a real income deflator that is parallel to the Konüs (1924) cost of living deflator, see Diewert and Bossons (1987).

50. More specifically, take Pollak's (1989, p. 131) social cost of living index as the correct theoretical index.

51. The bias resulting from the use of P_L of P_P is the difference between the right and left sides of (8.11) or (8.12).

52. Recall the discussion of this method in Section 8.7 above.

53. Recall our discussion of Hicks' (1940, p. 114) approach to this problem in Section 8.7 above.

54. This will still not eliminate the bias under normal conditions—that is, the bias represented by the inequalities (8.70) and (8.71) in Section 8.7 will still remain.

55. Of course there are many exceptions; see for example Romer (1994) for a model of economic development that is centered around the creation of new goods.

56. See Kendrick (1961), Jorgenson and Griliches (1967), Christensen and Jorgenson (1970), Mark and Waldorf (1983), Balk (1994b), and Kohli (1990, 1993) for hints on how these accounts could be constructed.

References

Afriat, S.N. (1972). "The Theory of International Comparisons of Real Income and Prices." In D.J. Daly (ed.), *International Comparisons of Prices and Output* (pp. 13–69). National Bureau of Economic Research. New York: Columbia University Press.

Afriat, S.N. (1977). *The Price Index.* London: Cambridge University Press.

Aizcorbe, A.M., and P.C. Jackman (1993). "The Commodity Substitution Effect in CIP Data, 1982–91." *Monthly Labor Review* (U.S. Bureau of Labor Statistics) (December): 25–33.

Allen, R.C., and W.E. Diewert. (1981). "Direct Versus Implicit Superlative Index Number Formulae." *Review of Economics and Statistics* 63: 430–435.

Allen, R.G.D. (1949). "The Economic Theory of Index Numbers." *Econometrica N.S.* 16: 197–203.

Allen, R.G.D. (1975). *Index Numbers in Theory and Practice.* London: Macmillan.

Anglin, P.M., and M.R. Baye. (1987). "Information, Multiprice Search, and Cost-of-Living Index Theory." *Journal of Political Economy* 95: 1179–1195.

Archibald, R.B. (1977). "On the Theory of Industrial Price Measurement: Output Price Indexes." *Annals of Economic and Social Measurement* 6: 57–72.

Armknecht, P.A., B.R. Moulton, and K.J. Stewart. (1994). "Improvements to the Food at Home, Shelter and Prescription Drug Indexes in the U.S. Consumer Price Index." Paper presented at the International Conference on Price Indices, October 31–November 2. Ottawa: Statistics Canada.

Arrow, K.J. (1974). "The Measurement of Real Value Added." In P.A. David and M.W. Reder (eds.), *Nations and Households in Economic Growth* (pp. 3–19). New York: Academic Press.

Baldwin, A. (1985). *The Treatment of Seasonal Commodities in the Consumer Price Index*. Ottawa: Statistics Canada, Prices Division.

Baldwin, A., P. Després, A. Nakamura, and M. Nakamura. (1994). "New Goods from the Perspective of Price Index Making in Canada and Japan." In T. Bresnahan and R.J. Gordon (eds.), *New Goods*. NBER Conference on New Goods. Chicago: University of Chicago Press.

Balk, B.M. (1980a). "A Method for Constructing Price Indices for Seasonal Commodities." *Journal of the Royal Statistical Society* A 143: 68–75.

Balk, B.M. (1980b). *Seasonal Products in Agriculture and Horticulture and Methods for Computing Price Indices*. Statistical Studies 24. The Hague: Netherlands Central Bureau of Statistics.

Balk, B.M. (1989). "On Van Ijzeren's Approach to International Comparisons and Its Properties." *Statistical Papers (Statistische Hefte)* 30: 295–315.

Balk, B.M. (1990). "On Calculating Cost-of-Living Index Numbers for Arbitrary Income Levels." *Econometrica* 58: 75–92.

Balk, B.M. (1992). "Axiomatic Price Index Theory: A Survey." Netherlands Central Bureau of Statistics, Department of Price Statistics, P.O. Box 959, 2270 AZ Voorburg, November 26.

Balk, B.M. (1993). "Multilateral Methods for International Price and Volume Comparisons." Department of Price Statistics, Netherlands Central Bureau of Statistics, P.O. Box 959, 2270 AZ, Voorburg, April.

Balk, B.M. (1994a). "On the First Step in the Calculation of a Consumer Price Index." Paper presented at the International Conference on Price Indices, October 31–November 2. Ottawa: Statistics Canada.

Balk, B.M. (1994b). "Micro-Economic Foundations for Industrial Price, Quantity and Productivity Indices." Paper presented at the Georgia Productivity Workshop, October 21–23. Statistics Netherlands, P.O. Box 959, 2270 AZ, Voorburg.

Barnett, W.A. (1987). "The Microeconomic Theory of Monetary Aggregation." In W.A. Barnett and K.J. Singleton (eds.), *New Approaches to Monetary Economics* (pp. 115–168). New York: Cambridge University Press.

Bell, W.R., and C. Hillmer. (1984). "Issues Involved with the Seasonal Adjustment of Economic Time Series." *Journal of Business and Economic Statistics* 2: 291–319.

Berndt, E.R. (1991). "The Measurement of Quality Change: Constructing a Hedonic Price Index for Computers Using Multiple Regression Methods." In E.R. Berndt, *The Practice of Econometrics: Classic and Contemporary* (ch. 4). Reading, MA: Addison-Wesley.

Berndt, E.R., and Z. Griliches. (1993). "Price Indexes for Microcomputers: An Exploratory Study." In M.F. Foss, M.E. Mansen and A.H. Young (eds.), *Price Measurements and Their Uses* (pp. 63–93). Chicago: University of Chicago Press.

Berndt, E.R., Z. Griliches, and J.G. Rosett. (1993). "Auditing and Producer Price Index: Micro Evidence from Prescription Pharmaceutical Preparations." *Journal of Business and Economic Statistics* 11: 251–264.

Bjerke, K. (1968). "Some Reflections on the Terms of Trade." *Review of Income and Wealth* 14: 183–198.

Bortkiewicz, L., von. (1923). "Zweck und Struktureiner Preisindenzahl: Ester Artikel." *Nordisk Statistisk Tidskrift* 2: 369–408.

Bowley, A.L. (1901). *Elements of Statistics*. London: King.

Bowley, A.L. (1921). "An Index of the Physical Volume of Production." *Economic Journal* 31: 196–205.

Caves, D.W., L.R. Christensen, and W.E. Diewert. (1982a). "Multilateral Comparisons of Output, Input and Productivity Using Superlative Index Numbers." *Economic Journal* 92: 73–86.

Caves, D.W., L.R. Christensen, and W.E. Diewert. (1982b). "The Economic Theory of Index Numbers and the Measurement of Input, Output and Productivity." *Econometrica* 50: 1393–1414.

Christensen, L.R., and D.W. Jorgenson. (1970). "U.S. Real Product and Real Factor Input, 1929–1967." *Review of Income and Wealth* 16: 19–50.

Christensen, L., D. Jorgenson, and L. Lau. (1973). "Transcendental Logarithmic Production Frontiers." *Review of Economics and Statistics* 55: 28–45.

Cleveland, W.S. (1983). "Seasonal and Calendar Adjustment." In *Handbook of Statistics* (Vol. 3, pp. 39–72). Amsterdam: Elsevier Science.

Court, A.T. (1939). "Hedonic Price Indexes with Automotive Examples." In *The Dynamics of Automobile Demand* (pp. 98–119). New York: General Motors.

Crawford, A. (1993). "Measurement Biases in the Canadian CPI: A Technical Note." *Bank of Canada Review* (Summer): 21–36.

Dalén, J. (1992). "Computing Elementary Aggregates in the Swedish Consumer Price Index." *Journal of Official Statistics* 8: 129–147.

Davies, G.R. (1924). "The Problem of a Standard Index Number Formula." *Journal of the American Statistical Association* 19: 180–188.

Davies G.R. (1932). "Index Numbers in Mathematical Economics." *Journal of the American Statistical Association* 27: 58–64.

Diewert, W.E. (1974). "Applications of Duality Theory." In M.D. Intriligator and D.A. Kendrick (eds.), *Frontier of Quantitative Economics* (Vol. 2, pp. 106–171). Amsterdam: North-Holland.

Diewert, W.E. (1976). "Exact and Superlative Index Numbers." *Journal of Econometrics* 4: 115–145.

Diewert, W.E. (1978). "Superlative Index Numbers and Consistency in Aggregation." *Econometrica* 46: 883–900.

Diewert, W.E. (1980). "Aggregaton Problems in the Measurement of Capital." In Dan Usher (ed.), *The Measurement of Capital* (pp. 433–528). Chicago: University of Chicago Press.

Diewert, W.E. (1981). "The Economic Theory of Index Numbers: A Survey." In A. Deaton (ed.), *Essays in the Theory and Measurement of Consumer Behavior in Honour of Sir Richard Stone* (pp. 163–200). London: Cambridge University Press.

Diewert, W.E. (1983a). "The Theory of the Cost-of-Living Index and the Measurement of Welfare Change." In W.E. Diewert and C. Montmarquette (eds.), *Price Level Measurement* (pp. 163–233). Ottawa: Statistics Canada.

Diewert, W.E. (1983b). "The Theory of the Output Price Index and the Measurement of Real Output Change." In *Price Level Measurement* (pp. 1049–1113). Ottawa: Statistics Canada.

Diewert, W.E. (1983c). "The Treatment of Seasonality in a Cost-of-Living Index." In W.E. Diewert and C. Montmarquette (eds.), *Price Level Measurement* (pp. 1019–1045). Ottawa: Statistics Canada.

Diewert, W.E. (1986). "Microeconomic Approaches to the Theory of International Comparisons." Technical Working Paper No. 53, National Bureau of Economic Research, Cambridge, MA.

Diewert, W.E. (1987). "Index Numbers." In J. Eatwell, M. Milgate, and P. Neuman (eds.), *The New Palgrave: A Dictionary of Economics* (Vol. 2, pp. 767–780). London: Macmillan Press.

Diewert, W.E. (1988). "Test Approaches to International Comparisons." In W. Eichhorn (ed.), *Measurement in Economics* (pp. 67–86). Heidelberg: Physica-Verlag.

Diewert, W.E. (1992a). "Fisher Ideal Output, Input and Productivity Indexes Revisited." *Journal of Productivity Analysis* 3: 211–248.

Diewert, W.E. (1992b). "Exact and Superlative Welfare Change Indicators." *Economic Inquiry* 30: 565–582.

Diewert, W.E. (1993a). "The Early History of Price Index Research." In W.E. Diewert and A.O. Nakamura (eds.), *Essays in Index Number Theory* (Vol. 1, pp. 33–65). Amsterdam: North-Holland.

Diewert, W.E. (1993b). "Symmetric Means and Choice Under Uncertainty." In W.E. Diewert and A.O. Nakamura (eds.), *Essays in Index Number Theory* (Vol. 1, pp. 355–433). Amsterdam: North-Holland.

Diewert, W.E. (1993c). "Duality Approaches to Microeconomic Theory." In W.E. Diewert and A.O. Nakamura (eds.), *Essays in Index Number Theory* (Vol. pp. 105–175). Amsterdam: North-Holland.

Diewert, W.E. (1995a). "Axiomatic and Economic Approaches to Elementary Price Indexes." Discussion Paper No. 95-01, Department of Economics, University of British Columbia, Vancouver, Canada V6T 1Z1.

Diewert, W.E. (1995b). "Functional Form Problems in Modelling Insurance and Gambling." *Geneva Papers on Risk and Insurance Theory* 20: 135–150.

Diewert, W.E., and J. Bossons. (1987). "Adjusting the Consumer Price Index for Changes in Taxes." Discussion Paper No. 87-09, Department of Economics, University of British Columbia, Vancouver, Canada, April.

Diewert, W.E., and C.J. Morrison. (1986). "Adjustng Output and Productivity Indexes for Changes in the Terms of Trade." *Economic Journal* 96: 659–679.

Diewert, W.E., and C.J. Morrison. (1990). "Productivity Growth and Changes in the Terms of Trade in Japan and the United States." In C.R. Hulten (ed.), *Productivity Growth in Japan and the United States* (pp. 201–227). Chicago: University of Chicago Press.

Diewert, W.E., and A.M. Smith. (1994). "Productivity Measurement for a Distribution Firm." *Journal of Productivity Analysis* 5: 335–347.

Diewert, W.E., and T.J. Wales. (1987). "Flexible Functional Forms and Global Curvature Conditions." *Econometrica* 55: 43–68.

Dikhanov, Y. (1994). "Sensitivity of PPP Based Income Estimates to Choice of Aggregation Procedures." Paper presented at the Conference of the International Association for Research in Income and Wealth, St. Andrews, New Brunswick, August.

Drechsler, L. (1973). "Weighting of Index Numbers in Multilateral International Comparisons." *Review of Income and Wealth*, Series 19 (March): 17–47.

Dulberger, E.R. (1989). "The Application of a Hedonic Model to Quality-Adjusted Price Index for Computer Processors." In D.W. Jorgenson and R. Landau (eds.), *Technology and Capital Formation* (pp. 37–75). Cambridge, MA: MIT Press.

Eichhorn, W. (1976). "Fisher's Tests Revisited." *Econometrica* 44: 247–256.

Eichhorn, W. (1978). *Functional Equations in Economics*. London: Addison-Wesley.

Eichhorn, W., and J. Voeller. (1976). *Theory of the Price Index*. Lecture Notes in Economics and Mathematical Systems 140. Berlin: Springer-Verlag.

Eisner, R. (1989). *The Total Incomes System of Accounts*. Chicago: University of Chicago Press.

Elteto, O., and P. Köves. (1964). "On a Problem of Index Number Computation Relating to International Comparison." *Statisztikai Szemle* 42: 507–518.

Eurostat. (1988). *Purchasing Power Parities and Gross Domestic Product in Real Terms Results 1985*. Luxembourg: Statistical Office of the European Communities.

Fisher, F.M., and K. Shell. (1972). *The Economic Theory of Price Indexes*. New York: Academic Press.

Fisher, I. (1911). *The Purchasing Power of Money*. London: Macmillan.

Fisher, I. (1921). "The Best Form of Index Number." *Journal of the American Statistical Association* 17: 533–537.

Fisher, I. (1922). *The Making of Index Numbers*. Boston: Houghton Mifflin.

Fisher, I. (1923). "Professor Bowley on Index-Numbers." *Economic Journal* 33: 246–252.

Fixler, D.J. (1993). "The Consumer Price Index: Underlying Concepts and Caveats." *Monthly Labor Review*, BLS (December): 3–12.

Fixler, D., and K.D. Zieschang. (1991). "Measuring the Nominal Value of Finacincial Services in the National Income Accounts." *Economic Inquiry* 29: 53–68.

Fixler D.J., and K.D. Zieschang. (1992). "User Costs, Shadow Prices and the Real Output of Banks." In Zvi Griliches (ed.), *Output Measurement in the Service Sectors* (pp. 219–243). Chicago: University of Chicago Press.

Frisch, R. (1930). "Necessary and Sufficient Conditions Regarding the Form of an Index Number Which Shall Meet Certain of Fisher's Tests." *American Statistical Association Journal* 25: 397–406.

Frisch, R. (1936). "Annual Survey of General Economic Theory: The Problem of Index Numbers." *Econometrica* 4: 1–39.

Geary, R.G. (1958). "A Note on Comparisons of Exchange Rates and Purchasing Power Between Countries." *Journal of the Royal Statistical Society* A 121: 97–99.

Gerardi, D. (1982). "Selected Problems of Inter-Country Comparisons on the Basis of the Experience of the EEC." *Review of Income and Wealth* 28: 381–405.

Gini, C. (1931). "On the Circular Test of Index Numbers." *Metron* 9(2): 3–24.

Gordon, R.J. (1981). "The Consumer Price Index: Measuring Inflation and Causing It." *The Public Interest* 63: 112–134.

Gordon, R.J. (1989). "The Postwar Evolution of Computer Prices." In D.W. Jorgenson and R. Landau (eds.), *Technology and Capital Formation* (pp. 77–125). Cambridge, MA: MIT Press.

Gordon, R.J. (1990). *The Measurement of Durable Goods Prices.* Chicago: University of Chicago Press.

Gordon, R.J. (1993). "Measuring the Aggregate Price Level: Implications for Economic Performance and Policy." In K. Shizehard (ed.), *Price Stabilization in the 1990s* (pp. 233–276). London: Macmillan.

Griliches, Z. (1961). "Hedonic Price Indexes for Automobiles: An Analysis of Quality Change." In *The Price Statistics of the Federal Government* (pp. 137–196). General Series No. 73. New York: Columbia University Press.

Griliches, Z. (1971). "Introduction: Hedonic Prices Revisited." In Z. Griliches (ed.), *Price Indexes and Quality Change* (pp. 3–15). Cambridge, MA: Harvard University Press.

Griliches, Z. (1979). "Issues in Assessing the Contribution of Research and Development to Productivity Growth." *The Bell Journal of Economics* 10: 92–116.

Griliches, Z. (1988). "Capital Stock in Investment Functions: Some Problems of Concept and Measurement." In Zvi Geriliches (ed.), *Technology, Education and Productivity* (pp. 123–143). Oxford: Basil Blackwell.

Griliches, Z., and I. Cockburn. (1994). "Generics and New Goods in Pharmaceutical Price Indexes." *American Economic Review* 84: 1213–1232.

Hamada, K., and K. Iwata. (1984). "National Income, Terms of Trade and Economic Welfare." *Economic Journal* 94: 752–771.

Hancock, D. (1985). "The Financial Firm: Production with Monetary and Nonmonetary Goods." *Journal of Political Economy* 93: 859–880.

Hausman, J. (1994). "Valuation of New Goods Under Perfect and Imperfect Competition." In T. Bresnahan and R.J. Gordon (eds.), *The Economics of New Products.* Cambridge, MA: NBER.

Hicks. J.R. (1940). "The Valuation of the Social Income." *Economica* 7: 105–140.

Hicks, J.R. (1946). *Value and Capital* (2nd ed.). Oxford: Clarendon Press.

Hicks, J.R. (1981). *Wealth and Welfare.* Cambridge, MA: Harvard University Press.

Hill, P. (1982). *Multilateral Measurements of Purchasing Power and Real GDP.* Luxembourg: Eurostat.

Hill, P. (1984). "Introduction: The Special Conference on Purchasing Power Parities." *Review of Income and Wealth*, ser. 30: 125–133.

Hill, P. (1988). "Recent Developments in Index Number Theory and Practice." *OECD Economic Studies* 10 (Spring): 123–148.

Hill, P. (1993). "Price and Volume Measures." In *System of National Accounts 1993* (pp. 379–406). Brussels, Luxembourg, New York and Washington DC: Eurostat, IMF, OECD, UN, and World Bank.

Hill, R.J. (1994a). "Chained Multilateral Comparisons Using Graph Theory Algorithms." Department of Economics, University of British Columbia, Vancouver, Canada, October.

Hill, R.J. (1994b). "A Taxonomy of Multilateral Methods for Making International Comparisons." Department of Economics, University of British Columbia, Vancouver, Canada, October.

Hofsten, E. von. (1952). *Price Indexes and Quality Change*. London: George Allen and Unwin.

Hylleberg, S. (ed.). (1992). *Modelling Seasonality*. Oxford: Oxford University Press.

Iklé, D.M. (1972). "A New Approach to the Index Number Problem." *Quarterly Journal of Economics* 86: 188–211.

Industry Commission. (1993). *Government Trading Enterprises Performance Indicators 1987–88 to 1991–92*. P.O. Box 80, Belconnen ACT 2616, Australia.

Johal, K. (1991). "A Study of the Flow of Consumption Services from the Stock of Consumer Goods." *National Income and Expenditure Accounts*. 4th Quarter, Catalogue No. 13-001, 1–20. Ottawa: Statistics Canada.

Jorgenson, D.W. (1963). "Capital Theory and Investment Behavior." *American Economic Review* 53: 247–259.

Jorgenson, D.W. (1989). "Capital as a Factor of Production." In D.W. Jorgenson and R. Landau (eds.), *Technology and Capital Formation* (pp. 1–35). Cambridge, MA: MIT Press.

Jorgenson, D.W., and Z. Griliches. (1967). "The Explanation of Productivity Change." *Review of Economic Studies* 34: 249–283.

Kendrick, J.W. (1961). *Productivity Trends in the United States*. Princeton, NJ: Princeton University Press.

Keynes, J.M. (1930). *Treatise on Money* (Vol. 1). London: Macmillan.

Khamis, S.H. (1970). "Properties and Conditions for the Existence of a New Type of Index Number." *Sankhya* Series B 32: 81–98.

Khamis, S.H. (1972). "A New System of Index Numbers for National and International Purposes." *Journal of the Royal Statistical Society*, A 135: 96–121.

Kohli, U. (1978). "A Gross National Product Function and the Derived Demand for Imports and Supply of Exports." *Canadian Journal of Economics* 11: 167–182.

Kohli, U. (1990). "Growth Accounting in the Open Economy: Parametric and Nonparametric Estimates." *Journal of Economic and Social Measurement* 16: 125–136.

Kohli, U. (1991). *Technology, Duality and Foreign Trade*. Ann Arbor: University of Michigan Press.

Kohli, U. (1993). "GNP Growth Accounting in the Open Economy: Parametric and Nonparametric Estimates for Switzerland." *Swiss Journal of Economics and Statistics* 129: 601–615.

Konüs, A.A. (1924). "The Problem of the True Cost of Living" (trans.). *Econometrica* 7, 139: 10–29.

Konüs, A.A., and S.S. Byushgens. (1926). "K. Probleme Pokupatelnoi Cili Deneg." *Voprosi Konyunkturi* 2(1): 151–172.

Kravis, I.B. (1984). "Comparative Studies of National Incomes and Prices." *Journal of Economic Literature* 22: 1–39.

Kravis, I.B., R. Summers, and A. Heston. (1982). "Comments on 'Selected Problems of Intercountry Comparisons on the Basis of the Experience of the EEC.'" *Review of Income and Wealth*, Series 28: 407–410.

Kurabayashi, Y. (1971). "The Impact of Changes in Terms of Trade on a System of National Accounts: An Attempted Synthesis." *Review of Income and Wealth* 17: 285–293.

Laspeyres, E. (1871). "Die Berechnung einer mittleren Waarenpreissteigerung." *Jahrbücher für Nationalökonomie und Statistik* 16: 296–314.

Lawrence, D. (1992). *Measuring the Total Factor Productivity of Government Trading Enterprises*. Belconnen, Australia: Industry Commission.

Lehr, J. (1885). *Beiträge zur Statistik der Preise*. Frankfurt: J.D. Sauerländer.

Leontief, W. (1936). "Composite Commodities and the Problem of Index Numbers." *Econometrica* 4: 39–59.

Lowe, J. (1823). *The Present State of England in Regard to Agriculture, Trade and Finance* (2nd ed.). London: Longman, Hurst, Rees, Orme, and Brown.

Malmquist, S. (1953). "Index Numbers and Indifference Surfaces." *Trabajos de Estatistica* 4: 209–242.

Manser, M.E., and R.J. McDonald. (1988). "An Analysis of Substitution Bias in Measuring Inflation, 1959–85." *Econommetrica* 56: 909–930.

Mark, J.A., and W.H. Waldorf. (1983). "Multifactor Productivity: A New BLS Measure." *Monthly Labor Review* (December): 3–15.

Marshall, A. (1887). "Remedies for Fluctuations of General Prices." *Contemporary Review* 51: 355–375.

Martini, M. (1992). "A General Function of Axiomatic Index Numbers." *Journal of the Italian Statistical Society* 3: 359–376.

Moulton, B.R. (1993). "Basic Components of the CPI: Estimation of Price Changes." *Monthly Labor Review* (U.S. Bureau of Labor Statistics) (December): 13–24.

Nicholson, J.L. (1960). "The Effects of International Trade on the Measurement of Real National Income." *Economic Journal* 70: 608–612.

Nordhaus, W.D. (1994). "Do Real Output and Real Wage Measures Capture Reality? The History of Light Suggests Not." In T. Bresnahan and R.J. Gordon (eds.), *The Economics of New Products*. Cambridge, MA: NBER.

Paasche, H. (1874). "Über die Preisentwicklung der letzten Jahre nach den Hamburger Börsennotirungen." *Jahrbücher für Nationalökonemie und Statistik* 23: 168–178.

Pollak, R.A. (1971). "The Theory of the Cost of Living Index." Research Discussion Paper 11, Bureau of Labor Statistics, Washington, DC; and in W.E. Diewert and C. Montmarquette (eds.) (1983), *Price Level Measurement* (pp. 87–161). Ottawa: Statistics Canada.

Pollak, R.A. (1989). *The Theory of the Cost-of-Living Index.* Oxford: Oxford University Press.

Reinsdorf, M. (1993). "The Effect of Outlet Price Differentials on the U.S. Consumer Price Index." In M.F. Foss, M.E. Manser and A.H. Young (eds.), *Price Measurements and Their Uses* (pp. 227–254). Studies in Income and Wealth (Vol. 57), NBER. Chicago: University of Chicago Press.

Reinsdorf, M., and B.R. Moulton. (1994). "The Construction of Basic Components of Cost of Living Indexes." In R.J. Gordon (ed.), *The Economics of New Products.* Conference on Research in Income and Wealth. Cambridge, MA: NBER.

Romer, P. (1994). "New Goods, Old Theory and the Welfare Costs of Trade Restrictions." *Journal of Development Economics* 43: 5–38.

Ruggles, R. (1967). "Price Indexes and International Price Comparisons." In W. Fellner et al. (eds.), *Ten Economic Studies in the Tradition of Irving Fisher* (pp. 171–205). New York: J. Wiley.

Saglio, A. (1994). "Comparative Changes in Average Price and a Price Index: Two Case Studies." Paper presented at the International Conference of Price Indices, October 31–November 2. Ottawa: Statistics Canada.

Samuelson, P.A. (1947). *Foundations of Economic Analysis.* Cambridge, MA: Harvard University Press.

Samuelson, P.A., and S. Swamy. (1974). "Invariant Economic Index Numbers and Canonical Duality: Survey and Synthesis." *American Economic Review* 64: 566–593.

Sato, K. (1976). "The Meaning and Measurement of the Real Value Added Index." *Review of Economics and Statistics* 58: 434–442.

Schultz (Szulc), B.J. (1994). "Choice of Price Index Formula at the Micro-Aggregation Level: The Canadian Empirical Evidence." Paper presented at the International Conference on Price Indices, October 31–November 2. Ottawa: Statistics Canada.

Shephard, R.W. (1953). *Cost and Production Functions.* Princeton, NJ: Princeton University Press.

Sidgewick, H. (1883). *The Principles of Political Economy.* London: Macmillan.

Silver, M., and K. Mahdavy. (1989). "The Measurement of a Nation's Terms of Trade Effect and Real National Disposable Income Within a National Accounting Framework." *Journal of the Royal Statistical Society,* Series A 152: 87–107.

Stone, R. (1956). *Quantity and Price Indexes in National Accounts.* Paris: Organization for European Cooperation.

Summers, R., and A. Heston. (1988). "A New Set of International Comparisons of Real Product and Price Levels Estimates for 130 Countries, 1950–1988." *Review of Income and Wealth*, Series 34: 1–25.

Summers, R., and A. Heston. (1991). "The Penn World Table (Mark 5): An Expanded Set of International Comparisons, 1950–1988." *Quarterly Journal of Economics* 106: 327–368.

Szilágyi, G. (1986). "Procedures for Linking International Comparisons." *Statistical Journal of the United Nations ECE* 4: 165–181.

Szulc, B.J. (1964). "Indices for Multiregional Comparisons." *Przeglad Statystyczny (Statistical Review)* 3: 239–254.

Szulc, B.J. (1983). "Linking Price Index Numbers." In W.E. Diewert and C. Montmarquette (eds.), *Price Level Measurement* (pp. 537–566). Ottawa: Statistics Canada.

Szulc, B.J. (1989). "Price Indices Below the Basic Aggregation Level." In R. Turvey (ed.), *Consumer Price Indices: An ILO Manual* (pp. 167–178). Geneva: International Labour Office.

Törnqvist, L. (1936). "The Bank of Finland's Consumption Price Index." *Bank of Finland Monthly Bulletin* 10: 1–8.

Triplett, J.E. (1986). "The Economic Interpretation of Hedonic Methods." *Survey of Current Business* 86(1): 36–40.

Triplett, J.E. (1987). "Hedonic Functions and Hedonic Indexes." In J. Eatwell, M. Milgate and P. Newman (eds.), *The New Palgrave: A Dictionary of Economics* (Vol. 2, pp. 630–634). London: Macmillan.

Triplett, J.E. (1989). "Price and Technological Change in a Capital Good: A Survey of Research on Computers." In D.W. Jorgenson and R. Landau (eds.), *Technology and Capital Formation* (pp. 127–213). Cambridge, MA: MIT Press.

Triplett, J.E. (1992). "Economic Theory and BEA's Alternative Quantity and Price Indexes." *Survey of Current Business* 72 (April): 49–52.

Triplett, J.E. (1993). "Comment." In M.F. Foss, M.E. Manser and A.H. Young (eds.), *Price Measurements and Their Uses* (pp. 197–206). Studies in Income and Wealth (Vol. 57). National Bureau of Economic Research. Chicago: University of Chicago Press.

Turvey, R. (1979). "The Treatment of Seasonal Items in Consumer Price Indices." *Bulletin of Labour Statistics* (4th qtr.) (International Labour Office, Geneva): 13–33.

Turvey, R. (1989). *Consumer Price Indices: An ILO Manual.* Geneva: International Labour Office.

United Nations. (1993). *System of National Accounts 1993.* New York: United Nations.

United States Bureau of Labor Statistics. (1983). *Trends in Multifactor Productivity 1948–81.* Bulletin 2178. Washington, DC: U.S. Government Prining Office.

United States Bureau of Labor Statistics. (1993). *Labor Composition and U.S.*

Productivity Growth, 1948–90. Bulletin 2426. Washington DC: U.S. Government Printing Office.

Van Ijzeren, J. (1983). *Index Numbers for Binary and Multilateral Comparison*. Statistical Studies No. 34. The Hague: Netherlands Central Bureau of Statistics.

Van Ijzeren, J. (1987). *Bias in International Index Numbers: A Mathematical Elucidation*. Eindhoven: Dissertatiedrukkerij Wibro.

Van Yzeren, J. (1956). *Three Methods of Comparing the Purchasing Power of Currencies*. Statistical Studies No. 7. The Hague: Netherlands Central Bureau of Statistics.

Van Yzeren, J. (1988). "Weighting and Additivity Problems of Multilateral Comparison." In W. Eichhorn (ed.), *Measurement in Economics* (pp. 157–164). Heidelberg: Physica-Verlag.

Wald, A. (1939). "A New Formula for the Index of Cost of Living." *Econometrica* 7: 319–331.

Walras, L. (1874). *Elements of Pure Economics* (trans. by William Jaffé, 1954. London: George Allen and Unwin.

Walsh, C.M. (1901). *The Measurement of General Exchange Value*. New York: Macmillan.

Walsh, C.M. (1921a). *The Problem of Estimation*. London: King.

Walsh, C.M. (1921b). "Discussion of the Best Form of Index Number." *Journal of the American Statistical Association* 17: 537–544.

Walsh, C.M. (1924). "Professor Edgeworth's Views on Index-Numbers." *Quarterly Journal of Economics* 38: 500–519.

Wold, H. (1944). "A Synthesis of Pure Demand Analysis, Part III." *Skandinavisk Aktuarietidskrift* 27: 69–120.

Wynne, M.A., and F.D. Sigalla. (1994). "The Consumer Price Index." *Economic Review Federal Reserve Bank of Dallas* (2nd qtr.): 1–22.

Young, A.H. (1992). "Alternative Means of Change in Real Output and Prices." *Survey of Current Business* 72 (April): 32–48.

DISCUSSION OF CHAPTER 8

Robert J. Gordon

Introduction

Erwin Diewert has written an impressive and insightful review of Peter Hill's paper on "Price and Volume Measures" in the *System of National Accounts, 1993*. This piece is classic Diewert-as-interpreter, taking a verbal discussion, identifying the key issues, and formalizing them in a thicket of equations, complete with a huge set of references going back to the dawn of the subject more than a century ago. In fact, as formidable as this paper may appear to the uninitiated, it is relatively sparse of equations and abundant in words compared to Diewert's many other original contributions.

While Diewert's paper has many virtues, I would have preferred less formalization and more of an attempt to assess the quantitative importance of some of these issues. While the paper concludes with a short survey of quantitative estimates of the bias in the U.S. Consumer Price Index (CPI), its earlier sections are notably lacking in guidance to the reader as to which of these issues really matter and why.

Index Numbers and Additivity

The most important point about weighting schemes and index numbers is that weights should change frequently. There is a class of index numbers that Diewert has classified as "superlative" and that allow weights to change frequently but differ in minor ways, depending on the duration of the period over which weights are averaged and how the averaging is carried out.

The U.S. National Income and Product Accounts (NIPA) are unique, in comparison with other countries, in their steadfast insistence on a *single* base year that applies to all calculations of real variables—that is, real GDP, real consumption, real investment, and so on, from the dawn of the data through to the present. This leads to fallacious data that are widely used and analyzed and yet that the producers of the data (the Bureau of Economic Analysis, or BEA) know are misleading and, for some purposes, lead to the opposite conclusions of the truth.

Why has the BEA maintained the single-base-year approach for so long? As Diewert points out, there is a fatal theoretical contradiction between shifting weights and additivity. Simply put, if we shift weights every quarter, then the sum of the components of real GDP will not add up to total real GDP for more than a single quarter (Diewert identifies particular superlative index numbers for which additivity holds for two consecutive periods). The obvious retort to the additivity dilemma is, "Who cares?" For any question involving shares of one component in the total economy or a subcomponent in a major part of the economy, the correct answer comes from shares of nominal (current dollar) spending or income, not real (constant dollar income). There is no additivity problem in nominal magnitudes and thus no problem in discussing shares of any component within any other component.

Perhaps we could agree that there is a dichotomy in the use of national income statistics. Some people are interested in the cross-section relationships—that is, relative magnitudes. For this, nominal magnitudes are the correct measure. More often, we are interested in growth rates of real magnitudes, such as productivity growth (which in turn is the growth rate of output minus the growth rate of hours of labor input). Here we want the growth rates to be based on moving weights, a Fisher-ideal, Törnqvist, or chain-weighted measure. For growth rates, additivity does not matter.

Not only is the additivity dilemma irrelevant for nominal magnitudes, but it is meaningless for real magnitudes. If we want the share of consumption in total real GDP (consisting of components $C + I + G$), we can measure that as $C/(C + I + G)$. It is irrelevant whether the level total real GDP compouted with a chain-weighted procedure differs from the total of $C + I + G$. Besides, with rapidly changing weights, shares in real GDP are unlikely to differ appreciably from shares in nominal GDP. Again, additivity does not matter.

The real issues in this area involve weighting schemes. First, let us review the simple logic behind the error of using a single base year and then examine some of the consequences. The official U.S. measure of real GDP in 1987 prices weights subcomponents of output by their relative prices in 1987. To focus on the effect, consider the different impact of government expenditures, which have an increasing relative price over the decades, and of producers' durable equipment, in which there is an important component of computing equipment, which has a (rapidly) declining relative price over the decades.

Consider first the years prior to 1987, when government expenditures were relatively cheaper than in 1987. The official 1987 weights based on 1987 relative prices will *overweight* government expenditures for years prior to 1987 and will *underweight* government expenditures for years after 1987. Since government expenditures always increase in wartime, the relative size of government (and of World War I or World War II wartime expenditures) is much larger using 1987 as a base year than, say, 1944 or 1917. Further, the size of the exaggeration of wartime expenditures is not fixed, since the base year is regularly moved to a later date, from 1972 to 1982 to 1987. To dramatize the importance of this error in weighting procedures, I have often said "that every time the BEA moves the base year back, World War I gets bigger."

Similarly, the 1987-base-year procedure *understates* the importance of computers and other high-tech equipment prior to 1987. Since these have rapidly declining relative prices, prior to 1987 any component of GDP that includes computers is understated as a share of GDP, and the growth rate of GDP itself is understated. Everything is reversed after 1987. The relative size of government (or any other sector with a rising relative price) is understated. The relative size of computer investment, or any aggregate (like producers' durable equipment—PDE—or manufacturing output) that includes computer output, is overstated.

But the size of relative shares is a small part of the overall problem. Anyone who wants to check the movement of true shares is free to use nominal magnitudes. Instead, the real damage is done to measures of the *growth rate* of real magnitudes, essential ingredients in measures of productivity and our standard of living. Oddly, while the BEA publishes both fixed 1987-base-year measures of real output magnitudes and superior magnitudes based on chain-weighting and benchmark-weighting, almost no one pays any attention to the superior measures.[1] Yet everyone, following Diewert, agrees that they dominate the conventional fixed 1987-base-year measures, so much so that the latter are invalid measures of economic performance.

Does this make any difference? Table 1 shows that important conclusions about the true behavior of the economy can be reversed when the official fixed 1987-base-year data are used in place of the theoretically preferable chain-weighted or benchmark-weighted indexes. To understand this table, note that the columns display annual rates of growth over four periods—1972–1987, 1987–1990, 1990–1994, and 1987–1994. That is, column 4 does not provide new information but rather provides a weighted average of the information in columns 2 and 3. Much of the following will be based on a comparison of the growth rates in columns 1 and 4.

Table 8.1. Growth rates of real output measures with alternative weights, various time periods, 1972–1994

	1972–1987 (1)	1987–1990 (2)	1990–1994 (3)	1987–1994 (4)
Real GDP:				
Fixed 1987 weights	2.75	2.68	2.00	2.29
Chain-type weights	3.03	2.70	1.72	2.14
Benchmark weights	3.10	2.68	1.74	2.14
Real consumption of durable goods:				
Fixed 1987 weights	4.69	2.48	3.92	3.30
Chain-type weights	5.05	2.45	3.30	2.94
Benchmark weights	5.09	2.45	3.34	2.96
Producers' durable equipment:				
Fixed 1987 weights	4.69	3.25	7.90	5.91
Chain-type weights	5.79	3.18	6.00	4.79
Benchmark weights	6.69	3.45	6.20	5.02
Nonfarm private output per hour:				
Fixed 1987 weights	0.95	0.15	1.94	1.17
Chain-type weights	1.23	0.17	1.66	1.02
Benchmark weights	1.30	0.15	1.68	1.02

Sources: GDP, consumption, PDE from Survey of Current Business, various issues. Output per hour from Economic Report of the President and Economic Indicators, various issues.

Note: Chain and benchmark versions of output per hour calculated by applying the differences for real GDP in the first three lines of the table.

The lines of the tables appear in four sections representing real GDP, real durable goods consumption, producers durable equipment (PDE), and nonfarm private output per hour (Q/H). In every case, the theoretically predicted difference appears between the indexes based on fixed 1987 weights, and the indexes based on chain-type weights or on benchmark weights. That is, the fixed 1987 weight measures understate the growth rate of real magnitudes prior to 1987 and overstate them after 1987.

For two key issues the change in weighting schemes, from the unsatisfactory BEA scheme based on fixed (1987) prices to one of the moving-weight schemes favored by Diewert, makes enough difference so that conclusions are reversed. Let's start at the bottom of Table 1, where data on the growth rates of nonfarm output per hour (Q/H) are displayed. Comparing column 1 and column 4, we reach the conclusion—associated with such optimistic business economists as Stephen Roach of Morgan Stanley—that productivity growth has accelerated. Fixed 1987 weights indicate that between 1972–1987 (column 1) and 1987–1994 (column 4) productivity growth accelerated from 0.95 percent per year to 1.17 percent per year.

However, this conclusion turns out to be quite decisively wrong when recalculated with either chain-type weights or benchmark weights. Comparing 1972–1987 with 1987–1994, chain-type weights indicate a productivity deceleration from 1.23 to 1.02 percent per year. In other words, the correct moving-weight index indicates a productivity *slowdown* of the same order of magnitude as the incorrect fixed-weight index indicates a productivity *acceleration*. The difference is even greater for PDE, where the fixed-weight (official) indexs indicates an acceleration from 4.69 to 5.91 percent per year, while chain-type weights indicate a deceleration from 5.79 to 4.79 percent per year. The difference between one measure and the other amounts to 2.2 percent per year, a big deal when compounded out over 10 or 15 years.

One of Diewert's conclusions is that differences between index numbers with moving weights should be relatively small. In this light, it is puzzling that there is such a large difference for the growth rate of PDE in the 1972–1987 period among the three measures. It may be that the benchmark measure, which uses the averages of weights five years apart, is flawed, since one of the benchmark years for that measure is at the trough of a business cycle when the behavior of investment was highly atypical.

International PPP Comparisons

Diewert's comments on Hill regarding international price and volume measures largely represent a summary of what Hill said, translated into equations. However, an important point is neglected by Diewert and perhaps by Hill. From the work that I have done, measures of purchasing-power-parity (PPP) exchange rates create a very fragile basis on which to assess the relative standards of living of various countries. Taking PPP exchange rates alternatively from OECD and other sources, I have been able to calculate that France in 1992 had a level of aggregate output per hour of anywhere from 105 percent of the U.S. level to a mere 75 percent. I have no idea why the sources differ so much, but for some questions these differences are extremely large. I wish both Hill and Diewert had addressed the fragile state of international PPP comparisons.

Sources of Bias in Aggregate Price Indexes

Diewert's section refers to bias in the CPI. What matters for output and productivity growth is bias in the GDP deflator. It is conceivable that these biases could go in the opposite direction because of the base-year bias discussed above. Real GDP growth is upward biased after 1987 because of the use of fixed 1987 weights rather than a moving-weight system like chain-weighting or benchmark weights. Yet the CPI is widely believed to be upward biased throughout the postwar period. This issue, for which no one has yet provided quantitative measures, implies that the direction of bias in aggregate measures of output after 1987 is uncertain, since weighting bias that raises the growth rates of real magnitudes is or may be overwhelmed by CPI bias that reduces the growth rates of real magnitudes. Obviously, before 1987 both sources of bias work in the same direction and imply that the growth rate of real GDP and of productivity is understated. This is not good news for those attempting to explain the infamous productivity growth slowdown.

Diewert's discussion of sources of bias in consumer price indexes provides many useful citations but is opaque for the purposes of many readers. Why are we now quite certain that the CPI incorporates a substantial upward bias? There are at least four reasons.

Traditional Substitution Bias

The CPI is known as a Laspeyres price index. That is, it measures price changes for many different products and then aggregates these thousands of separate measures of price change using weights that apply *to a base year (or years) that is prior to the period being measured.* Over much of the postwar period, these weights in the CPI have been based on consumer expenditures from five to fifteen years prior to the year of price measurement. In the traditional example, even if the price of chicken rises much less than the price of beef so that consumers shift their expenditures to chicken, the relative weight of chicken and beef in the CPI is based not on current spending patterns but rather on expenditures in that long-ago base year. Economists used to study this traditional substitution bias quite a lot, until they found out that it didn't amount to much. The consensus estimate for this first source of bias is 0.25 percent per year.

Quality Change

It is widely recognized that the CPI fails to adjust adequately for the improved quality of new products and new models. To set this problem in context, students of business history have drawn attention to the "product cycle." New products—whether autos, air conditioners, or VCRs—are initially made in small volumes and sold at high prices. Soon, firms figure out how to increase volumes and reduce prices. Eventually products mature, sales fall off, and prices increase more rapidly than the average product. The sequence is easily visualized as a U-shaped curve: the price of any given product relative to the consumer market basket starts high, then goes down, is flat for a while, and then goes back up.

Nobody debates the reality of this product cycle, and nobody debates the fact that the CPI introduces products late, thus missing much of the price decline that typically happens in the first phase of the product cycle. This is the first aspect of quality change bias. For example, room air conditioners were widely sold in 1951, available in the Sears catalogue and rated by *Consumer Reports* in 1952, but not introduced into the CPI until 1962, twelve years late! More recently, the microwave oven, VCR, and personal computer were all introduced into the CPI years after they were sold in the marketplace. In short, the CPI introduces new products too late and tracks obsolete products too long.

The second aspect of quality change bias results from a narrow definition of a commodity. Before 1970 precise multiplication and division required noisy and expensive rotary electric calculators; after 1970 electronic pocket calculators became available and are now in the pocket or dormitory of every college student. The price fell quickly from $1,000 to $10, and the new product could do exponents, logarithms, and lots of things the old product could not do. But the price decline was completely ignored by the government price indexes, which treated the old and new calculators as separate products. People flock to rent videos, but the declining price of seeing a move at home, as compared to going out to a theater, is entirely missed in the CPI. Similarly, the CPI missed the replacement of manual typewriters by electronic typewriters and then personal computers with word-processing capability.

The third aspect of quality change bias results from a narrow definition of quality. New improved models are often introduced with new features that are missed by the CPI. Changes occur in energy efficiency and repair frequency, but these are rarely if ever valued in compiling the CPI. Here is a brief list of some of the quality improvements that have been "missed" by the CPI over the postwar years:

- Improved ability of refrigerator-freezers to hold a zero temperature;
- Reduced electricity consumption of all applicances, particularly refrigerators and TV sets;
- Reduced repair costs on TV sets and indeed all appliances;
- Reduced vibration, noise, and discomfort in air travel as jets replaced piston planes and as air travel became safer;
- The enormous improvements in the audio quality of home and auto stereo equipment;
- The shift from metal to plastic that reduced corrosion and increased lifetimes for so many consumer products;
- The reduced weight of home power tools;
- The reduction of noise, weight, bulk, and installation cost of room air conditioners; and
- The immeasurable increase in picture quality of color TV sets compared to the dim, flickering images of the mid-1960s.

How much does this second source of CPI bias amount to? For some products it is huge—6 percent per year for the radio-TV category over the thirty-seven years studied in my book (Gordon, 1990). For other products, much less. I estimated that for consumer durables the upward bias was 1.5 percent per year for the postwar period, assuming that the half of consumer durables that I didn't study were measured perfectly. I'll bet that an inquiry into that other half would turn up additional bias. Even in such traditional products as apparel, there seems to be a substantial bias. In recent unpublished historical research I have identified a 2.1 percent per year upward bias in the CPI for apparel between 1920 and 1947. If the only quality bias was in the durables I measured in my book, the implied bias for the total CPI would be 0.3 percent per year. Adding in plausible bias in nondurables and services, we could easily double that to, say, 0.6 percent per year.

Outlet Substitution Bias

Just as the CPI has a narrow definition of a product, it has a narrow definition of where a product is sold. A banana is not a banana. If a pound of bananas initially costs $0.69 at Ace supermarket, and Ultra Discount Superstores comes to town and starts selling bananas for $0.49 per pound, the consumer enjoys a price decline of 29 percent, but the CPI registers a price decline of zero. Why? Each outlet is assumed to provide a separate set of services. But consumers have been leaving ma-and-pa stores in droves to shop at Wal-mart, Toys 'R Us, and Home Depot. So we know that individual consumers have enjoyed a price decline that is not measured in the CPI.

The Logarithm Bias

The most embarrassing source of bias in the CPI was brought to light by the BLS itself. To put it bluntly, the CPI doesn't understand logarithms. Using the methodology of the CPI, if a piece of apparel goes on sale from $100 to $75, that represents a price decline of 25 percent. When the item goes back to the regular price of $100, that represents a price increase of 33 percent. The true change in price from beginning to end is zero, the answer that would be obtained by using logs, but the CPI measures the change in price as plus 8 percent. Careful BLS research has shown that this contributes a bias of about 2 percent per year for produce and female apparel and a bias for the total CPI of about 0.35 percent per year.

Can We Believe This?

Even the radical estimate presented here of the CPI bias is surely an understatement of the true bias, for new products raise the standard of living in ways that go far beyond simple price changes for a single product. The price of light was reduced enormously by the invention of electricity, but until recent pioneering work there was no price index that directly compared the price per lumen of a primitive 1890s electric light bulb with that for a whale-oil lamp. And even such an adventuresome price index makes no attempt to measure the value to families of extending day into night or for firms in being able to extend the hours of production from a given set of facilities.

Whatever invention we take—whether the automobile that allowed limitless flexibility in the time and destination of rapid transportation, or the jet plane and communications satellites that tied together far-flung nations into a single international community, or the television and VCR that allowed almost any motion picture to enter the home, or the PC with CD-ROM that promises ultimately to bring the Library of Congress into every home—these new developments have made human life better on a large scale. The ultimate test of the change in the cost of living over the last twenty-five years is to do the following exercise. Take the market basket of goods and services available in 1970 and labeled with 1970 prices. Take the market basket available in 1995 and labeled with today's prices. Ask the consumer, how much more income would you require to be as satisfied with the 1995 basket and prices as with the 1970 basket and prices? The CPI says four times as much income would be necessary because the CPI has quadrupled since 1970. But that 1970 market basket has no VCRs, microwave ovens, or computer games; its color TV sets break down all the time; and its refrigerators use a lot of electricity. Consumers who answer this question will value the benefits of modern life and will say that two or three times as much income would be necessary but not four times. That's the ultimate test of bias in the CPI.

Conclusion

The topic of Hill's survey, and of Diewert's review of Hill, is price and volume measures of aggregate and sector output. While Diewert's review takes a neutral view and concentrates on the conversion of informal remarks into formal results, this comment has emphasized the practical importance of these issues. Two matters of enormous practical importance emerge from this discussion.

First, the United States is almost unique among developed countries in imposing a fixed base year on the whole history of real aggregates. This implies a substantial understatement of the growth rates of output, productivity, and other aggregates prior to the 1987 base year, and a substantial overstatement since the base year. As shown in Table 1, the amounts are not trivial. Official measures that indicate an acceleration of productivity (when 1972–1987 and 1987–1994 are compared) are replaced, once the superiority of chain-weighted measures is recognized, by alternative measures that indicate a deceleration of productivity. Similarly, the much-heralded acceleration of investment expenditures is replaced by the sad news that investment expenditures have decelerated.

In short, index number theory may appear formidable when expressed in all of its algebraic coat-of-armor, but it has a down-to-earth importance in telling us whether measures of growth in our standard of living are valid or not. The unhappy truth is that properly measured indexes indicate that the U.S. economy is doing far less well than is implied by official fixed-weight measures of real GDP and productivity.

Notes

1. The BEA's benchmark weighting system weights the growth rates of real subaggregates (such as real durable consumption) by the average of nominal expenditure shares in benchmark years five years apart, such as 1982 and 1987.

References

Gordon, Robert J. (1990). *The Measurement of Double Goods Prices*. Chicago: University of Chicago Press.

9 ADAPTATION OF THE REVISED *SNA* FOR DEVELOPING ECONOMIES

Uma Datta Roy Choudhury

9.1. Introduction

Many countries are still trying to reach the stage of development where they can reap the harvest of modernization. In such countries, traditional and household industries still predominate. This situation not only leaves them underdeveloped but pushes them backward because of slower rates of growth. These developing countries make an effort to improve and modernize, but their particular economic and social institutional demands require special policies that are not easy to implement. This suggests that generalizing about the characteristics of developing countries is not easy.

To identify the structural differences between these countries and also to trace their development process over time, it is essential to carefully formulated the system of national accounts for these countries. These accounts should give priority to the detailed classification and tabulation that will meet these requirements. It is not enough to identify these characteristics, but it is desirable to identify similarities among these features between developing countries so that some generalization becomes possible.

In this paper an attempt has been made to identify special charac-teristics of developing countries, generalize them to the extent possible, and discuss the extent to which these have been integrated within the new *System of National Accounts 1993*. The paper then goes on to examine those aspects of developing countries that are important for a meaningful representation of the economics of these countries and that do not find a place in the revised *system of National Accounts*. Finally the paper con-cludes suggesting that a few of these modifications may be incorporated in the new *SNA*. These, the paper suggests, would make the system much more meaningful for developing countries.

9.2. Special Characterisitics of Developing Countries

The first and formost feature that distinguishes these countries is the side-by-side existence of both traditional and modern technically advanced production systems. The technology, organization, and productivity of the two modes of production differ to such a great extent that the situation can be described as dualism within the same economic system. The classification within the *System of National Accounts* would therefore require a clear distinction in terms of different modes of production (modern and traditional) and organizational and management differences (formal and informal or organized and unorganized). For some countries even location might become an important point for consideration in the sense the economic development may not be uniform over the whole geography of the country but differ according to the nature and technology of the industries situated therein. Thus, areas with large-scale modern industries may be substantially developed coupled with high rates of growth while the rest of the country might be stagnating with the existence of subsistence agriculture and unorganized industries of a traditional nature with very little development of infrastructural facilities.

Further, the disposition of traditional production has a pattern different from that of products emanating from the modern sector even when the items produced are similar. A substantial proportion of production from traditional institutions is consumed by the producers themselves as final or intermediate products or used for asset formation without passing through the market. They are quite often also bartered by the producers in exhange for other goods. However, such forms do not necessarily exhaust the types of transactions in such products, and such products are also sold in the market in exchange for money. The primary purpose of production could be just to satisfy subsistence needs and hence be nonmarket in some cases or to maximize cash income rather than aggregate income in some other cases. Production in the modern sector, on the other hand, passes through the market before it reaches either the final consumers or the producers for intermediate consumption and asset formation. For reasons such as these, for a number of flows encountered in developing countries it becomes necessary to modify the definitions as well as the procedures of measurement from those generally adopted in national accounts. It is also necessary to present the results in a manner that highlights such structural features. Further, the details of supply and disposition of gross input and gross ouput of production within each individual sector should be presented separately for different production techniques to the extent possible.

In the capital account, similarly, for a balanced picture of the measures of total savings and total investment, the estimates of savings should include savings of household industries and of the population in the form of physical assets that do not have corresponding "sources of finance" measures as they do not pass through the money market. This would mainly comprise capital formation in rural areas undertaken with own labor and materials where no corresponding financial transactions exist. Such estimates are important both for grasping the structural details and for planning. They help in obtaining a comprehensive measure of the size of the subsistence economy at any point of time and also consequently indicate the extent of financial resources required for investment. In rural areas and in the traditional industries in the urban areas, even when sources of finance for capital formation are finanical institutions, they are quite often the financial intermediaries of a traditional type. These insitutions, by and large, do not maintain proper accounts and, in addition, carry on other business. These special features suggest that for developing countries, the role of financial institutions and banks is different from that in the advanced countries and the national accounts need to be modified for a meaningful presentation of the transactions.

Quite often traditional production in the rural areas uses own-account output of raw materials as inputs in addition to own labor and thus is very similar to production for own consumption qualitatively. The ownership of such industries is generally limited to households and individuals. In such cases it is extremely difficult to obtain a satisfactory measure of distributed factor incomes and primary incomes. Even when such enterprises employ labor, the payment quite often is in kind and not in cash or partly in kind and partly in cash.

Again, in developing countries where agriculture and allied activities frequently contribute a major share of the domestic product, production and employment are seasonal in character. Households are often engaged in activities like subsistence agriculture and handicrafts in which all the members of the household are joint contributors of labor. Thus, the occupational pattern becomes seasonal to enable the household labor to tide over periods of seasonal unemployment. Such diversified occupations often form the major source of income of large sections of households, and it becomes necessary to evaluate all such activities of the households for a complete and proper measure of total income generated by all economic activities. To solve the problem, it is not only necessary to define and introduce a new sector comprising household enterprises and new transactions in the production accounts of the sector but also to waive the conventional industry classification, reckoning households as composite enterprises where a number of economic activities take place at the same time. Industry classification can come later, when need arises and data permit, as a subsidiary partition of aggregates relating to this sector.

Finally, the existence of pluralism must be accommodated in the basic institutional sectoring of the economy. In the accounts for developing countries, households have to appear as a distinct institutional sector of the economy, meaning thereby that all traditional and quasi-traditional productive activities are to be accommodated in the household sector. It might also become necessary that the household sector will have to be subclassified, say, by urban and rural or by stages of development, such as traditional and nontraditional, and so on.

The problems of size distributions of income, consumption expenditure, and so on and distributions of relevant variables by social classes are more important for developing countries than for developed nations. Income disparities are normally larger in developing countries than in developed countries, and such inequalities in countries where average income is low imply subnormal levels of living in lower income brackets. It is imperative, therfore, for such countries to take action so that the disparity is not increased and, if possible, reduced. In view of this, developing countries can ill afford to neglect size distributions of income in their accounting systems even from the very beginning. While size distributions may not be explicitly included in the accounts, they need to be incorporated in the system, in concept, in the form of associated tables giving size breakdowns of the relevant flows.

Certain peculiarities of the external transactions of the developing countries may also be noted in this context. Exports usually include a lot of primary output and imports emphasize capital equipment and industrial products. Thus, policies to promote a more balanced pattern of export may be needed alongside a policy of import substitution. But apart from this, there remains the problem of foreign aid for economic development. Most developing countries seek rapid industrialization, and for this they have to solicit aid and loans both for capital and know-how, eventually giving rise to the problem of repayment. Frequently, the industries started on the basis of profitability considerations do not prove to be socially desirable. There is therefore a need for information to analyze the problem from the point of view of society. It should be possible for a country to satisfy itself as to when it is desirable to start an enterprise with foreign loans, aid and collaboration, and the economic information system has to provide data helping one to answer these questions. In the accounting system as well as in the interflow table there should be provision for these.

To summarize, special features of developing countries that need to be highlighted in a generalized system of accounts include (1) separation of unincorporated enterprises as an informal part of the household sector; (2) a few key commodities or industries that dominate economic activities in developing countries to be shown in separate accounts, preferably as subsectors within broad sectors; (3) separate accounts within individual sectors or within the economy as a whole for particular types of organizations (such as multinational corporations); (4) within each sector classification of enterprises by ownership because it is useful for public and private sectors to be distinguished by industry to the entent possible; (5) separate listing of the self-employed with their income classified as mixed income. The classification should also make a distinction between modern and traditional forms of production. However, the transactions appearing under these categories are not always uniform. Thus, for example in the unincorporated household sector, compensation of employees has to be subclassified into payment in cash and payment in kind. Similarly, gross product has to be classified as sold in the market, bartered, or used for the producer's own consumption, and private final consumption expenditure has to be classified as purchased or self-produced. Such classifications are particularly important for studying structural and organizational shifts over time in developing economies.

"Income of self-employed" comprises total income-generated net of wage payment (in cash or in kind) and other factor payments like interest and includes the imputed labor income of proprietors and family workers as well as the operating surplus generated in the case of unincorporated enterprises.

In the capital formation account, similarly, gross domestic fixed capital formation has to be shown to include asset formation out of "own production." Asset formation in the traditional sector can be either through the market economy or from "own production." In the former case, asset formation is a result of the purchase of either capital goods or material inputs and services from the market for production of goods of a capital nature, including newly constructed residential houses. Such additions to capital assets are classified as "purchased." In the traditional sector, however, capital formation can also occur as a result of use of one's own labor and materials that either are produced by the enterprises or are of no economic value and hence available freely. Examples of such asset formation are land improvement, minor irrigation projects, and rural houses constructed by the use of materials like mud, straw, grass, and so on. The value of capital formation in this case would consist of the imputed value of one's own labor together with the imputed values of such materials as bamboo that have recognized market value. Such additions to capital stock would obviously involve no market transactions and hence no corresponding financial measure. For a complete accounting, therefore, it is essential that such asset formation is also included as a part of the savings of the unincorporated household sector. In the subclassification, saving has to be defined to occur in the form of increases in "financial assets" and "physical assets." The subcategorizations under saving, however, are expected to be mutually exclusive and within well-defined boundaries.

9.3. Proposed *System of National Accounts*: *Relevance for Developing Countries*

The revised *System of National Accounts* now being recommended by the United Nations Statistical Division is revolutionary in several respects though interestingly it retains the basic theoretical framework of the 1968 *SNA*. Many of these features introduced make the system more meaningful for developing countries though it does not meet all the requirements elaborated above.

The most important innovation in the new system of national accounts is the extension of the classification of institutional units to the complete sequence of accounts—that is, the production accounts, distribution and use of income accounts, accumulation accounts, and balance sheets. Thus, in the revised *SNA* prodution accounts are suggested for all institutional sectors in addition to production accounts for the usual establishment-base industries. In order to link these two types of production account, the revised *SNA* suggests a cross-classification of gross value added and its components by type of institutional sector and by type of activity.

The household institutional units and particularly the unincorporated enterprises integrated within the households would normally behave the same way as corporations and partake in economic activities and transactions in their own right and would therefore be justified in having separate accounts.

Although households are primarily consumption units, in practice they may be engaged in any kind of conomic activity. In this respect, their economic behavior may be more complex than that of legal entities whose activities may be restricted to the purposes for which they are created. In particular, members of households play a major role in production either operating their own unincorporated enterprises or by supplying labor to other unincorporated or corporate enterprises by working as employees. They perform other activities like lending or borrowing funds. When members of households engage in activities other than consumption, they are still treated as acting on behalf of the households to which they belong and not as separate entities. Thus, when a member of a household owns singly or jointly with other members of the household an enterprise, which is not a corporation or quasi-corporation, that enterprise forms an integral part of the household itself.

Production in the household sector takes place within the unincorporated enterprises that are directly owned and controlled by members of households either indiviually or in partnership with others.

The owner of a household unincorporated enterprise usually has a dual role to play: first as the entrepreneur who is responsible for the creation and management of the enterprise and second as a worker who contributes labor inputs of a kind that could be provided by paid employees. Thus, in some cases, the principal role of the owner is to act as entrepreneur, innovator, and risk-taker, in which case the surplus from production that eventually accrues to the owner represents a return to entrepreneurship. In other cases, the principal function of an owner is likely to be of providing labor, in which case most of the surplus would, in effect, represent remuneration for work done.

Thus, the surples arising fromthe productive activities of a household unincorporated enterprise usually represents a mixture of two different kinds of income and it therefore described as "mixed income" of the self-employed and not "operating surplus."

Such household enterprises that are created for the purpose of providing goods or services primarily for sale or exchange in the market are to be classified as "household market enterprises." They can be engaged in any kind of production activity, such as agriculture, mining, manufacturing, construction, trade, or any of the srvices. They can range from single-person enterprises engaged in activities like shoe cleaning or retail trading with very little or no capital to large-scale manufacturing, construction, or service enterprises with several employees and large capital. They can also be highly modern using sophisticated techniques or traditional household enterprises.

Household market enterprises would also include unincorporated partnerships that are engaged in producing goods and services for sale or exchange in the market. The partners may belong to the same household or different households. The liability of the partners for the debts of the businesses must be unlimited for the partnership to be treated as unincorporated enterprises. In such cases where partners enjoy limited liability, they are effectively separate legal entities and should be treated as corporations.

Some of the outputs of these market enterprises may be retained for own consumption by members of the household to which the owner beongs. Such goods and services would also be included in the total output of the enterprises just as they would be part of the final consumption of these households. Similarly, buildings or capital equipments (such as transport equipments) may be partly used for production and partly for consumption and for proper accounting they need to be split up accordingly.

Household enterprises created for the purpose of producing goods or services for own final consumption or own gross fixed capital formation are to be classified as nonmarket enterprises (such as kitchen garden, poultry, weaving of textile or construction of residential premises for own use). The value of output of such enterprises has to be imputed using prices of similar goods and services in the market.

Goods produced by such enterprises for own use may be partly sold when they are surplus after meeting the households own requirements. In case, however, such sale take place quite regularly, these enterprises should be classified under market enterprises.

In the case of nonmarket services only two types of services produced by households for own final consumption are to be included under productive activity. These are (1) services of own-occupied dwellings (imputed houseing services for own consumption produced by owner occupiers in their capacity as unincorporated enterprises) and (2) domestic services produced by paid employees who are to be treated as independent unincorporated enterprises serving households.

The own account production of the above two services do not produce "mixed" income but "operating surplus" in the form of rent in the case of the former and pure labor income in the case of the latter.

All goods produced within the households—even though for own final consumption—are treated within the production boundary of the system and if non-marketed, they are then evaluated at equivalent market prices. These, for example, would include (1) agricultural products and their subsequent storage, gathering of uncultivated crops for own consumption, wood cutting, collection of firewood, hunting and fishing, (2) mining supply of water, (3) processing and curing of leather, production and preservation of meat and meat products, production of dairy products (butter and cheese), and (4) weaving of cloth, tailoring, production of mats and baskets, furnitures and furnishings and all other productive activities of similar type. Storage of goods produced within the household is to be included and so is supply of water, which is a kind of activity similar to extracting and piping of crude oil. In the case of services, however, only the two types of services just mentioned are to be treated as being within the productive system. Production of other types of domestic and personal services by the members of the household for their own consumption fall outside the production boundaries. Thus, no outputs, incomes, or expenditures are to be imputed when the services of the following type are produced by the members of the same household for their own use. These are cooking, cleaning, decoration, and so on of dwellings occupied by the household; cleaning and servicing of durables including transport vehicles; care, training and tuition of children, and the like.

Dividing the whole economy into sectors makes the accounts more meaningful for analytical purposes, as in this case insitutional units with similar objective and types of behavior are grouped together. Thus, the classification by sectors and subsectors makes it possible to monitor or target particular groups of institutional units. This is more important for the household sector where further division into subsectors enables one to study and observe how different sections of the community are affected by or benefit from economic development or from econmic and social policy measures.

Each of the five sectors may be further divided into subsectors. The division of a sector into subsectors depends on the type of analysis to be undertaken, the needs of the policy makers, the availability of data, and the economic circumstances and the institutional arrangements within the country. The subsectoring that will be optimal for all purposes and for all countries is difficult to find, and it may have to be left to the countries to chose the subsectoring that would be most meaningful. However, it is desirable that all countries work within a given overall framework of subsectors to make it possible to draw meaningful comparisons.

Besides subsectoring with reference to the characteristics of the household, for some countries—particularly the developing countries—distinguishing the character of the unincorporated enterprise in terms of techniques of production may be important. One could consider the question of classifying the enterprises in terms of modern or traditional: an household unincorporated market enterprise might use highly sophisticated techniques and need to be classified as modern, while a quasicorporate could be traditional in terms of techniques of production. Similarly a classification of the economy into formal and informal may be important and desirable though not easily definable. A generally acceptable definition of formal and informal that is applicable across a wide range of countries may not be easy to find, but a definition similar to that of an unincorporated enterprise may be meaningful. In other words, all enterprises for which a complete set of accounts, including a balance sheet of assets or liabilities, exist or for which it is possible and meaningful from both an economic and legal viewpoint to compile a complete set of accounts if they were required could be classified as a part of the formal sector with the rest as a part of the informal sector. In other words, if such a definition is adopted, household market and nonmarket enterprises as well as some in government could all be categorized under the informal sector and the rest under formal.

Within the informal household sector it is also envisaged that unincorporated financial enterprises such as individuals engaged in financial intermediation or in services auxiliary to financial intermediation will be included. Thus, money lenders who make loans from their own resources are also to be considered as producers of financial services within the household sector.

Coming to the question of accounts, the household sector would have a production account to the extent that unincorporated productive enterprises are included irrespective of whether the goods are produced for the market or for self-consumption or for own-account fixed capital formation. The value of output and value added will be measured following the standard procedure distinguishing only between the market output and non-market output if so desired. The generation of income account will then show the residual from value added after taking account of compensation of employees as mixed income and not operating surplus as has already been discussed and defined. In the primary generation of income account for household institutional units under compensation of employees, it is possible to separate out payment in cash and payment in kind just as under value of output one could distinguish sale and barter.

Disposable income is not all available in cash. The inclusion in the above two accounts of nonmonetary transactions associated with production for own consumption or barter, or with remuneration in kind, means that households do consume certain kind of goods and services for which the expenditures are imputed.

9.4. New SNA for Developing Countries: Points for Further Consideration

The details indicated thus make it clear that the revised *System of National Accounts* now being proposed is more extensive than the 1968 *SNA* and meets a substantial part of the requirements of the developing countries. It suggests a classification of establishments and their production according to the mode of production (modern and traditional) and also management type (formal and informal). It has, however, not been possible to include explicit definitions of either of the criteria. Though it may not be difficult to evolve relevant and meaningful definitions of modern and traditional, there is no doubt that even this definition has to be carefully formulated to be applicable to individual countries in different stages of development. Evolving meaningful definitions of formal and informal or organized and unorganized is not equally straightforward. The revised *SNA* need to provide meaningful definitions for all the new concepts that are being introduced so that the presentation of results using such classifications become relevant and meaningful.

It is also important to consider whether such bifurcation by mode of production should be restricted to the household sector. Even if dichotomy in terms of management type or organizational type may be argued to be limited within the household sector with the classification for the other two sectors being formal and organised, the differences in technology might certainly exist in the case of public sector or even private corporate sector and it would be desirable to provide classifications in a manner that would give a complete picture for the economy as a whole under any of these criteria.

To obtain a comprehensive measure of the subsistence economy, the new *SNA* suggests the recording of the output according to the nature of its disposal, such as sold in the market, bartered, or as own-account final or intermediate use. Similarly separation of payment to labor into cash or kind, final consumption, and fixed capital formation into bartered, own account, and purchased from the market may occur. For each of these transactions that are not directly observable the question of valuation has to be considered and settled. Barter of goods and services and own account consumption and capital formation are examples to the point. In all such cases, depending on the nature of the nonmarket transaction, the value is to be determined either according to costs incurred (nonmarket services produced by government, such as education services provided free of charge by the government and consumed by the student) or by reference to prevalent prices of similar goods or services in the market (services of owner-occupied dwellings). For ensuring correct and economically meaningful valuation it is desirable that proper guidelines are provided regarding principles to be followed.

In the course of separating monetary and nonmonetary transactions it is essential that gross fixed capital formation include barter transactions and own-account capital formation besides acquisition through purchases. By definition gross capital formation (fixed capital plus change in inventories) plus net acquisition of valuables and nonproduced nonfinancial assets adjusted for net lending and net borrowing is equivalent to gross saving plus capital transfers (net, from abroad). Inclusion of barter transaction or own-account capital formation in the capital account would imply that all capital formation transactions would not pass through the money market and would not therefore have corresponding sources of finance. This would mean that for balanced capital formation account it will be necessary to introduce on the savings side of the account an item of "savings in the form of physical assets." Such transactions would primarily be capital formation in rural areas undertaken with own labor and materials that are either own production or bartered and therefore done without any financial transactions taking place. The new *SNA* does not cover this aspect though nonmonetary capital formation has been taken note of.

Finally, it is essential to recognize that presentation of the accounts with locational breakdown is important and essential for developing countries. Typical example of such bifurcation is urban and rural in case of developing countries where the urban part of the economy may be highly developed and technically advanced with modern industries and rural areas very much different with large subsistence sector coupled with traditional systems of production. The presentation of accounts by areas in this case will not be limited to production only but should extend to interregional transactions in all their details. Discussion in Chapter 19 of the new *SNA*: "Application of the Integrated Framework to Various Circumstances and Needs" touches on the problem in the section on Regional Accounts but does not concretize the proposals. The 1968 *SNA* had included a supporting table on receipts and disbursements of the rural sector, but the table had a combination of capital and current transactions within the same table and was not of much use from the technical angle. It would therefore be desirable to have an articulated system of accounts for the rural sector where urban sector will be external sector for purposes of completing the accounting. The accounts would thus distinguish between the transactions within the rural sector and transactions (purchase or sale) with the urban sector in the case of, for example, production and intermediate consumption. Similarly, details of consumption or capital formation from within the rural sector or from the urban sector need to be identified. The external account for the urban sector would then help in complete articulation.

9.5. Conclusion

The revised *SNA* thus meets a large number of the requirements of the developing economies, and a few more elaborations and extensions would make the system much more useful for them. Once such modifications are integrated within the SAM (which is a part of new *SNA*), the U.N. recommendations may be seen to go a long way making the system of direct relevance for developing countries. None of the changes suggested would make the system less useful for advanced economies and can therefore be integrated without condition.

Before finally closing it is important to mention that the new *SNA* has turned out to be at least as heavy reading as the earlier one even, if not heavier, though no doubt the presentation is more direct and simple. It is accepted that a topic of this nature caters to the needs of special technical groups only and a technically based text with a large amount of jargon cannot be avoided. It will, however, be extremely useful to users in developing countries if a supplement containing clearer and more comprehensive definitions of all the important measures can be brought out without much delay so that the users do not have to scan through the pages again and again to comprehend and master the concepts built into each of the measures.

DISCUSSION OF CHAPTER 9

Anne Harrison

One of the first formal meetings connected with the revision of the *SNA* invited participants from developing countries to say whether they wished to have a special version of the *SNA* for use in their conditions. The unanimous and emphatic conclusion was that this was not appropriate. Developing countries vary quite as much between themselves as between the most prosperous of these and the industrialized countries, and it was felt much more appropriate to have a single system with degrees of flexibility in it rather than to have one system for the rich and one for the poor.

In the first section of her paper Mrs. Choudhury articulates the needs of particular relevance to developing countries, and then in the second part shows how these have in fact been incorporated into the *1993 SNA*. It is interesting to note that while they may be of particular concern to developing countries, they, in fact, affect all countries to a greater or lesser extent, and this underscores the appropriateness of having a single system for all countries.

One matter of considerable importance is the more explicit treatment of unincorporated enterprises and, in particular, the need to have a production account for the household sector. Concomitant with this is the decision that the returns to someone working on own account in an unincorporated enterprise should not be classified either as compensation of employees or operating surplus but given a distinctive name "mixed income" to make clear that this is both a return to labour and a return to entrepreneurial flair and capital. Mrs. Choudhury assumes that most unincorporated enterprises will be using traditional methodologies, such as handicrafts, but in many countries, rich and poor alike, there are an increasing number of people working from home in quite sophisticated activities, such as real estate, cosmetic selling and computer services. These too should be covered by unincorporated enterprises within the *SNA*.

One issue that was discussed on a number of occasions during the revision of the *SNA* was the introduction of the distinction between market and nonmarket activity. Discussion of the borderline revolved around the treatment of products that were marketable but not marketed and at different points different suggestions were made as to whether these should be treated as market or nonmarket activities. In the end it was decided that a simple dichotomy was not appropriate and, rather, that three types of output should be identified: market output, output produced for own final use, and other nonmarket output that would be restricted to the goods and individual or collective services produced by nonprofit institutions serving households and governments. Subsistence farming clearly falls into the middle category, as does production of housing in rural areas using self-help techniques. However, some large construction and other investment activity by enterprises may also fall in this category with similar problems of valuation and treatment in the account. Mrs. Choudhury suggests that own capital formation should be separately identified in the capital account with a matching part of saving, which implies making a similar subdivision in the production account so that the amount of value added arising from these activities can be identified in that and subsequent balancing items up to saving.

Production for own final use is obviously a special type of largely nonmonetary activity, and Mrs. Choudhury makes a plea to identify the distinction between monetary and nonmonetary transactions throughout the accounts. An attempt to indicate how the standard classification of the *SNA* can be extended to incorporate such considerations is given in the complementary classification in Part E of Annex V of the Blue Book, which, it is hoped, will be implemented to the extent that the subdivisions suggested are of major importance to individual countries. One problem with a complete distinction between monetary and nonmonetary activities, however, is exemplified by the case of a production account where either output or intermediate consumption may be nonmonetary but the other has a significant monetary component. Should value added then be deemed to be monetary or non-monetary? It should be noted, though, that reference to barter transactions and transactions in kind do occur throughout the text of the Blue Book, so ambiguity about how to treat these should be largely avoided in the future.

Mrs. Choudhury also points to the desirability of separating modern from traditional production techniques that are not, as she herself has pointed out on a number of occasions previously, the same as the distinction between formal and informal activities. A large handloom operation may be formal and traditional, while some of the unincorporated enterprises described above may be both modern and informal. The desirability of introducing this distinction extends not just to the household sector but may be relevant, for example, in the context of an input-output table for enterprises also.

Mrs. Choudhury sees the distinction between urban and rural parts of the economy as being key for many developing countries, and so it is. However, it closely parallels the increasing interest in regional accounts in many countries. One of the major problems in developing regional accounts is to know how to deal with interregional transactions ("imports" and "exports" on a regional basis) and national functions (such as transport and utilities). Although the *1993 SNA* was a major achievement, there are no claims that this represents the last word in the development of national accounts and the elaboration of satisfactory regional accounts may be one of the next developments to which we can look forward.

10 ADAPTATION OF THE *SNA* FOR TRANSITION ECONOMIES

Y. Ivanov and T. Homenko

10.1. Introduction

The purposes of this chapter are to review briefly the current status of work undertaken in countries in transition in order to introduce the *System of National Accounts (SNA)*, to discuss selected conceptual and practical problems that arise in connection with adaptation of the new *SNA* to the conditions in countries in transition, to review the matters pertaining to collecting and processing primary data needed for compilation of major accounts, and to review related topics pertaining to organization of sources of data.

It is also intended to discuss briefly the links between the *SNA* and the *Material Product System (MPS)*, which was used until recently in these countries for the purposes of macro analysis. Finally, an attempt will be made to assess the prospects for transition from the *MPS* to the *SNA* in the foreseeable future.

10.2. Current Status of Work on Introduction of the SNA in Countries in Transition

During the last two to three years the countries in transition (mainly the former CPEs) have undertaken energetic steps toward introduction of the SNA into their regular statistical practices. Approval of the revised SNA by the U.N. Statistical Commission at the beginning of 1993 has provided additional impetus to these efforts. The development in this area should be seen in the context of general polices of these countries aimed at transformation of the entire systems of socioeconomic statistics in accordance with international standards. These polices are clearly linked to the economic reforms carried out in order to ensure transition from the centrally planned economy to a market-oriented one. The plans of the countries in transition to integrate their economies into the world economic system as well as their membership in international organizations also require statistical data that are in conformity with the common methodology and are easily understood all over the world.

A number of countries in transition have undertaken revisions of statistical systems. These programs envisage, as a rule, a gradual (within five to eight years) transition to market-oriented statistics. The central element in these programs is the major accounts of the SNA. They are considered the key element in the entire process of transformation of the statistical systems and the timetable for the introduction of its major accounts and tables is, as a rule, broadly coordinated with the work on implementation of the international standards in the related areas—such as balance of payments, public finance statistics, price statistics, and economic classifications.

It is clear that countries in transition are not a homogeneous group in respect of the level of economic development, quality of the statistical services, familiarity with the SNA, advancement in economic reforms, and so on. Some of them (mainly the countries of Eastern and Central Europe) were in the past more exposed to the Western type of statistics. They have accumulated certain experience in the computation of GDP and have participated in the International Comparison Project (ICP) and in the U.N. study of the SNA-MPS links, and so on. The other countries in transition (mainly the former USSR republics) are taking only the first steps in this area. They have set up the Statistical Committee of the CIS, the principle function of which is to assist them in introduction of the new type of market oriented statistics. The Statistical Committee of the CIS works in close cooperation with international organizations and, in the field of national accounts, primarily with the OECD. The international organizations (OECD, EUROSTAT, and so on) also provide the technical assistance directly to the CIS member countries as well as to the other countries in transition, which is essential for speedy progress in the implementation of the *SNA* and other market-oriented statistics.

A review of the progress in the introduction of the *SNA* in countries in transition shows that the situation is not even among the countries but that, on the whole, work is at a very early stage. Only a few countries have started compilation of major accounts on a regular basis. Many countries have introduced selected accounts of the new *SNA* on an experimental basis; practically no attempts have been undertaken so far to introduce financial accounts or balance sheets. Some countries have advanced faster than others, and their progress has been achieved thanks to assistance from the international organizations as well as from national statistical offices of the developed economies with a long history of national accounts (such as France, Germany, and Sweden). The most visible progress has been achieved in countries of Eastern and Central Europe.

In *Hungary* a system of national accounting that was adopted in 1970 incorporated concepts of both the *SNA* and the *MPS*. This system was an important step toward the *SNA*. During recent years considerable progress in introduction of a comprehensive system of national accounts has been achieved. At the present time Hungarian national accounts include major accounts and tables as defined in the international standards. There are some deviations from the *SNA* in such areas as financial transactions, the government sector, and external transactions. However, in the process of estimation for 1992 new sources of data have been introduced, and some deviations from *SNA 1993* have been eliminated.

A great deal of work was done at the very beginning of the 1990s in *Czechoslovakia* and later in the *Czech* and *Slovak Republics*. In the *Statistical Yearbook of Czechoslovakia 1990* the data on GDP computed with the help of the conversion tables are published for 1980 and 1985–1988. The 1992 issue of the *Yearbook* includes more accurate estimates of GDP for 1989 and 1990. Work is under way now to introduce the major accounts of the *System*.

Poland participated almost from the beginning in the international comparisons of the GDP known as ICP and calculated for this purpose the GDP. New impetus to this work was given at the end of the 1980s due to political changes and economic reforms. More detailed and reliable figures of the GDP for 1990–1991 were produced and published recently (classified by major industries and categories of final use). Work on introducing major accounts is under way now, and efforts have been undertaken to provide a solid basis for this: a register of all institutional units has been introduced; new international classifications are being implemented; new methods of collection of data needed for compilation of the accounts are promoted. Efforts have been undertaken to compile major accounts for 1990 by sectors and for 1991–1992 by sectors and subsectors, and some figures are already available. There is also a plan to prepare an input-output table for 1992 on the basis of the new *SNA* definitions.

Remarkable progress has been achieved in *Romania*. The efforts were focused on experimental compilation of principal accounts for the sectors and for the General Economic Table as well as on compilation of production accounts for industries and input-output tables. During 1990–1993 the estimates were prepared for 1989–1992 on the basis of the ESA accounting framework and classifications. The reports of the enterprises were modified to provide data on output and intermediate consumption needed for compilation of input-output tables by 105 sectors. An input-output table was prepared for 1992 both in current and constant prices. The important feature of the work on introduction of the *SNA* during 1993–1995 will be implementation of the new *SNA*.

It should be mentioned that Poland and Romania have been receiving technical assistance from the INSEE (France) as well as from OECD.

In *Bulgaria* a program of introduction of the *SNA* was adopted in 1989. In accordance with this program production and generation of income accounts were compiled for 1990–1992 for industries and institutional sectors; efforts were also undertaken to compile the goods and services account and an input-output table. Compilation of income distribution accounts and capital accounts was commenced in the 1993.

In the new lands of *Germany* derivation of reliable estimates of the GDP is considered as a task of high priority. Calculation of other aggregates of the *System* has been postponed for the time being. The first calculations of the GDP were prepared in the former GDR for 1980–1989 on the basis of conversion tables that made it possible to derive the GDP from the figures on the net material product by final use. After the unification of Germany, new estimates of GDP of the new lands for 1988 were carried out; they were arrived at on the basis of procedures elaborated together with the experts from the Federal Statistical Department. During 1990–1992 the estimates of the GDP were prepared for the second half of 1990 and 1991 both in current and constant prices; quarterly estimates for 1991 were also prepared. In 1993 the final estimates of GDP and GNI are intended to be obtained to supplement the series for the old lands. Comprehensive compilation of all major accounts are planned for 1991 after finalizing the estimates of the GDP.

In *Baltic* states, the introduction of the national accounts has been carried out simultaneously with work in the related areas. The new system of business accounting, ISIC and CPC, was well as business registers have been introduced in practice. Since 1993 these countries abandoned the MPS and started compiling the *SNA* major accounts by sectors and industries on a regular basis. Latvia has even attempted to produce financial accounts and balance sheets by sectors for 1992.

Many CIS member countries regularly publish the estimates of GDP in current prices; however, in most cases they are still produced with the help of conversion tables worked out earlier by the United Nations Statistical Office in the context of the study of the *SNA-MPS* links. The estimates of GDP at constant prices are derived with the help of implicit deflators computed for net material product. At the same time efforts are undertaken to compile major accounts on an experimental basis. The countries rely in this work on the methodological materials prepared by the Statistical Committee of the CIS in cooperation with the OECD; these materials constitute adaptation of the new *SNA* to conditions in CIS member countries and the available sources of data. Statistical offices of the countries are assisted by the OECD.

The current situation concerning the introduction of the national accounts in the CIS countries appears as follows.

Russia compiles on a regular basis major accounts of the *System* for the economy as a whole (production, generation of income, distribution of income, use of income, capital, and goods and services accounts). It also compiles production and generation of income accounts by sectors and industries and produces estimates of GDP as the sum of value added and by final use. These data are available since 1989.

Armenia, Belarus, Georgia, Kyrghyzstan, and Ukraine have undertaken efforts to compile on an experimental basis the major accounts for the economy as a whole as well as by sectors and industries (the latter refers to the production and generation of income accounts). Belarus and Kyrghyzstan have compiled these accounts for 1990–1992; Armenia and Georgia, for 1990–1991; Ukraine, for 1989 (accounts for 1990–1991 are under way now).

Moldova has compiled the major accounts for the economy as a whole and production accounts by sectors and industries for 1989–1990; the production accounts for 1991–1992 are under way now.

Azerbaijan has compiled the production and the generation of income accounts by sectors and industries for 1990–1992.

Kazakhstan has managed to compile the production accounts by sectors and industries for 1992–1993, while Turkmenistan has concentrated its efforts on compilation of production accounts by industries for 1992.

Tadjikistan has produced the estimates of the major accounts for the total economy as well as of the production account by industries for 1992.

Uzbekistan has compiled the major accounts for the total economy for 1990–1991.

It is necessary to mention that the consolidated accounts for the economy compiled by the CIS member countries often contain crude estimates pertaining to the external transactions in goods and services and even omissions as far as flows of primary income payable abroad are concerned; this is due to the absence of reliable balances of payments. The accounts obtained as a result of the above-mentioned experimental compilations should be considered as provisional and may be revised in the nearest future.

The common problem of the CIS countries is that the work on introduction of the SNA goes somewhat ahead of work in related areas that are supposed to ensure the basis for implementation of the SNA in practice. The latter refers to the development of a new bookkeeping system, international classifications, organization of business registers, and compilation of balance of payments. The different agencies that are responsible for this work do not always coordinate their efforts; the latter is especially noticeable in countries that have not yet adopted national programs of transformation of their statistics. Table 10.1 contains currently available statistics on the GDP of the CIS member countries for recent years.

Table 10.1.   Gross domestic product of CIS member countries, 1989–1992 (current prices in billion rubles)

	1989	1990	1991	1992
Azerbaijan	15.5	14.7	26.7	250.9
Armenia	9.5	9.7	15.9	59.1
Belarus	37.7	41.5	81.3	1,080.0
Georgia	—	—	—	113.7
Kazakhstan	40.6	46.4	81.0	1,218.6
Kirghizstan	—	9.6	20.0	172.0
Moldova	11.2	12.7	24.4	216.5
Russia	573.0	644.0	1,300.1	1,806.4
Tadjikistan	6.6	7.3	13.4	64.5
Turkmenistan	7.1	7.6	14.7	—
Uzbekistan	30.7	32.4	61.5	416.9
Ukraine	154.1	164.8	295.4	4,580.0

Note: Figures are provisional and can be revised.

10.3. Transition from the *MPS* to the *SNA*

As is well known, the countries in transition compiled in the not-so-distant past (for the purposes similar to those served by the *SNA*) estimates for the *Material Product System (MPS)*. The latter was designed for macroanalysis and management of the centrally planned economy, and its underlying concepts and accounting structure differ from those of the *SNA*. As a result the *MPS* aggregates are not directly comparable with their *SNA* counterparts. The general accounting structure of the *MPS* is simpler because many aspects of economic analysis essential for monitoring market economies are of less importance, if important at all, in a centrally planned economy. Thus, in the *MPS* the focus is on the analysis of commodity flows (material goods), whereas the analysis of income distribution and of financial flows is underdeveloped and highly simplified; the sources of capital finance are not identified in the *MPS*, and the category of saving (which is so important in the *SNA*) is not explicitly recorded. Contrary to the *SNA*, the *MPS* analysis of stocks of assets is restricted largely to nonfinancial assets. There is no sector analysis of stocks of assets in the *MPS* comparable to that in the *SNA*, and the national wealth is confined in practice to tangible produced assets. Although in theory land and some other nonproduced tangible assets are included in the national wealth according to the standard description of the *MPS* (originally published by the CMEA Secretariat), in practice they were normally omitted due to practical problems associated with valuation of these assets. The analysis of financial assets is confined in the *MPS* to the net claims on the rest of the world.

Having said this, we have to emphasize that there are many similarities between the two systems of national accounting and, above all, in the manner in which the data are arranged and classified in order to derive the major macroeconomic aggregates. Thus, in both systems a distinction is made between the flows and stocks, flows of products and flows of income, income originated from production and income received as a result of redistribution, and so forth. The countries in transition have accumulated a considerable practical experience in compilation of the *MPS* balances, and therefore this experience should be fully exploited in the process of introducing the new *SNA*. A comparative analysis of the *SNA* and the *MPS* (which this paper can not pursue in detail) is, in principle, useful for a number of purposes and reasons and, above all, because it helps statisticians of countries in transition to understand better the underlying concepts of the *SNA*.

The analysis of the differences between the *SNA* and the *MPS* makes it possible to identify several elements of the *MPS* that are of interest in the context of introduction of the *SNA*.

This refers, above all, to the material balance of the *MPS* (the balance of production, consumption, and accumulation of the global product). This balance is very similar to the goods and services account of the new *SNA* except that it is restricted to the flows of material goods and is based on the *MPS* definition of economic production. The rearrangement of the material balance into the goods and services account requires incorporation of the flows of nonmaterial goods (which are registered in different sections of the *MPS* and treated as redistribution of income). The *SNA* categories of resources and uses of goods and services will have to be adopted. What is important, however, is that the bulk of the data needed for compilation of this account is available in the *MPS* (with or without some rearrangement). A more detailed scheme of the material balance resembles very much the scheme of the supply and use table in the new *SNA*.

Another important table of the *MPS* is the financial balance (the balance of production, primary distribution, redistribution, and disposition of national income). It contains a lot of the data needed for the compilation of the *SNA* income distribution accounts and partially of the capital account and financial account; these data require some rearrangement, however, in order to make them consistent with the SNA definitions.

The estimates of the national wealth are confined in the *MPS* in practice to tangible produced assets plus the net claims on the rest of the world. It appears that countries in transition should retain in practice compilation of the balances of fixed assets that integrate the data on stocks and flows of fixed assets. These balances can be extended in the future to include the estimates of other components of national wealth as defined in the *SNA*.

To conclude, the work on introduction of the *SNA* in countries in transition should take into account the recent experience with the *MPS*; the *MPS* balances contain a lot of data necessary for compilation of national accounts and in a number of cases only limited rearrangement of these data might be needed.

10.4. Characteristics of the Countries in Transition Relevant for National Accounting

There are a number of conceptual problems associated with the adaptation of the *SNA* to the conditions of countries in transitions. It is essential to clarify these conditions and to specify the characteristics of these countries that need to be taken into account in the process of adaptation of the *SNA*.

As was noted above, countries in transition are not a homogeneous group, but, taken as a whole, they seem to possess a number of common features. Though economic reforms have been pursued rather vigorously, they are far from being completed, and market mechanisms and institutions are still underdeveloped, although some countries may claim faster progress than others. In many countries there is no genuine capital market yet, and transformation of banking into a two-tier system is not completed. Financing of investments is often carried out with the help of methods that are conventional for the CPEs (that is, with the help of allocation from the state budget). Banks are, as a rule, poorly adapted to the requirements of efficient financial intermediation. Despite privatization, a considerable number of enterprises are still owned by the state. In a number of countries transformation of state enterprises into companies does not represent a real change and does not promote a new ownership structure but is simply a pseudo transformation to enable the enterprises to continue as before but under a modern label.

Liberalization of prices has reduced noticeably the subsidization of enterprises, but the subsidies still remain an important instrument of management of the economy in many countries. Monopolization of production is very high, and this prevents normal competition and formation of market prices that would reflect costs of production and interaction of supply and demand. In some countries in transition prices of selected goods are still administratively controlled.

Many countries in transition are still relatively isolated from the world economic system. In most of them national currencies are not fully convertible.

To sum up, many administrative rules and financial regulations from the past are still in effect in many countries in transition, and they continue to distort market forces and hinder the adaptability of enterprises and households to requirements of modern economic system. Nevertheless new institutional arrangements typical for market economies become more and more visible.

10.5. Selected Conceptual Problems

It should be noted that in the process of revision of *SNA 1968* special efforts were undertaken to accommodate certain characteristics of the countries in transition and, broadly speaking, it is fair to say that the revised *SNA* is, in principle, applicable to any type of economy. Having said this, however, we should emphasize the importance of the analysis of the impact of the above mentioned peculiarities and characteristics of countries in transition on the monitoring of their economies with the help of new *SNA*.

10.5.1. Sectorization of the Economy

The above said refers, first of all, to sectorization of the economy. The major problem in this area is allocation of government-owned entities to the sector of corporations or to the general government sector. This allocation depends to a considerable extent on whether the government units can be deemed to be market or nonmarket producers. By definition the sector of corporations includes market producers, whereas the sector of general government comprises largely nonmarket producers. To distinguish between them the new *SNA* suggests using the notion of economically significant prices charged for the products provided to other units. The new *SNA* does not specify, however, what exactly economically significant prices are in practice and leaves it to the countries to decide on this.

The advantage of such a broad approach is that countries might be able to avoid mechanical solution (if some rigid quantitative criterion were established) to take into account peculiarities in the institutional setup as well as the forthcoming changes in the economy due to the reforms. The disadvantage is that some countries may feel that they do not have clear rules that they could apply for allocation of units to the sectors in the borderline cases. The most vivid example of such situation refers to the state-owned housing units that in many countries in transition are still highly subsidized. The relative amount of housing subsidies varies considerably from country to country as well as over a period of time (from 80 to 50 percent of the cost). Under these conditions allocation of housing units to the relevant sector is a somewhat controversial issue for the countries in transition. The review of their practices shows that they tend to allocate state-owned subsidized housing units to the sector of corporations rather than to the sector of general government, even though the subsidies may cover a considerable part of the costs. This solution seems to rely on the assumption that subsidization will be abolished or considerably reduced in the foreseeable future. Nevertheless, some countries, such as Rumania, allocate highly subsidized housing units to the general government sector.

In principle in the former CPEs a distinction was made between the budgetary and self-financing units (for example, for taxation purposes). This distinction still used in countries in transition is somewhat similar to the market and nonmarket producers distinction in the *SNA* and can be regarded as a starting point for allocation of units to the relevant sectors. However, many borderline cases may require a more careful analysis of the functions of the units and of the mode of finance of their costs. This refers, for example, to allocation of central banks. In the recent past in many CPEs banking was organized as a mono state system, and the state banks were closely integrated into the state budgetary system. The state banks acted as government entities whose principle function was, broadly speaking, general management of the economy.

In some countries in transition, especially at the earlier stage of economic reforms, the functions of central banks have not undergone significant changes and remain very similar to the functions of the state banks in the former CPEs. In other countries in transition central banks have acquired more independent status in theory but in practice continued to be subordinated to the government. This is true, for example, in the case of Russia. Thus, in 1993 the Central Bank of Russia was compelled to provide a huge loan to the government to cover the budget deficit practically free of charge (at 10 percent whereas the normal rate for the commercial enterprises was 200 percent). Under these conditions the allocation of the central banks to a separate subsector of the general government sector could be regarded as a reasonable solution.

The other situation difficult from the allocation point of view exists in countries in transition with respect of the units engaged in research and development. Some of them are officially regarded as self-financing but in reality are financed from budget allocations rather than from sales of their output on the market. The research institutions of the branch ministries often obtain a status of self-financing entities because it is assumed that they are financed from the budget of the ministries depending on the output furnished to them. In practice, however, it is very difficult to establish close links between the output and finance, and they obtain the funds just like ordinary budgetary entities. These units are referred to as pseudo-commercial, and therefore it is essential to identify them and to allocate them to the general government sector. The above situation with pseudo self-financing units is characteristic for Russia, some other CIS member countries, Poland, and possibly for some other countries of Eastern Europe.

10.5.2. Subsidies

The treatment of subsidies is an important issue for countries in transition for a number of reasons but, above all, because the subsidies continue to be used as an instrument of management of the economy. On the other hand, while abolishing or reducing subsidies the governments in many countries of this group introduce social grants to certain groups of households. These processes have a clear impact on the measuring of the GDP and related flows and have to be reflected in the accounts properly. There are several aspects here that are worth mentioning. First, a distinction between the subsidies from the government to enterprises and the current transfers to institutional units belonging to the government sector is not always immediately clear. Failure to make this distinction will result in distortion of the GDP and related aggregates. It is believed that sector classification provides a good basis for a consistent solution of this issue even though allocation of the units to the relevant sector may require the use of some conventions.

As noted above, the other aspect is a distinction between subsidies and grants to households. For example, in 1993 the government of Russia abolished the subsidies on bread but introduced instead grants to needy persons designed to compensate their losses due to increased prices of bread. This change in policy will have impact on the GDP and some other flows recorded in national accounts.

In some cases it is essential to make a distinction between subsidies and social transfers in kind. If, for example, government makes payments to the subway to cover the losses that arise due to free transportation for certain groups of households, this flow has to be recorded as subsidies. If, however, the government purchases subway tickets for people with disabilities, the payment is to be treated as a social transfer in kind. In principle the *SNA* provides a clear basis for drawing the above distinction and what is needed is a careful implementation of the provisions of the *System*.

Subsidies on products have to be taken into account when the output is valued at basic prices as recommended in the *SNA*. In some countries, however, there are pecularities in the mechanisms of the subsidization that should not be overlooked. For example, in Russia subsidies on agricultural goods (known as price differentials), which recently accounted for a considerable part of all subsidies, were not paid directly to the producers of agricultural goods but to procurement organizations in order to cover their losses arising due to low prices at which the procured goods were sold to the retail trade organizations. Under this arrangement the subsidies in question should not be added explicitly to sales in order to arrive at valuation of agricultural output at basic prices.

Valuation of output at basic prices implies that a distinction is to be made between the subsidies on products and other subsidies on production. The latter are negligible in most of the countries in transition for the time being but are likely to increase in the future. For example, in 1993 the government of Russia made a decision to pay subsidies to those enterprises that hire persons with disabilities.

Finally, a few words on the so-called consumption subsidies, which refer to subsidies on consumer goods and services. The treatment of these subsidies was a controversial issue during the work on the revision of the *SNA*. The proposal to treat these subsidies as purchases of goods and services by the general government was discussed but was rejected by the experts participating in the process of revision of the *SNA*. If it had been accepted, the GDP in current prices of countries in transition would have been relatively bigger.

10.5.3. Output of Banks

Problems of computation of output of financial intermediaries and allocation of this output to deifferent categories of uses are important for the countries in transition. In principle, recommendations of the SNA on computations of these flows are applicable for countries in transition, but there are some peculiarities that should not be overlooked. As was mentioned above, the central banks in some countries of this group may be allocated to the general government sector. The implication of this solution is that output of central bank is to be valued at cost and allocated to the final consumption expenditure of general government. The output of commercial banks should be computed as an excess of the property income receivable (other than property income receivable on investment of own funds of the banks) over the interest payable by the banks. The new *SNA* suggests allocating the output of financial intermediaries among different users (that is, among industries, household, and so on), but it also allows retaining the 1968 *SNA* approach, which implied allocation of the output to the intermediate consumption of a notional (dummy) industry, the output of which is taken equal to zero. It appears that countries in transition (as possibly many other countries) will have to use for the time being the old *SNA* procedure because an attempt to allocate the output to different types of uses may lead to estimates that will be difficult to interpret both by producers of statistics and by its users.

10.5.4. Social Services Provided by Businesses for Their Employees

Another essential topic for countries in transition is treatment of the cultural and social services provided by businesses for their employees at low or no cost. These services are normally provided to the population by budgetary units, but in some countries in transition the social functions of government are extended to businesses. The latter have their own hospitals, stadiums, recreating centers, and so on. The costs of the services provided by these units are normally financed out of allocations from the profit from the principal activity of enterprises. In some countries, such as Russia, expenses for the maintenance of the subdivisions of the enterprises engaged in the provision of nonmarket cultural and social services are tax exempt and identified in the business accounts and reports submitted to the statistical authorities. The new *SNA* contains clear recommendations for treatment of the services in question. These recommendations can be summarized as follows:

- The units of the enterprises engaged in provision of cultural and social services to the employees are treated as notional (dummy) units and allocated to the sector of NPIs serving households (as a subsector);
- The output of these units is to be valued at costs; partial payments that employees may have to make to cover a fraction of costs are treated as incidental sales;
- The disposition of these services in recorded first as final consumption expenditure of NPIs serving households and then as a social transfer in kind from the NPIs to the households;
- The financing of the expenses on provision of the services in question is to be shown as current transfers in cash from the enterprises to the notional NPIs.

The rationale behind this rather complex solution is as follows. First, according to the *SNA* businesses cannot have final consumption expenditure. The introduction of this category in the *SNA* was advocated several years ago by R. Ruggles and N. Ruggles but was not accepted in the revised *SNA*. Second, the treatment of social and cultural services in question as wages and salaries in kind is not an appropriate solution because the provision of these services is not linked to the amount of labor input provided and therefore cannot be regarded as a renumeration for work done. Inclusion of these services in compensation of employees would affect the disposable income of households, which by the definition and nature of this flow should not include such items. Finally, it would be wrong to allocate the services in question to intermediate consumption of the enterprises because it is obvious that the employees benefit from these services more than employers. The review of actual practices of countries in transition shows that at least some of them are capable of implementing the procedure suggested by *SNA 1993*. It is worth noting in this context that in the process of privatization businesses often try to get rid of their socially oriented subdivisions. The latter in many cases are transfered to the control of local government agencies. This institutional change leads to some changes in the national accounts, the most important of which is that expenses on the provision of the services will be recorded as final consumption expenditure of the general government (rather than of the NPIs). Actual consumption of households will not be affected. In some countries of this group, however, the amounts involved are relatively small and perhaps a simpler solution, such as allocation of the services in question to wages and salaries in kind, could be adopted.

10.5.5. Treatment of Privatization

Another important topic for countries in transition concerns treatment of privatization. The transactions pertaining to privatization affect the accumulation accounts and, above all, the capital account and the financial account. In principle, *SNA 1993* contains all the necessary mechanisms (definitions, classifications, as well as rules to record the transactions in the accounts) needed to monitor privatization. Thus, capital transfers are defined to include, among other things, transfers of the ownership. But, of course, implementation of these definitions may require their adaptation to specific conditions in individual countries, to peculiarities in the form of privatization. Thus, *SNA 1993* does not contain explicit recommendations on treatment of vouchers, which are used in some countries in transition as an instrument of privatization. The vouchers are special types of securities that are distributed among the population practically free (in some cases for a nominal fee) so that all groups of the population can participate in the process of privatization of state property. There are some peculiarities in the rules pertaining to distribution and use of vouchers among the countries, but, as a rule, the vouchers do not earn directly any income that resembles income from property, and they can be used to obtain shares of businesses. Such a situation exists, for example, in Russia, where privatization is progressing faster than in many other countries of the CIS.

The use of vouchers complicates the recording of transactions dealing with privatization. It appears that in principle vouchers should be treated as special types of securities. It can be easily demonstrated that if vouchers are shown as securities in the financial accounts, recording of all transactions (exchange of vouchers into shares, sales and purchases of vouchers, and so on) becomes clear and consistent. However, many countries in transition will not be in a position to compile financial accounts in the foreseeable future. One simplified approach to deal with such cases is to disregard recording of vouchers altogether and to show in the capital account only the net result of transfer of property achieved with the help of the vouchers. Privatization also can be carried out with the help of sales and purchases of property. In this case, positive and negative entries on capital formation in capital accounts of the sectors involved or subsectors of the same sector will be necessary.

10.5.6. Holding Gains or Losses

Treatment of holding gains or losses in the context of measurement of output and income is of particular interest for countries in transition with a high rate of inflation. The problem of measurement of output and income (which excludes holding gains or losses) arises in practice largely due to the fact that the methods of recording of movements of stocks used by the enterprises are not acceptable from the *SNA* standpoint. While the *SNA* recommends use for valuation of the withdrawals of goods from stocks the prices that exist at the moment when the withdrawal takes place, in business accounts of the countries in transition the withdrawals are often valued at historic prices.

This inconsistency in the methods of valuation of movements of stocks in business and national accounts implies the need to introduce adjustments to intermediate consumption if the records of the enterprises on the costs of production are used as a principal source of data for compilation of intermediate consumption (which is the case in a number, if not in all, countries in transition. Indeed, if in business accounts of countries in transition intermediate input of goods is normally valued at historic costs, in the natonal accounts this flow is to be valued at the prices that exist when the goods enter intermediate consumption (or at the prices that exist when goods are withdrawn from the stocks). For example, in Russia on the eve of price liberalization in 1992 enterprises managed to accumulate huge stocks of supplies and materials purchased at relatively low prices. Then later in the year they started using these stocks in production and valuing withdrawals and intermediate consumption at historic prices. Thus, if no appropriate adjustment is made to the data on costs collected from business accounts to secure consistency with the *SNA* rules of valuation of flows, the estimates of major aggregates would be distorted.

The other implication of the above inconsistency in the methods of recording of movements of stocks in business and national accounts is that the estimates of change in stocks originally arrived at on the basis of business accounts should be adjusted to make it possible to remove holding gains or losses. The problem, however, is that in practice it is difficult to estimate the holding gain or loss from the sources available to statisticians. Some simplified solutions such as estimation of change in stocks at the average prices of output might not achieve the objective completely under the conditions of erratic high inflation characteristic of a number of countries in transition. The attempt to solve the problem by inventing a magic formula has not been successful so far. Recording all additions to and withdrawals from the stocks valued at the prices existing at the time of addition and withdrawal of goods, respectively (which, theoretically speaking, could solve the problem) would be prohibitively expensive. Thus, working out some effective and simple procedures that can be used for estimating holding gains or losses remains one of the most serious practical problems for countries in transition with high inflation. Table 10.2 shows the disposition of Russia's GDP for 1990–1993 computed in accordance with the definitions of *SNA 1993*.

Table 10.2. Gross domestic product of russian federation by final use, 1990–1993 (current prices, percentage of total GDP)

	1990	*1991*	*1992*	*1993*
Final consumption expenditure	70	62	54	58
Households	49	46	40	43
General government	21	16	14	15
Gross capital formation	30	38	32	25
Gross fixed capital formation	29	24	20	20
Change of inventories	1	14	12	5
Balance of exports and imports	—	—	12	13
Statistical discrepancy	—	—	2	4
Gross domestic product	100	100	100	100

10.6. Old and New Souces of Data for Compilation of National Accounts

Another range of problems that countries in transition face in connection with the introduction of the *SNA* relates to securing primary data. Statistical systems of the CPEs were based on comprehensive compulsory reporting to the statistical authorities by all institutional units (enterprises, organizations, institutions, and so on), 95 percent of which were owned or controlled by the government. The data collected with the help of these compulsory reports provided the bulk of information needed for compilation of the *MPS*. Under these conditions the need to use sample surveys was minimal, and they were employed only occasionally (largely to collect data on households). The statistical reports of the enterprises possessed a number of flaws and limitations. Thus, the data on output were often distorted upward because they were used for the assessment of the fulfilment of the plan; the focus of the reports was output in physical units, and the measures of gross output were not always consistent with the data of business accounts on sales of products; data on different aspects of activity of the enterprise were not in many cases consistent with each other, and their reconciliation often required a great deal of guesswork.

The economic reforms during the early 1990s called for the revision of both the statistical reporting system and business accounting, which served as a basis for compilation of statistical reports. Many countries in transition recognized the need to transform their business accounting in accordance with some international standards or the experience of the developed countries. However, the work on transformation of business accounts is far from being complete in many countries in transition. Some changes and improvements that have been already introduced in some countries are useful from the *SNA* standpoint. Thus, in Russia new regulations for business accounts provide clear rules for recording of nonproduced intangible assets and their depreciation, as well as the rules for accounting of a number of other new categories (income from proterty, purchases of shares, land, privatization vouchers, and so on), which practically did not exist in CPEs. It is clear that improvement of business accounts is essential for upgrading statistical reports, which many countries in transition seem to intend to preserve for the immediate future in order to secure the flow of data from large and medium state enterprises and in some cases even from entities belonging to the private sector.

At the same time the appearance of numerous small private units has made it difficult to collect data from them even with the help of a compulsory reporting system; thus, it has become clear that the latter should be gradually replaced by periodic censuses and sample surveys. Some countries in transition (for example, Poland) have already taken some steps towards this objective and introduced registers of all units. In a number of CIS member countries introduction of business registers may take a number of years. In the immediate future sample surveys will be used in countries in transition largely to monitor activities of small private enterprises or informal activities of households. Family budget surveys are not something new for countries in transition. They existed in the CPEs, but their importance is likely to grow, and many countries are taking specific steps to improve this instrument.

One common problem of countries in transition is the lack of systematic and comprehensive information about transactions with the rest of the world. Though external trade statistics existed in the former CPEs, they were not entirely consistent with international standards and therefore required serious analysis. Liberalization of external trade has complicated the process of obtaining data: while in the past information on external trade was collected from a relatively limited number of external trade organizations; now external trade transactions are carried out on an increasing scale by the businesses producing goods.

There are some particular problems of estimation of external trade flows for countries of the CIS. They refer, above all, to the estimation of the interstate trade in conditions when customs between the members of the CIS do not exist yet, though Russian authorities are making energetic efforts to install them. Under these conditions data on interstate trade are collected from special reports of businesses that export goods to other member states of the CIS. However, the reports submitted by exporters to statistical services cover only flows of major commodities.

Balance of payments, as defined by the IMF, was never compiled in the former CPEs and is only now being introduced on a regular basis in many countries of this group with the assistance of the IMF. The items of balance of payments that require special attention refer to flows of services and income, reinvested earnings of foreign direct investments, and transactions with financial instruments. Careful estimates of the balance of primary income paid to nonresidents is essential for the estimation of national income.

The other important source of data for national accounts is the report on execution of the state budget prepared, as a rule, by the Ministry of Finance or similar government body. This source also requires revision on the basis of recommendations of the IMF. Presently, however, the typical flaw in these statistics is the failure to make a distinction between unrequired payments and borrowing and lending and between capital and current payments. Thus, in Russia the Ministry of Finance continues to treat borrowing as income despite criticism in the press.

Price statistics are essential for the derivation of reliable estimates of the DGP in constant prices. The methods that were used in this area in the recent past in conditions of the CPEs are not acceptable under new circumstances. Therefore internationally approved standards have to be introduced. In many countries in transition, assistance from international organizations has allowed a great deal of work to be done to improve reliability of price indices, but some problems still exist. In many countries in transition the goods are distributed to households through many channels at different prices. It is essential therefore to cover properly all major channels, including the resale of goods by the individuals who originally purchased them at state-owned and other shops. It is also important to decide whether changes in channels of distribution should be treated as price changes or volume changes.

It is worth noting that one of the important tasks for many countries in transition is to establish appropriate methods and sources of data necessary for valuation of nonmarket services in constant prices. It should be rememberted that these services are omitted from the MPS, and therefore practical experience in this field is next to nothing.

Finally, mention should be made of the need to transform branch statistics and introduce internationally approved classifications (ISIC, CPC, COFOG, and so on). Some countries in transition, such as Poland, for example, have managed to achieve noticeable progress in this area, but in many other countries a great deal of work is still to be done. For example, underlying definitions of agricultural statistics used in CIS member countries differ from those of the FAO.

10.7. Conclusion

In conclusion several words should be said about the most probable development in this area in the foresseable future. It is clear that over the next five to six years all countries in transition will intensify their efforts to introduce the *SNA*. It appears that their major objective will consist in transition from the experimental compilation of selected accounts to compilation of major accounts on a regular basis. *SNA 1993* is a very comprehensive system covering practically all transactions and stocks, and it would be unrealistic to expect that all accounts and tables of the *System* can be introduced within a short period of time. The decision to introduce specific accounts should take into account a number of factors. The most important among them are as follows:

- The demand for certain type of analysis (the capacity of the government to use information contained in the national accounts for policy making, forecasting, and so on),
- Progress in transforming a planned economy into a market-oriented one, and
- Progress in transforming related statistics and business accounts, and the availability of primary data needed for compilation of accounts.

The combination of these factors is not the same in various countries, and priorities in different countries may differ noticeably, but generally speaking they are likely to focus in the foreseeable future on introduction of current accounts for sectors and industries (production and generation of income), compilation of supply and use tables or input-output tables, computation of the GDP and its major components on a quarterly basis, improvements of constant price computation methods, and the resulting estimates. On the other hand, compilation of financial accounts and balance sheets will apparently have to be postponed until later stages of this work.

As noted above, there will be some variations between the countries in speed of progress and programs of work in this area. Some countries, such as Russia, for example, plan to introduce financial accounts and balance sheets, but most likely the work in this area will be carried out within several years, mainly on an experimental basis. The same refers to the plans that exist in Russia to introduce limited regional accounts.

In any case, by the end of the next five-year period the majority of the countries in transition will apparently abandon compilation of *MPS* balance and move to regular compilation of *SNA* major accounts and tables. The success of their efforts will depend very much on the progress they make in modifying statistics in related areas and in balance of payments, government finance, and banking and monetary statistics. Work on introducing these statistics in accordance with international standards is at the very earliest stage in many countries in transition, and therefore assistance from international organizations and countries with developed market-oriented statistics is essential for rapid progress. Transformation of basic statistics as well as of business accounting in accordance with international standards, which is already on the way in many countries in transition, will facilitate the formation of adequate sources of data needed for compilation of the major accounts. However, at least in some countries, collection of primary data will continue to be done to a considerable extent with the help of traditional reporting systems.

Progress with the introduction of the *SNA* in countries in transition will depend very much on the demand for statistics from government bodies for formulating economic policies, forecasting, and making decisions on important macroeconomic issues. This may require training of the potential users of data, which in many former CPEs seem to have relatively limited knowledge about the *SNA* and its potential. This may, in turn, also require creation of specific mechanisms, which would make it possible to translate the analysis of national accounts data into decisions on macroeconomic polices. It appears that little has been done thus far in countries in transition in this direction, and the limitted national accounts data that are published are often used largely for propagandistic purposes very much in the same manner as they were used in the former CPEs. It would perhaps be unrealistic to expect too much from the countries in transition so soon.

References

Arvay, J. (1992). The Material Product System (MPS). A retrospective. "A paper presented at the Twenty-second General Conference of the International Association for Research in Income and Wealth, Flims, Switzerland.

Brichacek, Rudolf, and Jiri Pelej. (1993). "Problems of Introducing *SNA* into Statistical Practice of the Czech and Slovak Federal Republic." In *The Value Added to National Accounbting*. Netherlands: Central Bureau of Statistics.

Harrison, Anne. (1990). "Major Changes Proposed for the Next *SNA*: An Overview." *Review of Income and Wealth* 4 (December).

Huttle, A., and P. Pozsonyi. (1992) "National Accounts in the Transition Period: Past Experiences and New Requiremenmts in Hungary." Paper presented at the Twenty-second General Conference of the International Association for Research in Income and Wealth, Flims, Switzerland.

Ivanov, Y., B. Rajbushkin, and Tatiana Homenko. (1993). "Introduction of the *SNA* into the Official Statistics of the Commonwealth of Independent States." *Review of Income and Wealth* 3.

Kondrat, Barbara, and Boguslav Szybiscz. "Eastern Europe: From *MPS* to *SNA*." In *The Value Added of National Accounting*. Netherlands: Central Bureau of Statistics.

DISCUSSION OF CHAPTER 10

Anne Harrison

Whereas concern for developing countries was clear from the outset of the revision of the *System of National Accounts* (*SNA*), it was quite late in the process in 1989 that it became clear that the countries that previously used the *Material Product System* (*MPS*) were interested, initially, in a merging of the two systems. By the time the *1993 SNA* went to print, the pace of reform in most previously planned economies was such that it was clear that the *SNA* would supplant the *MPS* in a very short space of time, and in the closing stages of the *SNA* revision particular attention was paid to countries making the transition from a planned economy.

The speed of transition from *MPS* to *SNA* has been astonishing, and indeed, what is written in this article is almost certain to be out of date by the time it is published. Almost no country in Europe or the former Soviet Union is now doing simple conversions from *MPS* to *SNA* aggregates but, rather, is building on the knowledge of the *Material Product System* and using the similarities of the two systems to reconstitute the basic data used for the *MPS* into an *SNA* format.

While the progress is impressive in terms of visible results and presentation of *SNA* results, there is an underlying problem where change is heppening much less quickly. The basic data reflecting the activity of institutional units within the economy is not changing fast enough to keep up with new developments. The means for recording the newly private companies, let alone informal and illegal activities, are barely developed, and the development of statistical infrastructures needed—such as business registers, the use of sampling techniques, and the better integration of administrative and statistical data—is still in its early stages. These problems are referred to in the paper but perhaps not given the emphasis they deserve.

Initially, there was much concern that there may be conceptual aspects of the *SNA* where implementation in a planned economy would cause major problems. A conference took place in Minsk in April 1993 to examine these problems, and it was discovered that in fact there are only half a dozen areas where special interpretation may be needed for centrally planned economies. Typically, the *SNA* did give a solution, though these solutions were not always the same as in the *MPS* and therefore, for lack of familiarity, did not always seem easily acceptable. One area that was discussed was sectorization. In some instances, the legal status of a unit may not coincide with what the *SNA* recommends as the institutional sectoring that is appropriate, and there is a reluctance to move away from the legal form that was the basis of classification in the *MPS*. Lest the countries in transition should be held culpable on this point, one may think of a number of OECD member countries where units are classified as nonprofit institutions serving households because of their tax-exempt status rather than according to the *SNA* criteria.

The common practice of providing social and cultural services to employees by enterprises is one case where *SNA 1993* contains recommendations specifically addressed to countries in transition because of the representations during the revision process. Another area that was considered was "consumer subsidies." In fact, and rather ironically, the concept of consumer subsidy might have been accepted into the *SNA*, but for the almost casting vote against it from representatives from the countries in transition at the expert group meeting where the decision was finally made. The problem, ultimately, was less whether such a concept could exist but where the dividing line between a consumer subsidy and government expenditure should be drawn.

Two further issues of special interest mentioned in the paper are the treatment of central banks and the handling of privatization operations. These can present particular problems, but they are not exclusively those of countries in transition, though they are of great significance there at the present time.

The paper concentrates almost exclusively on the theoretical problems of the transition from *MPS* to *SNA* and, to a much lesser extent, on the practical problems being faced in the countries in transition at the present time. Two burning issues are the problem of inflation and the measurement of informal activities. The problem of inflation is captured to some extent in reference to holding gains and losses, but this is by no means the only aspect of importance. In 1992 inflation in the countries of the former Soviet Union was of the order of 1,200 percent, and concerns arise about what current price figures mean in such circumstances. Should constant price data still be derived by deflation, or would it be better to derive estimates using volume measures directly? In building up data from the basic sources, estimates of consumption of fixed capital based on historic bookkeeping, entries become derisory, and the need for presentation of alternative interest flows becomes a real issue.

The problem of measuring informal activity points to a dearth of experience and robust practice in all economies, not just those in transition. The tradition in countries in transition was to measure activity meticulously with the care of a bookkeeper. The need to take into account small-scale informal activity that is mushrooming at an undreamed-of rate points to the need for the statistical offices to move away from past practices and to become statisticians instead of bookkeepers.

As the paper notes in the closing section, the need for reeducation applies not only to the statisticians who must compile the data but also to the users of new *SNA* material, who are at present not well-informed about how to make best use of the new data being set before them. In my view, the transition from the *MPS* to *SNA* will come much faster than the five years mentioned in the paper. Whether transition to the *SNA* serves the economic reform and the peoples of these countries well will depend, in large measure, on the success of the reeducation for both the compilers and users of the accounts.

11 EXTERNAL SECTOR TRANSACTIONS: TOWARD A WORLD ACCOUNTING MATRIX

Rob Vos

11.1. Introduction

The increasing internationalization of production and finance puts higher demands on the availability and quality of data on external transactions. Domestic economic policies increasingly have to internalize global economic events and require full consistency of detailed information on the international economy with that of the national economy. One of the main goals of the revised *System of National Accounts (SNA)* of the United Nations has been to harmonize the system with related systems of macroeconomic accounts, such as the IMF's balance of payments statistics (BOPS) and money and banking statistics (MBS). Conceptually the new *SNA* has come close to achieving this goal. In practice, in achieving greater harmony (and reliability) in the actual measurement of international economic transactions, there is still a long way to go. Where the *SNA* provides a framework for consistent accounting of supply and demand and of incomes and expenditures at the national level for individual countries, there is no standardized accounting system that chceks such consistency at the global level.

A summary indicator of the global consistency of the measurement of external transactions, is the aggregate, world current account balance (WCAB). By definition, this global balance should add to zero: what goes out in one part of the world comes in elsewhere. However, using national accounts data the WCAB added to a global deficit of US$48 billion, equal to 0.4 percent of world GNP, while IMF BOPS data showed a deficit of US$106 billion or about 1.0 percent of world GNP in 1990. This global statistical discrepancy may be small relative to the total size of international transactions, but numbers of this magnitude representing real trade or financial flows do and should worry policy makers and analysts of the world economy. The discrepancy is comparable to the size of the first oil price shock of the 1970s or that of the estimated (annual) costs of the German unification process when entering the 1990s, both events with far-reaching global macroeconomic consequences (see Marris, 1985; Masson and Meredith, 1990; Vos, 1993).

The purpose of this paper is twofold. First, it discusses the progress made in the harmonization in the accounting of external transactions at the national level and some issues for further improvement. Second, an outline is given of a global accounting framework that would allow for a permanent consistency check of the international transactions and at the same time provide an improved basis for the analysis of global economic linkages. A World Accounting Matrix (WAM) for 1990, based on existing data sources, is presented to illustrate the nature of the framework and as a basis for discussing the nature of the existing global accounting discrepancies.

This paper is organized along these two lines. The first part outlines the main features of the external account in the revised *SNA*, its link to other data systems (particularly the BOPS) and its link to other parts of the accounting system (Section 11.2). Subsequently, some remaining problem areas in conceptualization, classification, and measurement are discussed (Section 11.3). The second part of the paper elaborates a system of global accounts (the WAM) which should help to integrate the individual country recordings in the *SNA* and BOPS into a consistent global framework (Section 11.4). It is subsequently shown that such a system can be implemented even on the basis of existing data (Section 11.5), but also that a large number of construction problems remain (Section 11.6). The WAM gives a systematic framework to cross-check the external accounts for all countries. If one accepts the rules and assumptions applied to achieve global consistency, this will give rise to a major revision of the external balance estimates of the major economies that are currently used by analysts and policy makers (Section 11.7). The precise consequences for policy making and our understanding of the functioning of the world economy may not be immediately clear, but obviously the way to go would seem to be to incorporate the *SNA*/BOPS into an integrated system of world accounts that allows checking the consistency of trade and capital flow estimates on a cross-country basis (Section 11.8).

11.2. The External Account in the New *SNA*

The *SNA* records the economic transactions between transactors and holders of stocks who are resident units of a particular economy. However, since the *SNA* is a closed system, a segment must capture those transactions that involve uses or sources for nonresident units. This is done in the external transactions or *rest of the world account*. Residence is defined in an economic sense—that is, a resident unit is one that has a "center of economic interest" in the "economic territory" of the country in question. Both the terms *economic territory* and *center of economic interest* are fairly well defined in the revised *SNA*[1] and are identical to those applied in the IMF *Balance of Payments Manual* (Fifth Edition). Since the *SNA* is a closed system, the rest of the world account is constructed from the perspective of the foreign agents rather than from that of the compiling economy. The difference between the balance of payments and the rest of the world account of the *SNA* is purely presentational: they mirror each other in terms of credit and debit entries.

The external account is fully integrated with the accounts for the total economy and, consistent with balance of payments practices, is composed of a *current* and a *capital and financial account*. The system further defines an external assets and liabilities account showing the internaitonal investment position of the country and the opening and closing balance sheets of foreign assets and liabilities of the nation. Table 11.1 gives an overview of the main components of the external accounts. The current account transactions correspond to, respectively, the *SNA*'s production account (export and imports of goods and services), primary and secondary income distribution (interest and other factor income and payments), and income redistribution (current transfers). The external capital and financial accounts distinguish between capital transfers and financial transactions. In the *SNA* *transfers* are defined as the offsets to changes, which take place between residents and nonresidents, in ownership of real resources or financial items and do not involve a quid pro quo in economic value. *Capital* transfers are related to transfers of ownership of fixed assets, transfers of funds linked to, or conditioned on, acquisition or

Table 11.1.   Revised *SNA*: external account

Current account	Goods and services account Account of primary incomes and current transfers
Capital and financial accounts	Capital account Financial account Other changes in volume of assets account (uncompensated seizures, etc.) Revaluation account (nominal gains and losses; other changes in external assets and liabilities not attributable to transactions)
External assets and liabilities account	Opening balance sheets Changes in value of assets and liabilities due to transactions and revaluations Closing balance sheets

disposal of fixed assets and forgiveness, without counterparts received in return, of liabilities by creditors. All other transfers are current transfers. This distinction is now also applied in the IMF BOPS and is part of the full harmonization of the *SNA* and the BOPS; previously the BOPS treated all capital transfers as current. The *financial account* shows the acquisition of financial assets and liabilities, and its balancing item measures the net lending and borrowing for the total economy to and from the rest of the world. This holds not only for the financial account of the rest of the world but also for the consolidated financial account of the total economy, since domestic financial flows cancel each other in the aggregate.

The *other changes in volume of assets account* relates to both financial and nonfinancial assets. Regarding the latter, the account may record uncompensated seizures, such as for intangible nonfinancial assets, seizure of patents, software, and the like. For financial assets, there may be volume changes due to a variety of uncompensated seizures (such as writing off bad debts) or due to changes in classification and structure (for example, resulting from mergers between foreign companies in which residents hold shares or have outstanding loans). Also this account is now an integral part of the IMF BOPS and should be detailed as part of the *international asset position* (IIP) or balance sheet accounts.

The *revaluation account* for the rest of the world follows the same rules as revaluation of domestic assets and liabilities. It defines first so-called nominal holding gains/losses, which is the value accruing to nonresident creditors and debtors as a result of a change in the price or the relevant exchange rate applicable to their external assets and liabilties. The price or exchange-rate change refers to the difference in their respective levels at the times of recording of opening and closing balance sheet values. This differs from the pricing rule for flows (transactions) where current market prices and exchange rates at the time of the transaction should be taken (in practice, usually the annual average price and midpoint exchange rate). In the asset valuation procedures, both *SNA* and BOPS propose the application of flow prices next to stock prices. After having identified the nominal gains and losses, a distinction is made between neutral and real gains and losses. *Neutral* holding gains are defined as the value of the holding gain that would be required to maintain the domestic currency value of the asset—that is, the asset price should stay in line with the change in the overall price level (United Nations, 1993, ch. 14, para. 14.143–14.146, pp. 339–340). The *real* holding gain is then defined as the difference between the nominal and the neutral gain. Neutral and real holding gains may differ for creditors in one economy and corresponding debtors in another economy because the general price change may differ between the economies. The nominal gains and losses should, in principle, correspond assuming compilers in both countries dispose of the same information regarding asset prices and exchange rates. The balancing item in the external revaluation account is the item "changes in net worth due to nominal gains/losses"—that is, the difference between the sums of holding gains and losses.

The difference between opening and closing balance sheet values should equal the sum of the value of transactions in external assets and liabilities (flows), other volume changes, and revaluations. In the BOPS the balance sheet accounts are labeled *international investment position* (IIP), which—as indicated—is recorded from the perspective of the compiling country, rather than from the rest of the world as in the case of the *SNA*.

Algebraically, the difference between the national accounting aggregates and the external accounts can be accounted for as follows. Gross domestic product (Q) equals the sum of private and public consumption (C), public and private gross domestic investment (I), and exports of goods and services (E), less imports of goods and services (M):

$$Q \equiv C + I + E - M. \qquad (11.1)$$

Gross national disposable income (Y) is defined as GDP *plus* net factor income from abroad (R) *plus* net current transfers received from abroad (NT):

$$Y \equiv Q + R + NT. \qquad (11.2)$$

Turning to the external account, the current account balance of the balance of payments (CAB) is equal to the balance of the goods and services account $(E - M)$ plus net factor income and current transfers from abroad):

$$CAB \equiv E - M + R + NT. \qquad (11.3)$$

Defining gross national savings as the difference between gross national disposable income and consumption $(S = Y - C)$, it follows from identities (11.1), (11.2), and (11.3) that the current account balance equals the difference between national savings and investment:

$$CAB \equiv S - I. \qquad (11.4)$$

The capital account of the balance of payments identifies the net lending and borrowing to and from abroad:

$$S - I \equiv CAB \equiv NKT + \Delta OCA + \Delta FA - \Delta FL + \Delta RES, \qquad (11.5)$$

where

NKT = Net capital transfers to abroad,
ΔOCA = Net change in nonproduced external assets and other changes in volume of external assets,
ΔFA = Net change in external financial assets, excluding reserve holdings,
ΔFL = Net change in external financial liabilities, and
ΔRES = Net increase in international reserves.

The total net worth of the economy (W) is equal to the difference between the sum of assets and liabilities. In the consolidated accounts of the economy, domestic financial assets and liabilities will cancel each other, so that the economy's stock of financial assets and liabilities refer to the stock of external assets and liabilities or the international asset position. The net worth or national wealth of an economy in year t consequently consists of its stock of nonfinancial assets *plus* the net international investment position (including international reserves):

$$W_t \equiv K_t + OCA_t + (FA_t - FL_t) + RES_t$$
$$\equiv W_{t-1} + \Delta W_t, \qquad (11.6)$$

where K, OCA, FA, FL, and RES represent the end-of-period balance sheet values (stocks) of, respectively, produced (fixed) assets, nonproduced external assets, external financial assets and liabilities, and reserve holdings.

In the terminology of the revised *SNA*, changes in the net worth of the economy as a whole (ΔW) may be due to three factors—namely savings, capital transfers, and nominal holding gains and losses (revaluations):[2]

$$\Delta W_t \equiv S_t - NKT_t + REV_t$$
$$\equiv I_t + \Delta OCA_t + \Delta FA_t - \Delta FL_t + \Delta RES_t + REV_t, \quad (11.7)$$

where *REV* is the balancing item of the revaluation account, which—in relation to *external* assets—equals (valued at domestic currency values):

$$REV_t = \sum_i [(e_t - e_{t-1}) \cdot p_{t-1,i} + e_{t-1} \cdot (p_t - p_{t-1,i})] \cdot$$
$$[OCA_{t-1,i} + FA_{t-1,i} - FL_{t-1,i}] + (e_t - e_{t-1}) \cdot RES_{t-1}, \quad (11.8)$$

where *e* is the relevant nominal exchange rate, *p* is the relevant asset price for asset and liability type *i* and subscripts $(t - 1)$ and (t) refer to, respectively, opening and closing balance sheet values (stocks).

These accounting relations are consistent with the basic concepts as applied in standard macroeconomic theory (see Tobin, 1969, 1980).

11.3. Issues in Classification, Presentation, and Measurement

The general outline of the external account in the revised *SNA* and the new *Balance of Payments Manual* (Fifth Edition) leaves little to question. Foremost, the harmonization between the *SNA* and the BOPS is a major step forward from the preceding guidelines. Definitions of residence and accounting variables have been fully harmonized on the basis of a series of expert group meetings and recommendations of an Intersecretariat Working Group (see Galbis, 1991; World Bank/BIS/IMF/OECD, 1988; United Nations, 1993, annex 2; IMF, 1993, ch. 3, app. 1). This includes instructions on how to deal with units operating mobile equipment, such as shipping companies. Ownership, mode of operation, and chartering of shipment services may involve complex arrangements, where for tax or other considerations ships fly flags of convenience and country of registry may differ from that of the operator or owner. Recordings of shipment services tend to show large global discrepancies because of so-called missing fleets (see below). The *SNA* and BOPS provide the guideline that in such cases the shipping activity should be attributed to the country of residence of the operating enterprise.

Also matters relating to valuation (market prices, application of flow and stock rates for asset prices and exchange rates) and time of recording (accrual basis) have been harmonized. The *SNA* now also follows BOPS practice of treating reinvested earnings of foreign companies as a payment on the income and outlay account of enterprises and on the (current) external account and as a capital inflow (direct foreign investment) in the (capital) external account. Also accounting for arrears and debt cancellations, an important issue for many developing countries in the 1980s, have been harmonized. Again following BOPS practice, the *SNA* records interest payments on external debt that are contractually due in the current accounts; arrears are considered as a form of exceptional financing and appear as a counterpart item on the capital and finance account. Debt cancellations and debt forgiveness no longer appear in the *SNA* as an (imputed) unrequited transfer in the current account (thus affecting the measurement of gross national savings; see equation 11.2 above) but is recorded as a capital transfer or as a 'other volume change in assets' on the capital account. The capital transfer is subsequently booked as if repaying outstanding debt.

This is not the place to detail all accounting procedures. These are well explained in the corresponding manuals. Here, I will just briefly discuss a few issues for further improvement relating to concepts, classifications, presentation, and measurement:

- *Trade measurement:* The new manuals for a *SNA* and the BOPS do not include guidelines on how to deal with possible misrecordings in trade due to smuggling and over- or underinvoicing of imports and exports. Particularly in developing countries, illegal trade and trade misinvoicing tend to be substantial and are also seen as channels of capital flight. The integrated system of national accounts checks the balance of the supply and demand for commodities and thus forms a means to detect unrecorded trade flows. A further consistency check could be applied by looking at the bilateral export and import recordings of trading nations. Such a method, though not without flaws, has been applied to measure trade misinvoicing (Bhagwati et al., 1974; Gulati, 1987; and Vos, 1992). World trade matrices compiled by the United Nations (UNTMS) and a broader world accounting framework, such as elaborated in Section 11.4, would provide more comprehensive global consistency checks in the measurement of trade flows.
- *Classification of financial transactions* While the *SNA* and BOPS

have achieved full conceptual harmonization, there remain important differences in their respective classification schemes (IMF, 1993, app. 1; United Nations, 1993, annex 2). In the *SNA*, financial assets are classified primarily by type of *instrument* (currency, equity, securities, loans, and so on), while in the BOPS the main classification criterion is by *function* (direct investment, portfolio investment, other, and reserves). The BOPS further applies a fairly aggregate breakdown by institutional sectors (monetary authorities, general government, banks and other), which differs somewhat from that in the *SNA*. Both manuals indicate how to construct bridges between the two classifications of financial transactions. This is, however, only possible in practice if both sources provide all data at its full level of detail by main items and subcategories and by institutional sector. For the *SNA* it would be thus preferable that the financial and capital accounts are presented, for each instrument, by institutional sector of origin and destination (including the rest of the world) to know precisely which institution provides or borrows which funds to and from other domestic institutions and from abroad. The *Social Accounting Matrix* framework allows for that (cf. Vos, 1991; United Nations, 1993, ch. 20). This would further provide a cross-check of consistency of the balance sheet and financial transaction recordings between institutions and at the international level, analogous to the trade matrices; this could be done through the construction of world financial account, as proposed in the next section.

- *Net versus gross capital movement: SNA* and BOPS record financial transactions in principle on a *net* basis—that is, increases less decreases in assets or liabilities. *Gross* recording is provided on a selective basis as supplementary information, such as for disbursements and repayments on long-term loans. How selective this procedure should be in practice remains unspecified. For purposes of making global consistency checks (see below), it is, of course, important to pursue the greatest possible symmetry in recordings across nations, and this would argue in favor of recording all financial transactions in principle on a gross rather than on a net basis. Also, for analytical purposes gross recordings have importance for the study of the size of (global) capital markets and the structure of financial interactions between domestic and foreign agents (such as new financing versus refinancing of existing debts, and so on).

Clear accounting rules and measurement guidelines form the starting point of a reliable statistical system, but in the implementation many practical problems likely emerge. As hinted at in the above, it seems highly desirable to attach a system of global consistency checks to the external accounts of individual countries. As observed in various studies (IMF, 1987, 1992; Marris, 1985; Vos, 1989; Luttik, 1992), existing data show huge discrepancies at the global level when adding the external accounts of all countries. Transactions for each item of the external account should sum to zero for the world as a whole. Table 11.2 (first column) shows that the world current account discrepancy mentioned in the introductory section is in fact the balance of (positive and negative) discrepancies on the various types of current transactions and that even larger discrepancies show up in the main types of capital movements. In the remainder of this paper I concentrate on these statistical discrepancies and the required framework that should be attached to the *SNA*/BOPS to check these and to provide a consistent data framework for analysis of global interactions.

11.4. Toward a World Accounting Matrix (WAM)

Assuming, and there is no reason why one shouldn't, that the world is a closed economy, accounting rules require that at the aggregate level global commodity and financial flows should balance. The framework set out here, expands the *SNA* into a World Accounting Matrix (WAM), which connects international transactions of each economy with the internal balance (reflected in the savings-investment balance) and identifies the interactions between economies. The WAM framework rests on the following basic accounting relations:[3]

$$S_i - I_i \equiv E_i - M_i + R_i + NT_i$$
$$\equiv NKT_i + NOCA_i + \Delta FA_i - \Delta FL_i + (\Delta RES_i + EO_i). \quad (11.9)$$

Since at the world level all ingoings and outgoings must balance, it should hold that

$$\sum_i^n (S_i - I_i) \equiv \sum_i^n (E_i - M_i + R_i + NT_i) \equiv 0, \quad (11.10)$$

$$\sum_i^n [NKT_i + NOCA_i + \Delta FA_i - \Delta FL_i + (\Delta RES_i + EO_i)] \equiv 0, \quad (11.11)$$

where a term has been added for errors and omissions (*EO*).

Table 11.2. Summary table of global discrepancies and initial adjustments, 1990 (billions of U.S.$)

		BOPS and NA data 1990	Initially adjusted data 1990
GMS-GDI		−47.9	−20.5
Current account		106.0	−101.6
TX	Trade balance	2.0	0.0
C1X	Shipment and other transportation	−35.2	0.0
C2X	Travel	3.2	1.0
C3X	Interofficial	−0.0	−11.3
C4X	DFI income/payments flows	45.5	44.3
C5X	Other investment income	−108.3	−121.1
C6X	Labor and property income	−5.4	−5.9
C7X	Other goods, services and income	20.5	14.2
C8X	Private transfers	6.6	5.8
C9X	Official transfers	−34.8	−28.7
Capital account[a]		−105.6	−83.0
K1X	DFI net	33.7	37.2
K2X	Portfolio investment	−5.7	42.7
K3X	Other capital	−210.6	−135.7
K4X	Reserves: net[b]	104.7	−2.2
EOX	Net errors and omissions	−27.8	−25.1

Source: De Jong, Jellema, Vos, and Zebregs (1993b), based on IMF, Balance of Payments Statistics, computer tapes and World Bank, World Tables (first column); and, in addition, UN, Trade Matrices; World Bank, Debtor Reporting System; and other sources listed in Table 11.9, below (second column of adjusted data).

a Capital account balance defined as change in assets *less* liabilities—that is, negative figure means that existing data record a global excess of outward capital flows over inward flows.

b Including foreign-exchange holdings and reserve position in IMF.

Equations 11.10 and 11.11 state that the global savings-investment account should balance and that the global current account balance and the aggregate change in *net* external asset position should be both zero, ex post. Since reserves may be held abroad in various forms of financial assets one can write

$$\sum_{i}^{n} (\Delta FA_i - \Delta FL_i + \Delta RES_i) \equiv 0. \tag{11.12}$$

In principle, if all reserve changes would represent international transactions, it should also hold that $\Sigma \Delta RES_i \equiv 0$. However, this identity does not hold in the accounting procedures of international data sources, particularly those of the BOPS, as countries hold part of their reserves as portfolio investment and other financial assets and are recorded as the corresponding type of liabilities in the countries where such reserve assets are held.[4] Due to this asymmetry in the accounting of part of the reserve holdings, it would be an accounting identity (11.11) that applies in practice to existing data sources. However, in the WAM framework adjustments have been made to cope with this asymmetry (see De Jong, Vos, Jellema, and Zebregs, 1993a, app. 1).

Given equation (11.12), the global estimate of net errors and omissions should sum, in principle, to zero as well:

$$\sum_{i}^{n} EO_i \equiv 0. \tag{11.13}$$

Matrix presentation (Table 11.3) permits the identification of the origin and destination of each transaction included in the accounting identities of equations (11.9) and (11.10). This has a number of advantages:

- it allows one to obtain a more detailed picture of the structure of international trade and finance useful for analytical purposes;
- at the same time it allows for a detailed and systematic cross-check of the statistical consistency of commodity flows, international payments, and internal balances across countries; and
- since various data sources are required to construct a data base in this way, it allows for a systematic identification of discrepancies between different data sources.

In Table 11.3 the CA (Current Account) quadrant defines on the rows for country (group) $i = 1 \ldots n$ exports of goods and services plus all factor income and current transfers received from abroad, while the columns in CA define commodity imports plus factor and current transfer payments to abroad. The CA block is a consolidated matrix that is composed of a set of transactions matrices with the same dimensions. The S and I blocks are *diagonal* matrices defining national savings and domestic investment per country group. The FOF (flow of funds) block defines the total international financial transactions between countries, reading in the rows the change in external liabilities and in the columns the change in external assets. Also the FOF block is built up from a set of matrices identifying

Table 11.3. Schematic presentation of the world accounting matrix (WAM)

	Current account (country groups, 1 . . . n)	Capital account (country groups, 1 . . . n)	Change in reserves	Total
Current account (country groups, 1 . . . n)	CA (Matrix of current account transactions)	I (Diagonal matrix of domestic investment)		$CA_i + I_i = (E + R^R + TR^R + I)_i$ (Total current receipts)
Capital account (country groups, 1 . . . n)	S (Diagonal matrix of national savings)	$\Delta FA - \Delta FL$ (Flow of funds matrix, liabilities in rows, assets in columns)		$S_i + KT_i^R + \Delta OCA_i^R + \Delta FL_i$ (Total investment finance)
Change in reserves and errors and omissions		$\Delta RES + EO$ (Row vector of adjusted net changes in reserves[a] and E&O)		$\Sigma(\Delta RES_i + EO_i) = 0$ (Global net change in reserves[a] and E&O)
Total	$CA_i + S_i = M_i + R_i^P + TR_i^P + S_i$ (Total current payments to abroad and national savings)	$I_i + KT^{P_i} + \Delta OCA_i^P + \Delta FA_i + \Delta RES_i + EO_i$ (Total investment, domestic and foreign)		

a. The accounting of (changes in) reserve assets contains adjustment with respect to the standard balance-of-payments accounting rules to obtain symmetry in the recording of those reserve assets held abroad in the form of portfolio investment and other financial assets. The reserve holdings are a separate item in the flow of funds matrix, the remaining reserve transactions (gold, SDRs and use of IMF credits are in the special account for reserve changes. See De Jong, Jellema, Vos, and Zebregs (1993a, app. A.1) for further details on this adjustment.

origin and destination of different types of international capital flows (direct investment, long-term capital, short-term capital, and so on).

An exception to this form of presentation concerns the net changes in international reserves and errors and omissions, which for each country (group) are the closing item of the balance of payments but cannot be identified by origin and destination. These are presented in the FOF in a separate row vector with counterpart values only recorded where applicable (that is, SDR creation with the IMF).

The WAM as presented in Table 11.3 redefines the internal and external balances of each country (group) equation (11.9), as follows:

$$\left(\sum_j^n \sum_k^o E_{ijk} + \sum_i^n \sum_l^p (R_{ijl}^R + T_{ijl}^R) \right) + I_i$$

$$\equiv \left(\sum_j^n \sum_k^o M_{ijk} + \sum_j^n \sum_l^p (R_{ijl}^P + T_{ijl}^P) \right) + S_i \qquad (11.4)$$

$$S_i + \sum_j^n (KT_{ij}^R + OCA_{ij}^R) + \sum_j^n \sum_m^q \Delta FL_{ijm}$$

$$\equiv I_i + \sum_j^n (KT_{ij}^P + OCA_{ij}^P) + \sum_j^n \sum_m^q \Delta FA_{ijm} + (\Delta RES_i + EO_i), \qquad (11.15)$$

where

$i = 1 \ldots n$ = exporting or recipient country (group),
$j = 1 \ldots n$ = importing or transferring country (group),
$k = 1 \ldots o$ = type of goods and services transaction,
$l = 1 \ldots p$ = type of factor payment and current transfer, and
$m = 1 \ldots q$ = type of external asset (liability),

and where

superscripts R and P refer to, respectively, receipts and payments of factor payments and current and capital transfers.

The *FOF* block in Table 11.3 refers to international financial transactions only—that is, to changes in external ("cross-the-border") assets and liabilities. The WAM uses the same definitions as *SNA* and BOPS, implying that the core table records in principle transactions (*flows*). Asset and liability positions (*stocks*) are presented separately in the WAM framework but use the same format as the flow of funds tables for each financial instrument.

11.5. An Illustration: An Aggregate and Reconciled WAM for 1990

By way of illustration, an aggregated WAM for 1990 is presented in Table 11.4. The WAM is a nine-country group aggregation from a fully balanced WAM for twenty-three country groups.[5] The table shows full consistency with the accounting rules defined above—that is, row and column totals are equal for each account—but it can also be checked that the current account balance of each country equals the savings-investment balance and the net change in external assets. For instance, identity (11.9) holds as shown in Table 11.5 for, respectively, the U.S. Japan, and the group of developing countries (LDCs).

According to the reconciled WAM for 1990, the U.S. external deficit was U.S.$65.0 billion, while the Japanese surplus added to U.S.$19.4 billion. LDCs (including major oil exporters) showed a *surplus* of U.S.$40.7 billion. These numbers deviate substantially from the original figures after the global consistency check and the adjustments made to eliminate the world discrepancies. In the case of the United States, the WAM estimates a significantly lower deficit compared to official sources (over U.S.$20 billion less), but then also the WAM suggests the Japanese current account surplus may be overestimated in the publicized data (by some U.S.$37 billion in 1990). Below, more is said about the nature of these adjustments and the construction methodology of the WAM. Of course, if the suggested adjustment procedure is, by approximation, acceptable, then these revised and globally checked figures may have important consequences for applied international macroeconomic analysis an policy decisions.

The WAM also allows for an immediate identification of the bilateral balances on current and capital account transactions. Table 11.6 extracts these balances for the economic relations between the United States and Japan and the United Stated and LDCs. The table indicates that the United States runs current account deficits with both Japan and the group of developing countries, that it borrows from Japan to finance its external deficit, but that it nevertheless remains a net creditor to developing countries. These numbers suggest a significantly smaller United States deficit in trade and factor payments with Japan than officially recorded and also a smaller inflow of Japanese capital.

From the asset and liability matrix (Table 11.7) it is also possible to identify the (bilateral) net international investment positions for all countries—that is, their net worth, excluding domestic physical capital.[6]

Table 11.4. Balanced world accounting matrix for 1990 (U.S.$ billions)

	Current account										Capital account										Total
	USA	JAP	DEU	GBR	ODC	EEU	LDC	OBC	INT	SUBTOT	USA	JAP	DEU	GBR	ODC	EEU	LDC	OBC	INT	SUBTOT	
Current account																					
USA	0.0	106.0	40.0	60.7	248.6	6.0	181.7	22.4	2.1	668.1	879.0									879.0	1,547.1
JAP	103.7	0.0	24.8	27.3	107.9	4.0	119.3	25.4	9.3	421.8		974.4								974.4	1,396.2
DEU	51.4	18.0	0.0	52.8	305.6	19.1	63.0	6.0	6.8	522.8			349.1							349.1	871.9
GBR	67.3	39.7	39.2	0.0	184.2	6.8	44.4	6.7	2.2	390.5				174.0						174.0	564.5
ODC	240.8	95.1	286.3	196.0	735.7	34.2	219.2	26.4	23.1	1,856.8					1,196.8					1,196.8	3,053.7
EEU	4.8	4.7	16.7	3.9	37.3	38.6	29.3	0.6	0.2	136.1						316.5				316.5	452.6
LDC	218.1	118.1	67.5	38.1	228.4	24.1	154.5	62.5	11.5	922.8							777.0			777.0	1,699.8
OBC	40.8	17.5	10.6	13.9	17.3	1.2	55.6	8.1	3.9	168.9								34.2		34.2	203.1
INT	6.0	2.7	6.1	4.1	24.1	0.3	15.3	0.5	16.2	75.3									0.0	0.0	75.3
Subtotal	733.1	402.4	491.1	396.8	1,889.1	134.5	882.1	158.7	75.3	5,163.2	879.0	974.4	349.1	174.0	1,196.8	316.5	777.0	34.2	0.0	4,701.0	9,864.2
Capital account																					
USA	814.0									814.0	0.0	15.0	9.5	28.5	44.7	0.7	3.4	-3.2	1.7	100.3	914.3
JAP		993.8								993.8	2.6	0.0	16.3	32.8	50.8	1.3	10.5	1.4	-1.2	114.5	1,108.3
DEU			380.8							380.8	3.2	-0.0	0.0	21.2	31.6	0.0	2.9	3.9	1.3	64.2	445.1
GBR				167.6						167.6	4.5	6.9	25.5	0.0	89.4	-0.0	10.5	3.3	1.0	141.1	308.7
ODC					1,164.5					1,164.5	29.7	62.0	50.4	55.4	176.4	0.8	79.8	11.9	6.9	473.4	1,637.9
EEU						318.1				318.1	0.0	-0.1	4.5	-2.3	-1.6	-0.4	0.1	-0.1	0.6	0.6	318.7
LDC							817.7			817.7	20.9	16.6	2.2	4.2	19.2	-0.5	0.6	2.4	14.2	79.8	897.5
OBC								44.4		44.4	4.5	2.0	0.4	0.9	4.0	0.0	0.4	0.1	0.2	12.4	56.8
INT									0.0	0.0	2.1	5.1	2.8	4.1	11.0	0.1	3.1	0.3	0.6	29.2	29.2
Subtotal	814.0	993.8	380.8	167.6	1,164.5	318.1	817.7	44.4	0.0	4,701.0	67.4	107.5	111.6	144.7	425.5	2.2	111.2	20.0	25.4	1,015.5	5,716.6
Other reserves											-0.2	-0.3	-0.7	0.0	0.1	1.0	-2.1	-0.1	2.3	0.0	0.0
Errors and omissions											-32.0	26.8	-15.0	-10.0	15.5	-1.0	11.3	2.8	1.5	0.0	0.0
Total	1,547.1	1,396.2	871.9	564.5	3,053.7	452.6	1,699.8	203.1	75.3	9,864.2	914.3	1,108.3	445.1	308.7	1,637.9	318.7	897.5	56.8	29.2	5,716.6	15,580.7

Note: USA = United States; JAP = Japan
DEU = Germany
GBR = United Kingdom
ODC = Other Developed Countries (Groups 2, 5, 6, 8, to 11)
EEU = Eastern Europe (Groups 12 and 13)
LDC = Development Countries (Groups 14 to 21 and 99)
OBC = Offshore Banking Centers (Group 22)
INT = International Organizations (Group 23)

Table 11.5. Internal and external balances for the United States, Japan, and LDCs (in billions of U.S.$)

	Current account balance	Savings – investment	Change foreign (assets – liabilities) + (Res. & EO)	Total
USA	668.1 – 733.1	= 814.0 – 879.0 =	67.4 – 100.3 – 0.2 – 32.0	= –65.0
Japan	421.8 – 402.4	= 993.8 – 974.4 =	107.5 – 114.5 – 0.3 + 36.8	= 19.4
LDCs	992.8 – 882.1	= 817.7 – 777.0 =	111.2 – 79.8 – 2.1 + 11.3	= 40.7

Table 11.6. Bilateral current and capital account balances, United States minus Japan and United States minus LDCs, 1990

	Current account balance	Capital account balance (net acquisitions of assets)
United States – Japan	103.7 – 106.6 = –2.9	2.6 – 15.0 = –12.4
United States – LDCs	181.7 – 218.1 = –36.4	20.9 – 3.4 = +17.5

Those for the United States, Japan, and the group of LDCs and their respective bilateral positions are presented by way of illustration in Table 11.8.

The table confirms the current net debtor status of the U.S. economy, but—surprisingly—suggests that also Japan had a negative net foreign investment position (IIP) in 1990. The IIP data published in the BOPS (*Yearbook 1992*) record a *positive* investment position of Japan of about U.S.$250 billion. The WAM data, which are cross-checked for global consistency, suggest that the individual country recordings for Japan would seem to grossly underestimate its net liability position with the major international financial centers (London, offshore banking centers). The group of LDCs has a net debtor position with almost half of its external liabilities outstanding with the United States and Japan. However, note the important external asset holdings (often associated with "capital flight"), particularly in the United States, the United Kingdom, and typical havens of capital flight money (Luxemburg, Switzerland, offshore banking centers).

WAMs with the same methodology and classifications have also been constructed for 1985–1989 (De Jong, Jellema, Vos, and Zebregs, 1993a, 1993b), while also WAMs going further back in time (1970, 1975, 1980, 1985) but with a somewhat different country group classification and lesser data coverage can be found in Luttik (1992). It should be noted

Table 11.7. WAM 1990: asset/liability matrix by aggregate regions (end of period; U.S.$ billion) (including reserves classified as "Liabilities Constituting Foreign Authorities" Reserves)

	US	JAPAN	GER	UK	ODC	EEU	LDC	OBC	INT	Liabilities total (1)	Assets total (2)	IIP (2) − (1)
United States	0.0	264.0	58.3	365.3	512.2	8.2	221.3	627.6	12.4	2,069.3	1,526.9	−542.9
Japan	224.0	0.0	62.4	283.3	443.0	3.7	90.4	302.8	77.9	1,487.4	1,468.2	−19.2
Germany	60.0	31.7	0.0	151.1	374.4	5.6	46.5	39.8	10.1	719.0	802.3	83.3
United Kingdom	252.0	141.9	147.0	0.0	583.4	6.4	184.1	146.2	7.4	1,468.5	1,687.6	219.1
ODCs	429.7	419.4	325.1	575.3	1,108.3	15.1	287.8	461.5	106.5	3,728.6	3,741.7	13.0
EEU	4.7	8.0	27.5	20.2	57.1	4.3	2.4	2.6	4.1	131.1	86.8	−44.3
LDCs	326.7	221.1	81.6	55.8	214.9	38.9	39.8	36.8	202.3	1,218.0	975.3	−242.7
OBCs	215.0	287.2	73.5	228.0	377.2	3.4	78.9	252.7	66.4	1,582.3	1,965.8	383.6
INT	14.4	94.8	26.8	8.7	71.2	1.2	24.1	95.8	20.6	357.5	507.7	150.1
Total	1,526.4	1,468.2	802.3	1,687.6	3,741.7	86.8	975.3	1,965.8	507.7	12,761.8	12,761.8	0.0

Table 11.8. WAM 1990—net investment position[a] of the United Stated, Japan, and the LDCs (U.S.$ billion)

	Total external Assets	Total external liabilities	Net IIP
U.S.	1,526.4	2,069.3	−542.9
with Japan	224.0	264.0	−40.0
with LDCs	326.7	221.3	+105.4
Japan	1,468.2	1,487.4	−19.2
with United States	264.0	224.0	+40.0
with LDCs	221.1	90.4	−130.7
LDCs	975.3	1,218.0	−242.7
with United States	221.3	326.7	−105.4
with Japan	90.4	221.1	−130.7

a. Including assets constituting foreign authorities' reserves.

that the WAM data presented here have not fully benefitted from the harmonization of *SNA* and BOPS, as this process started in the late 1980s and harmonized guidelines were made official as of 1993. For instance, the BOPS did not yet make the systematic distinction between current and capital transfers, nor did they identify revaluation account. More in general, the link between flow data and stock data is poorly covered, if at all, for most countries in both national accounts and balance of payments statistics. Furthermore, the WAM combines various data sources (see below) in order to (1) achieve (or, at least, approximate) the required geographical coverage for global consistency and (2) identify bilateral trade and financial linkages. While the WAM accounting framework is, as explained, fully consistent with that of the *SNA*/BOPS, the data resulting from these sources show discrepancies and are incomplete in coverage. In the next section, these issues are discussed in some detail, highlighting the difficulties in implementing theoretically sound accounting systems.

11.6. Construction of the WAM

The construction process of the WAM from existing data sources comprised the following five main steps: identification of data sources, identification of reference totals (marginals) of the WAM, initial global consistency checks and adjustments, construction of matrix interiors and second-round consistency checks, and overall balancing of the WAM.

Table 11.9.   WAM: primary and complementary data sources

	Primary data source	Complementary data source(s)
Current account		
TX Merchandise trade	BOPS	Individual country data
C1X Shipment, passenger services, other transport	UNTMS	BOPS, DOTS
C2X Travel	BOPS	UNCTAD
C3X Interofficial	BOPS	Individual country data
C4X Direct investment income payments	BOPS	Individual country data
	BOPS	Individual country data, and see capital account data sources
C5X Other investment income payments	BOPS, WDT/DRS	Individual country data and see capital account data sources
C6X Labor and property income	BOPS	
C7X Other goods, services and income	BOPS	
C8X Private current transfers	BOPS	Individual country data
C9X Official transfers (including grants)	BOPS, OECDGD	Individual country data
Investment and savings	WT	DAD
Capital account		
K1X Direct foreign investment	BOPS	Individual country data, UNDESD
K2X Portfolio investment		Individual country data
1. Bonds	BOPS	WDT/DRS (for groups 12–21)
2. Other equities	BOPS	Individual country data

	BOPS	Individual country data
1. Other long-term capital		
For Eastern Europe and developing countries (groups 12–99):		
1.1 Bilateral ODA	WDT/DRS	
1.2 Bilateral other official	WDT/DRS	
1.3 Multilateral ODA	WDT/DRS	
1.4 Multilateral other official	WDT/DRS	
1.5 Suppliers' credits guaranteed	WDT/DRS	
1.6 Suppliers' credits non-guaranteed	WDT/DRS	
1.7 Bank loans guaranteed	WDT/DRS	
1.8 Bank loans non-guaranteed	WDT/DRS	
For all countries:		
1.9 Other long-term capital	BOPS	Individual country data, BIS, IMF-IBS
2. Short-term capital	BOPS	WDT/DRS, Individual country data, BIS, IMF-IBS
K4X Reserves	BOPS	
EOX Net errors and omissions	BOPS	

Note:
BIS = BIS International Banking Statistics
BOPS = IMF, Balance of Payments Statistics
DAD = World Bank, DEC Analytical Database
DOTS = IMF, Direction of Trade Statistics
IFS = IMF, International Financial Statistics
IMF-IBS = IMF, International Banking Statistics
OECDGD = OECD, Geographical Distribution of Financial Resources to LDCs
UNDESD = UN-DESD, World Investment Directory, 1992
UNTMS = UN International Trade Matrices
WDT/DRS = World Bank, World Debt Tables/Debtor Reporting System
WT = World Bank, World Tables

11.6.1. Identification of Data Sources

The *SNA*/BOPS framework for the external account of the economy also forms the core of the WAM framework, and therefore the *SNA*/BOPS-related data sources formed the central database for the construction of the WAM. The basic classification of transactions of the BOPS was applied as this, in the *publicized* data, was the most detailed and useful for the purposes of the WAM. In the future, as indicated in Section 11.3, it should be no problem—in principle and if data are reported in adequate detail in both sources—to reclassify this to the new *SNA* classification. To enhance country coverage and data availability on certain types of transactions and to construct the international network (bilateral flows) of trade and payments, complementary data systems were used. These sources are listed in Table 11.9.[7]

The sources are classified as primary and complementary, indicating respectively which source in the first instance provides the reference total for the corresponding variable and which sources serve to complement this information to check estimates and provide additional information (particularly on origin and destination). As can be seen in Table 11.9, the BOPS served for most variables as the primary source. Obviously, given the observed global inconsistency of the BOPS, the complementary sources and the application of the WAM methodology inevitably require major adjustments of the BOPS reference totals (see Table 11.2). For some variables, such as merchandise trade, developing country official transfers and debt data (income, flows, stocks), the BOPS were replaced by other data sources considered more complete or more reliable, in general or for particular groups of countries.

11.6.2. Identification of Reference Totals

After having identified the principal data sources, the next stage in the construction process was to identify initial reference totals for the variables of the accounting framework. This was done in three steps. First, estimates for country aggregates for external (current and capital account) transactions were derived from the IMF Balance of Payments Statistics (BOPS) and for savings and investment from the World Bank's World Tables (WT). Second, reference totals from other primary data sources were calculated, replacing the BOPS reference totals where relevant and further complementary data sources were used for a number of variables to enlarge data coverage. The DRS data for external liabilities of developing countries replaced the BOP totals for the relevant types of capital flows. Third, a number of adjustments to these reference totals derived from primary data sources were made on the basis of complementary data sources in order to increase coverage (such as data for countries not covered in the primary sources). The main adjustments are detailed below.

11.6.3. Initial Global Consistency Checks

A first consistency check on the reference totals was to look at the global aggregates and consequently at the aggregate statistical discrepancy. Table 11.2 showed the global discrepancies between gross national savings and gross domestic investment, between exports on the one hand and imports and net factor payments and transfers on the other, and, finally, between the change in financial assets and the change in financial liabilities. The first column of the table showed that in 1990 the global savings-investment balance was $47.9 billion. The global current account discrepancy, which about equals the capital account discrepancy in the IMF BOP, is 106.0.[8] Combining the BOPS with the other major data sources led to a number of adjustments to these raw data (the second column in Table 11.2). The main adjustments include, among others:

- Inclusion of estimates for GNS and GDI from the more complete DEC analytical data base (DAD) of the World Bank for a number of countries not covered in the World Tables;[9]
- Replacement of the BOPS marginals for merchandise trade by the row and column totals of the trade matrix of UNTMS;[10]
- Replacement of the BOPS estimates of transactions related to income flows and changes in liabilities of portfolio and other capital (long-term external debt) for developing countries by the row totals of World Bank's Debtor Reporting System (DRS) and by data from IMF and World Bank studies for the (former) USSR;
- Adjustments to the accounts for shipment, passenger services and other transportation on the basis of UNCTAD data on shipment tonnage;
- Reclassification of part of reserve movements (Liabilities Constituting Foreign Authorities' Reserves) into changes in assets of portfolio investment and other capital (see De Jong, Jellema, Vos, and Zebregs, 1993a, app. A.1).

The adjustments have resulted in higher values for both savings and investment, but have led to a reduction of the global savings gap. In 1990, for example, the global savings-investment discrepancy is reduced from U.S.$ −47.9 to −20.5 billion. The global current account deficit is reduced initially through these adjustments from U.S.$106.0 to $101.6 billion. By definition, the replacement of the BOPS totals for merchandise trade by those of the trade matrix (based on import recordings)[11] renders a zero global discrepancy on merchandise trade. The remaining discrepancy on the current account thus stems from the, partially offsetting, imbalances on nonmerchandise trade current account transactions, especially on the account for other interest incomes. The indicated adjustments for the capital account items lead to a reduction of the global discrepancy (showing an excess of the change in liabilities over that in assets) from U.S.$105.6 to $83.0 billion.

11.6.4. Construction of Bilateral Trade and Payments Matrices

The next steps are to cross-check these global inconsistencies with data by origin and destination and to reconcile these data within the WAM framework. This is not the place to go into detail here (see De Jong, Jellema, Vos, and Zebregs, 1993a, 1993b), but the following were the main problem areas:

- *Merchandise trade* did not give major problems after deciding to use the U.N. trade matrices; only to enlarge coverage and reclassify certain country group data the IMF Direction of Trade Statistics (DOTS) were used as a complementary source.
- Basic data on the earnings from *Shipment, passenger services, and other transportation* were adjusted following the approach of the IMF Report on the Current Account Discrepancy (IMF, 1987), which mainly addresses the issue of the "missing fleet.[12] Data on this provides a table of the deadweight tonnage (dwt) by national flag and by foreign flag of the thirty-five most important maritime countries (as at July 1, 1989), as well as the true nationality by dwt of major open registry fleets (Liberia, Panama, Cyprus, Bahamas, and Bermuda).[13] It is assumed that the discrepancy on shipment (including the small discrepancies on passenger services and other transportation) relates to the "missing fleet." For the distribution of the discrepancy, the distribution (in dwt) according to country of

domicile of the five major open registry countries has been taken. Apart from estimates for specific individual countries for which direct estimates were available (Japan and France), the remainder of the interior of the shipment services matrix is constructed using the reference totals for receipts (row total in the WAM) and assuming a direct relationship between the geographical pattern of merchandise trade and services in shipment. It is thus implicitly assumed that *exporting* countries also carry out the transportation of merchandise. Obviously, this is a crude assumption, but almost inevitable because of lacking data. As a result of this approach discrepancies arise between the *column* totals of the derived shipment matrix and the reference totals for payments for shipment services. These are adjusted later as part of the overall balancing procedure (see below).

- The matrix for *travel* is based on direct data on receipts by most of the major industrialized countries, capturing a large share of the value of international transactions related to this item. Entries specifying the geographical distribution of incomes from travel of the other country groups were derived as a linear function of the geographical pattern of merchandise exports. Again, this is a crude assumption, of course, but required for lack of further information.

- Only a few countries provide data on the geographical distribution of payments related to *direct investment income*. The main part of the submatrix for direct investment income flows was constructed on the basis of an assumed link with the geographical distribution of the accumulated stock of foreign direct investment at the end of the previous year. The stock and investment income matrices were derived in three steps. First, a reconciled stock matrix (based on outward recordings as primary estimates and inward recordings as secondary estimates) is derived by applying the adapted Stone-Byron mathematical balancing technique to the unbalanced matrix obtained from the primary data sources (on this method, see below and De Jong, Jellema, Vos, and Zebregs 1993a, 1993b). The reference totals for direct investment stocks are taken from the BOPS and for some countries (like the United States) from national sources.

Subsequently, an average and uniform rate of return is assumed to apply to direct investment in a particular country (group).[14] These implicit average rates of return are applied to all the cells in a corresponding row of the reconciled stock matrix. This procedure was used only for those cases where no direct information was available on the geographical distribution of direct investment income flows. The result of this approach is that discrepancies arise between the row totals and the row sums of the interior. These discrepancies are dealt with, as the final step, in the overall reconciliation process.

- *Other investment income*: with the exception of the DRS, no systematic data of outstanding claims and liabilities and interest payments with a geographical breakdown are available. Most of the major industrialized countries provide banking statistics with a geographical breakdown of externally held assets and liabilities. However, the exact coverage of these data source is not always clear: for example; sometimes they do not only refer to bank deposits and credits, but also include portfolio investment and other long-term and short-term capital market instruments. Stock data of portfolio investment are scarcely available. Given these difficulties with the primary data sources, the following approach was taken to construct the matrix of interest payments and receipts. First, to the extent available, the reference totals of stocks of portfolio investment and of other long-term and short-term capital were lumped together.[15] Subsequently, the geographical break-downs of outstanding liabilities obtained from the banking statistics are applied to the row totals of portfolio plus other capital. For some countries both primary and secondary direct estimates were available and used to construct the corresponding matrix interiors. Portfolio and other capital stock data for multilateral institutions were derived from the IMF report on the measurement of capital flows (IMF, 1992). Consistent stock matrices are finally obtained by applying the adapted Stone-Byron mathematical balancing technique, whereby—for the reasons indicated below—the recording of liabilities to abroad is assumed to be more reliable than those of assets held abroad. This assumption also applies for interest payments compared to interest receipts (see further below and also IMF 1987, 1992). Next, as in the case of direct investment income, implicit rates of interest are calculated and these are subsequently applied to the cells in the corresponding rows of the matrix of outstanding liabilities in those cases where no direct information was available. For countries for which direct information on interest payments is available—as in the case of developing countries, Japan, and the United States—that information is applied directly.
- The interiors of the matrix of *private transfers* (mainly workers'

remittances) are constructed partly on the basis of recordings of recipient countries from the data available for some of the major industrialized countries. Taking receipts as the core reference total,[16] estimates for the remaining cells have been obtained on the basis of the marginal total of debits, which results in a discrepancy between the interior and the totals of debits. Such a procedure was required for a lack of acceptable data on international migration, expatriate workers and their remunerations and remittances rates. In the case of *official transfers*, the point of departure are the OECD data. These are supplemented by data on transfers from and to some of the major industrialized countries. Because the OECD data are reported by transferring countries, the debits of the BOPS have been distributed proportionally on the basis of the BOPS credits.

- In general terms, the construction methodology of the *flow-of-funds* (FOF) block (primary estimates) by type of capital flow is as follows. The FOF block consists of five components: three transaction matrices, direct foreign investment (DFI), portfolio investment (PFI) and other capital (OC); and two row vectors, net reserves (RES) and errors and omissions (EO). In the case of DFI, the matrix of primary estimates is based on recordings of investment abroad. In contrast, the data on inward PFI and inward Other Capital flows are the starting points in the construction of the matrices of PFI and OC.

Changes in external liabilities (bonds and other long-term and short-term capital) of developing countries by debtor and creditor country (groups) were derived from the World Bank Debtor Reporting System (WDT/DRS). Reference totals for the debtor countries were also derived from this source and replaced the BOPS reference total. Submatrices were constructed for capital transactions items 2.1.1–8 and 2.2 (see Table 11.9). Primary estimates by debtors and creditors are available with good coverage for long-term, public, and publicly guaranteed debt. Specific assumptions were applied to derive flow of funds matrices (net disbursements) for private nonguaranteed debt and short-term debt (excluding IMF credits).

11.6.5. Overall Balancing of the WAM

The process of data reconciliation took place in two steps. First, manual adjustments to complete and adjust the capital transactions matrices were made using complementary data sources, most of which derived from official statistics for individual countries. The nature of these adjustments was discussed above. Second, as a final procedure a mathematical balancing technique was applied, adapting the Stone-Byron methodology developed for balancing input-output tables and social accounting matrices.[17]

Obviously, given the large remaining discrepancies, mathematical balancing procedures of this kind should be used with extreme caution. Nevertheless, the results may be considered to be an advance, since data are adjusted within a narrowly defined system of accounting identities and constraints. Further, the adapted balancing method takes account of the full information incorporated in the overall WAM database, including the use of more than one observation per cell, and to manipulate preset degrees of reliability for each observation. The latter should be (and has been) based on a cautious assessment of the nature and quality of the different data sources used in the WAM. In broad terms, the following main assumptions about the reliability of the primary estimates were used:[18]

- Merchandise import recordings are considered more reliable than export recordings (see note 11);
- Recordings of outward direct foreign investment (stocks and flows) and related income flows are considered more reliable than inward recordings following assessments of other studies (IMF, 1987, 1992, and related background papers). One reason behind this assumption is that the largest foreign investors reside in the major industrialized countries (United Stated, Japan, Germany, United Kingdom), which have detailed and, seemingly, reasonably accurate DFI data. Further, a major component of DFI flows consists of reinvested earnings, which tend to be recorded with greater reliability in the country of origin (IMF, 1987);
- In contrast, recordings of capital *inflows* related to portfolio investment, bank lending, and other capital and related flows of interest payments are generally considered more reliable than the recording on the asset side. Bond issues as well as external debt data tend to be better recorded at the debtor side, since purchases may be spread over many creditors.
- Exceptions to these rules are made for the entries for specific (groups of) countries (see De Jong, Jellema, Vos, and Zebregs, 1993a).

Sensitivity analysis for these data source reliability assumptions indicates that results may differ significantly if the broad assumptions would be reversed, such as giving higher reliability to outward than inward recordings, and so on. Altering the degree of differential reliability within a given broad assuption, such as inward recording is twice or four times as reliable, would not yield significantly different results.

On this basis, it could be said that if one can accept the general assessment of the quality of the various data sources, then the WAM balancing procedure should adjust the global discrepancies, roughly speaking, in the right direction. Roughly, because the indicated short-comings in the primary data would still leave a potentially significant margin of error. However, as is generally also the case with input-output tables and social accounting matrices, cross-checking data as in the WAM framework not only helps to detect the flaws in the data on international trade and payments, but also allows to make well-informed adjustments.

11.7. The Balanced WAM for 1990 and the Adjustment of the Global Statistical Discrepancies

Table 11.2 showed the large global discrepancies on the various items of the external current and capital accounts. The WAM has reconciled inward and outward recordings at the global level. To achieve this global consistency major adjustments have been made to all accounts affecting the size and structure of the external balance of the major economies in the global system. Since the underlying causes of the discrepancies in the various components of the external account differ, as explained in the previous section, the adjustments do not follow a clearcut and unidirectional pattern toward the elimination of the officially recorded global current account deficit. Without entering in great detail here,[19] the major adjustments to deal with the (net) world current account deficit of U.S.$106 billion in 1990 include

- A substantially lower current account deficit for the *United States* than that is recorded. The United States external deficit as (re)estimated by the WAM is U.S.$65 billion in 1990, which is about U.S.$20 billion lower than the recorded deficit after the first corrections and combination of data sources. National accounts estimates already indicated a much lower savings-investment gap for the United States, but according to the global consistency check of the WAM this source seems to *underestimate* the United States deficit and the savings-investment gap is adjusted upward by about U.S.$30 billion. The main adjustments on the external account show up in the accounts for reinvested earnings from DFI and other investment income. The balanced world asset and liabilities matrix indicates a smaller net debtor position of the United States and a lower estimate of interest payments on external liabilities and a higher income on external finacial assets (partly, related to underrecording of asset holdings of residents from developing countries). On the other hand, the WAM gives a lower estimate for United States repatriated earnings on DFI, but this correction is less than the downward adjustments on the expenditure side. The capital account counterpart to these current account adjustments is principally an upward correction of United States external lending (OC).

- The *Japanese* external surplus in fact may have been much smaller in 1990 than officially recorded. The WAM estimates a surplus of about U.S.$20 billion, some U.S.$37 billion below the primary data. The adjustments appear principally on the account for merchandise trade, as the U.N. trade matrices give a lower estimate for Japanese exports, and on the investment income account, which relates to the smaller net creditor position for Japan through WAM measurement. Lower estimates for Japanese portfolio investment abroad (PFI) and external lending (OC) form the counterpart to the trade and income adjustments.

- For the *United Kingdom*, the WAM records a smaller external deficit for 1990, principally resulting from a higher estimate of interest incomes on outstanding portfolio investment and other foreign financial assets. This probably has to do with inadequate official recording of the capital movements in the international financial market in London. After cross-checking the origin and destination of global capital flows, the WAM produced a more favourable net investment position for the United Kingdom, which—in part—formed the basis for the adjustments in the investment income data.

- *Other industrialized countries* show on balance larger current account surpluses (or smaller deficits), particularly where large financial centres reside (such as in Switzerland). Adjustments concentrate again in the investment income account.

- External accounts of some developing country groups also required major adjustments. For *Latin America*, the WAM shows higher current account surplus in 1990: U.S.$27 billion compared to U.S.$10 billion according to primary data (after the first round of corrections). The WAM gives a higher estimate for Latin American merchandise exports, as the cross-checking by origin and destination may have corrected for some of the mismeasurement in official sources due to underinvoicing of exports and illegal trade. One cannot be sure, however, that this adjustment fully captures drugs trade and other illegal exports, as such transactions are typically poorly recorded at both the origin and the destination. Another major adjustment in the Latin American accounts is for underecorded earnings on external asset holdings, likely related to capital flight money. The WAM further gives a significantly lower estimate of merchandise exports from *China* (down by about U.S.$15 billion), but—for possibly similar reasons as in the Latin American case—gives a somewhat higher estimate for commodity exports of Sub-*Saharan Africa*. The external (current account) deficit of the latter region is adjusted further downward than the WAM estimates, after cross-checking with OECD data, as official transfers to the region may be underestimated in the BOPS. Finally, *East Asian* trade surpluses are slightly scaled down in the WAM compared to the individual country recordings in the BOPS.

- Finally, an important part of the adjustment in the global discrepancy in the investment income account takes place in the books of the *Offshore banking centers*. Much of the capital that finds a (temporary) haven in these usually small countries goes unrecorded in the BOPS and other data sources. For some of these countries BOPS and national accounts data are incomplete or not available. Combining international banking statistics and origin-destination estimates leads us to believe, through the WAM, that these centres have a strong positive net investment position (see Table 11.7) and larger current account surpluses due to investment income than officially recorded.

11.8. Conclusion

The full harmonization of the *SNA* and the BOPS is good news for students of problems of international trade and payments. With the two revised systems, the construction of consistent balance sheet accounts by institutional agents will become, hopefully soon, widespread and standardized practice and will allow for improved applied analysis of the impact of (domestic and international) portfolio adjustments on production and income distribution. Yet many of the practical problems in the measurement of trade and payments will not automatically disappear with the revised *SNA*/BOPS. The existing data frameworks still show huge discrepancies when set to the test of global accounting consistency. The main proposal of this paper is that the revised *SNA*/BOPS should be extended towards a system of integrated accounts for the world economy. This could be done along the lines of the WAM framework outlined in the second part of this paper. There it was also shown how such a framework can be applied. The resulting set of reconciled global accounts gave substantially revised estimates for the external accounts of the major economies: a U.S. deficit much lower than that shown in the BOPS and U.S. national data sources, but the WAM also suggests that the Japanese savings surplus is grossly overestimated, while groups of developing countries may have had smaller external deficits in 1990 than recorded by the official data.

This has potentially large implications for the analysis of trade, finance and global macroeconomic interactions. As indicated in Section 11.6, the results of the WAM still have to be taken with great caution given the prevailing data weaknesses and the assumptions required to balance the global accounts. Yet one is inclined to believe that the accuracy of the data can be enhanced this way, as the information of the global accounting constraints is added to the external accounts of individual countries.

Global model systems which have some influence in international policy decision making, such as Project LINK (see Pauly, 1993), IMF's MULTIMOD (Masson et al., 1990), OECD's INTERLINK (Richardson, 1988), World Bank's GEM (Petersen et al., 1991), and the MSG model (McKibbin and Sachs, 1991),[20] generally ignore the global inconsistencies or have implicitly residualized them in a "rest of the world" country group or otherwise. These models obviously require working from a consistent set of global accounts, which could be provided through the WAM. The WAM moreover could provide a basis for a more comprehensive modelling of the global linkages. Currently, many models, including LINK, only define endogenous commodity trade linkages and implicitly assume that all other items of the external account accommodate in one way or another to the modeled trade balances. Others, including MULTIMOD and MSG, provide only a partial modeling of global financial interactions. The WAM would provide a starting point for a more comprehensive approach. The work presented here is just a beginning. One would hope the United Nations, the IMF, the World Bank, and other international organization will take up this challenge and expand the *SNA*/BOPS framework into a true system of consistent global accounts. In this paper I have attempted to show how this could be done.

Acknowledgments

I am indebted to Niek de Jong and Harm Zebregs for valuable research assistance in the construction of the World Accounting Matrix, to the UN-DESIPA for research funding, and to Graham Pyatt and John Kendrick for helpful comments on an earlier draft.

Notes

1. *Economic territory* of a country is defined as "the geographic territory administered by a government within which persons, goods, and capital circulate freely" (United Nations, 1993, ch. 14, para. 14.9, p. 319; IMF, 1993, p. 20). *Free circulation* is defined as free from any kind of customs or immigration formalities. With this addendum this probably is a workable definition in practice. The quoted definition could give rise to debate over what is meant by "free circulation"; government controls of all kinds may also apply within an "economic territory" impeding a completely free circulation.

Institutions are said to have a center of economic interest in a country "when there exists some location—dwelling, place of production, or other premises—within the economic territory of the country on, or from, which it engages, and intends to continue to engage in economic activities and transactions on a significant scale" (United Nations, 1993, ch. 14, para. 14.12, p. 319; IMF, 1993, p. 20). As an operational guideline, an institutional unit should be considered to have a center of economic interest when it engages in economic activities or transactions for one year or more or if it intends to do so for one year or more.

2. The references to revaluations (REV) below strictly refers to revaluation of external assets. Revaluation or depreciation of the domestic physical capital stock (K) is not accounted for explicitly.

3. See Vos (1989, 1994) for the original (simplified) formulation of these global accounting rules. For other, but less comprehensive, attempts to achieve a global accounting framework, see Weale (1984), McCarthy et al. (1989), and Gray and Gray (1989). The work by Luttik (1992) is built on the same framework as is outlined here.

4. Such reserve holdings can be identified in the balance of payments statistics as "Liabilities Constituting Foreign Authorities' Reserves."

5. See De Jong, Jellema, Vos, and Zebregs (1993a, 1993b) for the presentation of the complete twenty-three country/region WAM. The complete classification embraces (1) USA, (2) Canada, (3) Japan, (4) Germany, (5) France, (6) Italy, (7) United Kingdom, (8) Other EC, (9) Other European OECD countries, (10) Australia and New Zealand, (11). Other developed countries (Israel, South Africa), (12) Former Soviet Union, (13) Eastern Europe, (14) Developing Europe, (15) North Africa, (16) Sub-Sahara Africa, (17) Latin America & Caribbean, (18) West Asia (Middle East), (19) South Asia, (20) China, (21) East Asia and Oceania, (22) Offshore Banking Centers, (23) Multilateral agencies, (24) Rest of the world.

6. The asset-liability matrix registers end-of–year stock values, including revaluations. A separate revaluation accounts matrix could be derived as a residual by taking the end-of-year stock matrix *less* the beginning-of-year stock matrix *less* the net flow of funds matrix of the WAM. However, in its bilateral specifications, such a "revaluation accounts matrix" would incorporate not necessarily only asset changes that be brought back to price change and exchange rate adjustments, but may also incorporate some statistical adjustments resulting from the balacing procedure of the WAM and the asset/Liability matrices (see below).

7. See De Jong, Jellema, Vos, and Zebregs (1993a, 1993b) for extensive discussions of the nature, coverage and reliability of all data sources used for the WAM.

8. The primary data source for the world current and capital account balances is the IMF Balance of Payments Statistics. Since the balance of payments for each country is consistent in this source, the global current and capital account discrepancies should be equal. The small difference in Table 11.6 is due to incompleteness of the balance of payments for a few countries.

9. In practice, the additional figures for GDI are taken from the indicated source, while GNS estimates are derived as a residual. DAD was not used for the other countries, since this data system is an *analytical* system by itself has procedures of its own to adjust and reconcile primary data from different sources. For some countries no data are available for the most recent years. In those cases the figure of a previous year has been duplicated. This is not likely to lead to gross distortions, because it generally concerns small countries.

Further, external accounts estimates for Taiwan, Other Asia, Other Africa, Eastern Europe and Middle East as well as those for International Organizations were added using individual country sources and BOPS *Yearbook 1992*, Part 2.

10. Some corrections were made to the U.N. trade matrices using the IMF's Direction of Trade Statistics (DOTS) in order to adjust for country coverage deficiencies.

11. The United Nations which compiles the trade matrices, now considers import recordings generally as more reliable than export recordings.

12. In IMF (1987, p. 90) it is concluded that: "the relative stability over time of the ratio between the discrepancy on shipment and total 'shipment' debits indicates that the principal cause of the discrepancy has probably been correctly identified as the 'missing' fleets."

13. These data can be obtained from the *Review of Maritime Transport* (UNCTAD, various years).

14. Calculated by taking total direct investment income flows paid by country i (including reinvested earnings) in year t as a share of the total stock of foreign direct investment in that country in year $t - 1$.

15. Where appropriate, stock data from BIS/IFS have been used to supplement BOPS stock data. Note that these stock data include revaluations for asset price and exchange rate changes. However, not enough detail has been available on currency composition and asset structure by origin and destination to actually estimate a reliable revaluations account matrix (see also note 8 above).

For portfolio investments, flows have been accumulated over 1974 to the year in question if no stock data are reported.

16. The argument to take *receipts*, rather than payments as the basis for the construction of this sub-matrix is that the number of countries that are main recipients of workers' remittances is likely smaller than the number of countries that host expatriate workers.

17. See De Jong, Vos, Jellema, and Zebregs (1993a) for a formal exposition of this methodology, which has an origin in a procedure developed by Stone, Champernowne and Meade (1942) for national accounts and was adapted to reconciling unbalanced SAMs by Stone (1977) and Byron (1978).

18. See De Jong, Vos, Jellema, and Zebregs (1993a, sec. 6.4 and app. A.3) for a detailed description of the methodology and the assumptions on data source reliability used in the reconciliation procedure.

19. See De Jong, Jellema, Vos, and Zebregs (1993a, 1993b) for detailed accounts of the adjustments in the WAMs for 1985–1990.

20. See Vos (1993) for a review of existing global model systems and their policy relevance.

References

Bhagwati, J., A. Krueger, and C. Wibulswasdi. (1974). "Capital Flight from LDCs: A Statistical Analysis." In J. Bhagwati (ed.), *Illegal Transactions in International Trade*. Amsterdam: North-Holland.

Byron, R. (1978). "The Estimation of Large Social Accounting Matrices." *Journal of the Royal Statistical Society*, Series A, 141 (3): 359–367.

De Jong, N., R. Vos, T. Jellema, and H. Zebregs. (1993a). "Trade and Financial Flows in a World Accounting Framework. Reconciled WAMs for 1985–88." Paper prepared for UN-DESIPA and Project LINK, The Hague and Rotterdam: Institute of Social Studies and GDUI, Erasmus University.

De Jong, N., R. Vos, T. Jellema, and H. Zebregs. (1993b). "Trade and Financial Flows in a World Accounting Framework. Reconciled WAMs for 1989–90." Paper prepared for UN-DESIPA and Project LINK, The Hague and Rotterdam: Institute of Social Studies and GDUI, Erasmus University.

Dunning, J., and J. Cantwell. (1987). *IRM Directory of Statistics of International Investment and Production*. London: Macmillan.

Galbis, V. (ed.). (1991). *The IMF's Statistical Systems in Context of Revision of the SNA's A System of National Accounts*. Washington, DC: IMF.

Gray, P., and J. Gray. (1989). "International Payments in Flow-of-Funds Format." *Journal of Post-Keynesian Economics*, 11(2): 241–260.

Gulati, S.K. (1987). "A Note on Trade Misinvoicing." In D. Lessard and J. Williamson (eds.), *Capital Flight and Third World Debt*. Washington, DC: Institute for International Economics.

IMF. (1977). *Manual to the Balance of Payments*. Washington, DC: IMF.

IMF. (1987). *Report on the World Current Account Discrepancy*. Washington, DC: IMF.

IMF. (1992). *Report on the Measurement of International Capital Flows*. Washington, DC: IMF.

IMF. (1992). *Balance of Payments Yearbook 1992*. Washington, DC: IMF.

IMF. (1993). *Balance of Payments Manual* (5th ed.), Washington, DC: IMF.

Luttik, J. (1992). "Trade and Finance in a World Accounting Matrix." Ph.D. dissertation, University of Amsterdam, Institute of Social Studies, Amsterdam.

Marris, S. (1985). *Deficits and the Dollar: The World Economy at Risk*. Washington, DC: Institute for International Economics.

Masson, P., and G. Meredith. (1991). "Domestic and International Consequences of German Unification." In L. Lipschitz and D. McDonald (eds.) (1990),

German Unification. Economic Issues (pp. 93–114). IMF Occasional Paper No. 75. Washington, DC: IMF.

Masson, P., S. Symanski, and G. Meredith. (1990). *MULTIMOD Mark II: A Revised and Extended Model.* IMF Occasional Paper No. 71. Washington, DC: IMF.

McCarthy, F.D., B. Laury, E. Riordan, and J.-P. Zhou. (1989). "Global Accounting Framework (GAF). The Basic System." In F.D. McCarthy (ed.), *Developing Economies in Transition* (Vol. 1). World Bank Discussion Papers No. 63. Washington, DC: World Bank.

McKibbin, W., and J. Sachs. (1991). *Global Linkages. Macroeconomic Interdependence and Cooperation in the World Economy.* Washington, DC: Brookings Institution.

Pauly, P. (1993). "Transfers, Real Interest Rates and Regional Development." In UNCTAD, *International Monetary Issues for the 1990s.* New York: United Nations.

Petersen. C. et al. (1991). "The Structure of a World Bank Global Economic Model." International Economic Analysis and Prospects Division, World Bank, Washington, DC (mimeo).

Richardson, P. (1988). "The Structure and Simulation Properties of OECD's INTERLINK Model." *OECD Economic Studies,* 10: 57–122.

Riordan, M. (1990). "Global Accounting Framework (GAF). DEC Analytical Data Base." In F.D. McCarthy (ed.), *Developing Countries in the 1990s* (Vol. 1). World Bank Discussion Papers No. 97. Washington, DC: World Bank.

Stone, R. (1977). "Foreword." In G. Pyatt and A. Roe et al. (1977), *Social Accounting for Development Planning with Special Reference to Sri Lanka.* Cambridge: Cambridge University Press.

Stone, R., D. Champernowne, and J.E. Meade. (1942). "The Precision on National Accounts Estimates." *Review of Economic Studies,* 9(2): 111–125.

Tobin, J. (1969). "A General Equilibrium Approach to Monetary Theory. *Journal of Money, Credit and Banking,* 1: 15–29 (February).

Tobin, J. (1980). *Asset Accumulation and Economic Activity.* Oxford: Basil Blackwell.

United Nations. (1968). *A System of National Accounts.* Studies in Methods Series F No. 2 Rev. 3. New York: United Nations.

United Nations. (1993). *Revised System of National Accounts.* New York: United Nations.

Vos, R. (1989). "Accounting for the World Economy." *Review of Income and Wealth,* 35(4): 389–408.

Vos, R. (1991). "Social Accounts and Capital Accumulation." In J. Alarcon, J. van Heemst, S. Keuning, W. de Ruijter, and R. Vos, *The Social Accounting Framework for Development.* Aldershot: Gower/Avebury.

Vos, R. (1992). "Private Foreign Asset Accumulation, Not Just Capital Flight." *Journal of Development Studies,* 28(3): 500–537.

Vos, R. (1993). "Prospects of Financial Flows to Developing Countries in the

1990s. The Global Macroeconomic Trade-Offs." In UNCTAD, *International Monetary Issues for the 1990s*. New York: United Nations.

Vos, R. (1994). *The World Economy, Debt and Adjustment. Structural Asymmetries in North-South Interactions*. London: Macmillan.

Weale, M. (1984). "Quantity and Price Effects in an Analysis of World Trade Based on an Accounting Matrix." *Review of Income and Wealth*, 30(1): 85–117.

World Bank. (1991). *World Debt Tables, 1990–91*. Washington, DC: World Bank.

World Bank/BIS/IMF/OECD. (1988). *External Debt: Definition, Coverage and Methodology*. Paris: OECD.

DISCUSSION OF CHAPTER 11

Yoshimasa Kurabayashi

This note is intended to supplement Dr. Vos's incisive approach to a World Accounting Matrix (WAM) by comparing it with related systems such as *SNA 1968*, *SNA 1993*, and BPM (International Monetary Fund, Balance of Payments Mannual). Four points will be discussed: the rest of the world sector as a constituent of *SNA*, from *SNA 1968* to *SNA 1993*, reconciliation of *SNA 1993* with BPM, and toward a WAM. In writing this note, I greatly benefited from Professor Hiroshi Matsuura's 1994 work, "A Comparison of Accumulation, Financial and the Rest of the World Accounts Between 1968 and 1993 SNA."

A schematic overview of *SNA 1993* is illustrated in Figure 1. It goes without saying that the rest of the world accounts, which form a basic cornerstone of WAM, play an essential role as a constituent of the integrated economic accounts. In passing, one should note that the framework of *SNA 1993* as illustrated in Figure 1 closely resembles the French framework of SECN (le Systèm élargi de comptabilité nationale) in its structure and presentation. Although this is not the place to go into the details of the intimate correspondence of the structures between *SNA 1993* and SECN, I have to recapitulate the importance of this correspondence, which necessarily casts a long shadow on the nature and

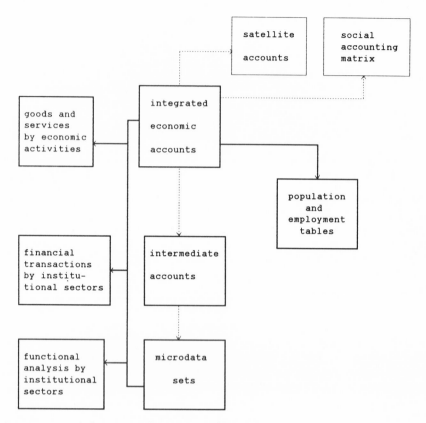

Figure 11.1.   A Schematic Overview of *SNA 1993*

significance of WAM. Returning to our original question, it is important to recognize, as *SNA 1993* clearly points out (para. 2.23), that the rest of the world plays a role as an institutional sector, implying that transactions between resident and nonresident units are external transactions to the total economy and are grouped into the accounts of rest of the world. It is essential for the design of the rest of the world accounts that the definition of *resident* (and *nonresident*) is clearly formulated. *SNA 1993* (para. 2.22) indicates that an institutional unit is said to be a resident unit of a country when it has a center of economic interests in the economic territory of that country—that is, when it engages for an extended period in economic activities on this territory. This definition of residents differs from that of resident economic agents in *SNA 1968* (see, in particular, paras. 5.100–5.111, 5.115–5.117). Moreover, we have to note that the rest of the world accounts are established from the viewpoint of the rest of the world, which diverges from what is taken by BPM. It is interesting to see that the perspective of the foreign sector in the U.S. national income and product accounts (NIPAs) is reversed from the viewpoint of *SNA* (see, in particular, Young and Tice, 1985). It should be remembered that this reversal of the viewpoint of the rest of the world should necessarily influence the design and formulation of WAM.

I have already noted that the definition of residents in *SNA 1993* diverges from the corresponding notion in *SNA 1968*. In the structure of integrated economic accounts, *SNA 1993* emphasizes institutional sectoring more than *SNA 1968* does. It appears that this characteristic of sectoring in *SNA 1993* is preferable to *SNA 1968* for fitting a sequence of the rest of the world accounts into the framework of integrated economic accounts. In this regard, several points can be made for favoring the sectoring of *SNA 1993*. In the first place, the firm consistency both in concepts and in accounting structure can be established by the characteristic of sectoring. Second, as a corollary of the first point, there exists a one-to-one correspondence of transactions between the total economy and the rest of the world. It naturally follows from this one-to-one correspondence that a close interrelationship in the entries of a sequence of the rest of the world accounts can be secured, as Table 2.3. for the rest of the world account of *SNA 1993* clearly indicates. Third, the logical consistency in concepts and in accounting structure is extended so that it may encompass not only flow concepts but also stock concepts. This is particularly the case in the way that the current external balance in the external account of primary incomes and current transfers is interrelated with changes in net worth in the external accumulation accounts. Finally, some new entries are introduced into the sequence of the rest of the world accounts for supplementing the logical consistency. Thus, changes in net worth are further broken down according to their causes, being subdivided into changes in net worth due to saving and capital transfer and changes in net woth due to other changes in volume of assets. It is interesting to see that the latter entry records such exceptional events that cause not only the value but also the volume of assets and liabilities to change. Examples of these exceptional events for the rest of the world are changes of the holding of SDRs caused by their reallocation or holding gains or losses caused by volatile fluctuations of exchange rates derived from some international agreements.

The conceptual reconciliation between *SNA 1993* and the *Balance of Payments Manual* (fifth edition) has been advanced in several respects. They are briefly referred to below. In the first place, in *SNA 1993* exports and imports of goods and services are recorded on the basis of FOB prices, which is quite in line with the treatment of *BPM*. Note that in *SNA 1968* exports of goods and services are valued by FOB prices, but imports of goods and services are valued by CIF prices. Second, while *SNA 1968* conceptually differentiates national consumption expenditure from domestic consumption expenditure, the conceptual distinction of consumption expenditure ceases in *SNA 1993*. Thus, direct purchases in the domestic markets by nonresident households or direct purchases abroad by resident households that appear in the entry of external transactions of *SNA 1968* (see Table 26) are considered as exports or imports of services concerning tourism in *SNA 1993*. Third, in *SNA 1993* monetary gold is recorded only as the entry of the financial account, whereas *SNA 1968* admits that a portion of nonmonetary gold may be recorded as an entry of net incurrence of foreign liabilities in external transactions (see Table 26).

As a result, the corresponding item for nonmonetary gold is dealt with imports of nonmonetary gold and included in imports of goods and services in the external account of goods and services in *SNA 1993*. In spite of the progress of conceptual reconciliation between *SNA 1993* and BPM, we find difficulty with the treatment of financial intermediary services and their impacts on the rest of the world accounts. In place of the imputation of financial services recommended by *SNA 1968*, *SNA 1993* admits that the role of financial intermediaries is to channel funds from lenders to borrowers by intermediating between them. Thus, *SNA 1993* argues that financial intermediation may be defined as productive activity in which an institutional unit incurs liabilities on its own account for the purpose of acquiring financial assets by engaging in financial transactions on the market (para. 4.78. of *SNA 1993*). The *SNA* recommends that interest payable and receivable by financial intermediaries be partitioned into two components so that financial services may be defined as the difference between the two components. This partitioning necessarily affects intermediate and final consumption and their allocation into industries and institutional sectors. Hence, exports or imports of financial intermediate services are also allocated to the rest of the world. Difficulty with this treatment might arise. It is true that exports or imports of financial intermediate services for the external account of goods and services can be derived from the standpoint of the production activities of the total (domestic) economy. But it is not at all clear that the counterpart of exports or imports of these financial intermediaries can be easily identified because the allocation of financial intermediate services is generated from the transaction account for goods and services which does not show direct relations between transacting sectors (see *SNA 1993*, para. 2.152). The difficulty would put great obstacles in the way of WAM, particularly from the viewpoint of the rest of the world.

Nobody would deny that the approach to WAM proposed by Dr. Vos has, in its own right, an important significance and contribution to the analytical purpose of a system of national accounts and that the approach should be further encouraged. To conclude this short note, I feel that a few general comments would be appropriate for advancing discussions on WAM. First, a question where the position of WAM is properly placed in *SNA 1993* might be raised. In this regard, it immediately occurs to me that two options might be open for WAM. In the first place, WAM may be considered as a constituent of the family of satellite accounts in *SNA 1993*. But as we can easily discover from the design and structure of satellite accounts, it appears that WAM might not be easily fited into the framework of satellite accounts whose idea has entirely originated from SECN to which I have referred in the earlier section of this note. As the second option, WAM may be considered as a constituent of three-dimensional analysis of financial transactions of *SNA 1993*. I am inclined to agree with this option. In this connection, the attention of Mr. Vos might be called to our article in English (Kurabayashi and Matsuura, 1989). Our idea has been further developed in the network of inter-national flow-of-funds and its link with the interactions of national and international transactions by Matsuura's work (Matsuura, 1992). In referring to these works, I would simply like to stress that international cooperation and coordination of research works between countries in an international forum would be indispensable for advancing the approach to WAM.

Second, a question in what aspects WAM contributes to the progress of *SNA 1993* might be raised. Two aspects for the progress of the *SNA* are immediately distinguished. They are deepening and widening the scope of *SNA*. Here, deepening the scope of *SNA* refers to completing the compilation of integrated economic accounts and surrounding frame-works, which are interrelated by direct arrows in Figure 1. On the other hand, widening the scope of *SNA* is related to expanding the scope of *SNA* that is indicated in supplementing frameworks interconnected by dotted arrows in Figure 1. As one of the collaborators for the revised *SNA 1993*, again I am inclined to favor deepening the scope of *SNA*.

Finally, a question whether WAM effectively plays a role for *SNA* purposes might be raised. In this respect, it is interesting to see that in *SNA 1993* two views on the purposes of *SNA* are contrasted (see, in particular, *SNA 1993*, p. xiii). One is that the national accounts are primarily an organizational scheme for economic statistics. A contrasting view is that the national accounts serve primarily to facilitate analysis of the economy and decisionmaking. Though it appears that the WAM approach seeks for the latter view, I feel that the question is still open and should remain "the unanswered question." In closing this note, let me quote a few lines from Leonard Bernstein's "The Unanswered Questions": "All particular languages bear one another, and combine into always new idioms, perceptible to human beings. Ultimately these idioms can all merge into a speech universal enough to be accessible to all mankind."

References

Kurabayashi, Yoshimasa, and Hiroshi Matsuura. (1989). "Progress of Japanese National Accounts in an International Perspective of the *SNA* Review." In Takashi Negishi and Ryuzo Satao (eds.), *Developments in Japanese Economics*. New York: Academic Press.

Matsuura, Hiroshi. (1992). "The Structure of Financial Markets Viewed from National and International Flow of Funds" (in Japanese). *Capital Market Researsch* 5 (April).

Matsuura, Hiroshi. (1994). "A Comparison of Accumulation, Financial and the Rest of the World Accounts Between *SNA 1968* and *SNA 1993*" (in Japanese). In Economic Research Institute of the Economic Planning Agency (ed.), *The Report of the Special Research Committee for 1993 SNA*.

Young, Allan H., and Helen Stone Tice. (1985). "An Introduction to National Accounting." *Survey of Current Business* (March): 67–68.

12 THE UNITED NATIONS SYSTEM OF NATIONAL ACCOUNTS AND THE INTEGRATION OF MACRO AND MICRO DATA

Richard Ruggles

The United Nations *System of National Accounts* (*SNA*) has been an evolutionary development over a period of fifty years. It was born in the world of macroeconomics, but statistically its roots have been in the data relating to individual decision-making units of the economy. Since its inception, both the complexity of the economic system and the concern with social problems have increased. Currently, governments are faced with the need to evaluate both the macro and micro aspects of their policies relating to old age entitlements, health care, education, the environment and poverty. The national accounts alone are not sufficient for this task. Both the need and the technical feasibility of linking the macro framework with micro data have increased. The following discussion attempts to trace the evolution of the system with respect to the macro/ micro linkage and to indicate how the macro accounts and micro data bases can be integrated.

12.1. The U.N. *SNA* View of Micro Data

12.1.1. National Income Concepts and Measurement Prior to the U.N. SNA

Before World War II, national income concepts consisted of various macro constructs relating to national output, final sales, and income payments. The split between macro and micro theory was reflected in empirical terms by the macro estimates of national income concepts and the detailed micro data collected from enterprises, households, and government by statistical and administrative agencies.

The technology used for data processing prior to World War II precluded any significant use of micro data in the estimation of national income. Punch cards were used to reduce the large masses of detailed micro data into more manageable sets of summary cross-tabulations. Those estimating national income prided themselves on their ability to piece together diverse and often fragmentary sets of information to derive their estimates of aggregates. A wide variety of statistical sources were used to provide the basic estimates. For example, tabulations by statistical and regulatory agencies of the value of product or sales for various industries provided the basis for estimating output. Social security and labor force tabulations were used for estimating wages and salaries originating in various industries, and tabulations of financial data and tax returns provided information for estimating interest and property income.

12.1.2. The 1947 U.N. Proposal and the 1952 SNA

In 1947 Richard Stone on behalf of the United Nations proposed a radically different approach to national income measurement (United Nations, 1947, p. 23):

> It has come to be realized that for different purposes certain related but distinct aggregates are useful and that beyond a given point it is only possible to specify a unique set of operations to define the content of one of these aggregates by adopting certain conventions.
>
> This view based upon experience is reinforced since the ideas can be expounded and presented more lucidly if the elementary transactions rather than the final aggregates are made the starting point of the enquiry. Transactions, whether actual or imputed, take place between accounting entities such as business enter-prises and individuals, and the accounts of these entities are much easier to grasp than the consolidated accounts of the whole system.

Thus by studying the different class of accounting entity in an economy and the different types of transaction in which they engage, we shall at once obtain a clearer picture of how the national totals are built up and at the same time exhibit the relationship between the constituent transactions and the implications of setting up the accounts in one way rather than another. This approach will also ensure consistency in the treatment of different transactions and will show the implications in other parts of the system of any treatment proposed.

This 1947 U.N. presentation clearly viewed macroeconomic accounts as the systematic aggregation of the accounts of individual transactors. As an example of his proposal, Stone presented a set of fully articulated accounts for the institutional sectors of the economy—including business enterprises, financial intermediaries, persons, government, and the rest of the world. But as Bos (1993, p. 6) points out, however, although the 1947 U.N. national accounts proposal was explicit about the importance of the transactor/transaction principle, it was also viewed as a flexible instrument for achieving more comprehensive and comparable national account figures. Therefore, provision was explicitly made for including imputations for such things as the services of owner-occupied housing, income in kind, and imputed banking charges.

At about this same time, however, the Economic Cooperation Administration (ECA) decided to utilize national income accounting as a framework for distributing Marshall Plan aid and monitoring European economic recovery. For this purpose, it developed a five-account system consisting of (1) national income and product account, (2) personal income and expenditure account, (3) government current receipts and outlay account, (4) a rest of the world account, and (5) a consolidated gross saving and investment account (Ruggles, 1949).

The ECA national accounts were functional rather than institutional in their nature. The national income and product account included all productive activities in the economy irrespective of their institutional characteristics, and the personal income account was essentially a residual account showing the private income and consumption in the economy. This functional approach to the national accounts was due to lack of institutional information on the one hand, and the need for international comparability in the national accounting data for countries with different institutional characteristics.

At the request of the Economic Cooperation Administration, Richard Stone was asked to set up a "National Accounts Research Unit" in Cambridge to train statisticians from the participating countries in the development of their national accounts and to establish for the OEEC a standardized national accounting system. As a result of this Stone developed a *Simplified System of National Accounts* (*SSNA*) (OEEC, 1950). The OEEC *SSNA* was quite similar to the ECA system of accounts except that, like Stone's 1947 proposal, it had an additional account for the transactions of the enterprise sector.

The U.N. 1952 *SNA*—also designed by Stone—was, understandably, very similar the OEEC national accounting system. However, the 1952 *SNA* accounts like the ECA system did not have an enterprise sector and were functional rather than institutional in their nature. These were (1) domestic product, (2) national income, (3) domestic capital formation, (4) households and nonprofit institutions, (5) general government, and (6) rest of the world. To some extent the set of supplementary tables that were appended to the accounts went in the direction of relating institutional data to the economic constructs presented in the macro accounts. But in 1952 and the following decade, national accountants were still incapable of utilizing micro data sets. Thus, the transactor/transaction accounting approach proposed by Stone in 1947 was not a part of the national accounts. The cut, adjust, and paste method used for the estimation of macro economic constructs continued to be used.

12.1.3. The 1968 U.N. SNA

The 1968 revision of the United Nations *System of National Accounts* was a major step forward (United Nations, 1968). The revised system not only expanded the national income accounts into a much more comprehensive and detailed system, but it integrated within the national accounting framework input-output tables, financial transactions, and balance sheets. Richard Stone was the main architect of the 1968 revision, and he emphasized the importance of the transactor/transaction accounting principle as contained in the 1947 U.N. proposal, but the *SNA 1968* accounting framework was more comprehensive and complex. In effect a dual sectoring system was introduced that was designed to provide (1) production, consumption, and capital formation accounts for industrial activities and types of commodities, and (2) income and outlay and finance accounts for institutional sectors—nonfinancial enterprises, financial institutions, general government, private nonprofit institutions, and households.

In order to make the aggregates of production and consumption more comprehensive and comparable from country to country, *SNA 1968* (1) included imputations for nonmarket production, bank service charges, and owner occupied housing and (2) rerouted to household income and consumption government expenditures for transfers in-kind and enterprise expenditures for employee compensation in-kind. This inclusion of imputations and reroutings in the macro aggregates, together with the increased complexity of the accounts, precluded any attempt to develop micro data sets that would underlie and replicate the aggregates in the macro accounts.

12.1.4. The 1993 U.N. SNA Statement on Micro-Macro Links

The 1993 version of the U.N. *SNA* (United Nations, 1993a, p. 12) states, explicitly, its position concerning the relation of the macro accounts to micro data:

Micro-Macro Links
The sequence of accounts and balance sheets of the System could, in principle, be compiled at any level of aggregation, even that of an individual institutional unit. It might therefore appear desirable if the macroeconomic accounts for sectors or the total economy could be obtained directly by aggregating corresponding data for individual units. There would be considerable analytical advantages in having micro-databases that are fully compatible with the corresponding macroeconomic accounts for sectors or the total economy. Data in the form of aggregates, or averages, often conceal a great deal of useful information about changes occurring within the populations to which they relate. For example, economic theory indicates that changes in the size of distribution of income may be expected to have an impact on aggregate consumption over and above that due to changes in the aggregate level of income. Information relating to individual units may be needed not only to obtain a better understanding of the working of the economy but also to monitor the impact of government policies, or other events, on selected types of units about which there may be special concern, such as households with very low incomes. Micro-data sets also make it possible to follow the behavior of individual units over time. Given the continuing improvements in computers and communications, the management and analysis of very large micro-databases is becoming progressively easier. Data can be derived from a variety of different sources, such as administrative and business records, as well as specially conducted censuses and surveys.

In practice, however, macroeconomic accounts can seldom be built up by simply aggregating the relevant micro-data. Even when individual institutional units keep accounts or records the concepts that are needed or appropriate at a micro level may not be suitable at a macro level. Individual units may be obliged to use concepts designed for other purposes, such as taxation. The accounting conventions and valuation methods used at a micro level typically differ from those required by the System. For example, as already noted, the widespread use of historic cost accounting means that the accounts of individual enterprises may differ significantly from those used in the System. Depreciation as calculated for tax purposes may be quite arbitrary and unacceptable from an economic viewpoint. . . .

Most households are unlikely to keep accounts of the kind needed by the System. Micro-data for households are typically derived from sample surveys that may be subject to significant response and reporting errors. It may be particularly difficult to obtain reliable and meaningful data about the activities of small unincorporated enterprises owned by households. Aggregates based on household surveys have to be adjusted for certain typical biases, such as the under-reporting of certain types of expenditure (on tobacco, alcoholic drink, gambling, etc.) and also to make them consistent with macro data from other sources, such as imports. The systematic exploitation of micro-data may also be restricted by the increasing concerns about confidentiality and possible misuse of such databases.

It may be concluded therefore that, for various reasons, it may be difficult, if not impossible, to achieve micro-databases and macroeconomic accounts that are fully compatible with each other in practice. Nevertheless, as a general objective, the concepts, definitions and classifications used in economic accounting should, so far as possible, be the same at both a micro and macro level of facilitate the interface between the two kinds of data.

As a consequence of the 1993 *SNA*'s final conclusion that it may be difficult, if not impossible, to achieve full compatibility between micro data bases and macro economic accounts, the *SNA* recommends two alternative approaches—social accounting matrices (SAMS) and satellite accounts.

Social accounting matrices (United Nations, 1993a, ch. 20) are defined as the presentation of *SNA* accounts in matrix form. *SNA 1968* provided an example of the national accounts in a matrix form, and the matrix form is widely used for input-output analysis. For some countries, SAMs have been constructed to show the relationship between structural features of the economy and the distribution of income and expenditures among household groups. The design and construction of SAMs are not standardized; rather they are developed as disaggregations of the *SNA* accounts for specific analytic purposes. SAMs draw upon a wide variety of census, survey, and administrative data and utilize them for disaggregating the aggregates in the sector accounts.

Satellite accounts (United Nations, 1993a, ch. 21) are intended to expand the analytic capacity of the national accounts for selected areas of social concern in flexible manner without disrupting the central system. Typically, satellite accounts allow for (1) additional information of a functional or cross-sector nature, (2) use of alternative classifications, (3) extended coverage of costs and benefits, (4) further presentations of indicators and aggregates, and (5) linkage of physical data to the monetary accounting data. Although satellite accounts, unlike SAMS, are not viewed primarily as disaggregations of the macro accounts, they do provide alternative classification systems, additional datail, or supplementary data for the formal *SNA* accounts. As is true in the case of SAMs, there is no standardized form for satellite accounts; their only requirement is that they be statistically or conceptually related to the *SNA* accounts.

12.2. The Proposal for Core Macro Economic Accounts

12.2.1. The Problem of Conflicting Demands for National Accounting Data

In the discussions leading to the 1993 revision of the *SNA*, a number of Netherlands national accountants proposed introducing greater flexibility in the SNA (van Eck, Gorter, van Tuinen, 1983; van Bochove and van Tuinen, 1986). They argued that the *SNA* serves a wide range of different and often conflicting demands and purposes. For example, the definition of the production boundary of the economy depends on the needs of different users. Monetarists prefer a national product concept confined to output related to market transactions. Environmentalists would like the degradation of the environment reflected in the accounts. Development economists want to take into account nonmarket production, and those economists concerned with the measurement of welfare need even more comprehensive measures of production and consumption. For those economists wishing to analyze the effects of fiscal policy, a strict accounting of government receipts and expenditures may be desired, but, for purposes of international comparability a more functional classification of government activities may be more useful.

Much of the conflict in the alternative approaches centers around the question of whether the national accounts are constructed on an institutional or a functional basis. In this context *institutional* refers to defining the transactors of the system by their legal form of organization (enterprises, government, and households) and using the sector accounts to record their actual transactions. In contrast, the term *functional* looks behind and beyond the institutional sector accounts to focus on measuring certain activities (production, consumption, saving, and capital formation) that are felt to be analytically important. The *SNA* is basically a system of institutionally defined sector accounts that is made more functional by introducing imputations and by rerouting actual transactions. Because the imputations and rerouting of transactions impair the usefulness of the accounts as a framework for monetary and fiscal data, there has been an effort to limit the extent of these imputations. Such limitations have the effect, however, of reducing the analytic usefulness of the *SNA* for other purposes.

12.2.2. The Concept of Core Accounts

In order to resolve this dilemma, the Netherlands national accountants proposed that the core of the *SNA* should consist of a set of institutionally defined sector accounts restricted to the recording of actual market transactions. Wherever possible the conceptions and perceptions of the transactors would be accepted as they are and the transactions described as they appeared. Such a core would represent the economic statisticians exercise in restraint; the temptation of superimposing the economic statisticians own views would be resisted. This system of core accounts bears a striking resemblance to the 1947 national accounts proposed by Richard Stone.

It was recognized, however, that in order to develop more comprehensive measures of production and consumption and to achieve greater comparability between countries where there were marked institutional differences, it would be desirable to introduce imputations for nonmarket activity and to reroute some transactions among the various institutional sectors. For this purpose, it was proposed that special modules should be introduced that could serve as the building blocks for developing more functional and more internationally comparable measures (such as the imputation of the services of owner occupied housing). This separation of imputations and reroutings from market transactions makes the integration of micro data and the macro accounts theoretically possible and statistically feasible (Ruggles and Ruggles, 1970, 1975, 1977a, 1977b, 1982, 1983, 1984, 1986, 1992).

The core account approach would achieve conceptual comparability between the central macroeconomic accounts and the actual accounts of the individual transactors. Therefore, micro data sets that accurately and fully represented the transactions of institutionally defined sectors of the economy would aggregate to the totals shown in the core macroeconomic accounts.

12.3. The Development of Micro Data Bases

12.3.1. The SNA 1993 *View of Data Processing for the National Accounts*

SNA 1993 explicitly recognizes the analytical advantages of having micro data bases that are fully compatible with the corresponding macro economic accounts for sectors of the total economy. It is argued, however, that it cannot be expected that the aggregation of data in micro data sets will add up to the totals estimated for the macroeconomic accounts. Conceptual differences, missing data, underreporting, and missing cases will result in the aggregated micro data differing from the macro totals. The estimates in the macro accounts are considered to be more comprehensive since they are adjusted to reflect data from different sources. On this basis, *SNA 1993* (United Nations, 1993a, p. 12) concludes that

> it is impractical to try to adjust the individual accounts of thousands of enterprises before aggregating them. It may be much easier to adjust the data after they have been aggregated to some extent. Of course, the data do not have to be aggregated to the level of the total economy, or even complete sectors or industries, before being adjusted and it is likely to be more efficient to make the adjustments for smaller and more homogenous groups of units. This may involve compiling so-called intermediate systems of accounts. At whatever level of aggregation the adjustments are made, the inevitable consequence is to make the resulting macro-data no longer equivalent to simple aggregations of the micro-data from which they are derived. When the micro-data are not derived from business accounts or administrative records but from censuses or surveys designed for statistical purposes, the concepts used should be closer to those required, but the results may still require adjustment at a macro level because of incomplete coverage (the surveys being confined to enterprises above a certain size, for example) and bias from response errors.

This view accurately reflects the past practices and even the current practices of most statistical offices engaged in constructing national account statistics. Prior to the development of the computer, advanced sampling techniques and the development of registers, national accountants have had to rely on tabulations of censuses, fragmentary sample surveys, and various kinds of administrative data. Most of these sources were not exhaustive, and national accountants generally did not have access to the original micro data. Even where access to micro data was possible, the programming and processing costs made its use for estimating national accounts impractical.

12.3.2. Current Methods of Data Collection, Processing, and Utilization

In the past several decades fundamental changes have occurred in the nature of the basic micro data available and the technology of using it. For households, sampling frames and sample surveys have become much more sophisticated, and the variety and availability of surveys have greatly increased. For enterprises, complete registers have been built up so that the coverage of both sample surveys and administrative records can be ascertained. The records in different micro data sets can be matched with each other. In the more statistically advanced countries both sample survey data and administrative micro data can easily be accessed by statistical offices for their use in national accounts estimation. Computer processing has advanced to the stage where the individual analyst can access and process major bodies of micro data easily and cheaply without requiring special computer programming.

For the most part, however, *SNA 1993* does not view the macro/micro linkage in the context of the existing realities. Rather the *SNA* accounts have been designed in terms of the data collection and processing capabilities of a half century ago. In the coming decades, even the developing countries will find it more efficient to use modern computer methods to maintain and process their statistical and administrative information.

Just as the development of national accounts is the function of a central statistical office, so also is the creation of micro data bases that are compatible with the macro data in the national accounts. Contrary to the *SNA* assumption that editing should be done at intermediate levels of aggregation, experience indicates that it needs to be carried out at the micro level. Most statistical agencies use computer editing of micro data to correct inconsistencies, impute missing values, and introduce estimates for missing cases. To the extent that there are significant differences between the aggregated data for a specific micro data set and the corresponding estimates in the macro accounts, the statistical basis of the macro estimates needs to be examined to determine the reasons for the discrepancies. Only by understanding the reasons for data incompleteness or incomparability will it be possible to improve data. In many cases, it will be possible to use other micro data sets and exact or statistical matching to provide the missing values, adjustments, or alignment that is required.

12.3.3. Micro Databases and the Problem of Privacy

The question of whether or not the use of micro databases by statistical offices should be restricted in the interest of privacy does not relate to the development and use of micro data by a central statistical office, but rather it relates to the release of micro data to the users of the national accounts. In effect, a central statistical office by being responsible for censuses and sample surveys, and by having legitimate access to administrative and regulatory data, does have access to all micro data collected by the government. To deny them such access would mean that they could not collect or process censuses or sample surveys, or use, for statistical purposes, the records that are maintained and utilized by other government agencies.

However, it is very appropriate to question what micro databases should be released to the public. Many governments currently release household sample surveys where there is no significant problem of disclosure. Some other micro data sets of a public nature, such as the data collected by the Securities and Exchange Commission (SEC) and the accounts of governmental units are also released. However, in the case of censuses, tax returns, and other administrative data where individual respondents are identified, the micro data are not generally released. In these cases, only those tabulations or aggregated data that do not reveal the identity of individual respondents are provided. From the point of view of statistical offices, however, there are considerable advantages in developing micro databases even when these cannot be released for general use. For any given micro database a large variety of different tabulations can easily be generated that will be consistent with each other and with the aggregates in the macro accounts.

12.4. The Integration of Household Sector Macro Accounts and Micro Databases

12.4.1. The Definition of the Household Sector and Its Transactions

The household sector in *SNA 1993* is defined as including not only households but also unincorporated enterprises, owner-occupied housing, and persons living in institutions. The treatment of unincorporated enterprises primarily relates to their production accounts, and this aspect will be examined in the context of the discussion relating to the enterprise sector. However, with respect to the household income and outlay accounts the *SNA* treatment of owner-occupied housing and the inclusion of the institutional population in the *SNA* household sector need to be considered.

In the *SNA*, householders who own the houses they live in are considered to be renting their houses from themselves as unincorporated real estate enterprises. These fictitious unincorporated enterprises not only own the dwellings and pay all of the costs associated with them, but they also receive an imputed space rent from the households as occupiers. The difference between the imputed space rent and the current costs of providing the housing services is returned by the fictitious unincorporated enterprises to households, as net imputed rental income.

As a consequence of this treatment, what appears in the *SNA* household income and outlay account is (1) on the outlay side, the imputed space rent (effectively the shadow price) as a part of the household's consumption expenditure, and (2) on the income side, net imputed rental income on owner-occupied housing, as a part of household income. The actual costs of owner-occupancy, including maintenance expenditures, property taxes, insurance, mortgage interest, and imputed capital consumption, appears in the *SNA* accounts as costs paid by unincorporated enterprises. In the United States in recent years the costs of owner-occupied housing have exceeded the imputed space rent—hence the net imputed rental income of owner occupied housing has been nagative. This approach does not take into account that in the United States homeowners can deduct their mortgage interest payments and their property taxes from the taxes they owe the government whereas renters have no such deductions. Therefore, contrary to imputed space rental approach, the homeowners' actual costs may not exceed what they would have to pay in rent.

Although this *SNA* method of imputation gets the imputed services of owner-occupied housing into output and household consumption, it does so at the cost of distorting the accounts of both households and enterprises. In fact, it is households that pay the property taxes, the interest on the mortgage debt, and the expenses of repair and upkeep, not unincorporated enterprises, and it is households, not enterprises, that do the gross saving reflected by the imputed capital consumption. The distortion may be particularly evident in an inflationary period, when the shadow price that is imputed for space rental may rise much more than the homeowner's actual costs. The homeowner in such a situation is more comparable to that of a renter who benefits from rent control. In the case of rent control, the *SNA* would report the actual rent paid, not its shadow market price, and it would seem logical to do the same for the expenses of owner-occupied housing.

Household survey data usually adopt an approach that is quite different from that of the macro accounts. Costs of owner-occupancy are considered to be household outlays like any others. Neither space rent nor income from owner-occupancy is imputed. Capital consumption is not usually asked for directly, but information from which it could be estimated is often collected.

The inclusion in the household sector of those individuals residing in institutions violates the transactor/transaction principle. The *SNA* notes that the individuals in the institutional setting have "little or no autonomy of action or decisions in economic matters" (United Nations, 1993a, p. 105). Some of the institutions that are included are prisons run by the government and hospitals or religious institutions run by nonprofit organizations. A preferable treatment of these populations would be to include their consumption as part of the final consumption services provided by government and nonprofit institutions rather than as outlays by the households. The sampling frames for household surveys rarely include the institutionalized population.

12.4.2. The Development of Household Micro Databases

Many different sources are available for developing household micro databases. Although no single micro data set contains in full detail all the data needed for the household macro accounts, taken together, they can provide highly detailed micro databases that directly correspond to the household macro accounts.

As already indicated in the discussion of data processing, the editing of data for inconsistencies, missing data, and missing cases currently takes place at the micro level. In creating a comprehensive micro database, therefore, the edited micro data will be in alignment with the national accounting macro data. In fact, in many instances, it is the macro estimates that will be based on the more carefully edited sources of basic micro data.

In the United States there are a large number of micro data sets that relate to individuals and households. One of the most comprehensive sets of data relating to households is the Census of Population. From edited versions of the population census, micro data Public Use Samples (PUS) comprising both 1 percent and 5 percent samples of households are generated. Public use samples of household micro data have now been developed for almost every Census of Population going back to 1850. On a monthly basis, the Current Population Survey (CPS) sample of approximately 60,000 cases provides the basis for measuring employment and unemployment in the economy.

In addition, there are a large variety of specialized sample surveys and administrative data files that provide an abundance of data on households and individuals. The Survey of Income and Program Participation (SIPP) gives detailed information on household income and the participation of households in government programs. Wages and salaries in this sample survey covers approximately 99 percent of the wages and salaries reported in the national accounts. The social security files also give detailed data on wages and salaries and have been used to construct a 1 percent sample of Longitudinal Employer-Employee Data (LEED). This micro data set provides longitudinal information on the work history and earnings of specific individuals over extended periods of time (Ruggles and Ruggles, 1977a, 1977b). The income tax files have been used to provide samples of personal income tax returns, and these have been supplemented by representative samples for low-income individuals and households. Surveys of Consumer Finances provide data on the financial transactions, assets and liabilities of households, and the Consumer Expenditure Surveys give detailed information on consumer expenditures. The Annual Housing Survey contains longitudinal information on both owner-occupied and rental housing. Because the United States has a large number of statistical agencies unrelated to the national accounts, many of these micro data sets have not been edited and aligned so that they correspond to the macro data in the published national accounts, but given the abundance of information available and current computer processing methods, such editing and alignment is quite feasible.

A prototype micro-macro link for the Canadian household sector has been constructed by Hans Adler and Michael Wolfson (1988), using a household micro simulation database of the kind pioneered by Orcutt, Pechman, and Okner (Orcutt, 1973; Pechman and Okner, 1974). In this instance the micro data consisted of the Social Policy Simulation Database (SPSD) that had been based on the 1984 Survey of Consumer Finances (SCF). Approximately 40,000 households were included in this sample (about 100,000 individuals). Adjustments and reweighing of the original sample was undertaken to include the institutionalized population and to be consistent with the data drawn from a sample of 400,000 income tax returns. Information on expenditure patterns were imputed from a Family Expenditure Survey (FAMEX) of 10,000 households containing detailed data on annual expenditure patterns. Finally, the SPSD also included 30,000 synthetically matched cases from unemployment insurance records. Overall, the correspondence between the aggregated micro data and the corresponding household data in the national accounts was quite close. Total household receipts in the SPSD were 91 percent of the national accounts household receipts. The greatest discrepancy on the income side was the reporting of interest and dividends where the aggregated micro data totaled approximately 50 percent of that shown in the national accounts. It does not follow, however, that this difference was due to under reporting in the micro data. The national accounts data include in the household sector the interest and dividends received by nonprofit institutions and by estates and trusts aimed at sequestering funds for households not yet in existance.

A more recent study of the consistency between the macro and micro data for the Japanese household sector was undertaken by Atsushi Maki and Shigeru Nishiyama (1993). A comparison was made between the SNA household sector consumption macro data (adjusted for imputations) and the aggregated micro data generated from the Family Income and Expenditure Surveys (FIES) (annual samples of 8,000 cases) supplemented by National Survey of Family Income and Expenditures (NSFIE) (54,000 sample every five years). The results were comparable to that achieved by similar experiments for other countries: the micro data for consumption totaled about 80 percent of the *SNA* household sector macro data.

In 1979 the United Nations Statistical Office established the National Household Survey Capability Program (NHSCP), which has had as its major objective assisting developing countries in the collection, processing, analysis, and dissemination of household survey data (United Nations, 1993b). Over fifty countries participate in this program, and a variety of different household surveys are undertaken. The World Bank has given substantial support to the Living Standards Measurement Study (LSMS), which attempts to monitor malnutrition, poverty levels, inequality of income, and the characteristics of the poor. Other household surveys have included the saving behavior of households and their willingness to pay for education and health care. It is indeed regrettable that the U.N. Statistical Office did not take the opportunity to harmonize the 1993 revision of the *SNA* with its own Household Survey Capability Program. As a consequence of this lack of integration, household income, consumption, and saving as measured by household surveys in a given country will differ radically from that shown in the household sector account of the national accounts.

12.4.3. The Imputation and Rerouting of Household Transactions

In most cases, the imputation and rerouting of transactions for analytic purposes can be carried out more accurately and more meaningfully if they are based on edited and aligned micro databases. For example, the imputation of the services of owner-occupied housing over and above the actual outlays can more easily be made at the micro level where factors such as the characteristics of the housing, its location, its estimated value, and the rental value of similar properties can be taken into account. In a similar manner, imputations for government services in kind to households, such as education and health services, can be allocated on the basis of micro data relating to a household's characteristics or their known participation in specific government programs. The imputation of the services of financial intermediaries to individuals can be based on information relating to the income, expenditures, and financial transactions of households.

There may be instances, however, where there is little or no basis for attributing specific imputations to individual households. In such situations the validity of attributing such *SNA* imputations to the household sector as a whole needs to be questioned. For example, the *SNA* recommends that pension fund reserves be attributed to households as part of their net equity. These reserves may represent substantial overfunding or underfunding of the actual discounted value of future pension obligations: the individuals concerned may be totally unaware of such valuations and the actual pension fund reserves may not be directly relevant to their own specific future benefits. In such cases, the validity of attributing these pension fund reserves to households needs to be reexamined. A more logical approach would be to use some other method for valuing pension entitlements to households and to treat the reserves held by pension funds as undistributed pension fund reserves much in the same manner as the SNA treats the undistributed profits of corporations. Undistributed profits are not included as a part of household equity; instead, the market value of the corporate stock is used as the basis for valuing the equity of stockholders.

In some other cases, such as social security schemes, it may be analytically useful to introduce into individual household accounts imputations for the value of public entitlements. It seems unreasonable, from a household's point of view, that private pension schemes should be considered to be of value, whereas publicly funded social security pensions should be considered to have no value. Of course, it would be possible to carry the imputation of future government benefits and taxes even further: economists concerned with "rational expectations" or politicians wishing to emphasize the burden of the government debt might wish to attribute to the grandchildren in households their share of the federal debt as well as their future inheritance of government bonds.

12.5. The Integration of Enterprise Sector Macro Accounts and Micro Databases

12.5.1. The Definition of Enterprises and Establishments

SNA 1993 defines enterprises as those institutional units that engage in production. Thus corporations, quasi-corporations, unincorporated enterprises, and nonprofit institutions all are included as enterprises. A single enterprise such as a corporation, however, may simultaneously engage in a number of different kinds of economic activity and be active in various locations. Thus for analyzing production or regional activity it is necessary to partition some of the institutional units into smaller and more homogeneous units, which the *SNA* defines as establishments. Furthermore, in the *SNA* system the production accounts and generation of income accounts for establishments are then compiled into industries as well as into the institutional sectors. From the point of view of the integration of micro data and macro accounts, therefore, both enterprise and establishment data need to be considered.

12.5.2. The Development of Enterprise and Establishment Micro Databases

To a major extent the operation of the economic system depends on the record keeping of enterprises and establishments. Such records are not only needed for the operation of business, but they are also needed for tax returns and in the case of publicly held corporations as statements for the stockholders. In addition, the government conducts periodic censuses and surveys of enterprises and their establishments, and specialized agencies such as the Social Security Administration, the Bureau of Labor Statistics, and regulatory commissions require periodic reports.

In the United States, the Bureau of the Census maintains a register, the Standard Statistical Establishment List (SSEL), that identifies each enterprise and its related establishments. Similarly, the Internal Revenue

Service identifies each corporation, partnership, nonprofit institution, and unincorporated business. Every employer is assigned an Employer Identification Number (EIN), which is used as the basis of the Social Security System. Even small family enterprises that have no employees must report their receipts, costs, and income on Schedule C of the Personal Income Tax Forms. Thus, the government maintains complete and comprehensive registers and data on all enterprises and their establishments in the economy.

Tabulations of the tax records of enterprises have served as the basis for much of the national accounting estimates. In fact, the official U.S. national accounts publish reconciliation tables showing the detailed adjustments made to the IRS tabulations of the tax files for deriving the national accounts estimates of capital consumption, proprietor income, interest taxes, dividends, and corporate profits. Almost all of the adjustments made to the aggregate tabulations of the tax files could be implemented at the level of the micro data.

The Security Exchange Commission (SEC) requires that every publicly held corporation provide standardized quarterly financial reports. Until recently, the computerized micro data sets of these SEC reports were primarily used by large financial and commercial institutions, but currently, with the support of the NSF, these micro data are being released on Internet free to users.

The specific problems involved in creation of micro databases are well illustrated by the Longitudinal Establishment Data (LED) project. In the mid-1950s, when the Bureau of the Census obtained its first large computer and put the Census of Manufactures and the Annual Survey of Manufactures on Computer tape, a joint project was developed in conjunction with the Social Science Research Council to create a longitudinal file of manufacturing establishments. The task of this project was to match the records of individual establishments for different years so that changes could be observed at the micro level of the establishment. Thousands of computer tapes were involved, and the project lasted for more than five years. At the end of that time the project was abandoned for three reasons. First, the aggregates of the individual records for each year did not add up to the published data, since the tabulated data had been adjusted at an aggregate level for missing data, missing cases, and incorrect data. Second, the percentage of establishments that could be successfully matched from year to year was not as large as desired since the identification of plants, their mergers, and industry changes were not systematically maintained. Finally, the matched file of establishments was so large it was not economically feasible to analyze it on the computers available at that time.

However, twenty-five years later in the early 1980s, the handling of the Manufactures Census and the Annual Survey of Manufactures had changed, thanks in large degree to Shirley Kalleck, who was in charge of the Census of Manufactures. The Bureau of the Census had developed the Standard Statistical Establishment List that was a complete register of all enterprises and their establishments. Every manufacturing establishment was assigned a permanent plant identification. The editing and imputation of missing data was carried out at the level of the micro data. Finally, computers had advanced to the stage where they could handle large data sets economically. As a consequence, with the support of the National Science Foundation, a second attempt was made to create a LED file. This time the attempt was successful and the Bureau of the Census now maintains on a current basis a longitudinal file for all manufacturing establishments. Special arrangements are made at the Census Bureau to give researchers access to this data base within the restrictions of confidentiality.

Another example relates to the micro data base developed by the Small Business Administration in the 1980s. This agency was charged by Congress with the task of creating a micro database for small business (including names and addresses) much in the same manner as the Department of Agriculture maintains a micro data file of individual farms. Because of the confidentiality of both Internal Revenue Tax records and data on enterprises and establishments collected by the Bureau of the Census, the Small Business Administration was forced to use records from the private sector. By using the data in the credit files of Dun and Bradstreet supplemented by telephone listings in the yellow pages, the Small Business Administration was able to piece together a file of large and small businesses that matched in its comprehensiveness the Standard Statistical Establishment List maintained by the Bureau of the Census.

In an article on macro economic accounting and micro business accounting, Postner (1986) explores the limits to consistency between macro and micro data and urges that national accountants preserve as much as possible the initial sets of data that go into the construction of the published accounts. He argues, quite reasonably, that the preadjusted data provide valuable insight about the nature and extent of the inconsistencies and their implications for the specification of the macro economic identities.

In a more recent article, Postner (1988, p. 239) points out that much of this problem lies in the nature of micro data itself: "There is considerable evidence that two or more parties involved in a common market transaction may have inconsistent views and knowledge of the same transaction. The views and knowledge of individual transactors are reflected in their respective accounting records and inevitably affect their respective economic behavior. So inconsistency embodies an important aspect of the real economic world. If such strands of inconsistency are preserved in our national accounting procedures, then it is more likely that accounting relations will furnish information that could be used to eventually 'explain' economic behaviour and thus also be of value for purposes of economic policy."

This points up some of the reasons for the imbalances and inconsistencies observed at the macro level. For example within the flow of funds accounts of the Federal Reserve Board, the total amount of financial assets held in the economy is not equal to the amount of financial liabilities outstanding, and in part this results from the creditors and debtors placing different values on their financial assets and claims.

12.5.3. The Imputation and Rerouting of Enterprise Transactions

In the discussion of micro-macro links, *SNA 1993* indicates that one of the difficulties involved in linkage is that concepts such as depreciation as used for tax purposes may be quite arbitrary and quite unacceptable from an economic point of view. This, however, is not a barrier to the integration of macro aggregates and micro data. Nothing prevents the national accountant from imputing his concept of economic depreciation at the micro level. In fact this imputation probably could be made more logically and accurately at the micro level where relevant information is available to support such an alternative measure of depreciation. In this context, however, Postner's argument is also quite appropriate. The depreciation charges for tax purposes are relevant to the behavior of the individual micro unit. In this case the depreciation charges affect the tax payments the enterprise has to make in the current period, and will also affect future tax payments. This information is relevant to understanding the operation of the enterprise, and it needs to be preserved in the accounts rather than flushed down the drain. By excluding actual depreciation charged, and showing only imputed "economic depreciation," the *SNA* precludes the analysis of the effect of such tax policies as "accelerated depreciation" upon the economy.

Another area where both imputations and reroutings of transactions are carried out by the national accountant is in the financial intermediation services indirectly measured (FISIM). Since a number of different alternatives are permitted in the *SNA*, explicit imputations and rerouting at the micro level would increase an understanding of the implications of the various approaches.

SNA 1993 takes the position that enterprises and nonprofit institutions serving households cannot have expenditures on consumption. In the case of enterprises all consumption expenditures are attributed to employees as part of their compensation. This assumption may violate the transactor/ transaction principle or treat as an intermediate cost of production consumption goods that are actually provided by enterprises. Some goods or services made available by enterprises may be of a collective nature or, at least, not easily assignable to specific individuals. For example, enterprises may provide services to the community, environmental benefits, or even food and entertainment for customers, and suppliers as well as employees. It is interesting to note, however, that the *SNA* does recognize that, in principle, the recognition of enterprise consumption is appropriate in certain situations (United Nations, 1993a, p. 425): "Under a planned economy enterprises frequently provided health, education and recreational services for their employees (and sometimes the general population) not primarily to attract employees but as an extension of a government policy of providing these services through out the economy."

In the case of nonprofit institutions serving households, the *SNA* also attributes all of their final expenditures to be transfers of consumption in kind to households. However, in those instances where the nonprofit institution is concerned with broader expenditures such as improvement in the environment, preservation of wild life, or scientific and medical research, it would seem more appropriate to treat these as collective consumption in the same manner as when such goods are provided by general government.

12.6. The Integration of Government Sector Macro Accounts and Micro Databases

12.6.1. The Definition of the Government Sector and Its Transactions

In many respects the task of integrating the macro accounts of the government sector and the micro data of different governmental bodies and units is simpler and more straightforward than for other sectors. This is due to (1) governmental units are required by law to provide detailed accounting of their receipts and expenditures and (2) such accounts are available for public use. The government sector consists not only of central, state, and local governments with their related departments, agencies, and commissions, but in addition there are a wide variety of semi-independent bodies such as school districts, water districts, or other specialized authorities. *SNA 1993* provides consolidated accounts for central, state and local governments, but for many types of analysis, it is important to be able to access the more detailed and deconsolidated data that are available for individual governmental units.

In publishing the United States national accounts, the Bureau of Economic Analysis provides special tables that show the reconciliation between (1) the data as given in the federal government budget documents and federal sector in the national accounts and (2) the tabulations of the Census of Governments and the state and local government sector in the national accounts. The adjustments contained in these reconciliation tables could, of course, be carried out at the level of the micro data for these governmental units.

12.6.2. The Development of Government Micro Databases

In the mid-1970s a research project on "The Measurement of Economic and Social Performance" was undertaken with the support of the National Science Foundation (NSF, 1978). This project had as one of its major objectives the development of micro databases for enterprises, households, and governments. The micro data sets for enterprises and households were limited by the publicly available micro data files at that time (Compustat for enterprises, Census Public Use and IRS Income Tax samples for households), and the ability of mainframe computers to handle large files. In the case of government, however, the 1972 Census of Government computer tapes provided information on 78,000 governmental units. By adjusting the data in the Census of Government micro accounts to reflect accrual accounting rather than cash accounting, recognizing intergovernmental transfers, and distinguishing purchases of goods from the compensation of employees and payments of transfers and subsidies, it was possible to develop data at the level of the individual governmental units that consolidated quite closely with the macro data in the government sector of the national accounts. One of the other objectives of this project was to provide a spacial distribution of public-sector activity. For this purpose, the federal, state, and local receipts and expenditures were disaggregated to the county level, and data provided on their activities for 3,000 county and standard metropolitan statistical areas (Quigley, 1977a, 1977b). No attempt was made, in this project, to construct longitudinal micro data sets for governmental units.

A more recent and comprehensive account of establishing a link between the micro data on government accounts and the government sector in the national accounts has been provided for the Netherlands (Bloem, 1988). Over an extended period of time, the Netherlands Statistical Office has been involved in the development of two connectable data sets of government statistics—one from the administrative point of view and one fitting in the national accounts. Many of the same problems encountered in the NSF project such as the conversion from cash to accrual accounting and reclassification of transactions to correspond with the national accounting classifications were required. Transformation tables provided a relatively simple and concise connection between the micro data sets relevant from the accounting point of view and the government sector in the national accounts. With respect to the national accounts, however, the link was still somewhat incomplete since a more disaggregated sectoring was needed in the national accounts to fit with the administrative data. This problem, however, was remedied in the course of the revision of the Netherlands national accounts.

12.6.3. The Imputation and Rerouting of Government Transactions

The major imputation in the government sector macro account is related to the consumption of fixed capital. *SNA 1993* requires that the consumption of fixed capital be charged for a wide variety of fixed assets owned by the government. It is explicitly stated (United Nations, 1993, p. 228) that "All buildings and other structures are assumed to have finite service lives, even when properly maintained, so that consumption of fixed capital is calculated for all such fixed assets, including railways, roads, bridges, tunnels, airports, harbors, pipelines, dams, etc. Service lives are not determined purely by physical durability, and many buildings and structures are eventually scrapped because they have become obsolete. However, the service lives from some structures such as certain roads, bridges, dams, etc., may be very long—perhaps a century or more."

Increasingly, governmental units are instituting capital budgets, and renewal accounting or are amortizing their capital costs over extended periods (Postner, 1992). Although such accounting information is important and relevant for many purposes, including the measurement of government surpluses and deficits from the point of view of public policy, it would not necessarily meet all the needs of the macro accounts. In order to conform to *SNA* macro concepts it would be necessary to develop, in addition, imputations based on a perpetual inventory method of keeping track of fixed capital, applying appropriate economic service lives, and computing in current market values the amount of capital consumption taking place. Most governmental units would not maintain their accounts on such a basis, but the data provided by the detailed governmental unit accounts on fixed capital formation could be utilized to make such imputations.

12.7. Summary and Conclusions

SNA 1993 is a major accomplishment. It represents a further development of *SNA 1968*, embracing within a single integrated system all the major forms of national economic accounting—input-output, national income accounting, financial accounts, and balance sheets. Richard Stone would have been pleased at the successful harmonization within the *SNA* of the macro economic data requirements by the major international statistical organizations.

In commenting on the proposed revision of the *SNA* in 1986, however, Stone stressed four other issues that he felt deserved attention even if they were not ready for international standardization. First, Stone attached importance to the integration of macro and micro data and argued for more country experience in this area. Second, he urged that more recognition should be given to the statistical procedures for estimating and adjusting entries in the national accounts by least squares or other methods. Third, he felt the efforts to form links between the *SNA* and *MPS* should be continued. Fourth, he hoped that the U.N. Statistical Office would see what could be done in formulating economic, sociodemographic and environmental statistics in a related manner (Stone, 1986).

SNA 1993 has only partially followed Stone's recommendations. First, although the *SNA* explicitly recognizes the theoretical desirability of integrating macro and micro data no provision is made for it, and actual integration is considered to be impractical. Second, there is no discussion within the *SNA* concerning statistical procedures for the estimation or adjustment of entries in the accounts. Third, although some attention is given to the special problems of transition economies, the linkage between the *SNA* and *MPS* has become moot. Finally, formulations of economic, sociodemographic and environmental statistics have been relegated to ad hoc social accounting matrices and satellite accounts that lie outside the main framework of the *SNA*.

Macro accounts and micro data are highly symbiotic, and their integration is basic to both statistical measurement and the analysis of economic, sociodemographic and environmental data. National accountants, however, have not been accustomed to using micro data. In the past, data processing by both statistical and administrative agencies has primarily consisted of data reduction—that is, aggregating micro records to produce summary tabulations. It is such sets of tabulations that have constituted the databases with which national accountants have worked. To the extent that different tabulations have been found to be inconsistent with each other or incomplete, adjustments have been carried out at the level of the aggregate tabulations. In turn, the national accountants have provided users with a consistent macro data set of national accounting tables that gives a general overview of the economy but does not provide the distributional, regional, social, and demographic data needed for analyzing most problems of economic and social policy.

In the past several decades the major advances in the technology of data processing and data storage have altered the way data are developed, maintained, and analyzed. It has now become practical to edit and adjust data explicitly at the micro level. For individual respondents, corrected data can be introduced for inconsistencies or extreme values, and estimates derived from similar respondents can be made for missing data. Sampling frames or registers covering the complete universe of all existing respondents can be used to determine the completeness of data, and imputations based on past information or on data from similar cases can be added at the level of the micro data. In this manner, a given micro data set can be made internally consistent and aligned with other sources of data. In light of this development, to an increasing extent, statistical and administrative agencies are creating, using, and providing to users a large variety of micro databases.

It is simplistic to suppose that the integration of macroeconomic accounts and micro databases requires that all the variables in a macro sector account be contained within a single micro database. Rather what is required is (1) that the reporting units included in the macro sector directly correspond to the reporting units represented in the micro database and (2) that for any variables appearing in both the macro accounts and the micro database the totals should match. There are, potentially, for every sector, a large number of different micro databases that contain important and valuable data. Thus, a micro database of social security data can provide wage and salary information with considerable geographic and industry detail for all enterprises, whereas another micro database of corporate tax returns could give more complete data relating to the income accounts and balance sheets of corporations.

It should also be recognized that in some instances it will not be possible to provide micro data sets that are related to the estimates of specific aggregates in the national accounts. For example, the preliminary estimate of GDP on a quarterly basis may be extrapolated by applying an estimated percentage change to the previous quarterly GDP. This percentage change estimate, furthermore, may be based on a variety of "economic indicators" such as changes in pay rolls, retail sales, or purchase orders. In such cases, there may be no meaningful micro data that relate to the estimate, and it is only with time that such information will become available and the estimates of GDP can be revised.

The integration of macro accounts and micro data refers primarily to benchmark periods. In the past, the benchmark periods for estimating the macro accounts have coincided with years when there were complete censuses or when the basic tabulations provided by administrative agencies, such as the taxing authorities, became available. This has often meant that benchmark periods occurred only once in every five or ten years. With more comprehensive sampling methods and faster processing of administrative records, it should be feasible to provide for the integration of macro accounts and micro data on a more frequent and up-to-date basis.

National accountants cannot only utilize a large variety of different micro databases for constructing the market transactions of the household, enterprise and government sectors, but they will also find micro databases useful for making imputations and rerouting transactions. For example, a household or labor force database that showed the age, sex, occupation, and residence of the population would be useful in constructing estimates of nonmarket activity. A household expenditure database or a housing database would provide the necessary information for estimating the services of owner-occupied housing. Finally, a micro database such as the Survey of Income and Program Participation could assist in estimating benefits in kind received by households from the government. Many of the extensions suggested by Kendrick and Eisner for nonmarket activity of the household or for introducing alternative definitions of capital formation and depreciation can best be estimated by using micro databases of households and enterprises (Kendrick, 1976, 1979; Eisner, 1994). SAMs and satellite accounts would thus be aggregations of the basic micro data estimates.

The macro economic accounts not only benefit from their integration with micro databases, but, at the same time, the statistical system also benefits. By extending the *SNA* to micro data, it can serve as the vehicle for integrating economic, social, demographic, and regional data. One of the major difficulties in using micro data in the past has been that different micro data sets purporting to cover similar reporting units come out with very different results. As a consequence, analyses of micro data have become suspect. It is felt that by selecting appropriate micro data sets, analysts can arrive at any conclusion they so desire. By developing micro databases that match the control totals in the macro accounts, those using micro data will have greater assurance that the data they are using are representative, complete, and unbiased.

From an analytic point of view, the integration of macro accounts and micro data has become increasingly important for problems related to pubic policy. Thus, for example, in developing equitable tax laws, it becomes necessary to know how different provisions of the tax system affect both the distribution of the tax burden and the generation of tax revenue. Micro data sets of tax returns for individuals and enterprises can provide such information. Social welfare, health care, and pension programs require micro data relating to the social, demographic, and economic characteristics of households in order to assess their distributional impact and to develop the total cost of financing such programs. In analyzing the level and character of unemployment in the economy and its relation to the macro performance of the economy, micro data are needed relating to the social, demographic, occupational, and regional characteristics of the unemployed. Many environmental questions require data of a regional nature and are concerned with the cost-benefit effects on individual households. If there is not integration between the macro accounts and the basic micro data sets used for such analysis, it will not be possible to evaluate in a consistent manner both the overall economic effects and the distributional effects.

It is the contention of this paper that *SNA 1993* needs to provide explicitly for the integration of micro data. This can be accomplished by developing core transactor/transaction accounts for the institutional sectors with separate modules for introducing imputations and rerouting of transactions. Micro databases are important both for constructing national accounting aggregates and for providing users with detailed integrated economic, social, and demographic information. The cut and paste methods using tabulations of aggregated data are becoming obsolete. The complex social and political problems of the twenty-first century will require both the broad macroeconomic constructs and the underlying micro data relating to enterprises, governments and households. The technology exists: the much-heralded information superhighway has arrived, and the modern computer provides the individual analyst with the ability to access, manage, and analyze large data sets of macro and micro data. It is the responsibility of the national accountant to develop such databases in a coherent manner.

References

Adler, Hans, and Michael Wolfson. (1988). "A Prototype Macro-Micro Link for the Canadian Household Sector." *Review of Income and Wealth* 34(4) (December): 371–392.

Bloem, Adrian M. (1988). "Micro-Macro Link for Government." *Review of Income and Wealth* 34 (September): 289–312.

Bos Frits. (1989). "A Systems View on Concepts of Income in the National Accounts." *National Accounts*. Occasional Paper NA-033. Netherlands Central Bureau of Statistics.

Bos, Frits. (1992). "The History of National Accounting." *National Accounts*. Occasional Paper NA-048. Netherlands Central Bureau of Statistics.

Bos, Frits. (1993). "Standard National Accounting Concepts, Economic Theory, and Data Compilation Issues." *National Accounts*. Occasional Paper NA-061. Netherlands Central Bureau of Statistics.

Eisner, Robert. (1995). "Expansion of Boundaries and Satellite Accounts." In John Kendrick (ed.), *The New System of National Accounts*. Norwell, MA.

Kendrick, John W. (1976). *The Formation and Stocks of Total Capital*. New York: Columbia University Press for NBER: 349–364.

Kendrick, John W. (1979). "Expanding Imputed Values in the National Income and Product Accounts." *Review of Income and Wealth* 25(4) (December). IARIW, New York, N.Y.

Maki, Atsushi, and Shigeru Nishiyama. (1993). "Consistency Between Macro- and Micro-Data Sets in the Japanese Household Sector." *Review of Income and Wealth* 39(2) (June). IARIW, New York, N.Y.: 195–208.

National Science Foundation. (1978). "The Measurement of Economic and Social Performance." Report on Project, SOC74-21391. Yale University, January.

Orcutt, Guy H. (1973). *Microanalytic Simulation: A Tool for Policy Analysis*. Washington, DC: Urban Institute.

Organization for European Economic Cooperation. (1950). *A Simplified System of National Accounts*. Cambridge: National Accounts Research Unit.

Pechman, J.A., and B.A. Okner. (1974). *Who Bears the Tax Burden?* Washington, DC: Brookings Institution.

Postner, Harry H. (1986). "Micro Business Accounting and Macroeconomic Accounting: The Limits to Consistency." *Review of Income and Wealth* 32(3) (September): 317–344.

Postner, Harry H. (1988). "Linkages Between Macro and Micro Business Accounts: Implications for Economic Measurement." *Review of Income and Wealth* 34(3) (September): 313–336.

Postner, Harry H. (1992). "A Capital Budget, Renewals Accounting and Public

Accountability." Paper prepared for Government and Competitiveness Reference, February. Ottawa, Canada.

Quigley, John. (1977a). "The Spatial Distribution of Public Activity: A Preliminary Report." *Proceeding of the 1976 General Conference of the Society of Government Economists.* Washington, DC: SGE.

Quigley, John. (1977b). (with Gail Trask and James Trask). "Income and Product Accounts for the Local Public Sector." Institution for Social and Policy Studies, Working Paper 795. Yale University.

Quigley, John. (1977). (with Thanos Catsambas), "Spatial Redistribution Through General Government Activity." Paper presented at the fifteenth General Conference of the International Association for Research in Income and Wealth, York, England, August. Cambridge, MA: Balinger.

Ruggles, Richard. (1949). *National Income Accounting and Its Relation to Economic Policy.* Paris: Economic Cooperation Administration, Office of the Special Representative.

Ruggles, Richard, and Nancy D. Ruggles. (1970). "Macro Accounts and Micro Data Sets." *Proceedings of the Business and Economic Statistics Section.* American Statistical Association: 208–213.

Ruggles, Richard, and Nancy D. Ruggles. (1975). "The Role of Micro Data in the National Economic Accounts." *Review of Income and Wealth* 21(2) (June): 203–216.

Ruggles, Richard, and Nancy D. Ruggles. (1977a). "The Anatomy of Earnings Behavior: Analysis of the Social Security LEED Micro Data File. "*The Distribution of Economic Well-Being*, NBER Studies in Income and Wealth (Vol. 47). Cambridge, MA: Balinger: 115–157.

Ruggles, Richard, and Nancy D. Ruggles. (1977b). (with Edward Wolff). "Merging Micro Data, Rationale, Practice and Testing." *Annals of Economic and Social Measurement* (NBER) 6(4) (October): 407–428.

Ruggles, Richard, and Nancy D. Ruggles. (1982). "Integrated Economic Accounts for the United States, 1947–80." *Survey of Current Business* 62(5) (May): 1–65.

Ruggles, Richard, and Nancy D. Ruggles. (1983). "The Treatment of Pensions and Insurance in National Accounts." *Review of Income and Wealth* 29(4) (December): 371–404.

Ruggles, Richard, and Nancy D. Ruggles. (1984). "The Analysis of Longitudinal Establishment Data." Paper presented at the Conference on the longitudinal Establishment Data Files and Diversification Study, Alexandria, VA, October: 1–16.

Ruggles, Richard, and Nancy D. Ruggles. (1986). "The Integration of Macro and Micro Data for the Household Sector. "*Review of Income and Wealth* 32(3) (September): 245–276.

Ruggles, Richard, and Nancy D. Ruggles. (1992). "Household and Enterprise Saving and Capital Formation in the United States: A Market Transactions View." *Review of Income and Wealth* 38(2) (June): 119–163.

Stone, Richard. (1986). "Comments on the Overall Program." *Review of Income and Wealth* (Special Issue on the Review of the United Nations System of National Accounts) 32(2) (June): 118–121.

United Nations. (1947). *Measurement of National Income and the Construction of Social Accounts*. Studies and Reports on Statistical Methods, No. 7. Geneva: United Nations.

United Nations. (1953). *A System of National Accounts and Supporting Tables*. Studies in Methods, Series F. No. 2. New York: United Nations.

United Nations. (1968). *A System of National Accounts*. Studies in Methods, Series F. No. 2, Rev. 3. New York: United Nations.

United Nations. (1993a). *System of National Accounts, 1993*. ST/ESA/STAT/ SER.f/2/REV. 4. New York: United Nations.

United Nations. (1993b). "Technical Cooperation: National Household Survey Capability Programme (NHSCP)." Social Dimensions of Adjustment (SDA) and the Living Standards Measurement Study (LSMS), Joint Report of the Secretary General and the World Bank E/CN.3/1993/18, January.

van Bochove, C.A., and H.K. van Tuinen. (1986). "Flexibility in the Next SNA: The Case for an Institutional Core." *Review of Income and Wealth* 32(2) (June): 127–154.

van Eck, R., C.N. Gorter, and H.K. van Tuinen. (1983). "Flexibility in the System of National Accounts." Occasional Paper, NA-001. Netherlands Central Bureau of Statistics.

DISCUSSION OF CHAPTER 12

Harry H. Postner

1. Introduction

Richard Ruggles has contributed a chapter on an important topic that is almost, but not completely, overlooked in the *System of National Accounts 1993* (*SNA*). The topic of micro-macro data links and integration is briefly outlined in Chapter 1 of *SNA 1993* and that particular section is quoted at length in the Ruggles' contribution. There does not appear to be any other mention of this topic in *SNA 1993*. One possible reason for this position is that the *SNA* is meant to be an exposition of accounting and conceptual methodology; the topic of micro-macro links is evidently considered to be part of "compilation methodology"—outside the *SNA* scope of reference.

Richard Ruggles, often together with Nancy Ruggles, has been deeply concerned with micro-macro data links and related subjects for many years. It is, therefore, easy to understand his profound disappointment that the question of integration of micro and macro data is not taken seriously in *SNA 1993*. Do we have the right to expect, say, at least a five-page appendix on the subject in the present *SNA*, pending the ultimate release of a *Manual on Compilation Methodology for National Accounts*?

I would think that the topic does deserve a more formal treatment at this time. Thus the contribution of Richard Ruggles is particularly relevant now.

The main purpose of this present commentary is to extend the Ruggles' contribution especially in the light of (1) certain contemporary stresses on national statistical systems, (2) the behaviorial "rules of the game" under which statistical agencies tend to operate, and (3) how much we can really expect from the constraints of international standardization. Some mention is also made of the need for distinguishing and working out practical case studies of micro-macro linkages and their related technical problems. The conclusion of this commentary has some suggestions to make with regard to the question of where do we go from here. The references do not repeat those already included in the Ruggles' chapter.

2. The State of the Art

The Ruggles' paper is very much a concern of our times. It is, in effect, one important aspect of a more general aggregation problem in economics, some phases of which are currently the focus of research attention. For example, Kirman (1992) has questioned the conceptual validity of the "representative individual" from a theoretical point of view. Stoker (1993) provides a detailed survey of the econometric approaches to the problem of aggregation over individuals. There is also a paper by McGuckin and Reznek (1993) describing research possibilities with economic microdata available from the Census Bureau's Center for Economic Studies.

Here at Statistics Canada, the 1993 catalogue lists over thirty pages of different microdata files obtainable as part of electronic products and services. To quote from Statistics Canada (1993, p. 359): "Microdata files consist of unaggregated records of individual responses to Agency surveys. . . . Selected data sets in this form have been assembled to be used, along with necessary documentation, on users' own computer systems." The microdata files normally come fully edited to reflect their respective scopes.

Microdata files often serve as a basis for compilation of macroeconomic aggregates in national accounts. But as Richard Ruggles points out, the macroeconomic aggregates are not simply an unadjusted aggregation of related microdata sets. The aggregates, as deployed in national accounts, must be preadjusted and reconciled in order to satisfy national accounting concepts and balance identities. (We overlook the issues of consolidation in this commentary.) Richard Ruggles' main point is that the adjustments and reconciliations are rarely carried back to the microdata level. The two sets of data, micro and macro, are therefore not aligned and are not consistent to the extent that such alignment and consistency may be possible.

Why, then, do the statistical authorities neglect a good opportunity to put "their house in order"? There are a number of factors that probably play a role in this regard. The following discussion, however, is not meant to be complete and is, in fact, largely impressionistic.

The macroeconomic data that appear in national accounts not only embody a standard conceptual methodology, say, *SNA 1993*. The data also must be integrated and reconciled in order to satisfy a complex range of national accounting balance identities (as seen, e.g., in Van Tongeren and Hannig, 1989). One impression is that while purely conceptual adjustments could be carried back to the microdata level in a distinctive individual manner, there is strong opposition to carrying back the reconciliation adjustments to the microdata level. These latter adjustments have no microdata "handles" and so could turn out to be simply crude proportional adjustments. The adjusted microdata files would be disfigured and lack economic content.

Another impression is that national economic accounts undergo a sequence of revisions, both in current and constant prices, over time. Should we expect the relevant microdata sets to also undergo a sequence of revisions for purposes of alignment? There seems to be a feeling that microdata sets and macroeconomic aggregates serve different constituencies and so the case in favour of "forcing consistency" becomes weak and inappropriate. It should also be remarked that statistical data are collected and compiled according to institutional responsibilities within an agency—faced with quarterly and annual production deadlines (this theme is further developed in Postner, 1993).

One more impression must be added that is more in line with *SNA 1993*. A major purpose of the new *SNA* is to provide international standards for national economic accounting. This has been a feasible goal so long as we remain within the realm of accounting and conceptual standards. But once we move into issues of compilation and reconciliation, within an integrated system of national accounts, and attempt to relate these issues to micro-macro links, then the problems of reaching a consensus on international standards become much more profound. The problems, indeed, are particularly severe when there is so little practical experience even at the various national levels.

3. Does Two Plus Three Always Equal Five?

In principle it is often possible to align microdata sets and macroeconomic aggregates so that "two and three," the postadjusted microdata, equals "five," the macroeconomic aggregate present in official national accounts. This appears to be the case, in very simple form, emphasized by Richard Ruggles. In effect, the macroeconomic aggregates present in national accounts provide the "control totals" for corresponding microdata sets. This case can be extended to where the original microdata are infected by underreporting and where appropriate sample auditing is performed to further adjust the microdata records to conform with conceptual standards. The solution of the auditing problem, though, may turn out to be complex and dependent on certain assumptions.

There is, however, another case where the issue of micro-macro links of a consistent nature is not capable of resolution. This case arises when macroeconomic aggregates are meant to cover individual units that are out-of-scope with respect to microdata files while the remaining microdata that are available are in scope. For example, *SNA 1993* refers to the illegal economy, the underground economy, and even to the informal economy—all of which are essentially unrecorded. The sample auditing "solution" cannot be applied since the unit records that require auditing do not exist.

In this situation, synthetic coverage adjustments combined with commodity-flow type reconciliations are performed at the macroeconomic level. But the resulting macroeconomic aggregates that ultimately appear in national accounts can only provide clues for (partially) aligning the microdata records that are available. These records can be postadjusted to conform with conceptual standards and even crudely adjusted to conform with reconciliation standards provided that the reconciliation standards are identified. Unfortunately, there is no reasonable way to disentangle the purely reconciliation standard adjustments from the coverage-type adjustments that are required in the presence of a significant unrecorded economy.

The propositions put forward in this and the previous section essentially hold irrespective of whether microdata sets are derived from administrative files or from economic surveys.

4. Conclusion

I would prefer to interpret Richard Ruggles' contribution as one of opening a dialogue between the "two solitudes" of economic statistics.

(The term "two solitudes" has a special meaning for Canadians.) At the present time we have, e.g., microanalytic simulation models, based on microdata files, that have no real links to the system of national accounts (see, again, Stoker, 1993). On the other hand, macroeconomic models based on national accounts are difficult to relate to individual economic behaviour because the micro-macro links are not being supported. Richard Ruggles makes some concrete suggestions as to how we might proceed in the future, particularly in the light of enhanced computer power. In my opinion, there is still a range of statistical management and technical problems to be overcome before we can claim to have integrated microdata with macrodata. In the meantime, it would be beneficial if the relevant statistical agencies could provide documentation of the statistical gaps that now exist between the two great solitudes of economic statistics.

Finally, one big question still remains. Should national economic accounts be granted the exclusive role of the Grand Auditor of a nation's economic statistical system? Perhaps John Kendrick would like to edit an additional volume based on that underlying theme.

References

Kirman, A.P. (1992). "Whom or What Does the Representative Individual Represent?" *Journal of Economic Perspectives* 6(2) (Spring): 117–136.

McGuckin, R.H., and A.P. Reznek. (1993). "Research with Economic Microdata: The Census Bureau's Center for Economic Studies." *Business Economics* (July): 52–58.

Postner, H.H. (1986) "Microbusiness Accounting and Macroeconomic Accounting: The Limits to Consistency." *Review of Income and Wealth* 32(3) (September): 217–244.

Postner, H.H. (1993). "The Canadian Statistical Infrastructure System: Main Issues for the Public Sector." Paper prepared for Government and Competitiveness Reference, Queen's University Economic Project, Ottawa, January.

Statistics Canada. (1993). *Catalogue 1993*. Catalogue No. 11-204E, Library Services Division, Ottawa.

Stoker, T.M. (1993). "Empirical Approaches to the Problem of Aggregation over Individuals." *Journal of Economic Literature* 31(4) (December): 1827–1874.

Van Tongeren, J., and C. Hannig. (1989). *Compilation of Integrated National Accounts and the Use of Micro Computers* (4th rev.). New York: Statistical Office of the United Nations.

13 RELIABILITY AND ACCURACY OF QUARTERLY GDP ESTIMATES: A REVIEW

Allan H. Young

Most users are aware that national economic accounts do not provide precise measurements, given that the compilers release a stream of revisions. To make intelligent use of such measurements, the user needs to be aware of the nature and magnitude of the errors. Knowledge of the errors may also help compilers develop more accurate estimates. This essay concerns assessment of the reliability and accuracy of quarterly gross domestic product (GDP) estimates, illustrated by the quarterly expenditure-side estimates of GDP in the U.S. economic accounts. These estimates, which are compiled by the Bureau of Economic Analysis (BEA) of the Department of Commerce, are based on a wide variety of source data that originate in various government agencies and to some extent in private organizations.

Figure 13.1 presents an overview of the estimates of U.S. GDP for 1978–1992. For each quarter, it shows the first and each successive "current" estimate and the "latest available" estimate of the quarterly percentage change.[1] The chart shows that most of the time the current estimates correctly indicate the direction of economic activity and whether activity is accelerating or decelerating. There is no doubt, however, that the current estimates have been misleading on occasion. For example, in

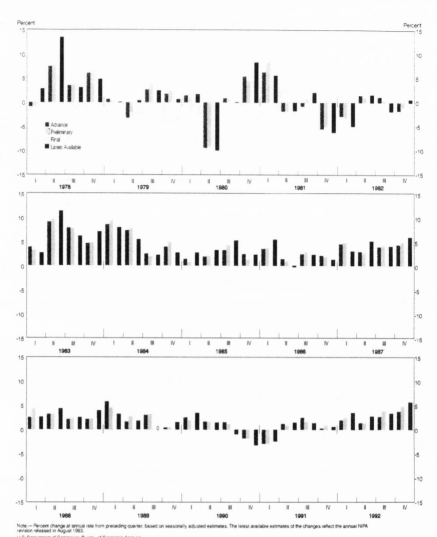

Figure 13.1.   Successive Estimates of Quarterly Changes in Real GDP

Source: U.S. Department of Commerce. Bureau of Economic Analysis.

Note. Percent change at annual rate from preceding quarter: based on seasonally adjusted estimates. The latest available estimates of the changes reflect the annual NIPA revision released in August 1993.

the second quarter of 1978, they showed a robust increase of 7.5 percent at an annual rate that was later revised up to an almost unprecedented increase of 13.5 percent. Of a more serious nature from the standpoint of a policymaker is that the current estimates understated the severity of the recent recession by missing the downturn in the third quarter of 1990 and understating the decline in the fourth quarter.[2]

Reliability refers to the revisions in the estimates. Revisions come about for four reasons: (1) replacement of preliminary source data with later data, (2) replacement of judgmental projections with source data, (3) changes in definitions or estimating procedures, and (4) updating of the base year in the constant-dollar estimates.

Accuracy refers to the total measurement error, which arises primarily from error in the source data and secondarily from the estimating procedures that utilize the source data. On the assumption that the later source data are more accurate, revisions provide a partial measure of the total measurement error in the initial estimates. The remainder of the error—what remains in the final estimates—can only be partially observed at best.

One should keep in mind that the usefulness of the national economic accounts for analysis and policymaking cannot be summarized entirely by a single, or by a few, measures of reliability or accuracy. Such an approach, which is the one taken in this essay, overemphasizes the use of GDP as a global indicator of the direction of the economy at the expense of another equally important use of the national economic accounts. This other use is as an analytical tool that conveys a summary picture of the interactions of the various sectors of the economy. To evaluate all aspects of the use of the accounts as an analytical tool is no easy matter. Development of statistical measures of the reliability of the composition of GDP, as discussed in this article, is a step in that direction.

This essay does not consider how the reliability and accuracy of the GDP estimates might be increased through the development and use of additional and improved source data. It generally assumes that the maintenance and improvement of estimating procedures and source data will be continued.

Given the nature of the source data and the estimating procedures, there is no clear distinction between maintenance and improvement. Maintenance may be defined as including (1) timely incorporation of source data from ongoing statistical programs, (2) development of substitute approaches using existing data sources, perhaps with minor extensions or modifications, when the preferred data source disappears or becomes inappropriate, and (3) extension of the estimates using existing data sources to cover emerging products and industries. Improvement may be defined as development and use of major new data sources or estimating techniques that close gaps in coverage or represent substantial improvement compared with existing methodologies. Deferred maintenance may be assumed to lead to less accurate estimates; catching up on maintenance or undertaking improvement may be assumed to lead to increased accuracy.

The importance of stepping up the rate of maintenance and improvement is recognized as a priority in U.S. economic statistics.[3] However, this priority competes with other statistical and nonstatistical priorities within the federal government that place limits on the extent of improvement that may realistically be expected. There also are limits from the lack of certain types of information in business and household records. For example, some smaller businesses do not keep inventory records on a more frequent than annual basis.

Finally, findings concerning reliability and accuracy of the existing national economic accounts will by and large continue to be relevant as BEA moves toward the *SNA*. Although a new set of accounts would contain new definitions and concepts, its statistical implementation to a large extent would use the same source data and estimating techniques as now used.

Section 13.1 briefly describes how the U.S. estimates are prepared. Section 13.2 considers the various sources of error. Section 13.3 reviews the results of a recent BEA study of the reliability and accuracy of the quarterly expenditure-side estimates of GDP. Section 13.4 briefly considers prospects for improving the reliability and accuracy of the estimates through use of existing information.

13.1. How the Estimates Are Prepared

13.1.1. Estimating Schedule

GDP estimates for each quarter are prepared in the United States on a schedule that calls for three successive "current" estiamtes—advance, preliminary, and final—and for subsequent estimates prepared as part of annual and comprehensive NIPA revisions. The advance estimate is prepared about twenty-five days after the end of the quarter. For most components, the estimate is based on source data for either two or three months of the quarter. In most cases, however, the source data for the second and third months of the quarter are not final and are subject to revison by the issuing agencies. Where source data are not available, the estimate is based primarily on the estimator's judgment.

One month later, the advance estimate is replaced by the preliminary estimate, which is typcially based on source data for all three months of the quarter. However, in some instances, the source data used for the preliminary estimates, particularly the data for the third month of the quarter, are subject to further revision.

One month later, the preliminary estimate is replaced by the final estimate, which incorporates revisions in source data for the third month of the quarter and quarterly source data for some components.

Each quarterly estimate is subject to three successive annual revisions. The first annual revision incorporates further revisions in the monthly or quarterly source data and introduces some annual source data. The second and third annual revisions incorporate a broad range of annual source data. Each quarterly estimate is also subject to one or more comprehensive revisions, in which information from the economic and demographic censuses is incorporated.

13.1.2. Types of Source Information

More complete and more accurate information is generally available on an annual basis than on a quarterly or monthly basis. In many cases, annual data are based on larger samples or represent a complete universe count. In addition, annual data often correspond more closely to the desired definitions and therefore require less adjusting, or they may contain more information for making the necessary adjustments. As a result of these factors, quarterly estimates are obtained either by interpolating between annual estimates or by extrapolating from the most recent annual estimate.

Similarly, the annual estimates in many instances represent interpolations or extrapolations of the more complete and accurate information available in the quinquennial economic censuses. This information provides the basis for the benchmark input-output tables prepared by BEA in which the output of each product is fully accounted for either as an input into further production or as final demand, thereby providing the most accurate estimates of the level of GDP.

The quarterly and monthly indicators that are used as interpolators and extrapolators are based largely on monthly or quarterly sample surveys conducted by various government agencies. Some exceptions are the budgetary data from the Treasury and Defense Department, which are used to estimate federal government purchases, and the tabulations of export and import documents filed with the Customs Service, which are used to estimate merchandise trade. Another type of exception occurs if no suitable monthly or quarterly data are available, for example, data for some types of consumer purchases of services and for most state and local government purchases. In such cases, the quarterly estimates are obtained by interpolation and extrapolation using annual data or related information.

The estimation is carried out at a very detailed level. There are about 2,500 annual components and 1,000 quarterly components. A summary of the source data used for the GDP estimates is included each year in the *Survey of Current Business* article that presents the annual GDP revision (see pages 31–42 of the August 1993 *Survey*). A list of methodological papers is available in "A Look at How BEA Presents the NIPA's" in the February 1994 *Survey* and in the annual *Users' Guide*, which is available on request from the Bureau.

13.2. Sources of Error

The GDP estimates contain several kinds of error. Error arises from the sampling errors and biases in the monthly, quarterly and annual surveys and from biases and other errors in the annual and periodic universe counts that provide source data. Error also arises because much of the source data do not fully meet the requirments of the national economic accounts in terms of coverage, timing, and valuation and because the stratagems employed by BEA to compensate in these situations can only partially succeed. In addition, although seasonal adjustment removes a type of unwanted variation, it introduces error into all the vintages. Finally, in the constant-dollar estimates, the procedures used to separate value change into its price and quantity components also introduce error.[4] The above types of error affect all the vintages of estimates—from the advance to the latest available. The only type of error that does not affect all the vintages is one that arises from the use of judgment in the advance and preliminary GDP estimates where source data are not yet available for some components.

The discussion that follows is not intended to be an exhaustive enumeration of errors but is intended, partly through the presentation of examples, to convey a sense of the complex nature of the error in GDP.

13.2.1. Sampling Error

Sampling error accounts for a large part of the revision between the successive current estimates of GDP, although nonsampling error and late responses are also factors. Sampling error is probably less important than other types of error as a determinant of the revisions between the final current estimates and the later estimates and as a determinant of the accuracy of all the estimates.

13.2.2. Other Survey Errors

A particularly troublesome and widespread type of error in sample surveys is the delay between the births and deaths of business firms and the reflection of these events in the survey. More often than not, such delays result in downward bias until corrected. In many surveys, such corrections are introduced only periodically when a new universe is established. At such a point, corrections are carried back to earlier periods by wedging the new level back to the previous universe level because there is no information available to establish the annual and quarterly pattern for the corrections. To the extent that the actual pattern of births and deaths differs from the assumed pattern, the procedure fails to correct for the cyclical pattern of the error and part it remains in the latest available estimates.

Table 13.1 illustrates the potential for error that arises if corrections for births and deaths are introduced only with considerable delay. The first three lines in the table compare the estimates of manufacturers' shipments for 1983–1986 as obtained in the Annual Survey of Manufactures and the estimates after they were revised to reflect the new universe level from the 1987 Census of Manufactures. The revisions shown in the third line—ranging from 0.8 to 1.0 percentage points of the annual changes—indicate the pattern of births and deaths assumed in the correction.

The next two lines show a hypothetical pattern in which the effect of births and deaths was less than the assumed correction in the first two years and more in the last two years. The last line shows the error that would arise from the use of the assumed pattern if the hypothetical pattern was correct. Given that the hypothetical pattern of births and deaths is reasonable, it is clear that delayed corrections can result in substantial revisions as well as errors that remain in the latest available estimates. The quarterly revisions would average the same size as the annual counterparts, but could be considerably larger in some quarters.

Table 13.1.   Manufacturers' shipments

	(Billions of dollars)					*(Percent change)*			
	1982	*1983*	*1984*	*1986*	*1987*	*1983*	*1984*	*1985*	*1986*
Published	1,960	2,055	2,254	2,280	2,260	4.8	9.7	1.2	−0.9
Revised Census	1,960	2,071	2,288	2,334	2,336	5.7	10.5	2.0	0.1
Revision Census	—	16	34	54	76	0.9	0.8	0.8	1.0
Revised hypothetical	1,960	2,062	2,274	2,324	2,336	5.2	10.3	2.2	0.5
Revision hypothetical	—	7	20	44	76	0.4	0.6	1.0	1.4
Error hypothetical	—	10	5	−5	−12	0.5	0.2	−0.2	−0.4

Source: Lines 1 and 2 are from appendix D of U.S. Bureau of Census Manufacturers' Shipments, Inventories, and Orders: 1982–1990 M3-1(90) (Washington, DC: U.S. Government Printing Office, 1991).

13.2.3. Coverage

Another particularly troublesome error—one that is perhaps best characterized as an error in coverage—arises from the misreporting of income and expenses and nonfiling of tax returns. Although BEA adjusts for misreporting and nonfiling, the adjustments are developed from information that is only available periodically—with the exception of corporate profits, the most recent information is for 1988 or earlier. Because little is known about how taxpayer misreporting and nonfiling may vary with respect to either changes in tax laws and regulations or business conditions, the annual and quarterly pattern, particularly since 1988, is based largely on judgement and is subject to considerable error. Unlike the problem of births and deaths of business firms, the effect of misreporting and nonfiling is largely confined to the income-side estimates.[5]

The emergence of new products and industries also leads to errors in coverage. There is likely to be a delay until such products or industries are adequately covered. Recent examples include the emergence of expenditures by consumers for VCR rentals and paid child care and the emergence of international trade in various types of services. With the exception of certain international financial services, new surveys have been developed or existing surveys modified to provide information on these new activities. As a consequence of the delay in coverage, especially in the case of international services, the historical GDP series will always contain extrapolations of the first survey-based estimates to earlier periods that introduce some degree of annual and quarterly error.

13.2.4. Timing

The recording of imports and exports of merchandise provide two examples of timing error. The trade flows are recorded by Customs when goods cross the border. To the extent that there is a discrepancy between the recording of the import or export and the corresponding recording of the withdrawal or addition in business inventories, one type of timing error is continually present. It is relatively unimportant as long as the "float" tends to be constant. The other error will arise if the Customs documents are not placed in the proper month when they are tabulated. Very large errors of this type occurred in the mid-1980s as Customs was faced with a rapidly increasing volume of imports and was unable to transmit all the documents promptly to the Census Bureau for statistical tabulation. The corrections to the quarterly GDP changes in 1983 and 1984, which were incorporated in December 1985, were quite large. For 1984, they averaged 2.4 percentage points at an annual rate; that for the fourth quarter of 1984 was 4.1 percentage points.

A third example is the error that arises from the reporting of some annual source data by business firms on a fiscal year, rather than a calendar year. Even though adjustments may be developed to place the data on a calendar year basis, the results differ from those that would be obtained with calendar year reporting. This error affects the estimates of personal consumption expenditures, producers' durable equipment and change in business inventories, which are based on source data from the Census Bureau, and estimates of some income-side components, which are based on tabulations of business tax returns by the Internal Revenue Service.

13.2.5. Seasonal Adjustment

Even if the source data were free of error on a seasonally unadjusted basis, seasonal adjustment would introduce error because of inherent limitations in modeling the underlying seasonal variation. Some reduction has been achieved over time in that part of the error represented by revisions to the seasonal factors through the use of concurrent seasonal adjustment and by combining ARIMA methods with the ratio-to-moving-average method of seasonal adjustment. However, this part of the error is still of considerable magnitude. The part that remains in the latest available estimates is indeterminate.[6]

The effect of revisions in seasonal factors may be approximated at the aggregate level by comparing two seasonal adjustments of total GDP where one adjustment contains additional years of data. When three or more additional years of data are added, the average absolute revision in the quarterly changes in the seasonal factors in the period 1983 to 1988 is 0.8 percentage point at an annual rate, which is about one-half the size of the total revision from the current estimates to the latest available estimate of GDP.

13.2.6. Separation of Price and Quantity Change

Some of the most difficult measurement problems associated with the national economic accounts arise in the derivation of real output, for which it is necessary to separate value change into its price and quantity components. Price change is defined as the change in the price of a good or service of fixed specification. In measuring the price change, it is necessary to remove the element of the observed price change that is associated with a change in the characteristics of the product—that is, with a change in quality. For products that are undergoing rapid technological change, the information required to make this separation may be substantial and difficult to acquire. The introduction of new products also presents difficult measurement problems. Such problems are discussed in a recent set of articles in the *Monthly Labor Review* of the Bureau of Labor Statistics and were also the subject of a workshop of the NBER Conference for Research in Income and Wealth (U.S. Department of Labor, 1993; Foss, Manser, and Young, 1993).

In addition to errors that arise in the measurement of price and quantity change at the detailed component level, the index formula used to obtain the GDP aggregate may not be appropriate and may be viewed as a source of error. This source of error is discussed in Section 13.4.

13.2.7. Judgmental Projections

The use of judgment where source data are not yet available is an obvious source of error in the advance and preliminary estimates. However, the importance of this error is smaller than many users may imagine.

If the contribution of each month of source data is given an equal weight, judgment is used in lieu of source data in the advance estimate for about 40 percent of the GDP value; in the preliminary estimate, for about 20 percent of the value; and in the final estimate, about 10 percent of the value. However, as discussed in the next part, the contribution of each monthly change does not receive equal weight in the determination of the quarterly change. Consequently, judgment plays a smaller role than suggested by the above percentages. Further, the judgemental projections are not subject to certain errors that are present in the later estimates.

13.3. GDP Revisions, 1978–1991

BEA completed a major study of the reliability of the expenditure-side estimates of GDP in 1993 (Young, 1993b). The study examined revisions between the current estimates and the latest available GDP estimates for the period 1978 to 1991 and analyzed revisions among the current estimates through 1992. The latest available estimates used in the study were those available before the annual revision in August 1993.

13.3.1. Historical Record of Revisions

As part of the study, revisions for 1978–1991 were compared with those from four earlier studies by BEA, some of which extended as far back as 1947 (for references to the earlier studies, see Young, 1993b). Table 13.2 compares two revision measures from the studies: dispersion and bias. The measures are calculated as follows. Let P represent the percentage change in the current estimates, L the percentage change in the latest available estimates, and n the number of quarterly changes.

Dispersion is the average of the absolute values of the revisions:

$$\Sigma|(P - L)|/n.$$

Bias is the average of the revisions:

$$\Sigma(P - L)/n.$$

Because of the shift from GNP to GDP as the featured aggregate in the 1991 comprehensive revision, the 1993 study examined revisions for both

Table 13.2. Measures of revisions in quarterly changes in GNP and GDP (percentage points[a])

	Current-dollar estimates						Constant-dollar estimates[b]					
	Dispersion			Bias			Dispersion			Bias		
	Advance	Preliminary	Final	Advance	Preliminary	Final	Advance	Preliminary	Final	Advance	Preliminary	Final
Gross national product												
Study I												
1947–56*	—	3.5	—	—	-1.0	—	—	—	—	—	—	—
1947–52	—	3.3	—	—	-1.2	—	—	—	—	—	—	—
1953–56	—	2.1	—	—	-0.8	—	—	—	—	—	—	—
1957–61	—	1.2	—	—	-0.1	—	—	—	—	—	—	—
Study II												
1947–63*	—	3.1	—	—	-0.9	—	—	—	—	—	—	—
1958–63*	1.6	—	—	-0.3	—	—	—	—	—	—	—	—
1964–71	1.2	1.0	—	-0.8	-0.6	—	1.0	1.0	—	0.1	-0.2	—
Study III												
1968–72*	1.1	1.1	—	-0.7	-0.6	—	1.4	1.3	—	-0.2	-0.2	—
1973–77	2.4	2.2	—	-1.0	-0.6	—	2.0	1.8	—	-0.6	-0.4	—
1978–83	1.9	1.5	1.5	-0.8	-0.5	-0.2	1.5	1.3	1.2	-0.7	-0.5	-0.1
Study IV												
1968–77*	2.1	1.8	—	-1.0	-0.7	—	2.4	2.4	—	0	0.2	—
1978–86	1.7	1.5	1.5	-0.5	-0.3	-0.2	1.5	1.4	1.5	-0.4	-0.3	-0.2
Study V												
1978–82*	2.0	1.8	1.8	-1.0	-0.7	-0.3	1.6	1.6	1.7	-0.6	-0.4	-0.1
1983–91	1.2	1.2	1.2	-0.3	-0.2	-0.3	1.3	1.2	1.3	0	0.1	0

Gross domestic product

Study V												
1978–82*	1.9	1.8	1.8	−0.9	−0.6	−0.3	1.6	1.7	1.8	−0.5	−0.3	−0.1
1983–91	1.2	1.1	1.2	−0.2	−0.1	−0.2	1.3	1.3	1.3	0.1	0.1	0

Sources: The table is adapted from Young (1993b).

*Estimates for this period incorporate one or more comprehensive revisions.

a Calculated from quarterly percentage changes at seasonally adjusted annual rates.

b For the constant-dollar estimates, revisions in the advance estimates are for 1966–1971, and those for the preliminary estimates, 1965–1971.

Note: See the text for definitions of the revision measures. The measures were calculated using the revisions between the current estimates and the latest available estimates. The latest available estimates used for each study are as follows:

Study I. The first line uses as latest available estimates those from the comprehensive revision in 1958, which incorporated information from the 1954 Economic Censuses. The next three lines use as latest available estimates those from the annual revisions in 1953, 1957, and 1963, respectively; in general, these estimates had not undergone a comprehensive revision.

Study II. The first two lines use as latest available estimates those from the comprehensive revision in 1965, which incorporated information from the 1958 Economic Censuses; the 1958–1963 period is included because the "preliminary" estimate was introduced in 1958. The third line uses as "latest available" estimates those from successive annual revisions.

Study III. The first line uses as latest available estimates those from the comprehensive revisions in 1976 and 1980, which incorporated information from the 1963, 1967, and 1972 Economic Censuses. The second line uses as "latest available" estimates those from the comprehensive revision in 1980, which did not fully incorporate economic census information in that the 1977 Economic Censuses had not yet been fully incorporated. The third line uses as latest available estimates those from the annual revisions in 1982 and 1984.

Study IV. The first line uses as latest available estimates those from the comprehensive revision in 1985, which incorporated information from the 1977 Economic Censuses. The second line uses as latest available estimates for 1978–1982 those from the comprehensive revision in 1985, which did not fully incorporate economic census information in that the 1982 Economic Censuses had not yet been fully incorporated, for 1983–1985 those from the annual revision in 1985, and for 1986 those available prior to the annual revision in 1987.

Study V. The first line uses as latest available estimates those from the comprehensive revision in 1991, which incorporated information from the 1982 Economic Censuses. The second line uses as "latest available" estimates for 1983–1988 those from the comprehensive revision in 1991, which did not fully incorporate economic census information in that the 1987 Economic Censuses had not yet been fully incorporated, and for 1989–1991 those available prior to the annual revision in 1993.

aggregates, so as to provide a basis for consistent comparisons as well as for an assessment of revisions in the currently featured aggregate. In general, revisions in the two aggregates are very similar.

Both the 1993 study and the one immediately preceding it did not incorporate two types of adjustments that were made in the earlier studies. These adjustments removed the effect of the changes in definitions of the GNP components and of the change in base year in the constant-dollar estimates that were made in comprehensive revisions. Consequently, the contribution to the revision that comes from source data was not as well isolated in the two more recent studies.

In order to interpret the revision measures, it is necessary to take into account two aspects of the estimation process. First, within a given study, reduction in revision size over time is not evidence that reliability is increasing. This type of reduction, which can be observed within each study, reflects different vintages of the latest available estimates.

Second, the effect on the revision measure of a change in source data or estimating procedure, which one may assume affects the accuracy of the estimates, depends on the vintage in which the change is incorporated. For example, an improvement in the current estimates results in a per-manent decrease in revision size, while an improvement in the latest available estimates results in a permanent increase in revision size. Improvement in both the current and latest available estimates results in little change. Improvement that is introduced retrospectively into the latest available estimates, *as is often the case*, results in an increase in revision size for a period of years until the improvement is also reflected in the current estimates. *Thus one cannot assume a close correspondence between changes in the size of revisions and changes in accuracy.*

To allow for the different vintages, revisions were calculated separately in each of the studies for the period in which the latest available estimates were taken from a comprehensive revision and for the more recent period in which they were from an annual revision. In the 1993 study, the most recent year for which the estimates fully reflect a comprehensive revision is 1982. The measures that reflect comprehensive revisions are identified in Table 13.2 with an asterisk following the time period designation.

It is much more difficult to allow for the effect of improvements incorporated in different vintages. The limited amount of detail retained in the historical record imposes a limitation. Further, consideration of the effect of improvements on the accuracy of the estimates necessarily involves informed judgment and speculation because, as noted previously, total error is unobserved.

13.3.2. *Accounting for the Variations in Dispersion,* *1947–1991*

The following review of the revision record is limited to the current-dollar estimates. For the shorter period for which they are available, the picture presented by the constant-dollar measures is similar.

One can observe considerable variation in Table 13.2 in dispersion in the revisions that fully reflect a comprehensive revision. The sharp decline following 1947–1956, no doubt, reflects both a learning curve faced by the estimators in the first years and improvements in source data. It is reasonable to conclude that the decline in dispersion corresponds with increase in the accuracy of both the initial and final estimates subsequent to 1957.[7]

The increase from the relatively low level in the 1960s reflects the volatile economic conditions in the mid-1970s, which required estimators to use more judgmental techniques in preparing the current estimates. One may deduce from the information in studies 3 and 4 that, if dispersion had been calculated in the fourth study for 1973–1977, it would have been about 3.0 percentage points.

As a result of the shortcomings exposed by the volatile conditions, new cource data and various improved techniques were introduced in the 1980 and 1985 comprehensive revisions. Some of these improvements, which were introduced retrospectively into the estimates for the 1970s and from then on incorporated in the current and latest available estimates, are best viewed as working to restore lost accuracy. Others worked to increase accuracy. The decline in dispersion in 1978–1982 may be viewed as a return to a more normal level.

The upward drift from 1968–1972 to 1978–1982 in dispersion is probably not evidence that the accuracy of the initial estimates declined over this period. It likely reflects a higher rate of development and retrospective introduction of improvements in the 1991 comprehensive revision than earlier. In light of the improved estimation procedures and source data that over time have been introduced, it is possible that the accuracy of the initial and final estimates of quarterly change have increased since the 1960s. In considering this question, it is important to note that *changes* are not affected as much as *levels* by long-term developments, such as the gradual shift to services, which, at least in real terms, may not be adequately measured.

The learning curve and the problems the estimators encountered in the 1970s are also apparent in the current-dollar revisions in which the latest available estimates do not reflect a comprehensive revision. However, from 1957–1961 to 1983–1991 there has been little upward drift. This is consistent with the fact that few retrospective improvements are introduced in annual revisions.

Assuming the future holds no volatile economic conditions of a type for which the statistical system is not well designed, such as occurred in the 1970s, it is reasonable to expect that revisions in the 1990s will be about the same size as in 1978–1991. If the rate of maintenance and improvement were to slack off, revisions would become somewhat smaller; however, one would have to assume that a price was being paid in terms of accuracy which would gradually become apparent.

13.3.3. Dispersion and Bias, 1978–1991

The most interesting finding in the 1993 study was that dispersion was about the same size in the advance estimates of GDP as in the preliminary and final current estimates. This was the case not only for total GDP but for the major components as well. This finding suggested that one or both of the later current estimates of GDP might be discontinued without much loss of information.

Table 13.3 summarizes some of the results that led to the conclusion that three current estimates may not be necessary. For current-dollar GDP, dispersion declines only slightly over the successive estimates. For the constant-dollar estimates, dispersion actually increases slightly. For the major GDP components, the advance estimates in many cases provided a smaller measure of dispersion than did the preliminary or final estimates. In 1978–1982, the advance estimates provided the smallest dispersion in four of the eleven current-dollar components—PCE nondurables and services, residential investment, and federal government purchases—which accounted for almost 60 percent of GDP. In 1983–1991, the advance estimates provided the smallest dispersion in three components—PCE services, residential investment, and state and local government purchases—which accounted for over 40 percent of GDP. The record for the advance constant-dollar estimates is about the same as that for the current-dollar estimates, though the share of GDP for which the estimates perform the best is smaller for 1983–1991.

Bias was not large enough in either the current- or constant-dollar GDP estimates to be statistically significant under assumptions of normality at the 5-percent confidence level. In the current-dollar estimates, bias was negative in both 1978–1982 and 1983–1991. In the constant-dollar estimates, bias was less negative than in current-dollar GDP for

Table 13.3. Summary of dispersion and bias of current estimates of GDP

	Dispersion (percentage points)[a]				Bias (percentage points)[a]			
	Current dollars		Constant dollars		Current dollars		Constant dollars	
Estimate	1978–1982	1983–1991	1978–1982	1983–1991	1978–1982	1983–1991	1978–1982	1983–1991
Advance	1.93	1.17	1.64	1.25	−0.93	−0.21	−0.53	0.09
Preliminary	1.82	1.14	1.72	1.27	−0.55	−0.12	−0.28	0.13
Final	1.82	1.15	1.75	1.33	−0.34	−0.24	−0.06	0.03

Components with smallest dispersion

	Number				Percent of GDP[b]			
	Current dollars		Constant dollars		Current dollars		Constant dollars	
	1978–1982	1983–1991	1978–1982	1983–1991	1978–1982	1983–1991	1978–1982	1983–1991
Advance	4	3	5	4	59	44	68	24
Preliminary	1	6	1	6	6	32	9	58
Final	6	2	5	1	35	24	23	18
Total	11	11	11	11	100	100	100	100

Source: BEA revision study (Young, 1993a).
a Calculated from quarterly percentage changes at seasonally adjusted annual rates.
b Calculated from the absolute 1991 values of the current-dollar components.

1978–1982 and slightly positive for 1983–1991. This damping of the current-dollar bias reflects the rebasing of the constant-dollar estimates.[8] The current estimates for 1978–1985 were stated in 1972 dollars, and those for 1986–1991 in 1982 dollars; the latest available estimates are stated in 1987 dollars. In both current- and constant-dollars, there were some instances of significant bias in major GDP components.

13.3.4. The Good Performance of the Advance Estimates

The 1993 study devoted considerable attention to why dispersion for the advance estimates is not considerably larger than that for the later current estimates. The explanation involves two seldom recognized factors: (1) the small role of source data for the second and third months of a quarter in determining the quarterly change and (2) errors in later estimates that are not contained in the advance estimates.

The role played by the data for second and third months of the quarter in determining the change from the previous quarter is small. The change from the second to the third month receives a weight of only one-ninth in the determination of quarterly change. The weight of the second and third monthly changes together is only one-third. The weight of the first monthly change is another one-third, and the second and third monthly changes in the previous quarter receive the remaining one-third.[9] Consequently, errors neither in the preliminary source data for the second and third months of a quarter nor in the judgmental projections used in lieu of source data affect the quarterly change as much as one might intuitively expect.[10]

One type of error that is not present in the judgmental projections is the error that seasonal adjustment introduces into the source data that replaces the projections in the final current quarterly estimate. The judgmental projections do not contain this type of error because they are developed on a seasonally adjusted basis. The seasonal adjustment factors for the current year are derived from the seasonal patterns of recent preceding years (and for concurrent seasonal adjustment, the seasonal pattern of the current year). The factors are revised as additional data become available, and they eventually reflect the average seasonal pattern of a period of years that extends symmetrically on either side of the given year. The difference between the initial estimate of the seasonal factor and the final estimate prepared some years later is an error that becomes part of the revision in the final current estimate. To the extent that they are based on judgmental projections, the advance and preliminary quarterly estimates do not contain this error. It is possible for this error to be the same size or larger than the error in the judgmental projection.

Other errors that are contained only in the later current estimates are component specific and they can arise only if the judgmental projection is replaced in the later current estimates with an interim quarterly estimating procedure (and source data) that is then replaced in the annual revision with still another procedure. In such a case it is possible for the revision of the advance estimate to be smaller than that of the later current estimates.

The study uncovered several examples of such situations in PCE services and in Federal Government purchases. In the case of PCE services, the interim procedures have been improved or replaced. However, the study also found a tendency for the advance estimates of PCE services to perform well in the most recent years of data, suggesting that either some old problems remain undetected or new ones are emerging in which the approach used for the later current estimates should be either improved or replaced with judgment.

It is possible that the advance estimates of GDP and its major components also benefit more from offsetting errors in the detailed components than the later current estimates; that is, the revisions of the advance estimates may be more negatively (or less positively) correlated than those of the preliminary and final estimates. An exploration of this avenue would have to await development of a more detailed database.

The question of whether all the later current estimates are necessary has been raised from time to time by other investigators (Cole, 1969; McNees, 1986; Duncan and Gross, 1993). In the past, BEA has chosen not to reduce the number of current estimates for several reasons. As may be observed in Table 13.2, in some periods the evidence was mixed. Also, it was apparent that many users would be concerned with whether the later estimates measure the composition of GDP in some sense better than the advance estimates. This is an especially important issue to forecasters because the composition of the latest quarter's GDP change can affect the trajectory of the forecast. In addition, it seemed likely that some users would want a current estimate each month in which there was a substantial body of new or revised source data that could be incorporated.

To sum up: The 1993 study provides considerable additional evidence in favor of discontinuing one or more estimates and explores for the first time why the advance estimate performs well. In light of the relatively good performance of the advance estimates at the major component level, the study also recommends that the issue of whether the composition is better measured in the later current estimates is worthy of empirical evaluation. To assess the demand for continuation of the three successive current estimates will require input from several types of users.

13.4. Prospects for Increasing Reliability and Accuracy Using Existing Information

Researchers have addressed the question of increasing the reliability and accuracy of the GDP estimates through use of existing information from several angles. One approach is to consider whether the early estimates are efficient—that is, whether there is information available at the time the estimate was made that could be used to modify it so that its subsequent revision would be smaller. Such a question may be asked of either the aggregate or the detailed component estimates.

Another approach attempts to make use of the statistical discrepancy, which is the difference between the expenditure-side estimate of GDP and the income-side estimate of GDP (gross domestic income), to derive a more accurate estimate. This approach may take the form of the user discounting the expenditure-side change to some extent when it diverges greatly from the income-side change. It could also take the form of averaging the income- and expenditure-side estimates and distributing the discrepancy among detailed components. The revised *SNA* is silent with respect to whether the compiling agency should conform the two measures by averaging them.

A third approach is quite different than the others. It is the use of a more appropriate index formula than the Laspeyres (fixed-weighted) formula to derive what may be considered to be a more accurate measure of real GDP.

13.4.1. Efficient Estimates

Various investigators have considered whether the GDP estimates are efficient estimates. In the late 1980s several investigators used the data base from BEA's third study of revisions to explore whether the GDP revisions were correlated either with economic information from outside the national economic accounts or with previous or current estimates or revisions of GDP. Of particular note was work by John Scadding that found through the use of Kallman filtering that the current estimates of real GNP contained a measurement error that might be removed to provide a more accurate prediction of the latest available estimate

(Scadding, 1988; this reference also reviews several earlier investigations).

In terms of dispersion, the measurement error that might be anticipated amounted to about 0.2 percentage point of the revision in the change in real GDP (estimated from the variance measures presented by Scadding). However, the results were not tested outside the sample period and subsequent calculations using more recent data from the fifth revision study do not indicate a similar relationship.

At the detailed component level, consideration of efficiency amounts to ascertaining whether the estimation procedures are as good as they might be. Obviously, a detailed consideration of this question is beyond the scope of the essay. Note may be taken, however, of a systematic examination of a small part of the question. Albert Hirsch and Michael Mann at BEA compared the advance estimates of certain import and export components with estimates in which econometric-based techniques were used in lieu of judgmental projections (Hirsch and Mann, 1993). The study found that the use of judgmental projections compared favorably with econometric techniques and did not indicate that revisions might be reduced. One should not attempt to generalize these results to other components of GDP.

13.4.2. The Statistical Discrepancy

Under ideal conditions, the statistical discrepancy would indicate the average size of the total error in the current-dollar estimates of GDP. Two factors, however, tend to invalidate the statistical discrepancy as an indicator of total error. First, errors on the income- and expenditure-sides are not completely independent, partly because some source data enter on both sides and partly because some of the estimation techniques may be assumed to give rise to similar errors on both sides. For example, seasonal adjustment may give rise to similar errors because of a common seasonal pattern on the two sides. Likewise, errors arising from births and deaths of business firms, may be reflected similarly in both sides.

Second, in the process of preparing the estimates, BEA takes various actions that affect the statistical discrepancy. The actions consist of modifying estimates where there is a troublesome swing in the discrepancy and at times concentrating efforts to improve the estimates, that is, uncover error, on one side of the account. Both types of actions operate to reduce the size of the statistical discrepancy relative to the total error. However, in modifying estimates BEA may reduce but does not eliminate large swings in the statistical discrepancy. Thus the statistical discrepancy may be viewed as retaining some value as an indicator of error.

Some users of the U.S. GDP estimates anticipate that the expenditure-side change will be revised in the direction of the income-side change when the statistical discrepancy shows a large swing. This approach rests on the assumption that, as the estimates are revised, the income- and expenditure-side estimates will converge and the statistical discrepancy become smaller. As shown in Table 13.4, there is some convergence between the preliminary and final current estimates and between those estimates and the first annual estimates. However, the later vintages do not converge. The average size of the change in the discrepancy in the second and third annual estimates and the latest available estimates is larger than that in the current estimates. Likewise, in terms of levels, the discrepancy in the latest available estimates is larger than the current estimates.

Thus the statistical discrepancy is a weak reed on which to base anticipations of future revisions. Over spans of one to several quarters, the swing in the statistical discrepancy anticipates the direction of the revision in the change in GDP no more than 60 or 70 percent of the time. The record for periods where the swings are large is about the same.

The lack of convergence in the statistical discrepancy is consistent with the estimation process that is used in which the later vintages of estimates are obtained by conforming the quarterly indicators to the annual and quinquennial source data. Such a pattern could also emerge if actions to control the statistical discrepancy affected the current estimates more than the later estimates. It is not clear whether BEA actions have such an effect. In any case, achievement of a "better behaved" statistical

Table 13.4. Average size of quarterly statistical discrepancy as a percent of GDP, 1978–1987

Estimate	Changes	Levels
Preliminary	0.65	0.18
Final	0.64	0.16
First annual	0.55	0.14
Second annual	0.72	0.20
Third annual	0.76	0.17
Latest available	0.91	0.36

Note: Quarterly changes are at annual rates. The averages are calculated without regard to sign.

discrepancy depends upon developing more accurate preliminary source data.

As noted previously, the income- and expenditure-side estimates may be averaged, thereby eliminating the statistical discrepancy. Given that the two estimates are of the same underlying measure, one would expect their average to be more accurate than either one alone. Martin Weale examined this approach using quarterly estimates of real GNP for 1947–1982 (Weale, 1992). He determined that, under certain error assumptions, the optimum averaging would assign a weight of 0.64 to the income side and 0.36 to the expenditure side. Calculations at BEA suggest that the procedure is not sufficiently robust with respect to the sample period or to the vintage of the estimates to prove useful without further research.

One may also inquire as to whether averaging the income- and expenditure-side estimates provide more reliable estimates. Calculations at BEA show that revisions between unweighted averages of the current estimates and the latest available estimates are 0.1 to 0.2 percentage points less than those in the expenditure-side measure for 1978–1987. The extent of reduction is not very sensitive to variations in the weights.

13.4.3. The Appropriate Index Formula

The importance of the index formula used to derive real GDP was highlighted with the introduction in 1985 of a hedonic price index for computers in the U.S. national economic accounts. To the extent that changes in prices and quantities are moderate, the choice of index formula is not of major importance. However, the computer price index did not move at all closely with other prices—declining steadily at about 15 percent per year—and the output of computers increased sharply. As a consequence, use of a single set of fixed price weights was no longer defensible in measuring growth over long periods or in comparing the amplitudes of business cycles.

BEA has introduced two alternative indexes that are more appropriate for these purposes than the featured fixed-weighted measure in which quantities in all periods are weighted with 1987 prices using the Laspeyres index formula (Triplett, 1992; Young, 1992, 1993a). It is likely that these measures will be used increasingly as users become familiar with them.

One alternative—the chain-type annual-weighted index—uses an adaptation of the Fisher ideal quantity index with annual weights to calculate both annual and quarterly changes. The other alternative—a benchmark-years-weighted quantity index—also uses an adaptation of the

Fisher Ideal quantity index but with adjacent benchmark years as weights. (Benchmark years are used because, for components of GDP that incorporate information from the quinquennial economic censuses, the price and quantity estimates are considered to be more accurate than those for other years.) So far, the alternatives have been extended back to 1959. The fixed-weighted measure is available on a quarterly basis to 1947 and on an annual basis to 1929.

The alternative indexes are consistent with the recommendations in the revised *SNA* (SNA 1993, pp. 379–383) for price and volume measures. The revised *SNA* calls for the use of either chain Fisher indexes or chain Laspeyres or Paasche indexes using annual weights as the preferred measures; it advises against quarterly weights in the chain indexes. Because there is a loss of additivity with the use of chain indexes, the *SNA* recommends the preparation of constant-dollar series using fixed weights for intervals of five to ten years as a supplementary measure. With such a scheme it is necessary to adjust either the components or the total to maintain additivity as the intervals are linked. The SNA does not recommend the use of a single set of fixed weights for a period of sixty plus years as has been the case in the U.S. national economic accounts.

For total GDP, the differences between the alternatives and the fixed-weighted measure may be summarized as follows. From 1959 to 1987, the alternatives increase at an average annual rate of 3.4 percent compared with 3.1 percent in the fixed-weighted measure. Such a difference over a span of almost thirty years represents a substantial difference in terms of economic growth. In terms of the business cycle, the alternatives show more severe contractions before 1987—more than twice as severe in 1960 and 1969–1970. Since 1987, the alternatives increase less rapidly than the fixed-weighted measure—the differences in the changes average 0.1 to 0.3 percentage point per year in the early 1990s and in some quarters are as large as 0.8 percentage point. The 1990–1991 contraction is about the same in all three measures.

Acknowledgments

This article was prepared while the author was Chief Statistician at BEA. Parts of the article were presented at the October 1993 meeting of the Atlantic Economic Society in Philadelphia PA and subsequently included in Young (1993b). Views presented in the article do not necessarily represent those of BEA or the Department of Commerce. Albert Hirsch, Martin M. Marimont, Clinton P. McCully, Robert P. Parker, Jack E.

Triplett, Teresa L. Weadock, and Richard C. Zeimmer contributed to the development of the article.

Notes

1. Quarterly percentage changes of U.S. GDP are presented at annual rates, and revisions are calculated as the difference between these changes. Annual rates facilitate comparisons of changes over spans of different length. Unfortunately, they have the potential of conveying an impression that a quarterly revision is approximately four times larger than actual size. A revision from a 4 percent annual rate to a 3 percent annual rate corresponds to an actual revision in the quarterly change of about 0.25 percentage points $(1.04^{0.25} - 1.03^{0.25} = 0.243)$.

2. It is difficult to establish whether a specific estimate that was subsequently revised misled policymakers. Carol Carson and George Jaszi examined the number of times this occurred in the 1960s and 1970s. They identified six instances in which policymakers stated that the preliminary estimates had been misleading. In four of these cases, Carson and Jaszi agreed that the estimates appeared to have misstated the picture. In their opinion, there was not a strong case for misstatement in the other two instances (see Carson and Jaszi, 1986; a summary appears in Young, 1987).

3. Both the need to improve the accuracy and reliability of the national economic accounts and to align them with the revised international *System of National Accounts* were recognized as priorities in the Economic Statistics Initiative in 1991 and the first year of a multiyear funding increase was sought in the FY 1992 budget (see U.S. Department of Commerce, 1991). This effort has been continued as a funding priority in subsequent budgets submitted to Congress; to date, the various parts of the initiative have been partially funded. See also the recent study by Martin Fleming, chairman of the Statistics Committee of the National Association of Business Economists (Fleming, Jordan, and Lang, 1993).

4. For most GDP components, the separation is made in the United States by deflating expenditures using a component of the consumer, producer, or international trade price indexes that are compiled by the Bureau of Labor Statistics. Thus actions taken by BLS as well as BEA with respect to defining price and quantity determine the constant-dollar estimates.

5. The adjustments for misreporting and nonfiling were 4.6 percent of gross domestic income in 1982, 5.2 percent in 1987 and 4.6 percent in 1990. For a description of the adjustments, see Parker (1984).

6. Seasonal adjustment removes from the time series the average impact of variations that normally occur at about the same time and in about the same magnitude each year—for example, weather, holidays, and tax payment dates. In general, BEA relies on the source agency to seasonally adjust the data. A comprehensive survey of seasonal adjustment methods is provided by F.A.G. den Butter and M.M.G. Fase (see den Butter and Fase, 1991).

7. In the comprehensive revision in 1958, which incorporated source data from the 1954 Economic Censuses, many techniques that had used pre–World War II information were updated or replaced and seasonal adjustment factors were thoroughly reworked (see U.S. Department of Commerce, 1958).

8. The effect of the damping of the current-dollar bias that results from rebasing will not come into play in the recently introduced alternative measures of GDP. The constant-dollar bias in these measures will likely be about the same size as the current-dollar bias (see Young, 1993a).

9. For the derivation of these weights, see Young (1993a).

10. An interesting consequence of the small role of the second and third months of the quarter is that the reliability of the "flash" estimate, which until 1986 was prepared about fifteen days before the end of the quarter, was about the same as that of the advance estimate. As stated in the GNP news releases, the dispersion of the flash estimate was the same as that of the advance estimate (1.7 percent in constant dollars for 1974–1983) and somewhat larger than that for the preliminary and final estimates (1.5 and 1.4 percent, respectively). This revision record contradicted the statement by the Secretary of Commerce that announced the discontinuance of the flash estimate (U.S. Department of Commerce, 1986). Apparently, the decision to discontinue the estimate, in which BEA was not consulted, was based on a mistaken perception of its reliability. As the statement suggests, the decision may also have reflected a concern with the effect on financial markets in the mid-1980s of a release of GDP in "real time," as opposed to after the fact, followed by a revision one month later. With hindsight, it is apparent that the timing errors that arose in the processing of import documents in the preceding quarters contributed to the decision. These errors affected the later current estimates much more than the flash estimates but the flash estimates were assumed to be incorrect. As a consequence of the discontinuance of the flash estimate and a subsequent two-week delay introduced in 1987 to provide additional time for tabulating merchandise imports, the first estimate of the quarter is now available six weeks later than previously. Only the user can say whether such a loss of currency is harmful.

References

Carson, Carol S., and George Jaszi. (1986). *The Use of National Income and Product Accounts for Public Policy: Our Successes and Failures*. Bureau of Economic Analysis Staff Paper 43. Washington, DC: Bureau of Economic Analysis.

Cole, Rosanne. (1969). *Errors in Provisional Estimates of Gross National Product*. National Bureau of Economic Research Studies in Business Cycles No. 21.

den Butter, F.A.G., and M.M.G. Fase. (1991). *Seasonal Adjustment as a Practical Problem*. Amsterdam: Elsvier Science.

Duncan, Joseph W., and Andrew C. Gross. (1993). *Statistics for the Twenty-first Century*. New York: Dun and Bradstreet.

Fleming, Martin, John Jordan, and Kathleen M. Lang. (1993). "Measurement Error in the U.S. National Income and Product Accounts: Its Nature and Impact on Forecasts." Paper presented at the thirty-fifth Annual Meeting of the National Association of Business Economists, Chicago, Illinois, September 19–22.

Foss, Murray F., Marilyn E. Manser, and Allan H. Young (eds.). (1993). *Price Measurements and Their Uses*. National Bureau of Economic Research Studies in Income and Wealth No. 57. Chicago: University of Chicago Press.

Hirsch, Albert A., and Michael A. Mann. (1993). *An Analysis of the Use of Time-Series Models to Improve Estimates of International Transactions*. Bureau of Economic Analysis Working Paper 7. Washington, DC: Bureau of Economic Analysis.

McNees, Stephen K. (1986). "Estimating GNP: The Trade-off Between Timeliness and Accuracy." *New England Economic Review* (January/February): 3–10.

Parker, Robert P. (1984). "Improved Adjustments for Misreporting of Tax Return Information Used to Estimate the National Income and Product Accounts, 1977." *Survey of Current Business* 64 (June): 17–25.

Scadding, John. (1988). "Getting the Noise Out: Filtering Early GNP Estimates." *Economic Review* (Cleveland Federal Reserve Bank) (3rd qtr.): 24–31.

System of National Accounts 1993. (1993). Brussels: Commission of the European Communities, International Monetary Fund, Organization for Economic Cooperation and Development, United Nations, and World Bank.

Triplett, Jack E. (1992). "Economic Theory and BEA's Alternative Quantity and Price Indexes." *Survey of Current Business* 72 (April): 49–52.

U.S. Department of Commerce, Bureau of Economic Analysis (formerly Office of Business Economics). (1958). *U.S. Income and Output*. Washington, DC: U.S. Government Printing Office.

U.S. Department of Commerce. (1986). "Statement by Secretary of Commerce on the GNP Flash." Commerce News Release, January 27.

U.S. Department of Commerce, Bureau of Economic Analysis. (1991). "Improving the Quality of Economic Statistics: The 1992 Economist Statistics Initiative." *Survey of Current Business* 71 (March): 4–5.

U.S. Department of Labor, Bureau of Labor Statistics. (1993). "The Anatomy of Price Change." *Monthly Labor Review* (December): 2–62.

Weale, Martin. (1992). *Education, Externalities, Fertility, and Economic Growth*. Washington, DC: World Bank Population and Human Resources Department, 50 pp.

Young, Allan H. (1987). "Evaluation of the GNP Estimates." *Survey of Current Business* 67 (August): 18–42.

Young, Allan H. (1992). "Alternative Measures of Change in Real Output and Prices." *Survey of Current Business* 72 (April): 32–48.

Young, Allan H. (1993a). "Alternative Measures of Changes in Real Output and Prices, Quarterly Estimates for 1959–92." *Survey of Current Business* 73 (March): 31–41.

Young, Allan H. (1993b). "Reliability and Accuracy of the Quarterly Estimates of GDP." *Survey of Current Business* 73 (October): 29–43.

DISCUSSION OF CHAPTER 13
Sir Jack Hibbert

Introduction

In his essay Allan Young considers U.S. experience in the fields of reliability (measured by reference to the degree of revision) and accuracy (measured by reference to total measurement error) of seasonally adjusted quarterly real GDP estimates. The ground covered will be familiar territory to those who have grappled with the problems of compiling such statistics, but the U.S. experience may well be unique, given the long period over which their estimates have been compiled and analyzed.

The Need for Assessments of Reliability and Accuracy

Much of the essay is concerned with the many different sources of error that affect reliability and accuracy. As noted in the very first paragraph, users need to understand the nature and magnitude of errors if they are to make intelligent use of the statistics. This is obviously true, although the results of analyzing past revisions may provide the user with an ambiguous picture about the present. This is because any competent

compiler tries to use the analysis of past errors to improve current estimation methods, and, in particular, evidence of systematic bias in the
past will clearly be a poor guide to the present if account has already been
taken of it in compiling the current estimates.

The Factors Determining Levels of Reliability and Accuracy

For many users their potential use of the estimates would require higher
levels of reliability and accuracy than those that are achieved.[1] Rather
than simply tailoring use of the statistics to their existing levels of reliability and accuracy, users will press for better measurements. This is not an
unreasonable position for the consumer of a product to take, but the
difficulty, of course, is that the nonmarket production process is not able
to respond to this demand in the way that a market producer might be
expected to.

A major, and most influential, set of users of these statistics, in terms
of deciding how large the resources devoted to the production of GDP
estimates should be, are government policy and decision makers. One
fundamental question that is touched on, but not taken further in the
essay, is the degree of reliability and accuracy that would be adequate for
these users (see note 2). This is not surprising because the question of
"fitness for purpose" is extremely complex. Nevertheless, it is a question
that ought to be addressed if organization of the task of compiling such
statistics is to be tackled in a rational manner.

The complexity arises because the process of compiling the "product"
to be considered (a quarterly estimate of seasonally adjusted real GDP)
generates many by-products that are of interest in their own right and can
itself be designed in many different ways with variations in costs of
production and in the quality and quantity of by-products. Thus, although
government policy and decisionmakers can be very much involved in
influencing the levels of resources devoted to the production process,
particularly following periods when they feel they have been seriously
misled by the statistics, this influence may be exercised in an irregular and
less than scientific fashion, so that the issue of "fitness for purpose" is
never addressed in a wholly satisfactory way.

Experience in the United Kingdom

There was a long period during which the approach to compiling quarterly
GDP estimates in the United Kingdom was to take the data to be used

largely as predetermined, its availability being mainly decided by the needs of those requiring micro, rather than macro, economic data. In purely practical terms, the task of the national accounts compiler was to make the best use of such data rather than to specify what was needed in order to compile adequate GDP estimates at minimum cost (including the costs of data provision falling on businesses).

The vulnerability of this approach became apparent in the 1980s as the needs of those requiring microeconomic data were given much lower priority and efforts were made to reduce significantly the statistical form-filling burdens on business. In due course this led to increasing dissatisfaction with the quality of U.K. macroeconomic statstics and the setting up of a formal scrutiny of government economic statistics (the report of which was published on April 5, 1989). Among the many changes that stemmed from the results of this scrutiny was the introduction of targets for the reliability and accuracy of major national accounts aggregates.

Some Special Problems in Defining the Accuracy of Quarterly GDP Estimates

Timing is referred to in the essay as one of the sources of error in the estimation of GDP. For obvious reasons this source of error is liable to be more serious in the compilation of quarterly, than of annual, estimates. A particular source of difficulty within an expenditure measure is the potential mismatching of foreign trade measurements and those for changes in inventories. Steps can sometimes be taken to eliminate mismatching in the measurement of specific categories of goods (for example, large items such as ships and aircraft), but in general the problems are likely to be intractable. This can lead to the heavy discounting of large implausible quarterly movements in order to achieve consistency with the picture implied by other evidence which may be available (for example, direct measurements of domestic production). In such circumstances the assessment of accuracy becomes increasingly subjective.

The well-known types of problem associated with partitioning value changes into price and quantity components—the introduction of new and disappearance of existing products, changes in the quality of existing products, and so on—are referred to in the essay. In general these problems loom less large in the estimation of quarterly changes than in the estimation of annual or longer-term changes. There are, however, potential timing problems that can give rise to serious error where sharp changes in price occur and the possibility of mismatches between value and price data exists. Another type of problem that may be encountered is where the detailed commodity composition of the available data is limited, and the assumptions necessarily made about this in order to be able to express the value data in constant dollar terms may be incorrect. If large changes in relative prices and quantities are taking place to the commodities within the available value aggregates, this may lead to significant error in the calculation of constant dollar estimates. The estimates for foreign trade and inventories especially may be liable to errors of this kind.

Do Policymakers and Other Users Need a Different Product?

There are some questions of a more fundamental kind than the reliability and accuracy of the existing statistics that we ought to consider. These concern the appropriateness of the statistics considered here as relevant indicators for economic policymaking and other purposes. Although economic decisionmakers are not so naive as to regard quarterly GDP estimates as the sole, or even the main, indicator on which to base their decisions, is a series of seasonally adjusted quarterly GDP estimates the most useful product for their purposes?

It is likely that many users would find a measure of underlying economic activity, and its projection into the future, a more valuable product than seasonally adjusted estimated of GDP for the past. How is it that such measures are not generally compiled?

One possible explanation is that the production of such a measure presents technical problems, the solution of which is by no means assured. Another explanation is the reluctance of compilers to take on the additional task of forecasting, not least because of the possible compromising of their neutrality as compilers of estimates for the present. Whatever the reasons may be, there is little doubt that such statistics, provided they were of an adequate quality, would be extremely welcome to many users.

In periods of short-term change in economic activity it is not the precise measurement of the latest quarter-to-quarter movement in seasonally adjusted real GDP that is of primary interest, but what this implies for the coming periods. For example, in April 1975 when the first measurements of U.S. GDP for the change between 1974 Q4 and 1975 Q1 appeared they showed a fall of 10.4 percent (at an annual rate), subsequently revised to 9.0 percent; and an estimate of the change between 1974 Q3 and Q4 of 9.0 percent, subsequently revised to 11.4 percent. The real concern was not whether these estimates were reliable to within (say) plus or minus 2 percent, but whether this fall in economic activity was likely to continue. (In 1975 Q2 U.S. economic activity roughly stabilised and in Q3 grew at an annual rate of over 10 percent).

Summary

Although assessments of the reliability and accuracy of GDP estimates are important, both to users and compilers, they are not easy to make in an unambiguous way and their implications need to be properly understood (or, as an inscrutable Japanese professor once said to me properly misunderstood), if they are to be of value.

The issue of the degree of reliability and accuracy that would be adequate for government policy and decision makers has to be addressed if the compilation process is to be carried out in a rational and cost effective way.

Measures of underlying economic activity for the past, present and future would be a more appropriate tool for many users provided they were of adequate quality. Greater attention should be given to the development of such meausres than to the improvement of the existing estimates of seasonally adjusted GDP.

Notes

1. An interesting example of this arises in the use of GNP as the basis for member states' contributions to the central budget of the European Union. The auditors are reputed to have requested figures to the nearest thousand ECU.

Author Index

Subject Index